2000

Springer Series on ETHICS, LAW, AND AGING

Series Editor
Marshall B. Kapp, JD, MPH
Director, Wright State University
Office of Geriatric Medicine and Gerontology
Wright State University, Dayton, OH

———

Marshall B. Kapp was educated at Johns Hopkins University (B.A.), George Washington University (J.D. With Honors), and Harvard University (M.P.H.). Since August 1980, he has been a faculty member in the School of Medicine at Wright State University, Dayton, Ohio, where he is the Frederick A. White Distinguished Professional Service Professor in the Departments of Community Health and Psychiatry and Director of the WSU Office of Geriatric Medicine and Gerontology. He holds an adjunct faculty appointment at the University of Dayton School of Law. In addition to being admitted to practice law in a number of state and federal courts, he is also licensed as a Nursing Home Administrator in the District of Columbia. He is the author of a substantial number of published books, articles, and reviews. He is a Fellow of the Gerontological Society of America. Mr. Kapp also is Editor of the *Journal of Ethics, Law and Aging* (Springer Publishing Company), as well as Editor of Springer Publishing Company's book series Ethics, Law and Aging.

Third Edition

Geriatrics and the Law

Understanding Patient Rights and Professional Responsibilities

Marshall B. Kapp, JD, MPH

 Springer Publishing Company

Springer Publishing Company, Inc.
536 Broadway
New York, NY   10012-3955

Cover Design by Janet Joachim
Aquisitions Editor: Helvi Gold
Production Editor: J. Hurkin-Torres

99 00 01 02 03 / 5 4 3 2 1

Library of Congress Cataloging-in-Publication Data

Kapp, Marshall B.
    Geriatrics and the law : understanding patient rights and
professional responsibilities / by Marshall B. Kapp.—3rd ed.
        p.   cm. (Springer Series on Ethics, Law, and Aging)
    Includes bibliographical references and index.
    ISBN 0-8261-4532-9 (hc.)
    1. Geriatrics—Law and legislation—United States.   2. Aged-
Medical care—Law and legislature—United States.   I. Title.
KF2910.G45K37   1999   98-54241
344.73'0326—dc21   CIP

Printed in the United States of America

To my family: Past, present, and future

"*May you live all the days of your life.*"
—Jonathan Swift (1738)

Contents

Preface to the Third Edition

Older individuals encounter a panoply of legal vicissitudes, as well as other types of challenges, in their daily lives. For older persons needing medical services, it frequently is impossible to separate the clinical aspects of care from the legal (as well as ethical, financial, and public policy) elements. Medical care of the elderly is intimately affected and extensively governed by the broad array of legal considerations that are applicable to the delivery of health services in general, and many of these considerations often are exacerbated in the care of older persons. Additionally, a variety of specific government programs has arisen for which the elderly are the primary or exclusive beneficiaries, and the legal rights and entitlements thus created frequently pose new and unique legal issues for the clinical caregiver attending to the needs of the older patient.

It was the aim of the first and second editions of this book to provide practical guidance for health care professionals—physicians, nurses, psychologists, health facility administrators, pharmacists, hospital and nursing home trustees, and allied health professionals—in successfully and productively meeting these legal challenges. This remains the goal of the third edition: both to inform and to sensitize the health care professional about some of the potential emerging legal issues he or she may encounter in providing clinical services to the elderly and to offer practical advice and guidance that will better enable the practitioner to grapple intelligently with legal issues and the responsibilities they impose. My approach remains one of trying to identify, analyze, and explain a complex series of human circumstances, legal rules, and social values in lay language and in terms that can be comprehended readily, assimilated, and applied by the busy health care professional with little prior experience or expertise in these matters.

As in the first and second editions, the focus here is on patients' rights and the correlative duties of health care professionals. Special attention is paid to the attitudes and behavior exhibited by such professionals in their interactions with older patients.

This revised edition of the text was necessary because the world of geriatrics and the law continues to change in many and substantial ways. New judicial decisions, legislative statutes, administrative rules and regulations, agency reports, and governmental and private guidelines exert a powerful and growing influence on the legal relationships presently played out among older patients, their families, health care professionals and institutions, private third-party payers, and the larger society. A flood of recent contributions to the legal, medical, and gerontological literature interpreting unfolding legal developments help to give texture and context to the legal environment prevailing in the late 1990s, an environment that is constantly and materially evolving. The current revolution in health care financing and delivery helps to shape a context in which legal obligations sometimes are enhanced but sometimes are placed in tension with ethical and other professional values.

The implications of the relevant statutes, regulations, judicial opinions, and private guidelines that have unfolded since the second edition, as well as the professional literature illuminating the new laws, have been woven into each chapter of the third edition. Every part of the book has been thoroughly updated and, where appropriate, expanded.

The admonition made in the prefaces to the first and second editions is truer today than ever: few health care professionals can afford to ignore the aging phenomenon. As significant changes in the law affect the patient rights and professional responsibilities entailed in serving this distinct and challenging patient population, this third edition of *Geriatrics and the Law* attempts to assist practitioners in a variety of disciplines in recognizing and responding appropriately to those changes.

Marshall B. Kapp, J.D., M.P.H.

Chapter 1

Introduction: Demography and Epidemiology of Aging

DEFINITIONS

Demography and epidemiology are sciences concerned with numbers of people and with changes and trends in their characteristics over time. Both of these sciences often, though not always, focus on specific populations, one of which is the so-called elderly population, commonly considered to consist of individuals who, in terms of chronological age, are 65 years or older. Thus, demography is the science of social and vital statistics and, in relation to the elderly, studies the numerical relationship between the "senior" group and the overall society and variations in that relationship (Olshansky, 1997). The epidemiology of aging studies diseases, health problems, or related conditions and their distribution in the elderly population as compared to the rest of the general population (Furner, Brody, & Jankowski, 1997).

While in both the demography and epidemiology of aging the chronological age range of 65 and over serves as the principal yardstick for the identification and description of the older population, it must be noted that this population is characteristically as heterogeneous as any other age group and that chronological age by itself neither describes nor explains variations among its members very well. Thus, for example, while an individual who is chronologically old is not necessarily also biologically, psychologically, and/or socially old, a chronically ill patient may be considered very old from a biological/physiological point of view regardless of that patient's chronological age and also much older than another individual of the same chronological age who does not suffer from chronic illness. Age 65 has no special scientific significance, owing its origins as an aging demarcation point to the pragmatic economic concerns of Prussian Chancellor Bismarck in the late 1800s. In a similar vein, if one were to compare the population aged 80 and older with that in their 60s, one would find many sharp differences with respect to such characteristics as health, living arrangements, marital status, work status, income, education, kinship support, and use of leisure time. It is worth keeping this in mind in the following discussion of the demography and epidemiology of aging.

THE GRAYING OF AMERICA

There are some very important reasons why the law pays increasing attention to the elderly in the United States and thus affects the way that health care professionals serving older patients practice. As one lawyer has noted, "Legal institutions and rules reflect changes in society; if law schools and legal research can anticipate social changes, they will be able to deal more effectively with them" (Levine, 1980). One such change is the nation's demographic profile involving the elderly.

In 1776, about 50,000 or some 2% of the total population of 2.5 million people then living in the United States were 65 years of age or older. By 1900, the population 65 years and over had risen to about 3 million people, or some 4% of the total. By 1975 that number had risen to about 22 million, or 10.5% of the total population, and it stood at about 33.5 million, constituting 12.18% of the total population in 1995 (AARP, 1996). Finally, various projections indicate that by the year 2030 Americans 65 and over will rise to 70 million (about 29% of the total population) (AARP, 1996).

The increase in the number of older Americans, as well as of elderly populations in other developed nations, is unprecedented in world history (Taeuber, 1992). For the United States, a report entitled *Future Directions for Aging Policy: A Human Service Model* (U.S. Congress, House Select Committee on Aging, 1980) put it as follows: "In one century, from 1900 to 2000, this segment of the population will have increased tenfold—from 3 million to 31 million. During the same century, the nation's total population will have increased at the very most fourfold."

In efforts to explain this large increase in the number of older Americans, it has become customary to point to advances in medical knowledge (e.g., in disease control) and facilities as a major contributory factor, if not the main cause. Frequently, the continuing role of research and development in medicine and medical technology, especially that of the life-prolonging kind, is taken for granted in this regard. Healthy lifestyle changes are also an important factor.

It is appropriate within the context of the increasing older population to consider two demographic processes: birth and death rates. The elderly of the future as far ahead as the year 2060 are already born. Thus, the baby boom generation of the post–World War II period (1946–1957) will produce a "senior boom" coupled with a decrease in births. Further, the babies of the 1960s and 1970s will be 65 and older after the year 2030.

Regarding death or mortality rates, life expectancy, which is the measure of years one has yet to live, is usually considered first. Life expectancy has increased dramatically since the beginning of the 20th century. People are living longer due, for example, to the decline in deaths from infectious diseases. Beyond that, more people are living long enough to grow old due, for example, to the decline in infant and childhood mortality rates during the past century. In 1900, life expectancy at birth was 49 years, and only approximately 40% of the total population reached the age of 65. In 1986, life expectancy at birth was approximately 75 years, and 80% of persons in their 30s in 1985 were expected to be alive in 2020.

The life expectancy of 75 years is, however, an average, and there are differences between sexes and races. Overall, the life expectancy since just before 1900 has been higher for women than for men because of declines in maternal death rates and in deaths from infectious diseases. This gap appears to be narrowing. Overall the life expectancy of the American population has increased during the 20th century, and mortality rates have tended to come down substantially.

THE OLDER POPULATION SPECIFIC

Up to this point, the discussion has been about the "graying of America" generally. Turning now to a consideration of some specific changes that have occurred and are occurring in the older population itself, it is useful to distinguish between three cohorts of older adults: those aged 65 to 74, those aged 75 to 84, and those aged 85 and over. The 75–84 and the 85+ cohorts are the fastest-growing segments of the population. In 1995, the 65–74 age group (18.8 million) was 8 times larger than in 1900, but the 75–84 group (11.1 million) was 14 times larger, and the 85+ group (3.6 million) was 29 times larger (AARP, 1996).

The vast majority of the total population aged 65 and over live in the community. At any point in time, only about 5% live in any kind of institution. In 1995, about 85% of persons aged 65 and older were White, 8% were Black, 4% were Hispanic, and 3% were Asian or Native American.

The changing age distribution of the U.S. population raises serious questions about patterns of work and retirement, health care costs, family structures and roles, intergenerational relationships, and societal structures (Atchley, 1994). The key factor is the "dependency ratio," the ratio of the number of persons aged 65 and older compared to the number of persons of the commonly accepted working ages (18 to 64). This ratio is expected to increase rapidly by 2030.

The likelihood of developing chronic health conditions increases sharply with age. Most older people have at least one chronic condition, and multiple conditions are not uncommon (Furner et al., 1997). The most common chronic conditions in persons aged 65 and older are arthritis, hypertension, hearing impairment, heart conditions, visual impairments, and diabetes. Finally, the three major causes of death for people aged 65 and older are heart disease, stroke, and cancer. Together, these three causes account for more than three fourths of all deaths in the 65 and older population.

IMPLICATIONS

These demographic factors concerning the elderly have, and will have in the future, significant implications for both health care and legal professionals who devote part or all of their efforts to the care of older patients/clients. The consequences of the graying of America are massive and inescapable for those who are involved in the intersection of geriatric practice and legal regulation. These consequences are the subject matter of this book.

Chapter 2

Introduction to Law and the Legal System

INTRODUCTION

Most health care professionals have to deal primarily with two aspects of law and the legal system. These are the areas of (1) medical jurisprudence and (2) forensic medicine.

Medical jurisprudence, or medical law, is the specialty area of law and law practice related to legal regulation of medicine and medical practice. This subject covers what the legal system does for, and to, the health care professional. Legal rules governing informed consent, refusal of treatment, termination of treatment, and confidentiality are examples of medical jurisprudence.

Forensic medicine (Wecht, 1998) is almost the mirror image of medical jurisprudence. It is defined as the specialty area of medicine, medical science, and technology concerned with investigation, preparation, preservation, and presentation of evidence and medical opinion in courts and other legal, correctional, and law enforcement settings. It concerns ways in which medical expertise and experience can be applied to aid in resolving certain specific legal questions that may arise. Health care professional participation, through the rendering of reports or the giving of live testimony, in cases involving such matters as guardianship, civil commitment, or disability determinations constitutes a part of the practice of forensic medicine.

The remaining chapters in this book will discuss in detail particular issues in medical jurisprudence and forensic medicine that are likely to arise in the clinical care of older persons. Policy issues that have legal implications are explored as well. Before proceeding to particulars, however, it is important for the health care professional to have some general understanding of what the law and the legal system as a whole are about and how they function (Hansen, 1998; Richards & Rathbun, 1993). This chapter provides an introduction.

TYPES OF LAW

A law normally may be classified as falling within one of the following general types: (1) constitutional law, (2) statutory law, (3) administrative law, or (4) common law.

Constitutional law refers to the general organization, plan, and principles of a government. It is organic law, subject to amendment, that is made by the people as a whole. In the United States, the federal, state, and local governments all have written constitutions. (City or county constitutions are called charters.) In some societies, such as Great Britain, the constitution is unwritten, depending for its force on formally recognized usage. Judicial decisions that interpret and apply constitutional provisions are also part of the body of constitutional law. For example, a patient's judicially recognized right to privacy, which encompasses the right to refuse medical treatment, is a matter of constitutional law, stemming in part from the "liberty" that is protected by the Due Process clause of the Fourteenth Amendment.

A constitution grants the elected legislature authority to enact different types of general laws. Legislatively enacted laws are termed statutes on the federal and state level and ordinances or codes on the local level. Statutory law must be written, expressed in general language, and promulgated or published so that affected individuals are put on notice regarding what is expected of them. A statute may be addressed either to the entire society or to a specified group. It can have only future effect. A statute may not make illegal past conduct that was legal at the time it occurred; such an *ex post facto* effect is impermissible under federal and state constitutions. A legislature, composed of elected representatives, may not pass a statute that violates any provision of the Constitution that empowers the legislature to enact statutes in the first place. When courts are called upon to decide the meaning of particular statutory language, these decisions become part of statutory law. Legislation establishing the Medicare and Medicaid programs (see Chapter 5) are examples of federal statutes; guardianship and civil commitment proceedings (see Chapter 8) are among the areas governed by state statutory schemes.

Administrative laws are called rules, regulations, or orders. They are enacted by administrative (executive) agencies, such as departments of health or public welfare, pursuant to powers delegated by the legislature. Administrative laws contain the specific content of programs and activities that are authorized by statute. This characteristic can be seen, for example, in federal and state regulations that have been promulgated to implement the broad Medicare and Medicaid statutes passed by the Congress and state legislatures. Rules, regulations, and orders have the full force of law behind them and, just like statutes, must be written, published, limited to future effect, addressed to all or a few, and consistent with the Constitution (as well as with the authorizing statute). Although there are certain constitutional limits to the amount of authority that a legislature may delegate to an administrative agency, it is the general practice of legislatures to give agencies the power to fill out with specifics the often very general shell of statutory programs. This practice is based on considerations of the agency's purported expertise, experience, and resources, as well as a political strategy to try to deflect the complaints of disgruntled constituents about particular program items. Administrative law also includes judicial decisions interpreting the meaning and effect of rules, regulations, and orders.

Common law is judge-made or court-made law. It is not based on the application of any specific constitutional, statutory, or regulatory provision but rather on shared values concerning social custom, tradition, usage, history, and, most important, legal precedent, or *stare decisis* (i.e., what previous courts have decided in similar cases). The goal of common law is justice, and the impact of a common law decision is binding only on those parties actually represented before the court in that particular case. Common law is reactive; that is, a court hears and decides a case only when particular parties ask it to do so. A legislature may react negatively to a common law decision by enacting a statute that abrogates, changes, or clarifies the common law principles announced. A legislature may give approval to a common law decision by passing a law that translates the common law principle into statutory form and thereby makes it applicable throughout the jurisdiction. Common law rules may be announced and modified by judicial systems in the United States on both the federal and state levels. The rules governing limitation of medical treatment (see Chapter 11) are generally handled by common law, although states also have enacted living will, durable power of attorney, and family consent statutes, and the courts have announced applicable constitutional principles regarding limitation of treatment as well.

SOURCES OF LAW

Both a vertical and a horizontal analysis of our governmental organization is instructive in understanding the sources of our laws. Vertically, government is organized in descending fashion in the following levels: (1) federal, (2) state, and (3) local.

Federal authority to legislate and regulate in the health sphere derives chiefly from two sources. First, the federal Constitution grants Congress the power to tax citizens, to collect revenues, and to spend that money for the general welfare of the citizenry. When Congress spends tax dollars through a particular program it has created to benefit the public, such as Medicare, it may attach conditions or requirements that accompany the receipt of such money. This is sometimes cynically referred to as "the Golden Rule" (as in "He who has the gold makes the rules") or the "poisonous tree" doctrine (as in "The whole tree goes along with the poisonous fruit you have tasted"). For this reason, if a health care professional wishes to participate in the Medicare program, for instance, he or she is obliged to obey the statutes and regulations that have been enacted as conditions to accompany the receipt of those public dollars.

The second major source of federal power in the health area is the constitutional clause authorizing Congress to regulate interstate and foreign commerce. In our complex health care system, virtually every medical substance, device, and service involves some element of manufacture, transportation, or sale that affects or is affected by more than a single state and that therefore comes under the Commerce clause. Under this vast authority, for example, the federal Food and Drug Administration (FDA), operating under the federal Food, Drug, and Cosmetic Act (FDCA) and implementing regulations, determines what drugs may be legally prescribed by health care professionals for their patients and the advertising that may be used in connection with the marketing of those pharmaceuticals.

At the state level, the government's power to control health affairs derives mainly from the state's (1) inherent police power to regulate for the general health, safety, welfare, and morals of the community and its (2) inherent *parens patriae* ("father of the land") power to benevolently protect those who cannot protect their own interests. State statutes mandating automatic reporting by physicians of infectious diseases or the involuntary commitment of mentally ill persons who are dangerous to others are examples of the police power exercise. State statutes regarding the reporting of cases of elder abuse or the involuntary commitment of or imposition of guardianship upon mentally ill individuals who neglect their own needs grow out of the *parens patriae* rationale.

Local governments ordinarily possess those lawmaking powers that are authorized by the constitution of the particular state in which they happen to be located. This category includes city and county governmental bodies.

Each of these vertical levels of government contains three horizontal branches. Theoretically, powers are distributed among these separate branches as follows: (1) The legislative branch is responsible for initiating laws, through the passage of statutes; (2) the executive branch (including administrative agencies, like health and welfare departments) is charged with enforcing the law; and (3) the judicial branch is expected to interpret constitutional, statutory, and regulatory provisions and to announce principles of common law. The actuality of government operations may vary significantly from this ideal version of the separation of powers, as the respective branch roles have become quite blurred over time.

CHARACTERISTICS OF LAW

There are certain aspects that characterize laws of any type or source. These characteristics distinguish laws from pronouncements that are purely moral or psychological in nature.

First, a law is a rule, requirement, or command that is addressed to an audience. It may be positive or affirmative, such as statutes mandating a professional to report to authorities cases of suspected elder abuse. It may be negative or prohibitory, such as a statute forbidding the practice of medicine or nursing without first obtaining a suitable license.

The purpose of a law is to control conduct and set limits on behavior. Lawmakers and enforcers are concerned primarily with *what* actors do, rather than *why* they do it.

An effective law must provide for the imposition of a specific range of sanctions or punishments if it is not obeyed. As an example, criminal or civil liability may be imposed for practicing medicine without a license. Conversely, a law may contain an incentive or reward for individuals who comply with it. Thus, a physician who complies with conditions set forth in the Medicare statute and implementing regulations is entitled to receive financial reimbursement from the federal government for covered professional services delivered to Medicare-eligible patients.

A law additionally is a statement of what is considered morally "correct" by a substantial proportion of society at a particular point in time. Totally apart from its enforceability or practical effect, the law is a mechanism for society to put itself on public record regarding particular controversial issues. Thus, for example, a number of state legislatures have been motivated to enact statutes authorizing the execution of living wills. This has been done as much to publicly proclaim their support for individual patient autonomy as to effect any specific practical changes or actions.

Finally, the law is a means of pronouncing and ensuring human rights. Rights may be placed in one of two basic categories, namely, liberty rights or entitlement rights. A liberty right may be thought of as a freedom to do a specific action, like the freedom to select whom one will accept as a patient, or as a freedom from governmental or private interference in one's affairs, such as the freedom from medical intervention without one's voluntary, competent, and informed consent. The federal Constitution's Bill of Rights (the first ten amendments plus the Fourteenth), for instance, is framed in terms of specific limitations imposed upon the federal or state governments in intruding into the lives of citizens.

Claims or entitlements are different. If a liberty right is thought of as a shield protecting the individual against unwanted intrusion, claim or entitlement rights may be envisioned as swords with which individuals seek to impose upon society affirmative obligations to provide them with some concrete good or service. Under the Medicare law, for instance, an eligible person is imbued with the entitlement to make a claim against the government to act affirmatively (i.e., to furnish financial resources) to provide that individual with a particular benefit (in this case, medical care).

It is essential to clear thinking about these matters that the idea of liberty rights be kept analytically distinct from claim or entitlement rights. Courts, legislatures, and administrative agencies have frequently applied these two sets of concepts to factual circumstances very differently. For example, under the federal Age Discrimination in Employment Act (ADEA), 29 U.S.C.§623 *et. seq.*, an individual possesses the liberty right to work as long as he or she is capable, free from discrimination by the government or private parties on the basis of age. This is very different from saying that an individual is entitled to a specific job forever and that a valid claim may be exerted against the government or private employers to provide that job for that individual. The latter type of right has not been legally recognized.

FUNCTIONS OF HEALTH LAW

Health law has classically served five separate but interrelated functions or roles. They are as follows:

1. *Health law prohibiting conduct injurious to health.* Examples of legal prohibitions aimed at protecting the health of the actor him- or herself or others include compulsory vaccination against infectious diseases, mandatory motorcycle helmet or automobile and airplane seatbelt wearing, quarantines, and sanitation and environmental controls.

2. *Health law authorizing programs and services to promote health.* Multiple and diverse federal, state, and local categorical programs of health services for specific purposes and specific persons have been devised. The emphasis of such programs is on the right of access to health care.

3. *Health law providing for social financing of health care.* Medicare and Medicaid are the most prominent manifestations of this function of health law. Here, too, the accent falls on the right of access to health care.

4. *Health law regulating the production and distribution of resources for health services.* Health facilities are regulated through government construction funding, fiscal reimbursement for depreciation of physical structures, and the health planning process. Health care staffing is strongly influenced

by government grants and loans for the education and placement of future and present health care professionals. Additionally, basic biomedical and behavioral research efforts have become highly dependent on public monetary support.

5. *Health law exercising surveillance over quality of care.* This function emphasizes the citizen's rights not only to health care but also within the health system. It challenges health care professionals by creating certain obligations on their part that correspond to the rights of the patient that are recognized. Most of my attention in this volume is devoted to this quality function of health law.

CONCLUSION

With this brief introduction to the structure and function of law and the legal system in mind, I now move to a discussion of specific medicolegal problems that are likely to arise in the clinical care of older persons.

Chapter 3

Informed Consent and Truth Telling

The subjects of informed consent and truth telling pose significant legal, as well as clinical and ethical, issues for all patients and all health care professionals. In this chapter, I explore both generic considerations and specific applications of these legal doctrines to the older patient population.

INFORMED CONSENT

Historical and Ethical Foundations

The relationship between patient and health care professional is at its heart a moral and legal, as well as a clinical, one. A respect for patient preferences is the moral and legal nucleus of that relationship (Jonsen, Siegler, & Winslade, 1998).

More than any other medicolegal doctrine, informed consent reflects the basic ethical responsibility to respect the personal autonomy of the patient (President's Commission, 1982). Autonomy stems from the Greek for "self-law or rule" and has been defined as the moral right to choose and follow one's own plan of life and action or the moral ability to identify and to pursue goals that we have set for ourselves. Within the health care provider/patient relationship, the provider's duty of fidelity, or faithfulness, compels respect for the patient's autonomy.

The legal counterpart to the concept of autonomy is the inherent right of self-determination, the recognition that each individual has the fundamental prerogative to control his or her own body and deserves to be protected from unwanted intrusions or unconsented-to touching (Applebaum, Lidz, & Meisel, 1987; Faden & Beauchamp, 1986). As a patient ages, this right of self-determination should become, if anything, stronger rather than weaker.

A second ethical basis for the informed consent doctrine is the encouragement of more intelligent and rational decision making. Medical decisions are based on more than biological data and laboratory values. They also involve important considerations of the patient's own life plan. Only the patient has access to these subjective factors, which, for older individuals with a wealth of life experiences and opportunities for value distillation behind them, can be especially weighty.

Informed consent can also help to instill a greater sense of partnership and active mutual participation within the patient/health care professional relationship (Charles, Gafni, & Whelan, 1997; Quill & Brody, 1996). It encourages more openness and less authoritarianism on the part of the professional. Other values served by the doctrine include a minimization of duress and a maximization of the patient's quality of life (Szabo et al., 1997), an increase in the public visibility of treatment decisions, and the encouragement of professional self-scrutiny with respect to medical decisions.

Contrary to popular opinion, the legal requirement of informed consent is not the recent invention of hungry lawyers, designed to reap great riches at the expense of unsuspecting health care professionals (Schouten, 1989). Several thousand years ago, in Plato's Laws, the distinction was made between the medical care provided to slaves and that accorded to freemen. The slave doctor, according to Plato, prescribed "as if he had exact knowledge" and gave orders "like a tyrant." The doctor who catered to freemen went "into the nature of the disorders," entered "into discourse with the patient and his friends" and would not "prescribe for him until he has first convinced him."

In more modern times, the informed consent doctrine has firm roots in the individualistic tradition of Anglo-American common law and is enforced in most democratic nations today. It is a concept that is embedded in the American culture and the American character (Glick, 1997; President's Commission, 1982) and endorsed by organized medicine (American Medical Association, Council on Ethical and Judicial Affairs, 1997). In 1914, Judge Cardozo proclaimed: "Every human being of adult years and sound mind has a right to determine what shall be done with his own body; and a surgeon who performs an operation without his patient's consent commits an assault for which he is liable in damages" (*Schloendorf v. Society of New York Hospitals*, 1914). The legal rules governing the doctrine of informed consent in the United States have undergone and still continue to undergo a slow metamorphosis and definition, beginning with what is usually recognized as the first true informed-consent case in 1957, through the rash of litigation and state legislation initiated in the 1970s and 1980s (Rozovsky, 1990).

Relationship to Substandard Care

Many health care professionals function under the mistaken impression that, once properly informed consent is obtained, they are then completely immune from any potential legal liability to that patient, even if substandard health care is rendered. This perception is dangerously inaccurate.

Figure 3.1 illustrates the clear analytical distinction between lawsuits (1) based on lack of effective consent and (2) those based on the other malpractice theories of negligence for substandard care and breach of contract. (A thorough discussion of malpractice law per se is outside the scope of this volume, although it is addressed indirectly in many chapters.) In essence, a patient never consents to receive substandard care; consent always implies permission to be given care of an acceptable professional level. Thus, if the care rendered falls below that level, the patient's consent is no defense to a claim of malpractice. Conversely, proper or even exceptionally fine care is no defense to a lawsuit based on lack of informed consent; the wrong in this case is not the quality of performance but the violation of the patient's right to self-determination.

While the consent/quality dichotomy is analytically clear, it is frequently blurred in practice. Few lawsuits are based solely upon failure of the defendant health care professional or facility to obtain satisfactory consent. Rather, the allegation of lack of informed consent usually is an extra

FIGURE 3.1 Sources of legal liability.

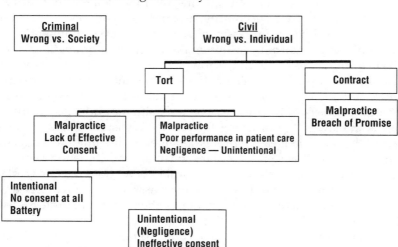

or additional count in the patient's complaint (Klingenstein, 1992). The basic theory is negligence, or giving care that falls below a minimally acceptable standard of quality. If the proof of negligence is inadequate, the patient may hope to prevail in the remaining cause of action, namely, lack of valid consent. If the injury to the patient is substantial but the evidence of negligence is weak, the stakes may be sufficient for the patient's attorney to litigate and even bring an appeal, stressing the consent count. Few cases are reported where the damages are modest and lack of consent is the only allegation made by the patient. This is especially noteworthy given strong empirical evidence of widespread deficiencies in the informed consent process.

Legal Theories

Traditionally, medical malpractice lawsuits alleging lack of effective consent have charged the health care professional with committing the civil wrong, or "tort," of battery. Battery is simply the intentional, offensive touching by one individual of another, in the absence of consent or privilege (e.g., the privilege to act to save another from suffering imminent harm). Battery violates the individual's time-honored rights to self-determination and bodily integrity.

In the past three decades, however, there has been a strong trend in informed-consent cases away from the battery theory and toward a greater reliance on claims of negligence. In most cases today, some form of bare patient "consent" is generally present. The modern negligence theory focuses on whether that consent contains all of the elements necessary to make it legally effective. Specifically, a patient alleging negligence must show that the health care professional was negligent (i.e., unintentionally failed to perform according to minimally acceptable professional standards) in fulfilling his or her duties toward that patient. The existence of a patient/health care professional relationship automatically imposes upon the latter certain "fiduciary," or trust, obligations to act in good faith and in the best interests of the former. The imposition of fiduciary responsibilities is the law's way of trying to rectify the vast disparity in power between the knowledgeable professional and the unknowledgeable, dependent patient. These fiduciary responsibilities include the assurance that any consent given to proposed medical interventions contains certain vital elements (discussed below). Failure to assure the presence of these elements constitutes a breach or violation of the health care professional's fiduciary duties and an act of negligence.

There are some types of cases that could arguably support both a battery and a negligence theory. Take, for example, the health care professional who obtains from the older diabetic patient a legally effective consent to amputate the right foot but who instead amputates the left foot by mistake. In that situation, battery would be appropriate because there was no consent at all regarding the left foot, and a negligence claim would be viable for the professional's failure to proceed with the degree of due care that would have been exercised by a conscientious professional peer in similar circumstances. A similar situation would arise if the patient consented to undergo an intervention by Dr. A, but Dr. B was the one who actually performed the intervention and the change was made without the patient's knowledge or consent.

Whether the suing patient relies on a battery or a negligence theory can make a very big practical difference to the health care professional who is being sued. First, the time limit for beginning the lawsuit (statute of limitations) is usually longer for negligence than for battery. However, the latter (because it is an intentional wrong) permits compensation, including punitive or exemplary damages (i.e., damages intended to punish the wrongdoer and set him or her up as an example to deter others) for things other than actual injury. Negligence requires proof of actual harm. Expert testimony is not required to prove battery, but it may be indispensable in a negligence suit because professional practice standards may need to be established. Finally, malpractice insurance may not cover a situation involving battery.

There is some authority holding that an action for fraud, as well as battery or negligence, may be maintained against a health care professional who knowingly and intentionally misrepresents important facts concerning a proposed medical intervention, *Nelson v. Gaunt,* 1981). A fraud lawsuit may subject the defendant to the possibility of punitive or exemplary damages as well as a longer statute of limitations than is found in ordinary negligence cases.

The remedy ordinarily available to the wronged patient in a negligence suit claiming lack of valid consent is an award of monetary damages. Compensation of the victim for losses suffered is the primary goal of contemporary tort law. Thus, patients able to show the violation of their rights under the informed consent doctrine may collect damages from health care professionals (or their insurance companies) for their actual out-of-pocket expenses occasioned by the risk that materialized but about which they were not forewarned. They also are entitled to damages for the pain and suffering consequent to this risk and for other economic items, such as lost wages or the cost of hiring a home health aide. Although judgments for lack of consent, rather than for other types of malpractice, are rare, sizable awards have been reported in cases presenting the appropriate configuration of circumstances.

The failure to obtain the patient's informed consent could conceivably lead to other sanctions against the offending health care professional. To the extent that hospital or nursing home bylaws require compliance with the law in general—or more specifically, with the doctrine of informed consent—a health care professional might lose staff privileges or be subject to other institutional sanctions for failing to obtain informed consent. Similarly, the health care professional might be subject to penalties by the state licensing authorities if the licensing statute or regulations make it an offense to fail to obtain informed consent. In a particularly rare and egregious situation, the health care professional could be subjected to prosecution for criminal battery.

The informed consent doctrine traditionally has been implemented through specific rules created by courts as a matter of common law. Since the 1970s, though, and particularly as a product of the "malpractice crisis" of the mid-1970s and 1980s, a number of state legislatures (now in the majority) have enacted statutes on this subject. These statutes vary somewhat in their specifics, in terms of form, substance, and effect. It is significant that none of these statutes and no reported judicial decisions regarding informed consent distinguish legal status among adult patients on the basis of chronological age.

There have been some halfhearted attempts to make informed consent requirements more uniform nationally. The American Hospital Association (AHA) proposed a Model Act on this subject in 1978, and the National Conference of Commissioners on Uniform State Laws (NCCUSL) proposed a national standard a decade later. To date, however, these efforts have not engendered much enthusiasm, and health care professionals therefore are advised to become familiar with whether their particular jurisdiction has enacted a statute on informed consent and, if so, what compliance with its specific provisions entails. In late 1997, the Department of Veterans Affairs promulgated a federal rule describing the requirements for obtaining and documenting informed consent in VA facilities (38 C.F.R. p. 17).

Express Versus Implied Consent

The most obvious way in which the patient can give consent to medical intervention is by stating it directly, either orally or in writing. This formal form of consent, through spoken or written words, is "express." The legal and clinical significance of written consent forms is discussed later in this chapter.

There are a number of situations where consent is not expressed, but the patient nevertheless may be said to have consented to the medical intervention. A patient's consent may be implied from the circumstances. Through actions, the patient may manifest a desire to receive the intervention by voluntarily submitting to it in a manner that the health care professional reasonably relies on to conclude that the procedure is authorized. For example, the patient implicitly authorizes a blood pressure check by unrolling a sleeve and extending an arm for application and reading of the sphygmomanometer. Likewise, consent for a vaccination may be inferred from the same patient actions where vaccination is the intervention that has been proposed. Implied consent is also found in some emergency situations.

Implied consent is not an exception to the general informed consent doctrine. All of the elements necessary to comprise a valid express consent are equally requisite where implied consent is applicable; the sole difference is that the patient's permission may be given by actions rather than by spoken or written words. Authorization comes by compliance but only after the health care professional has assured that the necessary preconditions for such compliance have been met.

Even though many clinical interchanges with older patients, particularly in the primary care sphere, are appropriate areas for implied consent, it (i.e., implied consent) is still a legal doctrine that should be relied on carefully by health care professionals. It presents certain evidentiary risks, and its use should be restricted to those interventions that are routine and relatively free of risk and to when it can reasonably be expected that the patient comprehends the nature of the intervention and the risks involved. When there is any doubt, a consent put into words should be obtained (Mitchell, 1995).

Responsibility for Obtaining Consent

Health care is generally delivered to older persons through a team approach involving a constellation of different health care professionals. This phenomenon raises the issue of which member or members of the team is/are ultimately responsible for assuring the presence of the necessary consent elements (see next section) and obtaining implied or express consent from the patient.

In general, each health care professional must obtain consent to the particular medical intervention or part thereof that he or she expects to perform. Where two professionals—for example, a surgeon and an anesthesiologist—have discrete functions, the division is relatively easy. The surgeon should disclose the relevant facts concerning the operative procedure, mentioning anesthesia risks but leaving a detailed explanation to the anesthesia specialist. The anesthesiologist should separately discuss the risks of anesthesia and alternative types and methods of administration and obtain the patient's consent to be anesthetized. If a patient has been referred by one physician to another, the specialist or subspecialist to whom the patient is referred is personally obligated to obtain the patient's valid consent to any proposed interventions. The referring physician should disclose as much as possible to the patient, but such disclosures are not a substitute for the more detailed explanation expected of the referee physician.

For reasons of both psychological preference and practical efficiency, there is a strong temptation for physicians to delegate the bulk of the task of obtaining consent to subordinates, especially nurses. This temptation exerts a particular pull where older patients, with whom the process of discussion frequently may be laborious and frustrating, are concerned. Physicians should temper this temptation, keeping in mind that the ultimate legal responsibility for assuring the adequacy of consent can never be effectively delegated away. The legal "buck" stops with the physician, as far as the patient and the courts are concerned.

Other health care professionals can and should, however, perform an important supportive and reinforcement role after the physician's initial discussions with the patient. Nurses, nurse's aides, pharmacists (Brushwood, 1997), and other health care professionals should endeavor to reassure anxious patients and families and to respond to their questions accurately and compassionately. When confronted by questions that properly should be answered by the attending physician, though, other professionals should firmly but sensitively refer the questioner to the physician and inform the physician that the patient or family has unanswered questions.

Health care professionals also should encourage and enable patients and their families to take advantage of other sources of health care information. Much could be taught, for example, through wider distribution of printed pamphlets on medications written specifically for lay people or through greater public use of medical libraries. Health care professionals should view such informational resources as complementary to, not competing with or replacing, their personal disclosure activities and should encourage their development (Meredith, Emberton, & Wood, 1995).

One approach to dealing with the question of who is responsible is to conceptualize informed consent as an ongoing process rather than as a series of separate events (Lidz, Appelbaum, & Meisel, 1988). So perceived, communication between patient, significant others, and members of the health care team would take place on a continuous free-flowing basis, rather than being connected to discrete physical interventions.

Often, it is not only the individual health care professional who is obliged to obtain the patient's consent before medically intervening. Although some jurisdictions put exclusive responsibility on the physician (*Kelly v. Methodist Hospital*, 1995), in others the health care facility, if any, where the care is being delivered also has certain duties in this area. These duties arguably fall under two theories.

First, a nursing home, clinic, hospital, or other health facility ordinarily is held legally answerable for any civil wrongs committed by one of its employees while functioning within the scope of the job. Thus, under the doctrine of *respondeat superior* (Latin for "Let the master answer"), which is a version of the general doctrine of vicarious liability, a patient may hold a health facility liable when a house officer, nurse, facility-employed physician, medical technologist, or other health care professional or student directly employed or sponsored by the facility invades the bodily integrity of the patient without first obtaining a valid consent. The error or omission of the subordinate (employee) is said to be "imputed" to the superior (employing facility). The individual health care professional also remains personally liable to the patient, under the doctrine of joint and several liability. The particular wrongdoer additionally may be forced to reimburse the employing facility for its lawsuit-related expenses, under the theory of indemnification.

Second, a health facility has an institutional relationship with each patient and the independent obligation to see that care of an acceptable level of quality is delivered. Thus, even where, as is still most frequently the case, the attending physician is an independent contractor rather than a salaried employee of the facility, the facility may be held liable for certain deviations from standards under the corporate liability theory. This theory has not been applied to any facility for the failure of an independent contractor/medical staff member to obtain valid patient consent, and such liability is precluded by statute in some states (e.g., Ohio). It is conceivable, however, that corporate liability may be extended to this area in the future, especially in cases where facility administrators knew or reasonably should have been expected to know that the patient expressly objected to the intervention or was incapable of giving effective consent. The facility also acts (or fails to act) at its serious peril when it violates informed consent provisions contained in state facility licensing codes, Joint Commission on Accreditation of Healthcare Organizations (JCAHO) standards, or the facility's own internal operating policies and procedures. At the least, each health facility should adopt and implement its own formal policies and procedures for securing consent from its patients, and these policies and procedures should, among other things, designate which particular health care professional within the organization is responsible for overseeing the consent process for any specific patient.

The institution's consent policy should be integrated into its overall risk management program. The quality of provider/patient communication very directly affects the patient's satisfaction with the quality of the overall provider/patient relationship. That satisfaction (or dissatisfaction), in turn, strongly shapes the propensity of the patient or family to file a

lawsuit in the event of a poor medical outcome (Levinson, Roter, Mullooly, Dull, & Frankel, 1997).

Elements of Valid Consent

Voluntary

The first requirement for a valid legal consent is that the patient's participation in the decision-making process and the ultimate decision regarding
care must be voluntary. The usual definition of voluntariness in the context
of consent is that the person giving or withholding consent must be so situated as to be able to exercise free power of choice without the intervention
of any undue element of force, fraud, deceit, duress, overreaching, or other
ulterior form of constraint or coercion. It means, simply, that the patient
must be free to refuse to participate in the proposed intervention.

Voluntariness in medical decision making is best understood as a
matter of degree (President's Commission, 1982). The most obvious vio-
ation of this requirement occurs when the intervention is "forced," that is,
when it is performed over the express opposition of the patient. This
happens relatively rarely in the case of adult patients, even when legal
decision-making power regarding that individual has been voluntarily or
involuntarily placed in another (see Chapter 8).

A more subtle but equally objectionable violation of the voluntariness
element occurs when the patient's consent is the result of "coercion." Coercion may come in a variety of forms, especially if the patient is vulnerable
and dependent, as are many frail elderly, or is caught by circumstances in
an inherently intimidating setting, such as a hospital, nursing home, public mental health facility, or other similar type of institution. Coercion may
emanate, consciously or unconsciously, from the patient's health care professionals, family, and friends. Coercion is particularly repugnant when it
extends beyond subtlety into manipulation (such as telling an older
patient that the content of a disability evaluation [see Chapter 6] may
depend on the patient's acceptance of a particular proposed treatment) or
even outright deception.

Thus, in the case of older persons, the test of voluntariness is com-
pounded by questions. For example, is an older person more likely to
give consent because, among other reasons, (1) he or she is in an institution or is in custody, (2) he or she is involuntarily detained or committed
(Kapp, 1998d), (3) he or she is overly eager to please and to do as others
ask; (4) he or she is more susceptible to inducements or threats because
of physical or mental impairment, or (5) he or she is unable to obtain
independent advice and consultation? Hence, it is necessary to ask
whether there are inducements or threats that might unduly affect the

older person's consent. Likewise, it is necessary to investigate the dimensions of the authority, power, and control of the person requesting consent, the identity of the person seeking consent, and the distribution of power in his or her relationship to the older individual. Similarly, one must take into account the degree of restrictiveness of the environmental conditions under which the patient is being asked to consent.

Voluntariness is an exceedingly difficult concept to nail down in practice, precisely because certain elements of coercion are inevitable and unavoidable in any real health care encounter. The facts of illness and the limited capabilities of medicine often constrict the choices available to patient and health care professional alike. In that sense, the condition of illness itself is sometimes spoken of as coercive. But the fact that no available alternative may be desirable in itself and that the preferred course is, at best, only the lesser of several evils does not render a choice coerced in the legal or ethical sense. No change in human behavior or institutional structure could remove this limitation. Such constraints are merely facts of life that should not be regarded as rendering a patient's choice involuntary (President's Commission, 1982).

Every express choice made by an adult is legally presumed to be voluntary, and this presumption, as a practical matter, is very difficult for a complaining patient or family to rebut or disprove. For example, courts generally have been much stricter in looking at the voluntariness of a commercial contract than they have been in the medical intervention context. Nonetheless, the health care professional is advised to do all that he or she can to minimize any coercion inherent in the therapeutic relationship and to give advice and make recommendations in as nonpressured and empathetic a manner as possible. Such a practice best respects the older patient as a person, promotes the therapeutic value of the intervention accepted, and protects the legal flanks of the health care professional.

Informed

The second essential requirement for valid consent is that the patient's agreement be informed (Richards & Rathbun, 1993). "Patients are persons generally unlearned in the medical sciences and therefore, except in rare cases, courts may safely assume the knowledge of patient and physician are not in parity" (*Cobbs v. Grant*, 1972). Therefore, the legal doctrine of informed consent requires that the health care professional, before undertaking a medical intervention, disclose certain information to the patient. The patient may then issue a "knowing" or "intelligent" consent or refusal.

This doctrine, in addition to its common law application, is embodied today in numerous state statutes and certain federal legislation dealing with patients' rights. Additionally, the informed consent requirement has been unambiguously endorsed by major voluntary health organizations, including the AHA, the American Health Care Association (AHCA), and the JCAHO.

The disclosure requirement is justified not just on ethical grounds but for therapeutic reasons as well. In most instances, thorough provision of information to the patient is good medical practice as well as good legal and ethical conduct. A patient on powerful medication, for instance, who is warned of possible symptoms he or she may experience will be able to cooperate better with the health care professional in treating those side effects, and the therapeutic process is thereby facilitated.

Standards for Disclosure. There are several competing standards detailing the amount and type of information that the health care professional should convey to the patient. The test selected has both philosophical and practical ramifications.

The most complete and hence most legally cautious and safe standard for informed consent is full disclosure, under which all known or knowable relevant information concerning the proposed intervention is communicated to the patient. Thus, if a physician is considering prescribing a specific treatment for an older patient primarily for its placebo effect, the full-disclosure standard would require that the physician disclose that fact to the patient. Although no jurisdiction has yet adopted this standard, full disclosure, coupled with sufficient documentation (see Chapter 4), is the best defense a health care professional could have against a claim of lack of informed consent. No higher standard can be expected than full disclosure.

The disclosure standard currently enforced in the majority of American jurisdictions is referred to as the "professional," "reasonable physician," or "community" standard. Under this test, the adequacy of disclosure is judged against the amount and type of information that other reasonable, prudent health care professionals would have disclosed to that specific patient under similar conditions. Where proof is adduced that the customary practice within the health care professional community, at least for a respectable minority if not the majority of the profession, would be to withhold the questioned facts from the patient, a defense is established in a professional standard jurisdiction.

As health care professionals become more familiar with the informed consent doctrine and more concerned with maximum protection against malpractice claims based on alleged lack of consent, the customary practice has evolved and continues to evolve to one of ever-widening disclosure. Further, courts at times (albeit infrequently) have imposed on the medical profession a higher standard of care than that set by customary practice. As the acceptable standard of care evolves toward disclosure, either voluntarily or by judicial imposition, it will become increasingly difficult to locate even a respectable minority of health care professionals that continues to practice widespread nondisclosure.

Almost half of American jurisdictions have officially accepted a more expansive standard of information disclosure: the "reasonable patient" or "material risk" standard. This standard dictates that the health care professional communicate the information that a "reasonable patient" in the same situation would need to make a voluntary and intelligent decision. Under this test, the patient must be told about all material risks—that is, those factors that might made a difference to a reasonable patient. This certainly includes answering fully and truthfully any questions asked by the patient. The determinative element is the patient's informational needs, determined from the patient's perspective (*Carr v. Strode*, 1995).

Since the focus is on a "reasonable" patient, this is sometimes referred to as an "objective" or "prudent person" standard (*Bernard v. Char*, 1995). A "subjective" or "individual patient" standard, asking what the particular (rather than a reasonable) patient would have wanted to know under the circumstances, has been advocated by some and accepted by at least one state court (*Scott v. Bradford*, 1979). Otherwise, though, the subjective standard has been rejected as unfair to the health care professional.

Arguments put forward on behalf of the reasonable-patient or material-risk standard of informed consent, as opposed to the professional or community standard, include (1) patient autonomy, (2) enhanced communications, (3) better health consumer awareness, (4) less litigation, and (5) improvement in the quality of medical care. Underlying these arguments is empirical evidence suggesting that most patients and their families wish to receive more information than many health care professionals would willingly choose to disclose (Deber, Kraetschmer, & Irvine, 1996; Degner et al., 1997; Nease & Brooks, 1995). Interestingly, this inquisitive-patient sentiment does not generally extend as much to the elderly (Mazur & Hickam, 1997; Petrisek, Laliberte, Allen, & Mor, 1997), who generally report a higher level of satisfaction with the amount of information disclosed to them (Adamson, Tschann, Gullion, & Oppenberg, 1989). This is probably because they feel more dependent on their health care professionals and more deferential toward their judgment (Beisecker, 1988).

When the health care professional has purposely withheld information about the nature of a medical intervention, the patient-plaintiff's burden of proof under the reasonable-patient standard is much more easily satisfied than under the professional standard. Under the latter, an expert witness would be necessary to establish the appropriate conduct; under the former, no expert witness is needed, because figuring out what information a reasonable patient would want to know is a matter well within the capability of lay jurors. The jury's tendency to identify with the patient in a material-risk jurisdiction is likely to lead to a finding that failure to disclose the nature of an intervention was a culpable professional omission. Even when the defendant health care professional develops strong evidence that the intervention employed did not create, in his or her professional opinion, an undue risk of physical or mental harm, this argument could be dismissed as irrelevant on the issue of the materiality of the information to that patient. The test is whether the disclosure might make a difference to a reasonable patient, not to the treating health care professional (*Daum v. SpineCare Medical Group*, 1997).

Elements of Disclosure. With these standards of disclosure in mind, I now move to an enumeration of the specific informational items that fall within any of these standards. The specific elements of disclosure usually have been listed as follows:

1. Diagnosis. The patient should know what the medical problem is that the health care professional intends to pursue, diagnose, and treat, either as a discrete medical entity or as a symptom complex.

2. Nature and purpose of the proposed intervention. In medical terminology, this equates to the indications for the intervention. The health care professional should discuss with the patient the diagnostic or therapeutic rationale, in language that is clear, nontechnical, and understandable to the patient (Lee, 1993).

3. Risks, consequences, or perils of the intervention. People differ in the risks that they are willing to take when choosing among treatments. Choices may vary according to age and gender (Goldschmidt & Bertram, 1994). Different patients attach different weights and values to various potential outcomes (Kassirer, 1994). Whether one is in a professional- or a patient-standard jurisdiction may influence the specific risks that must be disclosed. In general, patients are most interested in risks associated with death (Mazur & Hickam, 1994), disability, or discomfort. As either (1) the potential degree or severity or (2) the likelihood of a risk's occurrence (the incidence rate) (Hopper, Houts, McCauslin, Matthews, & Sefczek, 1992) increases, the balance tips more toward disclosure. As a matter of defensive practice, it is always wise to err on the side of more disclosure. It also is wise to keep away as much as possible from citing percentages in describing risks, as percentages are highly susceptible to misunderstanding and misquotation and often are inaccurate scientifically (Adelsward & Sachs, 1996; Calman, 1996; Mazur & Merz, 1994). It may be most useful to try to place risks in context, that is, to speak of relative or comparative risks instead of just treatment risks in isolation (Schuck, 1994). For instance, patients may differ in how they weigh and

balance survival versus quality of life considerations in assessing relative risks (Mazur & Hickam, 1993).

4. Probability of success. In medical terms, what would the prognosis be if the particular recommended intervention is undertaken (competently, of course) (Annas, 1994b)? In other words, what are the expected benefits of the intervention (Naimark, Naglie, & Detsky, 1994)?

5. Alternatives. What options are reasonable and available? If an option is medically advisable but the patient's insurer or managed care organization will not pay for it, the patient ought to be informed about that option nonetheless.

6. Result anticipated if nothing is done. In any situation, one of the alternatives to any plan of intervention is to let nature take its course (*Wecker v. Amend*, 1996). But this too may entail specific risks and consequences of which the patient must be told. Just as consent must be informed, so also must refusal of proffered intervention be informed if it is to represent a legally valid patient choice.

7. Limitations on professional or facility. It has been suggested that any relevant legal, clinical, ethical, or other limitations on the ability of a health care professional or facility to serve a particular patient should be clearly delineated. Thus, for example, a nursing facility that lacks staffing or physical or financial capacity to adequately care for the needs of a prospective patient should spell out its limitations, at or before the admission interview, to the applicant, family, and any referring professional, facility, or social service agency.

8. Advice. Although most patients strongly desire sufficient information and the right to make ultimate decisions, most also want (and expect) advice and recommendations from the health care professionals in whose hands they entrust their well-being (Meisel & Kuczewski, 1996). This is likely to be especially true for the older patient, who tends to be more respectful of authority. Giving an opinion is not necessarily coercion or the exercise of undue influence. Rather, if done in an objective yet compassionate way, mindful of the human characteristics and values of the particular patient, it is the proper fulfillment of one's professional duties. It emphasizes the dialogue nature of real informed consent (Schouten, 1989). Doubts and uncertainties existing in the mind of the health care professional regarding the proposed intervention also should be shared frankly with the patient and family.

9. The financial costs of choosing various treatment options (Wilkes & Schriger, 1996).

Many states have enacted statutes that specify a particular standard of disclosure, but most state statutes deal with particular items of disclosure in only a very general fashion, if at all. The basic outline is filled in through the evolution of state common law via individual judicial decisions rendered in litigated disputes. A couple of states (Texas and Hawaii) have experimented with statutory schemes that list with specificity those items that must be disclosed to the patient for any particular proposed intervention. These statutes immunize health care professionals from subsequent liability if the statutory requirements have been met.

Even if the patient can establish the absence of informed consent, no civil recovery can be had unless the patient can also prove that the health care professional's failure to inform was a proximate, or direct, cause of the injury suffered. "Such a causal connection arises only if it is established that, had the revelation been made, consent to the treatment would not have been given" (*Cobbs v. Grant*, 1972). Put differently, if the patient would have proceeded with the intervention anyway, he or she cannot subsequently complain about a risk that he or she would have found unpersuasive.

In judging causation, whether a jurisdiction follows a (1) "subjective," individual-patient or an (2) "objective," prudent-patient standard is very significant. As alluded to earlier, at least one state court (specifically, in Oklahoma) has adopted a subjective test, asking whether the particular, idiosyncratic patient would have judged a specific risk as material and would have rejected the intervention if disclosure had been made. Most courts that have considered the question, however, have rejected or abandoned the subjective test in favor of an objective one—whether a reasonable, average person in that patient's position would have undergone the proposed intervention if he or she had been more fully informed. Under such a test, the patient's testimony, if offered, is relevant to the proximate-cause issue, but such testimony is neither necessary nor controlling.

A number of scholars object to the causation requirement for recovery of damages based on lack of effective consent. They argue that violation of the patient's dignity by itself, regardless of its effect on the medical outcome, ought to subject the negligent communicator to liability (Meisel, 1988). Courts have not yet adopted this approach.

The informed consent doctrine has been criticized by certain commentators and empirical researchers on the grounds that it is virtually impossible for the vast majority of nonprofessionally educated patients to adequately understand, assimilate, and mentally process the often extensive and detailed information that must be disclosed. This argument is made with special vehemence in the case of older patients suffering from some form of mental dysfunction. The courts and legislatures have thus far generally managed to avoid confronting this problem head-on, by focusing their inquiries almost exclusively on the quantitative and qualitative nature of the information disclosed by the health care professional while essentially ignoring what is done with that information by the patient.

In other words, in practice, "informed" consent has usually not been equated with "understanding" consent (Katz, 1994), although one often can hear the terminology used (inaccurately) interchangeably.

Thoughtful commentators from both the legal and health care professional communities contend that both informed and understanding consent, while perhaps seldom achieved today (Braddock, Fihn, Levinson, Jonsen, & Pearlman, 1997), is a realistic possibility for most patients and should be the standard that is legally enforced. I support this view and the notion that comprehension is less a function of patient characteristics or the complexity of the medical problem than it is dependent on the commitment and effort of the communicator and the method of communication used to inform the patient (Barry, Fowler, Mulley, Henderson, & Wennberg, 1995). A dialogue that is open, nontechnical, compassionate, receptive to questions, and involving significant family members or friends (Pratt, Jones, Shin, & Walker, 1989), can, in most cases, bring about meaningful patient comprehension (Krynski, Tymchuk, & Ouslander, 1994) and can serve a valuable therapeutic purpose at the same time (Wolf & Becker, 1996). Especially in the case of geriatric patients, the health care provider has a moral obligation to strive to maximize patient comprehension to fulfill the spirit as well as the letter of informed consent. Some of the best results in patient comprehension have taken place in the context of treating chronic illness.

Much work remains to be done in perfecting provider/patient communication techniques (Peters, 1994), especially in light of findings that the method of eliciting patients' preferences strongly influences their expressed preferences and that these preferences may have predictable relationships with demographic characteristics such as age (Ainslie & Beisecker, 1994; Mazur & Merz, 1993).

Another misplaced but frequently cited criticism of the informed consent doctrine is that the disclosure of information tends to frighten away many patients from agreeing to undergo clinically indicated interventions. In fact, empirical research shows that ample disclosure not only does not increase the patient refusal rate but that most refusals are based on inadequate disclosure and that the refusal rate actually decreases as the amount and kind of information disclosed increases and patient uncertainty decreases (Sprung & Winick, 1989). Similarly, there is evidence that physicians can warn patients about potential side effects without bringing about those side effects (Lamb, Green, & Heron, 1994).

Moreover, a good argument may be made that the patient is making the "correct" decision for himself or herself—in terms of personal values—when pertinent information persuades the patient to decline potential intervention. This is especially true when the benefits and risks of the different alternatives are very subjective and/or uncertain (Fowler, 1995), for example, in the case of benign prostatic hyperplasia, which is so common among older men (Wagner, Barrett, Barry, Barlow, & Fowler, 1995).

Although informed consent often is associated with surgery (Mazur & Merz, 1996), the doctrine applies with equal force to all manner of non-surgical medical and psychiatric (Appelbaum, 1997a) interventions as well (Annas, 1989). This includes the administration of drugs. Because older patients are especially heavy consumers of prescription and over-the-counter drugs, especially of the psychotropic variety, and because they are at higher risk of adverse reactions from the drugs they take (Col, Finale, & Kronholm, 1990), health care professionals should be exceptionally conscientious about adequately informing older patients and their families of potential consequences and alternatives of prescribed or suggested pharmaceutical therapies (Morris, Tabak, & Gondek, 1997). For over-the-counter drugs, this burden falls particularly on the pharmacist. Disclosure should include specifics on at least the following points:

1. What is the name of the medication? Why should the patient take it? When can the medication be discontinued? Is there a feasible alternative to this drug or to drugs altogether?
2. How many times a day should the medicine be taken? What are the best times? How should the drug be taken?
3. What side effects should be watched for? Which ones are expected and which ones should be reported to the health care professional right away?
4. Can this drug be taken safely with other prescription and over-the-counter drugs that the patient is presently taking? Are there any foods to avoid while taking this drug?
5. Are there any special warnings the patient should know about while taking this drug?

Additionally, informed consent is vital in decisions about screening tests for the existence of various disorders (Flood et al., 1996; Pauker & Kassirer, 1997; Ubel, 1996; Wolf, Nasser, Wolf, & Schorling, 1996) or genetic susceptibility to them (Geller et al., 1997; Kapp, 1996e). Informed consent requirements also apply, at least in theory (Kapp, 1998d), to nursing facility placement. Because placement decisions often are made in an atmosphere of great stress, health providers must try especially hard to maximize the understanding of options by the patient and significant others.

Competent

The third essential element of legally valid consent is that the patient must be mentally capable of giving valid consent regarding personal medical care. As is explained at length in Chapter 8, every adult human being is presumed to be decisionally capable (*Ficke v. Evangelical Health Systems,* 1996; Sirmon & Kreisberg, 1996). This presumption is rebutted or done away with only when a judge expressly rules that the individual is incompetent. Chapter 8 also extensively discusses legal tests of capacity and methods for its clinical assessment, as well as various forms of voluntary and involuntary proxy decision-making arrangements. The particular application of these subjects to the care of dying patients is dealt with in Chapter 11.

A major problem, noted in Chapters 8 and 11, is the older patient who is incapacitated in clinical fact (*de facto* incompetent) but who has not been so adjudicated in a court of law (*de jure* incompetent) and for whom no guardian has been formally appointed. It is always wise, in such situations (and, in fact, whenever possible regardless of the patient's functional abilities) to involve interested and available family members or significant others as much as possible in the decision-making process. Such involvement represents the widespread practice in current health care delivery and generally serves a therapeutic purpose for the patient, fosters more thoughtful decisions, and at the same time perhaps psychologically discourages future lawsuits.

Relatives frequently lack express or formal authority to give legally binding consent on behalf of patients who have not been judicially declared incompetent. About half of the states statutorily empower relatives, through explicit family consent laws or general informed consent statutes, to make legally valid decisions for clinically incapacitated patients in the absence of a formal incompetency finding and guardianship appointment order. Several states have Living Will or Natural Death statutes (see Chapter 11) that specifically authorize proxy consent without judicial appointment. In other states, the technical legal status of relatives as proxy decision makers is unclear. Obtaining consent from relatives on behalf of a patient who still maintains a legal presumption of competence may or may not be legally appropriate. The better practical rule is for the professional, in the absence of a guardianship order, to seek consent both from the patient and available "next of kin," except when this is not feasible (e.g., when the patient is noncommunicative) (Dubler, 1990).

Additionally, as noted in Chapter 8, even a judicially appointed guardian may have limits placed on his or her authority to consent to medical intervention. The health care professional should be aware of any such limits.

I do not advocate, as do some, that absolute legal certainty be sought by the health care professional through initiation of formal guardianship proceedings for every patient needing medical attention for whom competence to consent is questionable. Such a practice certainly yields definitiveness and represents the most cautious and legally prophylactic approach. In most situations, however, this imposes an unnecessary financial, practical, and emotional burden on the patient, family, friends, and health care professionals. The majority of the time, families can be counted on to act in a manner either (1) consistent with the patient's own values and preferences (substituted judgment) or (2) consistent with the family's sincere appraisal of what is in the patient's best interests (Reust & Mattingly, 1996). Health care professionals should be willing to tolerate a certain small degree of legal ambiguity and should invoke the formal legal process only when they entertain a serious doubt regarding the decision-making motives or abilities of the patient's family.

Exceptions

A number of well-recognized exceptions exist to the general informed consent requirements. These are all applicable, in appropriate circumstances, to older patients. They include (1) legally required interventions, (2) emergencies, (3) waivers, (4) therapeutic privilege, and (5) commonly known risks.

Authorization by Law

Informed consent is not required in certain instances in which medical interventions are directed or authorized by law. These include certain tests performed pursuant to the authority of police officers or public health officials, such as testing motor vehicle drivers for inebriation. Because consent need not be sought in such circumstance, "informed consent" is a misnomer. Nonetheless, it is still appropriate to discuss with a person the nature of the intervention and the reasons for it, out of respect for that person, even though such discussion is not intended to assist the individual in making a choice.

Emergency Exception

The emergency exception applies when (1) immediate medical treatment is required to preserve life or to prevent a serious, perhaps permanent impairment to health, but (2) consent cannot be obtained from the patient (or from someone empowered to authorize treatment on the patient's behalf), and (3) there is no credible indication that the treatment would be refused were the patient then able to make his or her own wishes known. It is sometimes said that consent in such situations is "implied by law," by analogy to situations (referred to earlier in this chapter) in which a patient by his or her conduct implies consent without explicitly giving it. This terminology is misleading in the emergency context. More accurately, in an emergency the law sets aside the requirement of consent, based on the presumption that a reasonable person would want emergency aid to be rendered and that a particular patient has such wishes unless he or she has definitively indicated otherwise previously.

To justify reliance on the emergency exception, the health care professional has the burden of proving the presence of two factors in the case at issue. First, it must be shown that it was not reasonably possible prior to the intervention to obtain the express consent of the patient or the consent of another person authorized to decide for the patient. Second, it must be established that there was an immediate threat of death or of serious, permanent impairment of health.

Because the establishment of these factors is the health care professional's responsibility, he or she should make every reasonable effort to document the circumstances in such a situation (see Chapter 4). Adequate notes should be included in the medical record explaining the immediate threat to life or health and what efforts were made, if any, to obtain express consent. Consultation with other health care professionals, if they are available and time permits, is wise and helpful in justifying the treating health care professional's action.

One variation of the emergency exception is the "extension" doctrine. This doctrine applies when unanticipated conditions are discovered during a surgical procedure. It justifies the physician in extending the operation beyond the patient's original express consent, when the extension is necessary to obviate an immediate threat to life or a permanent impairment of health. Although the courts have been fairly liberal in interpreting the extension doctrine, it will be used sparingly by health care professionals who are truly committed to the concept of maximum patient self-determination.

Defense of Waiver or Delegation

Just as personal autonomy is the primary ethical underpinning of the patient's right to make medical decisions, it also is the foundation for the health care professional's defense of waiver. Implied contract and assumption of risk are related concepts.

Ever since the earliest judicial recognition of the doctrine of informed consent, it has also been acknowledged that, if a patient has the right to know a proposed medical intervention's nature, risks, alternatives, and probability of success, then the patient also must possess the prerogative to waive or relinquish that right or to delegate decision-making authority to someone else. It is not legally required that health care professionals oversupply patients with unwanted information, or "truth dump." Allowing a patient the opportunity to waive or delegate the right to be informed is "paternalism with permission" and is a necessary part of full recognition of the patient's claim to self-determination (Gordon, 1996).

This defense also could be asserted in terms of implied contract. The health care professional might argue that a combination of the conduct, past history, and statements of a particular patient may be fairly interpreted as an implied desire by the patient for the health care professional to withhold some or all information and to make necessary treatment decisions for the patient. A patient may nonverbally communicate to the health care professional a willingness to unquestioningly undergo whatever form of intervention the health care professional judges to be consistent with the patient's life experiences and expressed values and serving the patient's best interests. The health care professional's acceptance of that responsibility is arguably an implied condition of the patient's entry into or continuation in the professional/patient relationship. It is also possible for the patient's waiver of decision-making authority to be purely express, but this will be a rarer situation.

Patient waiver or delegation of informed consent undoubtedly reflects the tacit understanding and trust (Young, 1997) in a considerable percentage of professional/patient encounters. This is especially true for older patients, who often are in even greater awe of the status of health care professionals than are most others. Many patients are content to have the specifics of their medical treatment remain a mystery, as long as it works (Diem, 1997). Health, as a "good," is judged by many people as more important than rights. Many older persons, too, naturally rely on adult children—mainly daughters—to assist them in making medical decisions, sometimes to the point of virtually delegating decision-making authority to them altogether (Pratt et al., 1989).

However, to prevent the waiver defense from becoming the exception that rapidly obliterates the rule, it has been strongly urged in some quarters that the patient's right to decide not to be informed must be exercised unambiguously if it is to be given effect. Consequently, the waiver ideally should be expressed rather than implied and should be recognized only in circumstances where the health care professional has made clear that there are risks and alternatives associated with the advised intervention and that he or she is willing to discuss them fully with the patient (and family) if so requested. It also should be kept in mind that some older persons who may wish to delegate ultimate decision-making authority may still want to receive information about their care (Ende, Kazis, Ash, & Moskowitz, 1989). Further, many patients who prefer not to make initial therapeutic decisions do want to participate in the ongoing evaluation of their therapy.

Every health care professional is familiar with the problems of patient deviation from instructions. Studies estimate, for example, that one fourth to one half of all patients fail to faithfully take all drugs that have been prescribed for them. If a patient (and older people are high nonadherers) fails to take a drug that in turn fails to produce positive results, the health care professional may argue that the patient has assumed the risks of noncompliance with medical instructions. Failure of a competent adult patient to follow instructions, after a reasonable explanation as to the necessity of the orders, is generally a complete defense for the health care professional who is accused of malpractice. The usual response to this defense, though, is that the risk was not really voluntarily and knowledgeably assumed.

Therapeutic Privilege

The most controversial exception to compliance with informed consent requirements is the doctrine of "therapeutic exception" or "therapeutic privilege." The doctrine of therapeutic privilege is the medical branch of the long-recognized common law defense of necessity. This defense acts to justify conduct that would otherwise be deemed a civil or criminal wrong. A defendant who prevents an injury that is threatened from some force of nature or some other independent cause not connected with the plaintiff is said to be acting under necessity. For example, an individual may break into a private dwelling in order to save an occupant from perishing in a house fire without becoming liable for trespassing. The foundation of the necessity privilege has been said to be a mixture of charity, the maintenance of the public good, and self-protection. This privilege, as applied to health care, is found codified in the statutes of several states today and is recognized as a matter of common law in all others.

In the medial context, the defense of therapeutic privilege to a claim of nondisclosure of material information about a patient's diagnosis, prognosis, or treatment is applicable when, in the health care professional's good faith judgment, disclosure would be likely to complicate or hinder necessary treatment, cause severe psychological harm, and be so upsetting as to render a rational decision by the patient impossible. In such circumstances, it is permissible to proceed with the intervention in the absence of disclosure and informed consent.

The general privilege of necessity has been strictly limited to emergencies in which severe harm is threatened. The medical version, therapeutic privilege, has likewise been construed extremely narrowly by the courts, which have implied that it applies only when the patient is severely and emotionally unstable and when the mere sharing of the information itself would imminently imperil the patient's life. Moreover, the privilege can in no event last longer than the condition that justifies it. Once the patient has improved, disclosure must take place. In light of the weighty limitations that have been placed on the therapeutic privilege defense by the courts, any attempted use of this defense must be viewed with substantial skepticism.

The preferred rule is a presumption that the health care professional must inform the patient of all material information but that the manner and setting in which the information is conveyed (encompassing such factors as time, place, language used, and other people present) be permitted to vary depending on the patient's particular circumstances. Although some health care professionals insist that they might be held liable for telling the patient too much, no court has ever found a health care professional liable for giving a patient an excessive amount of accurate and relevant information.

Nor can intervention without adequate disclosure be justified merely because the health care professional thinks that the intervention would be in the patient's best interest. A physician might well believe that a form of treatment is desirable or necessary, but the law does not permit the physician to substitute that judgment for the patient's through lack of candor or deception. To argue that a health care professional is justified in withholding information because a patient might, on the basis of those facts, decline therapy that the professional deems desirable would be a complete perversion of the principle of therapeutic privilege. Besides, as noted previously, patient consent rates actually tend to increase in direct proportion to the amount of relevant information disclosed to patients.

Before opting to treat a patient under therapeutic privilege, the health care professional should at least consult a colleague to secure an independent determination that there is a clinical and ethical basis to act under the privilege. The health care professional should document exactly what information is being withheld from the patient and why. The professional is then best advised to disclose these facts to the appropriate next of kin, when available, and to document that disclosure.

These general restrictions regarding use of therapeutic exception apply to all types of competent patients and all types of interventions, psychiatric as well as nonpsychiatric. They apply with particular force to older patients, for whose personal values and preferences the health care professional should have the highest respect.

Known Risks

The final notable exception to informed consent requirements comes into play when the anticipated risks are of a commonly known variety. In general, a health care professional is not required to disclose a risk of which the particular patient is already aware from past experience (Brahams,

1992) or that is so widely known that the average patient would be aware of it. When a patient claims that he or she was not personally aware of a particular risk, juries often tend to react sympathetically, so health care professionals should try to justify nondisclosure of information based on this exception quite gingerly, if at all.

Significance of Forms

No greater confusion exists among both health care professionals and members of the public in the area of informed consent than that concerning the legal significance of the written consent form. This confusion is extremely unfortunate, as it leads in far too many cases to a tendency for the written form to be equated with and substituted for the consent itself. It cannot be stressed strongly enough that this thinking and practice are erroneous; valid legal consent is not achieved by a piece of paper, but rather requires compliance with the professional/patient communicative process detailed in the preceding pages. In fact, obsessive preoccupation with written forms at the expense of the process of consent can be counterproductive in terms of legal risk management (Schouten, 1989).

Except when the proposed intervention is part of a biomedical or behavioral research protocol (see Chapter 12), a written consent form ordinarily is not even legally required. Even when a written form has been signed by the patient, there are numerous ways for its legitimacy to be attacked. Among the most familiar patient claims are "I was nervous"; "I didn't understand because the doctor used big, technical words"; "I was in such pain that I would do anything to get rid of it"; "They had already given me a shot, so I wasn't clearheaded"; and "The nurse handed me this piece of paper at the last minute, and I signed it without even looking at it." Such claims are likely to carry extra weight in the minds of a jury that is contemplating the plight of an injured older patient.

In spite of all this, most health care professionals and facilities regularly use written consent forms in their everyday clinical practice, for both their older and younger patients. This is largely a result of the confusion between form and substance described above. Nevertheless, I fully encourage the appropriate use of written consent forms in clinical practice, as it serves a variety of legitimate purposes.

First, the regular use of consent forms is required by JCAHO standards. Although these standards are not, strictly speaking, legal authority, JCAHO accreditation is a prerequisite (or at least one way to qualify) for many forms of public and private third-party payment for health services rendered to covered patients (see Chapter 5). Thus, hospitals and certain other health care facilities desiring to participate in Medicare, Medicaid, Blue Cross, most managed care organizations, and other third-party payment programs must comply with the JCAHO's written consent standards.

Second, the written consent form can and should serve as a valuable source of information and education for the patient and family. If it is (1) written in clear, understandable, nontechnical language; (2) given to the patient and family as far ahead of the proposed intervention as possible for their study in a nonstressful, relaxed way; and (3) orally supplemented by thorough, responsive explanations by all concerned health care professionals, the written form can become an integral part of the professional/patient relationship. It can perform a tremendous cognitive as well as therapeutic function for the patient and family. Any educational strategy that reduces the possibility of surprise and anger at an unexpected outcome is good patient management.

Third, the written consent form does provide some measure of legal protection for the health care professional. Although it does not by itself constitute the totality of the required consent, the written form does have status, based either on state statute or court decision, as an important piece of proof or evidence that the required process of communication took place. The existence of a written form signed by the patient (or the patient's proxy) creates a legal presumption that valid consent was obtained; the burden then shifts to the patient to rebut or overcome that presumption by persuasively showing that one or more of the essential elements of consent were missing.

There are several different kinds of written consent forms. These, as well as additional means of documenting consent and other aspects of patient care, are described in Chapter 4. But the specific means of documentation are really secondary. The important thing is for the health care professional to make sure that the information set forth in the documentation has in fact been communicated to the patient in a way that is understandable to that patient. If the objective is to fill pieces of paper with signatures, the whole point of patient consent is lost and the forms become meaningless. If the objective is to recognize and respect the principle that the adult patient is, in the vast majority of cases, the rightful determiner of his or her own destiny, then the consent form becomes a meaningful documentation of the patient's legitimate authorization. The use of consent forms should be dealt with in the institution's formal internal consent policy suggested earlier in this chapter.

Effect of Patient Decision

Most patients, especially most easily awed older patients, will accept the advice of their health care professionals and consent to undergo recommended medical interventions. Such cases present few ethical or legal dilemmas, as the health care professional almost invariably acts as though the consenting patient (by virtue of agreeing with the professional) must be competent and has understood the professional's explanation of the intervention.

Some patients, though, including a small but significant segment of the elderly, at certain times reject specific suggested medical interventions. This may occur for a variety of reasons, including misunderstanding; religious objections; fear of embarrassment, invasion, or physical pain; machismo; cost concerns; or any number of other rational or irrational motivations (Jeremiah, O'Sullivan, & Stein, 1995). The health care professional has an ethical and legal obligation to strenuously seek to persuade recalcitrant patients and their families to consent to clinically indicated interventions. Every effort should be made to explain to the patient and family, in a gentle and warm way, why the particular intervention is imperative. If that fails, the patient and family should be reminded that by refusing they now accept the responsibility—clinical, ethical, and legal— for the consequences. Failure to try one's best to convince the patient and family is an indictment of the health care professional's persuasive ability and might be construed by others as an attitude of indifference to the patient that could place the professional in subsequent legal jeopardy.

Despite one's best persuasive efforts, however, some patients and families will persist in their refusal. In such circumstances, the health care professional has several options.

First, once he or she has verified that the patient is competent to make treatment decisions and that adequate explanations have been given that the patient understood, the health care professional may and ordinarily should respect the patient's refusal and refrain from performing the proposed intervention. This general rule regarding competent patients applies to emergency as well as nonemergency health care and extends to refusals made by properly appointed substitute decision makers in the case of incompetent patients (see Chapter 8). When the professional relies on refusal of treatment, such refusal should be thoroughly documented (see Chapter 4).

Second, an informed refusal of treatment sometimes may be viewed, from the vantage point of the patient and family, as one means of reducing suffering. Such a perspective could make some refusals more acceptable to those who now disagree with the idea of honoring them. If a health care professional finds that acceptance of a patient's or proxy's treatment refusal is personally objectionable in a particular case, he or she is free to exercise a second option: terminating the professional/patient relationship. To avoid legal liability for abandoning a patient in distress, the health care professional should formally notify the patient and family of the relationship termination and the reasons for it and should make all reasonable efforts to refer the patient to another competent health care professional, who agrees to care for the patient and whom the patient and family are willing to accept as their caregiver.

A third alternative, realistically available only in emergency (life-threatening) situations if at all, is for the health care professional or facility to initiate a formal legal proceeding in which a judge is asked to authorize a particular course of care over the patient's competent and informed objections, based on the existence of compelling state interests favoring intervention. Decision making by and for critically ill patients is the subject of Chapter 11.

Patient consent to recommended treatment and patient refusal of recommended treatment are only two sides of the patient decision-making triangle. The third side is insistence by the patient or family on some form of medical intervention that the health care professional judges to be clinically inappropriate, that is, nonbeneficial or futile. If the intervention is not harmful and may have some palliative or psychological supportive value for the patient or family, the health care professional usually should view the request sympathetically, although economic considerations cannot be dismissed as irrelevant. If, however, the intervention carries some adverse risk to the patient or to others, the health care professional has no ethical or legal obligation to indulge the patient's or family's misguided desires and may actually incur legal jeopardy by doing so. Clinical decision making should be a mutual, cooperative process of negotiation among reasonable alternatives by patient, family, and health care professional, a process in which no single party is either master or slave. The subject of futile medical treatment is explored in more depth in Chapter 11.

TRUTH TELLING

The foregoing discussion of informed consent presumes that there exist reasonable forms of medical intervention that are likely to benefit the particular patient from whom or for whom consent is sought. But there are times, particularly when older patients are involved, when the patient's condition is such that no curative or restorative form of medical intervention is reasonably available. This may occur when a condition is thought to be terminal (in the past, cancer has been the best example) or chronic, degenerative, and untreatable (Alzheimer's disease has been the prototype of this category until recently). In such cases, informed consent is not relevant (there being no treatment proposed), and many health care professionals have advocated silence or even outright deception in the psychological interests of the patient and family. Additionally, physicians frequently have deferred to families' paternalistic pleas to keep the afflicted patient in the informational "dark" (Maguire et al., 1996).

We have come a long way in our ethical and legal thinking on this subject since Oliver Wendell Holmes advised the graduating class of the Bellevue Hospital Medical College in 1871: "Your patient has no more right to all the truth than he has to all the medicine in your saddle-bags. . . . He should get only just so much as is good for him" (Holmes, 1911). Candor is strongly supported by most, although not all (Nyberg, 1993), ethical philosophers on the grounds of respect for patient dignity (Post & Foley, 1992). Truthfulness in these cases also is favored by an increasing number of modern clinicians, based on an understanding that most patients and families want and are able to handle effectively infor-mation about the patient's condition, even when the news is bad and the reasonable alternatives for cure or amelioration are dim or nonexistent (Buckman, 1996; Holroyd, Snustad, & Chalifoux, 1996; Meyers, 1997). In 1997, the Alzheimer Society of Canada endorsed formal guidelines telling physicians not to hide the diagnosis of dementia from a patient believed to have Alzheimer's disease.

No specific statute or regulation can be cited at present requiring dis-closure in situations in which informed consent is not necessary. Never-theless, several legal caveats (words of caution) are in order.

First, as medical science inexorably progresses and new forms of curative, ameliorative, or palliative interventions are invented for diseases and conditions previously considered hopeless and untreatable, the num-ber of situations in which informed consent is irrelevant continues to shrink (Drickamer & Lachs, 1992). If a realistic possibility for slowing dis-ease progression, for cure, or even for relief exists but is not offered to a patient, the health care professional may be exposed to legal liability for negligent omission. Alzheimer's disease is beginning to fall into this class of ailments.

In addition, the older patient may have many life decisions to make that have nothing to do with therapeutic medical interventions (Post & Whitehouse, 1995). The individual, for example, might need to make timely financial estate planning choices or actively consider participating as a subject in biomedical or behavioral research (see Chapter 12). Patients who are deprived, by the health care professional's silence, of the chance to make such decisions in a timely, thoughtful fashion may be able in the future to hold the less-than-frank health care professional liable for breach of fiduciary duties (Dickerson, 1995).

As another warning, whereas the law may now accept the with-holding of information under certain limited circumstances, it will not condone clear-cut misrepresentation. A health care professional who is asked a direct question would be well advised to answer truthfully. As noted earlier, no health care professional has ever been sued successfully for disclosing an overabundance of truthful, pertinent information to a patient or family.

For the modern American (Higuchi, 1992) health care professional, the issue is not whether honesty is the best policy with older patients and their families. Rather, the important questions are where, when, and how information can be communicated in a manner that is as candid, competent, and compassionate as possible (Freedman, 1993).

Chapter 4

Medical Record Keeping: Documentation, Patient Access, and Confidentiality

Medical record keeping is an essential aspect of quality patient care (AMA Council on Scientific Affairs, 1993b). It is the primary means of refreshing the memory of the health care professional about the facts surrounding care of a particular patient and the major source of communication among professionals about a patient who is under the care of a multimember health care team. There is a legal duty to properly document patient care, violation of which may constitute actionable negligence on the health care professional's part if injury to the patient results (*Fox v. Cohen*, 1980).

In addition to its clinical importance, the medical record also has potentially substantial legal purposes. It is the process and the product of tangible documentation for later scrutiny of the nature and quality of health care services delivered. The medical record may become a central piece of evidence in resolving a variety of issues in a panoply of legal contexts. Among the theories of recovery against health care providers for negligence in record keeping is the tort of spoliation of evidence (Goodnight & Davis, 1992; *Smith v. Sup. Ct. for City of Los Angeles*, 1984). The medical record often contains the power to significantly promote or impair the legal well-being of both the patient and the health care professional. One commentator has gone so far as to suggest that the 20th-century version of the Hippocratic oath should be amended to read: "Whatsoever I shall see or hear in the course of my profession, in my intercourse with men, if it is that which should not be broadcast abroad, I will never divulge it but consider it a holy secret . . . provided, however, there are no lawsuits, third-party payers, or attorneys who want to examine your records" (Brooten, 1982).

43

The Joint Commission on Accreditation of Healthcare Organizations (JCAHO) sets strict standards regarding medical record keeping in its various accreditation manuals guiding practice in both acute and long-term health care settings. Individual facilities and agencies establish procedures through adoption of internal bylaws and rules. Most states prescribe record-keeping specifics as part of institutional, agency, or individual licensure acts. Additionally, federal record-keeping requirements for publicly funded patients (see Chapter 5), many of whom are older, are created by the Medicare and Medicaid statutes and implementing regulations. A physician may be involuntarily terminated from these programs for records deficiencies (*Koh v. Perales,* 1991). Finally, courts have frequently enunciated common law principles relevant to the adequacy and appropriateness of medical record keeping. It is essential that the health care professional be aware of specific provisions within his or her own jurisdiction and practice site concerning record keeping. Because noncompliance with legal record-keeping requirements may jeopardize a facility's or agency's license, or its JCAHO or insurance status, a health care professional's job or staff privileges may well hinge on acceptable performance in this area.

In this chapter, I deal with several aspects of medical record keeping of general interest and focus on areas of particular pertinence to the care of geriatric patients. I explore here (1) legal uses of the medical record, (2) allocation of responsibility for record keeping, (3) practical guidelines for proper documentation of care, (4) particular safeguards to employ in selected problem areas, (5) patient access to records, and (6) confidentiality.

LEGAL USES OF MEDICAL RECORDS

It has been estimated that medical evidence, which relies heavily on written records, plays a part in about three fourths of all civil cases and in about one fourth of all criminal cases brought to trial (Kennedy & Jacobs, 1981). It is likely that these fractions are even higher for litigation in which older persons are parties.

One type of legal case in which the medical record is invariably crucial is the professional liability/medical malpractice civil action. This is a lawsuit brought by the individual patient seeking compensation for injuries suffered as the proximate or direct result of the health care professional's or facility's deviation from acceptable standards of care (i.e., negligence) (Feegel, 1998; Flamm, 1998). In the typical malpractice case, the available documentation of care determines the legal outcome at least as much as does the actual quality of care provided. The record becomes the health care professional's greatest friend or worst foe.

Another kind of legal case in which medical records generally influence the result is represented by patient legal claims for benefits under public disability programs (see Chapter 6), private disability insurance policies, workers' compensation systems, and private or public (see Chapter 5) health insurance provisions. Challenges to alleged age discrimination in employment that are met by a defense that the plaintiff can no longer function properly in terms of job performance may turn in part on medical records. Similarly, personal injury lawsuits brought by older patients on the basis of casualty (accident) occasioned by the fault of another (automobile crashes and slip-and-fall situations are the most usual, if mundane, examples) frequently turn on the nature of medical proof produced. These types of cases should remind health care professionals that their fiduciary duties to their patients extend well beyond purely objective, scientific clinical intervention and include reasonable efforts to promote the total (involving the legal, social, emotional, and economic) well-being of their patients. It may be argued that failure by the health care professional, through inadequate record keeping or otherwise, to vigorously advocate on behalf of the legal entitlements of the patient constitutes negligence, as an unintentional deviation from an acceptable standard of care or even as intentional abandonment of a patient in need. The health care professional's nonclinical fiduciary duties are, if anything, more compelling in the case of older patients, who often are in most immediate need of the legal, social, emotional, and economic advocacy that health care professionals are in a position to provide.

Medical records also are put to legal use as part of utilization review (UR) and quality assurance (QA) programs. In both fee-for-service and prepaid contexts, public and private third-party payment for health services is generally tied, at least in the institutional context, to the existence and operation of effective UR and QA programs that purport to carefully scrutinize and ensure the appropriateness, necessity, and quality of the health care delivered (see Chapter 5). These programs depend almost exclusively, at least in the first instance, on a review of the medical records, which will be judged on their face to either justify or not justify claimed financial payment for services rendered or expected to be rendered. As managed care increasingly dominates the health care marketplace, pressure on health care professionals to produce the type of medical record that can pass UR and QA muster and thus support a claim of cost-effective care will mount. This is especially true for older patients, in light of Medicare's prospective payment system (PPS) computed according to the diagnosis related groups (DRGs) into which older hospitalized patients fall and the movement of older patients into managed care.

Finally, medical records constitute an essential element of evidence in disputes between the patient and the health care professional over the propriety and amount of professional fees billed. In such unfortunate circumstances, the medical record is the best means of establishing exactly what care was provided and why.

The significance of medical records as evidence for these and other types of legal purposes lies mainly in the psychological aura that our society tends to attach to the written word. A tangible document generally delivers an extremely persuasive impact on the minds of lay (in the sense of nonmedically educated) judges and juries who examine and evaluate the circumstances and quality of health care after the fact. The written record is also accorded great weight on the part of government and private reviewers who do have health care backgrounds. The general presumption in legal review is, realistically, as follows: If it is written, then it happened; if it is not written, then it did not happen. Poor, sloppy, incomplete records inevitably raise a red flag and create the inference, whether grounded in fact or not, of poor, sloppy, incomplete health care.

RESPONSIBILITY FOR RECORD KEEPING

Specific directions identifying who is responsible for various aspects of medical record keeping should be found in the internal bylaws and operating policies and procedures of a health care office or facility. The health care professional functioning in any organized setting should be thoroughly familiar with any applicable internal rules fixing documentation responsibilities. A missing or incomplete record creates a rebuttable adverse presumption about the quality of care given (*DeLaughter v. Lawrence County Hospital,* 1992).

As a general operational principle, responsibility for documentation falls on the health care professional who has made the observation, done the test, or rendered the treatment that is to be documented. In other words, documentation should be based upon the documenter's firsthand, direct knowledge. For example, surgical notes would be written by the chief surgeon, nursing notes by each nurse involved in patient care (Weiler, 1994), consulting reports by the consultant, and so on. The same principle applies regardless of the type or size of practice setting.

As a practical matter, the growing trend toward a team approach means that many patients, particularly those being diagnosed and treated on an inpatient (acute or long-term) basis, will have a multitude of different health care professionals contributing to the written record. This is especially true for geriatric patients, who are more likely to possess a wider variety of related and unrelated medical and nonmedical problems and who thus are likely to receive the attention of more different members of the health care team. Due to this multiplicity of actors involved in providing and documenting geriatric patient care, good practice compels the professional to read regularly and carefully the record entries of all other team members in order to stay abreast of the entire clinical and social picture describing each patient.

Documentation responsibilities cannot be delegated away as, for example, from the physician to the nurse. Each health care professional is liable for documenting personal observations, impressions, and actions. Although oral orders are permissible when necessary, they must be verified as soon as possible afterward by a written record notation. In situations requiring countersigning of record entries (such as when the attending physician countersigns notes made by medical students or physician's assistants), the individual who countersigns thereby assumes legal responsibility for the content of that notation. This means that record entries should be scrutinized and, if necessary, amended before they are countersigned.

GUIDELINES FOR DOCUMENTATION

Medical records generally are admissible as evidence in legal proceedings under the business records exception to the rule against hearsay. That is, medical records ordinarily are deemed accurate and reliable because they are made in the regular course of business (patient care), contemporaneous with the occurrence of the matters reported, by persons with direct knowledge of the facts being documented. To the extent that records do not satisfy these conditions, less reliance is placed on them, frequently to the detriment of the health care professional who depends on those records to justify a course of conduct (Burnum, 1989; Marks, 1989).

The form of record keeping will vary depending on practice setting. JCAHO standards and state facility and agency licensing statutes describe with some particularity record-keeping requirements in hospitals, home care, and nursing homes. Other types of health care settings have wide latitude to style their own form of record keeping through design of internal policies and procedures. One popular form of record keeping is the "problem-oriented" medical record, although this format has some detractors (Donnelly & Brauner, 1992). The following general "do's and don'ts" for documentation are advisable regardless of the type of setting in which health care is delivered.

First, written patient records must be accurate and truthful. It is presumed that the care rendered will be of high quality; if this is not the case, falsifying records will only further injure both the patient and the legal position of the health care professional. Given scientific advances in the forensic specialty of questioned document analysis and the greater unwillingness of modern health care team members to "cover up" for their colleagues' misdeeds, it is increasingly unlikely that an attempt to falsely alter a medical record will go permanently undiscovered. Proof of such an attempt could subject the health care professional to potential federal and state criminal fraud prosecution, licensure disciplinary action, insurance termination (*Mirkin v. Medical Mutual*, 1990), and civil liability to the patient for improper care or fraud (*Moskovitz v. Mt. Sinai Medical Center*, 1994). These adverse legal consequences are in addition to the obvious ethical problems raised concerning deception and dishonesty toward the patient and the public to whom the health care professional owes an obligation of fidelity (Prosser, 1992).

Second, documentation of care should be thorough and complete. This does not require the writing of a full-length treatise for each patient encounter. I merely emphasize the lay (i.e., judge and jury) perception that if a fact is not included in the record, then it probably didn't happen. Partial record keeping implies partial health care (*University of Texas Medical Branch at Galveston v. York*, 1991).

Third, medical records must be legible. Abbreviations should be used sparingly and judiciously and only according to a facility's approved list. Incomprehensible medical notations may have a place in cocktail party banter but not in the actual delivery of health care. Sloppiness in documentation creates a presumption of sloppiness in patient care and of the health care professional's need to hide or obscure certain facts about his or her conduct. Additionally, considerable amounts of valuable time are lost when another member of the health care team (usually a nurse or pharmacist) must doublecheck the meaning of a written entry or order because it is illegible (Kozak, Dittus, Smith, Fitzgerald, & Langfeld, 1994). Worse yet, an illegible but unchecked order may result in a misunderstanding and improper care being rendered.

According to a 1994 AMA report, medication error secondary to misinterpreted physicians' prescriptions was the second most prevalent and expensive claim in 90,000 malpractice claims over a period of 7 years. In 1994, the average indemnity payment for the 393 most recent medication error claims was $120,722, with a range of $5,000 to $2.2 million per claim (Cabral, 1997).

Fourth, documentation must be timely. Because the health care professional's memory naturally fades over time, notes that are made near or at the time of the event are likely to be most accurate. Further, contemporaneous entries create a more favorable overall impression of the totality of patient care. Specific time limitations for updating medical records are established by Medicare regulations (currently 15 days from patient discharge), JCAHO standards, and internal organizational bylaws. The health care professional should be familiar with specifically applicable time limits but should consider them a maximum time frame to be bettered whenever possible.

Fifth, one must not overcorrect mistakes that are entered into a medical record. Corrections must be obvious and legible, consisting of a single line drawn through the otherwise readable error, with the correction written above the error, signed, and dated. White-outs, erasures, total obliterations, and destruction of complete pages create an inference of secrecy that can seriously undermine the health care professional's credibility, and they are highly inadvisable. What to a health care professional might seem innocent neatness, to an attorney, judge, or jury might be considered destruction of relevant evidence.

Finally, a patient's medical record is no place for jousting with or editorializing about the patient, family, facility, or other health care professionals (Hirsh, 1998b). Every entry in a record should serve a legitimate patient care purpose. Thus, appropriate notations consist of objective observations and reports and clinically significant impressions. These items should be expressed in a value-neutral, nonjudgmental manner. Frustrations and other subjective emotions should be indulged through other, more appropriate, forums. The importance of possessing a wide working vocabulary is an asset often overlooked by many health care professionals.

Medical records should be physically retained by the health care professional or facility for as long a period of time as possible in a secure storage place (Harris & Thal, 1991). In this modern era of microfilm and microfiche, it is easily feasible to maintain records for at least as long as the health care professional is in practice or the health care organization is in existence. In the rare situation where space or cost limitations would make this prohibitive, records should be retained at least past the jurisdiction's applicable statutory minimum, which in most states is around 7–10 years from the last patient contact. Medicare requires that records be kept for at least 5 years, 42 C.F.R. §482.24(b)(1). The statute of limitations for medical malpractice negligence actions (generally 1 or 2 years but sometimes longer) provides no guidance in this matter. In most jurisdictions, the statute of limitations does not begin to run until the patient discovers (or should have discovered) the existence of an injury, even when this is substantially later than the health care professional's alleged substandard act or omission. Of particular relevance to geriatric practice, a patient's medical records should not automatically be discarded at the time of the patient's death, because many of the legal rights that are dependent on those records may become exercisable by the patient's surviving relatives or other designated persons.

PARTICULAR PROBLEM AREAS
IN DOCUMENTATION

Although proper documentation is essential throughout the entire spectrum of patient care, there are certain areas where it takes on added importance. Several of these "red flag" areas involve significant numbers of older patients.

Informed Consent

If a patient (or legal surrogate) either gives or withholds informed consent for a recommended medical intervention, complete and accurate documentation is imperative in establishing that the legally necessary process of professional/patient communication preceded the patient's decision and that the patient acted voluntarily and competently. If these three conditions of legally effective consent or refusal are not sufficiently spelled out in the patient's written record, an after-the-fact reviewer may find that they were not present.

The clinical and legal significance of formal, written consent forms for medical interventions that are invasive, risky, or experimental is discussed at length in Chapter 3. I emphasize again that the form's value, from both a clinical and legal perspective, depends entirely on the degree to which it accurately reflects the facts it contains. It must be a health care professional's standard practice to actually do what the form says has been done. The written form serves an adjunct function, embodying the process of dialogue and interaction but never substituting for the process. The AMA (1991) has produced an excellent volume on this topic, with an array of model consent forms for various situations.

In addition to using a written form for medical interventions requiring express consent, the health care professional also should document directly on the patient's medical chart those facts establishing the voluntary, competent, and informed nature of consent or refusal. The advisable volume of such a note depends upon the particular circumstances. Usually, a substantive but brief summary statement is sufficient. If, however, the intervention itself is especially risky or invasive, it may be wise to err on the side of a more elaborate written description of the facts surrounding consent or refusal. Similarly, greater detail in the written note is advisable when the health care professional senses, based on prior general or specific experience, that the particular patient or family is of a type that is likely later to raise questions concerning the appropriateness of the professional's conduct, particularly if the results of intervention are unsuccessful. Some health care professionals follow the practice of having consent-related conversations with patients witnessed in the record by a third party (such as a nurse) and/or requesting the patient to initial the chart entry. There are even reports of videotaping (with the patient's permission) and storing professional/patient consent conferences.

All of these practices are legally permissible. The extent to which precautions of this sort are advisable depends on the degree to which one is willing to tolerate certain legal risks as a matter of delivering health care.

If a patient's consent or refusal is exclusively oral and not embodied in a written document signed by the patient, the medical charting described in the preceding paragraph takes on, if anything, added importance. The chart entries in that situation constitute the only tangible evidence regarding the voluntariness, competency, and knowledge basis of the patient's decision. Absence of such documentation may lead to a conclusion that informed consent failed to occur.

As was noted in Chapter 3, older persons are disproportionate recipients of drug prescriptions and run a disproportionately high risk of adverse reactions. It is essential that the health care professional disclose to the patient adequate information regarding the risks of and reasonable alternatives to pharmaceutical interventions proposed and that the particulars of that disclosure be fully reflected in the medical chart. The chart should also show the health care professional's conscientious efforts to monitor the patient for indications of adverse drug reactions. In 1997, the voluntary organization National Council on Patient Information and Education (NCPIE) began an implementation strategy for its "Action Plan for the Provision of Useful Prescription Medicine Information" (MedGuide).

Chapter 3 details several recognized exceptions to the general legal requirement of express patient consent to an invasive or risky medical intervention. If the health care professional elects to dispense with patient consent on the basis of (1) a legally required intervention, (2) an emergency, (3) patient waiver of the right to consent, (4) therapeutic privilege, or (5) the risk being one of common knowledge, the written medical record should include a thorough, explicit statement of the circumstances on which the claimed exception is founded.

One of the most difficult situations in the consent context arises when a patient leaves a health care facility or agency "against medical advice" (AMA). Competent older individuals sometimes avail themselves of this right, although at a much lower rate than do younger patients (Long & Marin, 1982). At the time of treatment refusal, the patient should diplomatically but forcefully be requested to sign a form indicating that the potential adverse consequences of treatment refusal have been fully explained and releasing the provider and any associated health care professionals from potential legal liability flowing from injuries sustained as a direct result of treatment refusal. If the patient declines to sign such a form, that action itself should be recorded in the medical chart, along with a description of the health care professional's efforts to dissuade the patient from leaving treatment AMA.

Treatment Abatement

Decisions to withhold or withdraw medical treatment are discussed in Chapter 11. The wishes of the patient (if ascertainable), any formal proxy, the family, and significant others should all be recorded. The judgments of involved health care professionals, as well as their underlying reasoning, should be fully and candidly documented, as well as any attempts to change the minds of patient, proxy, or family. Honesty and openness in record keeping in this sphere is the professional's best defense against subsequent allegations of negligence or malevolent intent. Failure to put decisions and orders in writing not only fails to protect the health care professional but invites inappropriate action by other team members based on the mixed and confused signals that are emitted. Failure to clearly and convincingly document patient wishes may deprive the patient of the right to have those wishes carried out.

The point needs to be underscored in the case of "No Code" or "Do Not Resuscitate" (DNR) orders. The American Medical Association (Council on Ethical and Judicial Affairs, 1991) and other relevant groups (e.g., Choice in Dying, 1995) have carefully considered this issue and strongly endorsed policies mandating that "No Codes" be written directly by the attending physician in the patient's medical record. A written order serves to explain and justify the decision to withhold resuscitation and to avoid confusion and consequent improper action by other members of the health care team. Nurses and other team members are well advised to initiate and continue resuscitative efforts in the absence of a clear, recorded directive from the attending physician. JCAHO hospital accreditation standards, as well as statutes in New York (Pollack, 1996) and several other states, now require that DNR orders be written in the patient's chart. The medical chart entry should contain the order itself, an enumeration of persons consulted, names of those who concurred in the decision, and the clinical facts and impressions supporting the order. The more specific the order, the less is the likelihood of errors in patient care (Mittelberger, Lo, Martin, & Uhlmann, 1993).

Elder Abuse

In Chapter 7, I deal with the role of the health care professional in identifying and reporting evidence of elder abuse. It is vital, for both the physical and emotional well-being of the older patient and the legal protection of the health care professional, that the patient's medical record contain complete and accurate documentation of all observations and impressions upon which a reasonable suspicion of elder abuse is or should be based. The chart should indicate all actions taken by the health care professional in response to this suspicion. Adequate charting in this area will help to make needed social interventions available to the victim and to safeguard the health care professional from subsequent charges of either hastiness or tardiness in reporting to authorities a suspected case of elder abuse (Quinn & Tomita, 1997).

Older patients may also present for health care with other types of reportable conditions, such as criminally inflicted wounds or communicable diseases. The health care professional must be aware of his or her jurisdiction's specific list of medical conditions triggering mandatory or voluntary reporting and should thoroughly document clinical observations and impressions derived from contact with a patient suspected of presenting such a condition.

Emergencies

Health care often is sought by and for older individuals on an emergency basis. In such cases, the volume of patients seen, the acute nature of each patient's condition, and the constricted time span of the professional/patient relationship combine to emphasize the importance of entering notes as contemporaneously as possible to the occurrence of the matters recorded. A separate chart should be created for every person presenting for emergency care. All relevant patient information, including vital signs, should appear in that single chart. Responsibility for record keeping in the emergency context resides, as it does more generally, with the health care professional making the observation or diagnosis or ordering or administering the treatment.

It is important to document how the patient arrived in the emergency room (alone, with family or friends, by ambulance, by private automobile driven by the patient, and so on). If no care is medically indicated or care is given on an outpatient (nonadmitted) basis only, the record should explain why that course was chosen. The health care professional should indicate the patient's condition when emergency care was terminated and in whose care the patient was left, to show that no abandonment took place. The record also should reflect communication between the emergency health care professional and the patient's personal physician, if any. If the patient is not admitted, follow-up instructions provided to the patient and family or friends should be recorded.

Any consents to or refusals of medical intervention should, as explained earlier, be carefully documented.

PATIENT ACCESS TO RECORDS

The tangible pieces of paper, films, and charts comprising a patient's medical record are the legal property of the health care professional (in the case of a private practice) or institution or agency that created those tangible documents. The original versions of those documents need never and should never, be relinquished to the patient or to anyone else, absent a specific court order.

However, as a growing number of recipients of health care services, often including the elderly, demand increased participation in the totality of their own clinical care, issues have arisen concerning the patient's right to access to the information that is contained in those tangible documents. The strong and steady trend is toward a broad legal expansion of this access right.

Patients treated in federal health care facilities (such as those operated by the Departments of Veterans Affairs and Defense) may seek and obtain access to the information in their own medical records under the authority of the Federal Privacy Act, enacted in 1977. State legislation (in about half the states) and judicial decisions (*Pierce v. Penman*, 1986; *In the Matter of Gerkin*, 1980) have made records available in a growing number of jurisdictions to patients receiving care in a variety of state, municipal, non-profit, and proprietary health care settings. The health care professional must be aware of specific legal provisions for patient access to records that are applicable to his or her own practice. The professional must also know about any exceptions (such as for psychiatric notations or therapeutically privileged comments) or special procedures (such as the mandatory involvement of a third-party buffer [e.g., an attorney] or permission for the provider to supply a summary rather than an exact copy of the record) that are recognized in those legal provisions. The health care professional must also consider voluntary guidelines, like the JCAHO standards or the AHA Patients' Bill of Rights, that support broad patient access to information about their own health care. Ultimately, almost any modern patient who strongly enough desires access to the medical record can satisfy that wish through the institution of litigation, and that avenue will continue and enlarge in the coming years.

The expanded access-to-information phenomenon has not been greeted with unanimous approval by the clinical community. Some have argued that record requests are generally symptomatic of mistrust and an expression of adversary professional/patient relations. This attitude is overly defensive and counterproductive. The better view is that patient access to the medical record can have a valuable salutary effect on patient satisfaction and the quality of the professional/patient relationship (McLaren, 1991).

The key determinant of the actual effect of patient access lies in the quality of the reaction of the health care professional to the patient's request to examine the record. If the professional interprets the request as a challenge to the clinician's authority and reacts with suspicion and distrust, it is often this reaction (rather than the patient's request itself) that risks engendering or exacerbating tension between the professional and the patient. The professional's anxiety and imagination about an adversarial relationship can easily develop into a self-fulfilling prophecy. On the other hand, a patient's request for access to the medical record may reasonably be interpreted as (1) a dissatisfaction with the level and character of the communication with the professional and/or (2) a sincere curiosity about and desire to more actively participate in monitoring the course of care being provided. In either event, the health care professional can and should take this as a signal to convert the patient's request into an important opportunity to enhance communication and to strengthen the nature of the relationship. It is a chance to encourage greater mutual trust and understanding, to exploit (in the positive sense) the role of the patient as full partner in the relationship.

Converting a potentially adversarial action into a beneficial aspect of patient care will take some attention and effort, as well as a mature and flexible attitude, on the part of both patient and health care professional. This may be particularly challenging when dealing with older patients, for whom effectively achieving meaningful comprehension of frequently complex facts and considerations may be difficult, especially in light of often well-settled values and viewpoints. As explained in Chapter 3, nurturing a full relationship with the older patient may call for extreme patience, creativity, and perseverance by the health care professional. As I argued there, such extra effort can, in the vast majority of cases, yield successful results that are well worth the professional's energies. Supplying desired access to information via the written medical record in a tolerant, understanding, sympathetic manner is one significant means of bettering the larger professional/patient dialogue and, consequently, the entirety of the relationship.

Once a patient has died, in most states the release of medical records is controlled by the decedent's personal representative, executor, executrix, or administrator. Some states also allow the spouse of the decedent to access medical information. Although the Uniform Probate Code (UPC), section 3.703 (General Duties of Personal Representative) is silent on the issue of disclosure, the accompanying comments to that section imply that access to medical records is within the scope of the personal representative's authority.

CONFIDENTIALITY

In the course of performing their professional activities, health care professionals consistently and unavoidably come into contact with very personal, intimate information about their older patients. This knowledge of personal patient information imposes certain duties of confidentiality upon the health care professional. Fulfilling these duties can, in specific factual situations, raise substantial legal and ethical questions. The confidentiality obligations and concomitant legal and ethical consequences will become ever more complex and challenging as medical records are increasingly computerized (Frasca, 1996; Reed, 1994; Rind et al., 1997; Sweeney, 1997; U.S. Congress, Office of Technology Assessment, 1993; Waller & Fulton, 1993).

As a general legal and ethical precept, health care professionals have the duty to hold in confidence all personal patient information entrusted to them, and the patient has a right to expect the fulfillment of that duty (Annas, 1989). Ethically, confidentiality finds its origins as far back as the Hippocratic Oath and as currently as the latest version of the AMA's Principles of Medical Ethics. This broad ethical standard has been given legally enforceable status through numerous civil damage suits (Weisman, 1990) and by being embodied in most, if not all, state professional practice acts and implementing regulations. These laws provide that violation of the duty of confidentiality is a potential ground for revoking, denying, or suspending a professional's license to practice in his or her field of health care.

There are several foundations for this general rule. First, there are reasons based upon the bad consequences that would result from the failure to maintain patient confidences. Confidential treatment of patient disclosures and records is essential for continued trust and confidence in the health professions by the patient. If the patient fears communicating candidly and completely, proper care is jeopardized.

A second negative consequence of disregarding confidentiality is to make the patient more like an object of scrutiny than a person, to qualitatively set the patient apart from the caregiver. This would reinforce the paternalism and manipulation that has been all too often a part of the relationship between patients (especially older patients) and health care professionals.

Besides these arguments based on adverse consequences, there are certain ethical principles that, regardless of actual consequences, support the basic confidentiality requirement. These principles rest upon two factors: (1) the nature of the information itself that the patient communicates to the health care professional; and (2) the setting of the communication, that is, the fact that the communication occurs in the course of a patient/ health care professional relationship.

Certain kinds of personal information are by their nature private. In our culture, most people regard much, if not all, information about the state of their bodies (and minds) as the kind of information that ought to be kept largely under their own control (Chapman, 1997). Thus, the generic right to privacy that each individual enjoys encompasses within its boundaries the confidentiality of health records and disclosures. This right is particularly important to older individuals who, as the products of a precomputer, pre–mass communication age, often assign an even higher value to personal privacy than do members of younger generations. Corresponding with this right of privacy is a generic duty of respect on the part of the health care professional. The professional's obligation to maintain a patient's confidence, under this theory, is merely a specific application of the duty of individuals generally to refrain from invading the privacy zone of others.

Aside from the kind of information involved, the setting of the communication can establish the predicate for imposing a duty of confidentiality. The context of patient/health care professional communication creates a two-pronged type of relationship, giving rise to the confidentiality requirement.

One prong of this relationship is contractual. The patient and health care professional make a series of reciprocal promises to each other as conditions of the relationship. Included is a promise, almost always implied rather than spoken, that information shared within the patient/ professional relationship is confidential and that the professional will not disclose it without the patient's permission unless required to do so by law. The professional's implicit promise engenders reasonable understandings and expectations on the part of the patient (especially the trusting, deferential older patient) that the health care professional in turn must respect. In this sense, the principle of confidentiality in health care law and ethics is really a specific instance of the principle of promise keeping in law and ethics in general.

The older patient's reasonable expectation of privacy and the health care professional's concomitant duty of confidentiality apply with regard to all members of the health care team who are involved with a specific patient. This reflects the fact that the provision of health care is considerably more complex and institutionalized than any simple single professional/patient account would suggest, but it does not cause the contract model to break down. The patient generally makes an agreement with a single professional or organization, and that agreement ordinarily is to have a complex of services performed by a variety of members of a health care team. All professional team members are indirectly parties to the agreement and become committed to it by contracting with the employing professional or organization to perform certain patient care roles.

The second prong giving rise to the health care professional's confidentiality duty is the fiduciary, or trust, nature of the professional/patient relationship. This is the understanding and expectation within the professional/patient relationship that the health care professional will, with limited exceptions, act so as to maximally promote the best interests of the patient. This patient expectation and attendant professional obligation stem from the tremendous differential in power that exists between the parties to the relationship. On one hand, the patient (especially when old and ill) feels an extreme vulnerability and apprehension, an incapacity to provide for herself the care that is perceived to be needed, and a very limited capability to evaluate whether a proposed course of treatment and care is in fact advisable. On the other hand, the health care professional's vastly superior expertise and experience make the professional seem omniscient and omnipotent by comparison. The only way to redress this power imbalance is to impose upon the health care professional fiduciary or trust kinds of duties, including that of keeping a patient's confidences.

A health care professional's violation of the duty of confidentiality is exacerbated legally when the unauthorized disclosure is both false and injurious to the patient's reputation in the community. In such a case, the patient could bring a civil action against the professional for the tort of defamation (libel if written, slander if spoken). Additionally, repeating to another a false and injurious claim uttered by a patient about a third person could also make the health care professional legally liable to that third party. Particularly with sensitive and potentially harmful information, then, extreme discretion is in order.

The preceding exploration of general rules regarding confidentiality is helpful as far as it goes. The problem is that, although such general proclamations often express admirable moral sentiments and legal principles, they can rarely be applied directly to concrete situations without the aid of further moral reasoning and legal analysis.

The difficulty in many situations is that the health care professional's duty to maintain the disclosures and records of the patient is not an absolute, immutable obligation. The fact that a duty is not absolute does not imply that it fails to occupy an important, even central, place in moral reasoning and legal status. But when a duty is only *prima facie,* or presumptively applicable, rather than absolute or always applicable, one must consider whether there are relevant factors present that justify or even compel that the *prima facie* obligation be overridden in a particular case (Jonsen, Siegler, & Winslade, 1998). Stating general rules is much easier than identifying and applying possible exceptions to them.

First, a patient may waive, or give up, the right to confidentiality, as long as this is done in a voluntary, competent, and informed manner. This is accomplished daily in the health care area to make information available to third-party payers (insurers, such as Medicare, and managed care organizations [MCOs]), quality of care evaluators and auditors, and other public and private entities, including the patient's legal representative. The health care professional has an affirmative obligation to cooperate fully in the patient-requested release and transfer of medical information. (See Chapter 13 regarding health care professional/attorney cooperation on behalf of the older patient/client.) Failure to transfer information in a timely fashion at the patient's request may jeopardize the continuity and effectiveness of patient care. The patient's informed, voluntary waiver of the confidentiality right and request for release of information should be honored only when it has been thoroughly documented in writing. Further, the identity and legitimate authority of the record seeker should be satisfactorily verified.

Many older patients implicitly or explicitly approve the sharing of information about them with involved family members. Although such permission should not be taken for granted (Benson & Britten, 1996), it should be respected when borne out by the situation (Kapp, 1991a, 1991b; Petrila & Sadoff, 1992).

Second, when the rights of innocent third parties are jeopardized, the general requirement of confidentiality may yield. For instance, the expressed threat of a dangerous psychiatric patient to kill a specific victim, coupled with the patient's apparent present ability and intent to make good on the threat, should be reported to the victim and to law enforcement officials in a timely fashion.

Third, the patient's expectation of confidentiality must yield when the health care professional is mandated or permitted by state law to report to specified public health authorities the existence of certain enumerated conditions suspected in their patients. The health care professional should be familiar with the content of mandatory and voluntary reporting statutes and regulations in force in his or her own jurisdiction. Such provisions may be based on the state's inherent police power to protect and promote the health, safety, and welfare of society as a whole. This rationale would support, for example, reporting requirements concerning infectious diseases, occupational diseases, or vital statistics (such as death).

As the number of older drivers has risen, there is increasing concern (Underwood, 1992) about the impact of age-related neurodegenerative illness and sensory impairments on driving. Most states have very lax standards for renewing a driver's license (Bodnar, 1994). The decision to stop driving may develop into an area of tension between patient and physician, if informal and noncoercive attempts at persuasion fail to bring about voluntary abstention from the roads. "Physicians are not responsible for revoking driving privileges, but they must be knowledgeable of medical-condition reporting requirements" (Martinez, 1995). States differ in the ways that they treat dementia in this respect (Reuben, 1991). Only a few have statutes that expressly mandate physicians to report impaired drivers to public authorities (Reuben & St. George, 1996). Even in the absence of a mandatory reporting statute, some physicians have been held civilly liable when they should have foreseen a patient's dangerous driving but did nothing to prevent it and the patient than harmed an innocent third party in a motor vehicle accident (Weintraub, 1996). Further, physicians should inform driving-impaired patients of their own legal responsibility to notify the state concerning their impairment (Potamitis et al., 1994).

Alternatively to the police power, reporting of certain conditions may be mandated or allowed under the state's *parens patriae* power to beneficently protect those individuals who are unable and unwilling to care for their own needs. Mandatory and permissible reporting of elder abuse (see Chapter 7) and other forms of suspected violence are justified on this ground.

Finally, health care professionals may be compelled to reveal otherwise confidential patient information by the force of legal process, that is, by a judge's issuance of a court order requiring such release. This is a possibility in any type of lawsuit in which the patient's physical or mental condition is an issue in dispute. It is important to distinguish here between a subpoena and a court order.

A subpoena is a directive from the clerk of a court to appear at a specified time and place for the purpose of giving sworn testimony. A subpoena *duces tecum* directs one to bring certain identified tangible items, such as medical records, at the time of testimony. A subpoena may never be safely ignored, but it may be challenged legally before compliance is required. When a health care professional is served with a subpoena (i.e., the subpoena is personally delivered to him or her), the concerned patient should be notified immediately and given the opportunity to ask a judge to quash the subpoena for requesting privileged information or on some other legal ground. The statutory health care professional/patient testimonial privilege, which is one aspect of the larger concept of confidentiality, varies substantially in its specifics (in terms of types of parties and information covered, as well as recognized exceptions) among jurisdictions. It is only if the patient declines to challenge the subpoena or the judge rejects the challenge and orders disclosure over the patient's objection that the health care professional is obligated to comply (*Rost v. Board of Psychology*, 1995). Noncompliance with a judge's order constitutes contempt of court and is criminally and civilly punishable.

It should be noted that patient medical information concerning alcohol or narcotic dependency or treatment is specifically protected by federal law against unauthorized disclosure. This extra legal caution reflects a recognition of the extremely sensitive nature of this kind of information and the serious potential deleterious effects of its inappropriate revelation. Firm criminal and civil sanctions may be imposed for improper release of such information. Alcoholism and drug addiction afflict not insubstantial numbers of older patients (Skodol, Shaffer, & Gurland, 1997), and health care professionals involved in the care of these individuals should be well acquainted with federal provisions concerning confidentiality.

Another huge area in which questions pertaining to confidentiality of medical records are especially vexing is the emerging one of presymptomatic genetic testing for Alzheimer's disease and other dementias and disorders (Berry, 1997). There is valid anxiety that unauthorized transmittal of genetic test results may foster discrimination against certain individuals, particularly regarding employment and various forms of insurance coverage (Kapp, 1996e; National Institute on Aging/Alzheimer's Association Working Group, 1996; Post et al., 1997). Consequently, particular vigilance must be exercised in the handling of genetic test information to protect against improper disclosure. As of late 1998, a plethora of bills were pending on this subject, with the chief impediment to passage of more stringent privacy protections being apprehension that onerous requirements would stifle scientific progress in diagnosing and treating genetic diseases.

The whole area of medical confidentiality is presently in a state of flux (Turkington, 1997). On September 11, 1997, the U.S. Department of Health and Human Services (DHHS) submitted to Congress an 81-page report entitled *Confidentiality of Individually-Identifiable Health Information*, calling for a national set of standards to replace—or at least supplement—the current patchwork of state and federal statutes, regulations, and judicial rulings. At the time this chapter was written, that recommendation was being hotly debated by health care providers, users of medical information, and patient advocacy groups (Bates, 1997). The 1996 Health Insurance Portability and Accountability Act (HIPAA), Public Law 104-191, requires that DHHS take some action in terms of medical privacy by February 21, 2000, if Congress had not passed suitable legislation by August 21, 1999.

CONCLUSION

Information generated during the course of a relationship between a health care professional and an older patient is clinically and legally important to both the patient and the professional. This importance is reflected in legal requirements concerning methods of documentation, responsibility for documentation, patient access, and confidentiality. Especially for the older individual, a complete, accurate medical record is, in many respects, the story of that person's life and should be treated accordingly.

Chapter 5

Financing Health Care
for Older Persons

INTRODUCTION

Issues concerning the financing of health services are of vital importance
to both older individuals and health care professionals. For patients, an
adequate source of financing is essential to ensuring continued access to
necessary and appropriate services. For professionals, receiving adequate
and timely payment for services rendered to older patients is of obvious
pragmatic interest.

Until the past half century, health services for the elderly, as well as for
other segments of the population, were financed as a matter of personal or
family responsibility. The result, in many cases, was impaired access to
needed care for many older individuals lacking adequate personal fiscal
resources. Around the time of World War II, the third-party payment
mechanism, operating through private for-profit or nonprofit corporations
selling individual or group policies, arose and began to cover some older
persons among its insured parties. Since the mid-1960s, however, governments—federal and state—have assumed the clearly dominant role as finan-
cers of health services for the nation's older population.

This chapter is not intended to serve as a manual for health care professionals to rely on in dealing with third-party fee-for-service payers
(public or private) and managed care organizations (MCOs) in attempting
to gain earned payment for services provided or prior approval for services recommended. Despite the overwhelming complexity and the ever-
changing nature of specifics in the financing labyrinth, there are a number
of helpful resources available to the professional seeking practical assistance. For aid with specific problems, expert individual legal and accounting advice always should be retained.

Rather, in this chapter, I am content to outline briefly some of the
most salient aspects of health care financing for older persons, with the
expectation that this introduction will enhance the capacity of health care

professionals to advocate on behalf of their geriatric patients. It is part of the professional's role to assist older patients to secure maximum enjoyment of the rights and entitlements that public and private financing programs are supposed to provide.

FINANCING PROGRAMS

There are two primary government programs intended to provide older individuals with access to and financing for personal medical care (DeLew, 1995). These are the Medicare (Iglehart, 1992) and Medicaid (Iglehart, 1993) programs.

Medicare

Enacted by Congress in 1965 as part of President Lyndon Johnson's Great Society initiative, Medicare (Title 18 of the Social Security Act, Health Insurance for the Aged) is a completely federal program that is authorized to reimburse health care providers for certain medical services for almost all older persons, as well as for some categories of disabled persons. In 1996, approximately 38 million people were covered. The Medicare program is divided into three sections. Part A (Hospital Insurance [HI] Benefits) pays mainly for inpatient care in acute care hospitals, skilled nursing facilities (NFs), and for hospice care. Funding for Medicare Part A comes from payroll taxes (Federal Insurance Contributions Act, or FICA) paid into the federal HI trust account. Medicare Part B (Supplementary Medical Insurance [SMI] Benefits) pays chiefly for physician-related care and home health care. It also pays for the services of nurse practitioners and physician's assistants when delivered in a nursing facility and under a physician's supervision. Part B also covers laboratory and other diagnostic tests, as well as hospital outpatient services. Financing for Part B comes from a combination of beneficiary-paid premiums and general federal revenues.

As part of the Balanced Budget Act (BBA) of 1997, Public Law 105-33, Congress created Medicare Part C, the Medicare+Choice Program (MCP). Eligible Medicare beneficiaries may still remain in the traditional fee-for-service programs under Parts A and B. However, they also have the option of enrolling in MCP, which offers a menu of three basic possibilities:

1. Coordinated care plans offered by a traditional health maintenance organization (HMO), a competitive medical plan (CMP), a preferred provider organization (PPO), or the newly established provider sponsored organization (PSO).

2. A Medical Savings Account (MSA) plan.
3. A MCP fee-for-service plan.

Each MCP plan, irrespective of type, receives a specified monthly payment from Medicare per enrollee.

The Medicare program presently is the major source of public funding for medical care of the aged in the United States. In 1995, total Part A and Part B payments were $175 billion, about $4,800 per enrollee. An astronomical increase in health spending for the aged is projected over the next half-century as the population continues to age, especially in the oldest cohorts.

Medicare beneficiaries still must pay deductibles and co-payments directly out of pocket or through the out-of-pocket purchase of private supplemental insurance policies (discussed below). Additionally, Medicare does not pay for nonsurgical dental care, outpatient prescription drugs, eyeglasses, routine physical examinations, hearing aides, custodial NF care, or skilled NF care beyond 100 lifetime days. Out-of-pocket health expenditures vary substantially among older persons (Rubin & Koelln, 1993). On average, though, out-of-pocket health spending for the aged represents 21% of family income. In 1994, excluding the significant health care costs of residents of NFs and other institutions, older Americans' out-of-pocket costs on average exceeded $2,500 per person. In 1998, prescription drug expenses alone averaged $500 out of pocket per Medicare beneficiary.

Although enrollment in Part A is automatic for eligible beneficiaries, participation in Medicare Part B requires payment of an annual premium. In 1998, this premium rose to $525. By statute, the total amount of premiums must be 25% of Part B program costs; hence, rising program costs mean rising premium payments for individuals.

The Health Care Financing Administration (HCFA), in the federal Department of Health and Human Services (DHHS), administers Medicare and establishes the policies under which the program operates (Hirsh, 1998a). For Part A, HCFA pays contractors, known as fiscal intermediaries (FIs), to process claims. The contractors who review and process Part B claims for the federal government are referred to as carriers.

The Medicare Catastrophic Coverage Act (MCCA), Public Law No. 100-360 passed by Congress in 1988, would have substantially expanded Medicare coverage for certain health care services and products, such as prescription drugs. However, because of unhappiness among most older citizens about the additional Part B premiums that this legislation would have imposed and its failure to address long-term care expenses adequately, Congress repealed the Medicare portions of this Act the following year (Public Law 101-234).

The methodology for federal payment to hospitals under Medicare underwent revolutionary change beginning in 1983. Under the authority of the Tax Equity and Fiscal Responsibility Act (TEFRA) of 1982, DHHS began in 1983 to move away from the retrospective, cost-based reimbursement system that had characterized federal payments for inpatient hospital care since the inception of Medicare. Today, a prospective payment system (PPS) sets predetermined payment amounts for each patient discharge through the use of diagnosis related groups (DRGs). Patients are classified into 23 major diagnostic categories (MDCs), which are based on the human body systems. The MDCs are further divided by other factors to ensure clinical and resource homogeneity within groups. Among these factors are diagnostic or surgical procedures, other clinical information, and patient characteristics. This results in nearly 500 individual DRGs.

Each DRG is assigned a weight, indicating the relative amount of resources usually used to treat a patient assigned to the DRG. The DRG weights are constructed so that they average 1.0 across hospitals. The payment to a hospital for a specific patient is determined by multiplying the pertinent DRG weight by the standardized amount. Standardized amounts were computed originally by determining the average amount per case that Medicare would have paid for that patient's hospital care in the absence of the new system and then adjusting this amount for a variety of factors related to other public policy considerations.

Congress excluded several types of hospital costs from the PPS. For example, payments for the direct costs of medical education and for capital costs continue to be based on cost reimbursement. Specialized hospitals and units, such as psychiatric, long-term, children's, and rehabilitation, were also originally excluded from the PPS system.

Although Congress made the PPS system of DRGs applicable only to hospital payment for Medicare patients, a number of states have adopted versions of a PPS system for paying hospitals under the states' respective Medicaid programs (see below) as well. Additionally, several private health insurers have implemented some form of PPS system for paying for the inpatient services received by their policyholders.

Just as the advent of PPS through DRGs revolutionized hospital reimbursement methodology in the United States, the resource-based relative value scale (RBRVS) system that began to be implemented in 1992 significantly changed the way in which physicians are compensated for their services to Medicare beneficiaries. This system was intended to reverse some of the perverse behavioral incentives inherent in the traditional CPR (customary, prevailing, or reasonable) rate-setting system, under which Medicare's financial rewards encouraged excessive use of invasive, risky technological procedures performed by subspecialists.

The RBRVS system was developed under contract to HCFA by a group of health services researchers at the Harvard School of Public Health (Hsiao, Braun, Dunn, & Becker, 1988). Their project ranked physicians' services according to the resource costs involved in providing them. Resource costs were computed on the basis of the following factors: (1) the time and intensity of the physician's effort in providing a service; (2) a practice expense component that includes such overhead as office rent, salaries, equipment, and supplies; and (3) a separate malpractice component that reflects professional liability premium expenses. Congress enacted legislation based on this research as part of the Omnibus Budget Reconciliation Act (OBRA) of 1989, Public Law 101-239. Specific elements of the RBRVS system continue to undergo modification (Vladeck, 1996a).

Medicaid

The other primary government program subsidizing health care for older persons is Medicaid, enacted in 1965 as Title 19 of the Social Security Act, Grants to States for Medical Assistance Programs. Medicaid is a joint federal-state scheme that pays health care professionals for rendering certain enumerated medical services to specified groups of people who satisfy a financial means test. Persons falling below a certain financial line have "categorical" eligibility for Medicaid.

Under general federal guidelines, states set income and assets standards for cash assistance and Medicaid eligibility. Because there is considerable variation in the coverage of optional groups and in income standards across jurisdictions, the degree to which individual programs cover the poverty population varies considerably.

Title 19 of the Social Security Act requires that every state Medicaid program offer certain basic services: hospital inpatient and outpatient care, laboratory and x-ray services, NF care, home health care for individuals eligible for NF services, physicians' services, and other services of less immediate concern to geriatrics. In addition, states may elect to include other services under Medicaid coverage, such as prescription drugs, eyeglasses, inpatient psychiatric care for the aged and persons under 21, physical therapy, and dental care. States determine the amount, scope, and duration of services they pay for; for example, they may limit the number of days of covered hospital care or the number of covered physician visits.

Medicaid operates primarily as a vendor payment program. Payments are made directly to providers of service for care rendered to eligible patients. Methods for reimbursing physicians and hospitals vary widely among states, but providers must accept the Medicaid reimbursement level as payment in full. In NFs, persons are required to spend any income in excess of their personal needs to help pay for their care. States may require cost sharing by Medicaid recipients, but they may not require the categorically needy to share costs for mandatory services.

A growing number of states have contracted with MCOs to provide comprehensive medical services to Medicaid recipients. In some states, recipients' participation in managed care is mandatory; in others it is a strongly encouraged option.

Medicaid provides substantial funding for older individuals who receive medical services not reimbursed under Medicare and who are not financially able to pay for those services out of their own pockets. Under the Qualified Medicare Beneficiary (QMB) program, states use the Medicaid program to pay the Medicare Part B premiums, as well as deductibles and co-payments under Parts A and B, to purchase Medicare eligibility for older persons who are eligible for both programs. Under the Specified Low-Income Medicare Beneficiary (SLMB) program, states pay all or part of an individual's Medicare Part B premium, but the individual remains responsible for applicable deductibles and co-payments. The greatest Medicaid expenditures (over 35%) for the aged come in the area of institutional long-term care, specifically for placement in NFs (Spillman & Kemper, 1995). Medicaid accounts for about half of all NF payments, covering two thirds of all NF residents (Levit et al., 1996).

Prior to August 21, 1996, Congress had established civil penalties for those people improperly transferring or divesting assets in order to qualify for Medicaid when admitted to an NF. Under the Medicaid law, there is a defined period of time (the "look back" period) during which a transfer of assets (e.g., giving money to a child or grandchild) results in a period of ineligibility for Medicaid payment of NF care (or care provided under a home and community-based waiver program, 42 U.S.C. §1396p(c)) (Wiesner, 1995). For most transfers, the look-back period is the 36 months prior to application for Medicaid coverage; for certain trusts, it is 60 months prior to application.

When the 1996 Health Insurance Portability and Accountability Act (HIPAA), Public Law 104-191, became law, it exposed to criminal punishment for fraud or abuse anyone who "knowingly and willfully disposes of assets (including by any transfer in trust) in order for an individual to become eligible for medical assistance under [Medicaid], if disposing of the assets results in the imposition of a period of ineligibility for such assistance." This provision quickly became popularly known as the "Granny goes to jail" law. In the 1997 BBA, Congress amended this provision (§4734). Instead of exposing the Medicaid applicant personally to criminal liability, the BBA singles out the person who "for a fee knowingly and willfully counsels or assists an individual to dispose of assets (including by any transfer in trust) in order for the individual to become eligible for medical assistance under [Medicaid], if disposing of the assets results in the imposition of a period of ineligibility for such assistance," 42 U.S.C. §1320a–7b. Now, it is Granny's attorney or accountant who may be prosecuted (at the misdemeanor level) regarding improper asset divestiture.

This provision has been challenged and invalidated on constitutional grounds of First Amendment freedom of speech in federal court in *New York State Bar Association v. Reno* (1997). Additionally, the DHHS inspector general, who is responsible for enforcing Medicare/Medicaid antifraud and abuse laws, has in OIG Advisory Opinion 97-3 interpreted the law to mean that the transfer of $7,785 from an NF resident to her nephew 3 months prior to her application for Medicaid, in a case where the average price of monthly NF care was $2,595, did not constitute a prohibited knowing and willful disposition of assets to become eligible for Medicaid, since no period of ineligibility would have resulted from the asset transfer.

Related to the issue of Medicaid eligibility for long-term care is that of estate recovery. The Omnibus Budget Reconciliation Act of 1993 (OBRA 93), Public Law 103-66, required states to establish estate recovery programs to take back the costs of NF and other long-term care services from the estates of Medicaid beneficiaries who have died and who were 55 years of age or older when they received benefits (ABA Commission on Legal Problems of the Elderly, 1995; M. A. Miller, 1994). States may obtain liens against a Medicaid beneficiary's property for this purpose.

Although most Medicaid long-term care dollars have flowed to NFs, states may apply to HCFA for waivers of the usual Medicaid rules in order to divert some of those funds toward home- and community-based long-term care services instead of institutional care alone. A waiver represents permission, authorized under 42 U.S.C. §1396n(b), from the secretary of DHHS for a state to disregard what would otherwise be a congressionally mandated legal condition to the receipt of federal matching funds.

Private Insurance

The third leg of the stool for health care financing for the aged (besides government programs and out-of-pocket payments) is private third-party insurance. This may come in the form of employer-purchased conventional coverage as a fringe benefit for currently working older persons and their dependents and for retirees and their dependents. It also may come in the form of commercial health insurance policies purchased out of pocket by older persons to fill in the coverage gaps left by the Medicare crazy quilt. The majority of older persons own at least one such Medicare Supplemental (Medigap) policy, and the sale of these policies to the aged has been subject to serious abuse. In OBRA 1990, Congress tightened oversight over this $15-billion-per-year industry. Insurers and agents cannot sell policies to persons already owning one, and insurers must pay out at least 65% of what they bring in on individual policies and 75% of income from group policies. Additionally, the National Association of Insurance Commissioners (NAIC) has established model national standards for Medigap policies.

Older persons may also be covered by employers or their own premiums for participation in managed care health programs, specifically, HMOs and PPOs (Lachs & Ruchlin, 1997). As noted earlier, qualified HMOs and other MCOs may receive Medicare payments to cover program beneficiaries. The number of older persons voluntarily participating in managed care options has risen steadily over the past several years.

Private long-term care insurance, covering NF and home care services, is still in a fairly incipient state of development for a variety of reasons (Murtaugh, Kemper, & Spillman, 1995). Only 4–5% of the aged currently own long-term care insurance (Wiener, 1996). The role of the private sector in developing and marketing long-term care insurance products that supplement or replace Medicare and Medicaid coverage is likely to increase considerably in the foreseeable future. Provisions in HIPAA give tax-favored status to employers contributing to premiums and to individuals who purchase private long-term care insurance policies.

LEGAL ASPECTS OF HEALTH CARE COST CONTAINMENT

The concerted efforts of both governmental and private payers to contain health expenditures has raised a variety of legally pertinent issues for health care providers serving older patients. This section briefly outlines cost-containment considerations relating to utilization review, medical malpractice in acute and long-term care settings, and the implications of clinical practice parameters.

Utilization Review

Utilization review (UR) has been defined as "evaluation of the necessity, appropriateness, and efficiency of the use of medical services and facilities" (Hyde, 1988). UR may take place prospectively or retrospectively to or concurrently with the provision of the medical services in question. Today, UR is an integral component of both managed care and fee-for-service arrangements.

Two presuppositions underlie the concept of UR: (1) that there still is a substantial amount of unnecessary and inappropriate health care being delivered and paid for and (2) that the patient cannot adequately judge the necessity and appropriateness of recommended medical services. Hence, there is a belief that peers of the patient's physician are the only ones who can make such a judgment accurately. In principle, UR ensures that health care resources are appropriately used, not just saved. However, many commentators argue that UR in practice has evolved into much more of a means for saving money than for controlling and contributing to quality.

Initially, UR was used exclusively to review hospital inpatient services. However, many outpatient services are now reviewed as well. Also, UR is widely used in mental health facilities and agencies other than acute hospitals (Zusman, 1990).

TEFRA 1982, the same legislation that created the DRG reimbursement system discussed earlier, included the Peer Review Improvement Act (Public Law 97-248). This law created the Utilization and Quality Control Peer Review Organization (PRO) apparatus to replace Professional Standards Review Organizations (PSROs), which had monitored Medicare hospital services since 1972 under Public Law 92-603. TEFRA authorized HCFA to enter into contracts with a PRO for each state. The PROs are required, based on negotiated objectives contained in each contract, to review the necessity and reasonableness of care, quality of care, and appropriateness of the setting in which care is provided to Medicare beneficiaries.

Under federal regulations (50 *Federal Register* 15330, April 17, 1985), PROs are required to perform the following determinations:

> Whether the services are or were reasonable and medically necessary for the diagnosis and treatment of illness or injury or to improve functioning of a malformed body member, or (with respect to pneumococcal vaccine) for prevention of illness, or (in the case of hospice care) for the palliation and management of terminal illness.
>
> Whether the quality of the services meets professionally recognized standards of health care.
>
> Whether those services furnished or proposed to be furnished on an inpatient basis could, consistent with the provision of appropriate medical care, be effectively furnished more economically on an outpatient basis or in an inpatient health care facility of a different type.
>
> Through DRG validation, the validity of diagnostic and procedural information supplied by the hospital.
>
> The completeness, adequacy and quality of hospital care provided.
>
> The medical necessity, reasonableness, and appropriateness of hospital admissions and discharges.
>
> Whether a hospital has misrepresented admission or discharge information or has taken an action that results in the unnecessary admission of an individual entitled to benefits; unnecessary multiple admissions of an individual; or other inappropriate medical or other practices with respect to beneficiaries or billing for services furnished to beneficiaries.

In addition to the regulatory requirements, each PRO has conditions written into its contract that address specific problems in its own state. The problems are first identified by the PROs and then reported to HCFA, which attempts to address the concerns by requiring that the frequency of the problems be reduced.

HCFA contracts with 54 PROs, each of which employs physicians, nurses, and other staff members to conduct reviews. Although there are uniform requirements in each PRO contract, the PROs operate separately and go about their business distinctively, pursuing national objectives in the context of the medical standards of the local community. PROs use physician reviewers from their own communities. Despite this reliance on local peer review, PROs are still governed by national quality standards prescribed by a model, the Quality Intervention Plan, which includes specific criteria for detecting quality problems, assigning a severity weight to those problems, and determining the most appropriate intervention for a given deficiency.

PROs are empowered to deny payment for unnecessary care and may recommend sanctions that could result in the exclusion of physicians or hospitals from Medicare or the levying of a monetary penalty. Enforcement of the sanctions imposed by the PROs is the responsibility of the DHHS Office of Inspector General (OIG). The OIG is authorized by the secretary of DHHS to impose sanctions on Medicare-participating physicians or other providers who have "grossly and flagrantly" violated the Medicare law by demonstrating a pattern of poor-quality care.

In operation, when a PRO identifies violations of federal quality-of-care standards, it is supposed to provide the practitioner in question with reasonable notice and an opportunity to discuss the findings and rebut them before a sanction recommendation is forwarded to the DHHS. The law provides comprehensive due process protection for physicians. They are supposed to be given numerous chances to refute the allegations against them by providing testimony from other physicians or evidence from medical records. Even in cases in which sanctions are issued, the law allows for an appeal before an administrative law judge of the Social Security Administration and ultimately in the federal courts.

Although Congress authorized PROs to sanction physicians found to practice poor-quality care, it did not initially provide PROs with the authority to deny reimbursement for services because of incompetence or neglect. The only quality-of-care enforcement tools available to the early PROs were either termination of the physician from participation in Medicare or the levying of a monetary penalty, but only in cases where a clear pattern of incompetence had been demonstrated and, of those cases, only where physicians were unwilling or unable to improve their treatment of beneficiaries.

The Consolidated Omnibus Budget Reconciliation Act (COBRA) of 1985 authorized PROs for the first time to deny Medicare payments in cases where substandard quality of care is identified. Specifically, the law requires PROs to determine, on the basis of review, whether the quality of services meets professional standards.

The primary method used by HCFA, through the PROs, to detect substandard care is the generic screening system, in which certain events trigger closer review:

1. Inadequate discharge planning
2. Patient being medically unstable at the time of discharge
3. Unexpected death
4. Nosocomial infections
5. Unscheduled return to surgery
6. Admissions involving trauma suffered in the hospital

The screens are applied initially by nurse reviewers employed by the PRO. If the nurse reviewer identifies a screen failure, the records are forwarded to a physician reviewer to determine if the failure represents a bona fide case of substandard care.

PRO performance is evaluated and monitored by HCFA's Peer Review Organization Monitoring Protocol and Tracking System, which reviews PRO operations at least twice during each 3-year contract cycle. HCFA also contracts with a national "SuperPRO" to monitor the effectiveness of each PRO.

As the foregoing description should make apparent, the basically paper-review nature of UR places a premium on good written documentation of patient care by physicians (see Chapter 4), for reimbursement as well as for liability prevention. Furthermore, the importance of active participation by practicing physicians in the UR process also should be clear; it is needed to maximize the likelihood that professional judgment will predominate over rigid, externally imposed guidelines that do not adequately accommodate the vagaries of actual cases.

Malpractice Concerns

The advent of DRGs, PROs, MCOs, and other cost-containment strategies has generated concern among older persons, their advocates, and health care providers that quality of care will be imperiled as strong financial incentives compel providers to skimp on various aspects of diagnostic and therapeutic care (e.g., premature hospital discharges) (Rodwin, 1993). Opinions range across a broad spectrum regarding the actual impact of cost-containment initiatives on quality of care thus far; not surprisingly, practicing physicians render the most negative assessments, whereas academic researchers, insurers, and government and quasi-government officials are considerably more optimistic about a positive quality/cost containment synergy.

Health care providers are especially anxious about the possibility of cost-containment pressures causing a diminution in quality of care that will in turn lead to a massive increase in medical malpractice litigation brought against cost-containment-driven providers. Physicians feel especially exposed personally in light of the U.S. Supreme Court's interpretation (*Pilot Life Insurance Company v. Dedeaux,* 1987) of the Employee Retirement Income Security Act (ERISA), Public Law 93-406, in a manner that essentially precludes most patients from suing their MCOs directly under a traditional medical malpractice theory; thus, the physician and/or other providers usually are the sole "deep pockets" available.

Long-term care providers are as worried as those in the acute care sphere, the former because of an uneasiness that NFs and home health agencies (HHAs) are poorly equipped and staffed to care optimally for the sicker, frailer patients who are being discharged from hospitals too early and in need of intense posthospital medical attention. Concern has also been expressed regarding the ethical ramifications, in terms of quality of care and equitable access to services, of the divided loyalties and conflicts of interest that may be present in an environment heavily influenced by an imperative to contain health care expenditures (Glaser & Hamel, 1997; Morreim, 1995). Legal scholars differ over the validity of increased liability fears, with speculation ranging from an agreement with predictions of a litigation onslaught to suggestions that the courts will alter acceptable standards of care to implicitly or explicitly account for economic forces (Hall, 1997).

One of the very few reported appellate decisions squarely ruling on a complaint that cost-containment pressures improperly resulted in substandard medical care and consequent patient harm is found in *Wickline v. California* (1986). The factual background is fairly straightforward. Mrs. Wickline was a Medicaid-eligible patient who was hospitalized for circulatory problems regarding her legs and back. The California Medicaid program required precertification for hospital admission and assigned an approved length of stay for the admission. Any extension of the approved length of stay had to be authorized in advance. The state of California UR program approved Wickline's surgery and authorized a 10-day hospitalization.

The patient suffered complications after the original surgery, and two additional surgeries were performed. Her attending physician determined that she should stay in the hospital for 8 days beyond her scheduled discharge date, and he filled out a Medicaid application requesting an extension. The Medicaid on-site nurse reviewer, after consulting with a state physician adviser, approved only a 4-day extension.

The attending physician discharged Mrs. Wickline to her home when the 4-day extension period expired. Although the physician knew that a process existed for appealing the Medicaid UR decision, he did not pursue an appeal. Nine days following discharge, Mrs. Wickline had to be readmitted to the hospital with severe pain and discoloration of her leg, which eventually had to be amputated. She brought a civil lawsuit against the state of California, contending that her injuries were caused by the Medicaid UR program's negligence in failing to authorize the full requested extension of the original hospitalization. A jury awarded her $500,000.

The California Court of Appeal reversed the jury verdict, however, reasoning that although the state's preauthorization program played a role in the discharge decision, this role was not determinative. Rather, the decision to discharge the patient was made by the attending physician, who was the only one who actually had the legal power to discharge the patient. The court held that the Medicaid program therefore could not be found liable even if the discharge decision had been negligently made. In refusing to find the state liable, the court placed responsibility for the hospital discharge on the attending physician and criticized him for not formally appealing the UR decision with which he disagreed.

The *Wickline* case is noteworthy for several lessons it conveys. First, it places the duty squarely on the attending physician to officially challenge, through any available appeals process, UR decisions believed to be adverse to the patient's best interests. The court in *Wickline* intimated that, had the attending physician unsuccessfully exhausted available appeals avenues, the state of California then might have been found liable. The court also intimated that, because the attending physician did not follow that route in this case, a negligence action brought directly against him might have been permitted to succeed. That point brings us to *Wickline's* second major lesson, the importance of cultivating a positive physician/patient relationship. In this case, Mrs. Wickline refrained from suing her physician largely because of the existence of such a relationship; she perceived her physician as her advocate, even though he otherwise would appear to be an obvious defendant.

This case is perhaps most revealing because of its relative uniqueness. As noted, despite much anxiety in the provider community and academic speculation about the potential adverse liability impact of cost-containment influences on health care providers, *Wickline* is virtually the only case of its kind (as opposed to lawsuits against MCOs predicated on breach of contract or fraud claims) thus far to be reported at the appellate level. Whether the onslaught of expected litigation will materialize in the future or fail to materialize because of a generally positive quality/cost containment synergy or because of features of the legal system having little to do with the impact of cost-containment forces on quality of care remains to be seen.

Practice Parameters

There is a growing movement in contemporary American medicine toward the development of flexible but explicit clinical practice parameters or guidelines to assist physicians in making clinical decisions about the use of particular diagnostic tests and therapeutic procedures. A number of practice parameters developed thus far are particularly relevant for the care of older patients (American Psychiatric Association, 1997). These practice parameters are being developed by professional organizations and associations based on consensus processes and health services research exploring the demonstrable effectiveness of various medical interventions; they represent a movement away from the common earlier situation of physicians basing many of their practices more on community custom and doctors' lounge "shop talk" than on hard data. Although cost-containment considerations about reducing the incidence of unnecessary, inappropriate tests and procedures have much to do with the impetus for practice-parameter generation, there also is a sincere conviction by many medical leaders that practice-parameter development has the potential for greatly improving the quality of patient care delivered on a daily basis. A fortunate by-product of developing and implementing credible, factually based practice parameters should be a reduction in legal uncertainty about the acceptable standard of care in a particular situation and a bolstering of the physician's legal position where applicable parameters have been properly taken into account (Kapp, 1996c).

DE FACTO RATIONING BY AGE

Despite powerful criticisms (Binstock & Post, 1991) of earlier proposals (Callahan, 1987; Daniels, 1988; Veatch, 1988) for explicit, overt ("hard") forms of health care rationing based categorically on the chronological age of patients, there is substantial emerging evidence that age-based rationing is *de facto* taking place every day on the basis of individual bedside decisions and actions by physicians and nurses regarding individual patients (Asch & Ubel, 1997; Bennett et al., 1991; Boyd, Teres, Rapaport, & Lemshow, 1996; Fried, Miller, Stein, & Wachtel, 1996; Hesse, 1995; Hynes, 1994; Jayes, Zimmerman, Wagner, & Knaus, 1996; A. M. Kramer, 1995; Krumholz et al., 1994; Topol & Califf, 1992). The evidence is overwhelming that such differential treatment among patients of different ages—implicit, covert ("soft") rationing—takes place regardless of comparable diagnoses, prognoses, or other potentially explanatory factors besides the particular patient's age.

The law is both theoretically and practically unhelpful in protecting older patients from this form of *de facto* age discrimination (Kapp, 1998a). Realistically, the equitable remedies (e.g., judicial injunctions) available to respond prospectively and to prevent covert, age-based rationing practice before it occurs are limited and weak, as are the legal remedies for compensating the victim after the fact and thereby discouraging similar medical practice in the future. Indeed, some advocates of covert rationing support it precisely because avoiding the need for government involvement in an overt rationing scheme eliminates the kind of legal, external interference that they believe can seriously impede the whole inevitable rationing process (Blumstein, 1981).

Given the law's limitations, *de facto* age-based rationing presents primarily an ethical challenge to the involved parties. A morally acceptable solution will depend mainly on the good faith and commitment to ethical principles of those who control particular medical decisions.

FINANCING REFORM PROPOSALS

As this chapter is being written, a number of proposals for continuing to alter the way that health care for older Americans is financed are on the public policy table for discussion (Altman, Reinhardt, & Shactman, 1997). Some ideas aim to address the predicted forthcoming shortfall in the HI trust fund (Angell, 1997; Thomas, 1995). On the other hand, in his 1998 State of the Union speech, President Clinton proposed an expansion in the eligibility pool for at least some Medicare benefits down to age 62, for some persons, down to age 55. A thorough analysis of current proposals is beyond the scope of this book (and a timely analysis would be impossible), but health care professionals should follow—and participate in—the discussion about these proposals with great interest, because any changes will no doubt affect both the direct financial status of caregivers and the structure and operation of the health care delivery system itself.

CONCLUSION

In many respects, considerations of health care financing grow in importance as the dominant "tail" that wags the "dog" of medical treatment, for older as well as other patients. An understanding of the details of health care financing and their underlying public policy principles and associated legal and ethical implications is essential for all health care professionals, not only so that they can protect their own legitimate legal, ethical, and financial integrity but also so that they can act as zealous protectors of and advocates for the welfare of their patients.

Chapter 6

Disability Programs and Protections for Older Persons

INTRODUCTION: THE DISABILITY SYSTEM

The clinical care of older individuals is highly likely to involve the health care professional in the processing of private or public disability claims on behalf of those older patients. The lion's share of these cases involving the disabled elderly concern claims for federal government benefits under the Social Security Disability Insurance (SSDI) program. More than half of the individuals on the beneficiary rolls are age 55 or older. Very few SSDI claims can be successfully processed without the assistance of the health care professional, particularly the patient's personal physician.

The SSDI program, upon which so many older individuals rely, came into existence less than half a century ago. In 1954, the Social Security Act was amended to preserve the Social Security work record of disabled persons; individuals who became disabled were made eligible for retirement benefits at 65 as if they had continued to work between the onset of their disability and their 65th birthday. In 1956, Congress provided that Social Security taxpayers between 50 and 65 years of age who became permanently and totally disabled should be eligible for monthly benefits as if they were already 65 and retired. In 1960, the age 50 requirement was removed.

The largest single percentage of SSDI claimants is represented within the 62- to 65-year age category. When a person applies for early Social Security retirement benefits (Old Age, Survivors, and Disability Insurance, or OASDI, which is Title 2 of the Social Security Act), questions are ordinarily raised about individual health, and the applicant may be encouraged to apply for worker disability benefits. There is an impetus to have people declared disabled before they become 65 because the SSDI legislation provides that all persons lose disability eligibility at that age. When the disabled person becomes 65, there is a switch to straight OASDI retirement payments but at the same (higher) rate received while one was a beneficiary of the disability program. This is because the earlier disability payments were figured as though the claimant were already 65 at the time of onset of disability.

Disability insurance payments thus annexed to the OAS programs are conditioned on the satisfaction of three eligibility requirements. Claimants must show (1) that they have worked at "covered" employment for the requisite number of quarters of years, (2) that their inability to work is "medical" in nature, and (3) that they are totally disabled from performing any work for a span of time that has lasted or that is predicted to last for at least 12 months. Benefit payments end if disability ceases or if the individual returns to regular work. "Covered" employment refers to jobs in which the worker and employer make contributions to the SSDI trust funds, that is, employment where payroll deductions for Social Security (i.e., Federal Insurance Contributions Act, or FICA, taxes) are taken. The quarters-of-years provision is intended as a protection for individuals who do not work continuously over time.

A claimant who meets the prior work requirement satisfies a basic condition imposed on all Social Security recipients, namely, substantial workforce participation. To qualify for disability insurance benefits, the claimant must also demonstrate that inability to work is a result of "medically determinable" disease, defect, or injury. Specifically, the SSDI law (20 C.F.R. §404.1505 and §416.905) defines "disability" as the "inability to engage in any substantial gainful activity (SGA) by reason of any medically determinable physical or mental [Bonnie & Monahan, 1997] impairment which can be expected to result in death or has lasted or can be expected to last for a continuous period of not less than twelve months." The law further delineates "a physical or mental impairment" as one that results from anatomical, physiological, or psychological abnormalities that are demonstrable by medically acceptable clinical and laboratory diagnostic techniques. Such abnormalities are medically determinable if they manifest themselves as signs or laboratory findings apart from symptoms. Abnormalities that manifest themselves only as symptoms are not "medically determinable" for legal purposes. The concept of imposing medical criteria for the purpose of establishing eligibility for government-sponsored benefits dates back at least to 17th-century English social history (Stone, 1985).

Even if a claimant has worked for the required number of quarters and has suffered a "medical" decline, benefits will be denied unless the impossibility of employability is complete. One must be not only mentally and physically unable (1) to do one's previous work but also, considering age, education, and work experience, (2) to engage in any kind of SGA that exists in the national economy, that is, that exists in significant numbers in the region where one lives or in several regions of the country. Medical vocational guidelines mandate that the number of jobs fitting the various exertional levels and skill requirements be carefully considered. Used in this determination are the *Dictionary of Occupational Titles* and the *Occupational Outlook Handbook,* published by the U.S. Department of Labor; the *County Business Patterns* and *Census Survey* published by the federal Bureau of the Census; and surveys of light and sedentary jobs prepared by the various state employment agencies. It is immaterial whether such work exists in the immediate geographic area where the applicant lives, whether a specific job vacancy exists for that applicant, or whether the job would be offered if an employment application were to be submitted.

Generalized medical-vocational guidelines were adopted by the Department of Health and Human Services (DHHS) in 1978, replacing a system under which vocational experts had testified in individual proceedings. Use of the present standardized approach, rather than an individualized determination of each applicant's ability to work at particular types of available jobs for which the applicant could qualify, has been upheld by the U.S. Supreme Court as a reasonable administrative interpretation of the Social Security Act in *Heckler v. Campbell* (1983).

Within this setting, a finding of medical disability serves the function of admitting a recipient to a favored status in our welfare system. The applicant who has paid SSDI premiums for a sufficient number of quarters has a right to benefits, but coverage is limited and specific criteria must be met. In many respects, it is health care professionals who guard the key to this public horn of plenty (or at least, horn of something). However, before discussing the role of health care professionals, and especially the individual's personal physician, in helping an older person to turn that key, it is necessary to set out briefly the mechanism under which disability determinations are made.

THE SSDI CLAIMS PROCESS

The claimant who asserts disability begins the process by applying to the local district Social Security office (DO), which supplies the claimant with necessary forms and accepts them when filled in (Gonzalez, 1993). The DO office refers the claim to a designated state office (the Disability Determinations Services [DDS] office), which is under contract to the federal government, 56 *Federal Register* 11012, for an initial determination of eligibility based on federal criteria. This state agency then requests the production of a medical report on the issue of medical disability from a physician of the claimant's selection. If the report is extracted from an already existing medical record, the physician is reimbursed for professional efforts by the state, and the physician is free to supplement this payment by imposing an extra charge on the claimant. This extra charge may be a substantial financial burden for the older person involved. If a physical examination must be performed as well as a report prepared, the state compensates the physician with a larger amount, calculated on the basis of the physician's specialty and the prevailing state Medicare and Medicaid rates. If the claimant does not express a preference for any specific physician, or the claimant's treating physician is unavailable or cannot or will not provide sufficient evidence regarding impairment, the state DDS agency refers the claimant to a private physician listed on a consultant panel maintained by the state agency for a consultative examination (CE). Physicians may contact their own state DDS agency to request information regarding how they may become members of this consultant panel.

Regardless of who prepares it, the medical report must be based on the listing, appended to the SSDI regulations, of acceptable impairments and the criteria for each of these impairments that constitute evidence of a disabling level of severity. The current "Listing of Impairments" is found at 20 C.F.R. §404.1525 *et seq.*

If a claimant's condition is not included in the listing, a finding is still possible that the severity of the condition equals the severity intended by the listing, in which case an allowance of disability can be made. If the impairment meets the 1-year duration requirement and is included in, or equivalent to, the medical listings, the applicant is presumed to be disabled (*Sullivan v. Zebley*, 1990).

When multiple impairments exist, no one of which alone meets the listed criteria, the aggregate severity of all of the impairments documented may be found to equal the listing level of severity of one impairment. If the aggregate severity of all impairments is short of the listing level, nonmedical factors such as age, education, and vocational experience then are considered in conjunction with the limitations imposed by the impairments to see whether the aggregate effect of the medical and nonmedical factors precludes SGA. If this evaluation of the individual's "residual functional capacity" (RFC) indicates that the impairment does not prevent the applicant from performing past work, there must be a decision that the person is not disabled. If the applicant cannot carry out a former occupation, the question then becomes whether any SGA that exists in the national economy is possible for the particular applicant. If it is, the finding must be "not disabled." If not, the applicant may be considered disabled.

Approximately two thirds of initial applications are disallowed by state DDS agencies. However, about 50% of the SSDI applications submitted by claimants over age 55 are approved. If the initial application is rejected, the claimant may apply to the same state agency for reconsideration. At this stage, the state officers ordinarily will update the file with further medical or vocational data and reevaluate the application utilizing the same criteria of disability. In about 35% of claims, documentation will be supplemented by requesting that the claimant submit to an examination by a physician chosen and compensated by the agency.

If, after reconsideration, the claim is still denied, the claimant may request a hearing. It is usually at this stage that the claimant seeks professional legal advice and begins to be represented by legal counsel, who ordinarily is working on a contingency fee basis. The trier of fact, a federal administrative law judge (ALJ), is mandated to consider all of the evidence and make a fresh, original (*de novo*) decision. This decision becomes the final administrative decision if no exceptions are taken to it. A majority of claimants who were initially denied benefits gain awards at this point.

If either party—that is, (1) the Social Security Administration (SSA) or (2) the claimant—takes exception to the hearing examiner's decision, appeal is permitted to the SSA Council. The decision of the council is the final administrative determination of the claim. If the claimant remains dissatisfied, a civil lawsuit may be brought against SSA in the federal District (trial level) court and pursued through the federal appeals process, 42 U.S.C. §405(g).

THE ROLE OF THE PHYSICIAN

The foregoing discussion should leave no doubt about the central role of health care professionals, particularly the personal physician, in aiding older patients to obtain entitlements under the SSDI program. Furthermore, proper medical evaluation is essential not only for the initial obtaining of SSDI benefits but also for assisting the patient to retain them.

In 1980, Congress passed a law requiring SSA or the state DDS agency to conduct continuing disability reviews for each SSDI beneficiary at least once every 3 years, beginning in 1982, to make certain that the beneficiary remained disabled. In October 1984, DHHS placed a moratorium on these continuing disability reviews because of concern about the high number of negative benefit determinations. Between 1982 and April 1984, SSA reviewed 1.2 million disability cases and found 491,000 beneficiaries no longer disabled. Of these, 291,000 were restored to the rolls after appealing to an ALJ or the federal courts.

To address the public controversy that had developed over these reviews, Congress enacted the Social Security Disability Benefits Reform Act of 1984, Public Law 98-460, requiring, with certain exceptions, that medical improvement be shown before benefits could be terminated. In 1986, the state DSSs resumed their continuing reviews under the medical improvement standard, which stipulates that no beneficiary should be removed from the disability roles without either (1) "substantial evidence" that medical improvement in his or her medical condition has occurred and that he or she is now able to engage in substantial gainful activity or (2) evidence establishing that the previous determination of disability was erroneous. Recent studies have found only limited success in rehabilitating disabled SSDI beneficiaries (U.S. General Accounting Office, 1996c).

Because, as observed earlier, the SSDI law defines a physical or mental impairment as a condition "which results from anatomical, physiological, or psychological abnormalities which are demonstrable by medically acceptable clinical and laboratory diagnostic techniques," it follows that a claimant's reciting of mere symptoms about the impairment is insufficient by itself to establish that the impairment exists. By contrast, medical evidence by itself may be dispositive (i.e., may be the grounds for a decision) of a claim in either of two situations, namely, (1) when it establishes that the claimant has an impairment or a combination of impairments that meet or equal the criteria contained in the impairment listings or (2) when it establishes that the claimant's alleged impairment is not severe enough, in that it does not significantly limit the individual's physical or mental capacity to perform basic work-related functions. In all other situations, medical evidence is considered in conjunction with vocational factors.

Medical evidence to be used in the evaluation of a disability claim must include, at a minimum, a report signed by a licensed physician and other probative (i.e., tending to prove or disprove a fact in issue) medical reports, records, laboratory findings, and measurements. The physician's report should contain the person's medical history relating to the alleged impairment, together with the results of a recent physical and mental examination (performed within 3 months of the report date), and any supporting laboratory data in the physician's possession that would help define the nature and severity of the impairment. One format for documentation consists of sections covering history, physical and mental status, daily activities, diagnosis and prognosis, and general remarks. The report should be in sufficient detail to permit the agency evaluators, who will not have seen or examined the claimant, to independently determine the severity and expected duration of the impairment, and it need not be limited to those findings enumerated in the Medical Evaluation Criteria appended to the SSDI regulations.

The medical report should address the existence of an impairment or combination of impairments and the probable duration and severity in functional terms, describing the individual's capacity to perform significant activities such as being able to sit, stand, move about, travel, handle objects, hear, see, speak, and—in cases of mental impairment—the ability to reason or to make occupational, personal, or social adjustments. The crucial issue is not the diagnosis of a specific disease that may be afflicting the patient but rather how the ability to work may be impaired (American Medical Association, 1993). It is particularly important in mental disability cases for the physician to address the immediate and long-range functional effects of the patient's current and past medications.

There are thus three types of medical evidence to be considered in making a disability determination. The first two types emanate from the patient's physician: (1) objective medical facts, which are clinical findings divorced from expert opinions as to the significance of those clinical findings; and (2) expert diagnoses and opinions of the physician on subsidiary, or secondary, questions of fact. The third kind of medical evidence, subjective proof of pain and disability, is supplied by the claimant and corroborated by family, friends, and neighbors. Although it is preferable, once a case has reached the hearing stage, for the physician to render live testimony rather than a written report alone, in the vast majority of cases the technically acceptable practice of proceeding without the reporting physician's personal appearance is followed.

A statement in the physician's report that the examined individual either is or is not totally medically disabled for at least a 12-month period is not conclusive as a matter of law. Reaching that ultimate judgment is the responsibility of the SSA and may not be delegated away to any individual or group. One author has complained that the physician's opinion on the patient's disability is "definitely nondeterminative, administratively irrelevant, and occasionally counterproductive" (Hadler, 1982). This reaction, however, is unjustified. The opinion of the claimant's personal physician does carry weight to the extent that it is supported by specific and complete clinical findings and is consistent with other evidence as to the severity and probable duration of the claimant's impairment or impairments.

The hearing examiner does not exercise unfettered discretion in evaluating and weighing the evidence and is bound to view the evidence as a whole rather than isolating certain medical findings to support the decision. Nor is the hearing examiner permitted to ignore medical evidence that is uncontroverted by other substantial evidence. Further, the hearing examiner may not substitute a personal evaluation of a claimant's condition in place of competent medical evidence. Finally, even though medical evidence is not necessarily determinative of the ultimate issue of disability, it can, where objective findings are adequate, support the hearing examiner's inference regarding that issue.

In order to prevent the creation of an adversary relationship between the physician and patient, the SSA does not even request the physician's opinion on disability or motivation. Instead, objective medical findings are solicited so that an independent opinion can be reached. Any adversary relationship, with either the patient or the claims system, stems from a failure of the private physician to understand the need and function of objective clinical data in this process.

In evaluating medical evidence submitted regarding a disability claim, great preference is accorded to reports coming from the claimant's own treating, primary care physician (*Lester v. Chater*, 1995; Sutton, 1996). The SSA has advised the respective state agencies responsible for conducting initial evaluations and reconsiderations that "the attending physician occupies a unique place in the development of . . . medical evidence. Whenever possible, he should be utilized to furnish the . . . evidence needed for evaluation because of the relationship he has to the claimant's medical problems through diagnosis and treatment." Case law has accepted the standard that the opinion of a claimant's own physician is entitled to the most weight because it reflects an expert judgment based on continuing observation of the claimant's condition over a prolonged period. The length of this period and the number of times the physician has seen the claimant are relevant to the physician's familiarity with the claimant's overall condition. Particularly when multiple impairments are alleged, the federal courts reviewing disability determinations have recognized that the opinion of the claimant's personal primary care physician may be more reliable than that of a medical specialist who enters the case for evaluation purposes only, because the primary care physician is better equipped to take into account the total circumstances of the claimant.

The argument that the treating physician's report should be viewed with skepticism because the claimant's physician is inclined to be sympathetic toward the patient, in no small measure because the payment of professional fees may be influenced by the outcome of the disability claim, has also been rejected by the judiciary. The deference in which the primary care physician's judgment is held is illustrated by the fact that state-employed physicians who review submitted disability claims frequently personally contact and consult with the claimant's personal physician to obtain supplementary information that may aid in clarifying the legal viability of the claim.

There has been a substantial amount of criticism over a long period of time directed toward the SSDI program by both private commentators and public officials. The administration of the program has been roundly attacked for inefficiency and lack of control and accountability (U.S. General Accounting Office, 1997b). These criticisms are not the immediate concern of this book. What is the concern of this volume are the shortcomings that are sometimes found in the level of performance by older patients' personal physicians when it comes to helping the older patient (when warranted) to successfully apply for and receive SSDI benefits.

PROBLEMS AND POSSIBLE RESPONSES

Strains within the physician/patient relationship frequently occur in disability cases. Many physicians find this an area in which forging and maintaining an alliance with the patient is sometimes extremely difficult. This difficulty, exacerbated by the persistent roadblocks that arise generally in the path of productive relationships between physicians and the legal advocates who represent their patients, is manifested in a number of ways.

The primary care physician should ideally be well versed in the workings of the SSDI program and should be the first person to suggest to the older patient that he or she might be eligible for benefits under SSDI and should apply for them. Further, the physician should encourage the patient to persist even after a claim has been initially rejected and should direct the patient toward appropriate legal counsel.

All too often, though, the physician waits until the issue of work incapacity is raised by the patient, when it becomes an undeniable problem for him or her, or until being contacted by the patient's attorney. At that point, as previously discussed, the physician's role as primary documenter of the severity of the claimant's condition becomes foremost. The quality of the documentation produced, though, frequently leaves much to be desired.

A number of disability reports prepared by claimants' personal physicians are, to a greater or lesser degree, incomplete, inaccurate, and untimely. The reports are not always directly probative (helping to prove) of the legal issues to be adjudicated; in other words, the physicians often miss the mark in terms of addressing the specific questions asked. There is also a tendency for some medical reports to be expressed as ultimate conclusions only, with an inadequate or absent presentation and explanation of the objective data underlying the conclusions announced. The submission of naked conclusions sometimes is made worse by the style in which they are written, one that may be only minimally comprehensible even to other physicians. The technical jargon that sometimes characterizes these reports may be largely meaningless to the nonphysicians who must make and review the disability determination at various points along the process, as well as to the attorney charged with preparing and presenting the claimant's case. Perhaps most distressing is the extreme reluctance of some physicians to waiver from their self-imposed role as pure "objective" scientists and actively advocate for their elderly patients on behalf of their legitimate disability claims. Detachment from the patient's legal outcome has too often been the physician watchword.

There are several potential explanations for these shortcomings. First, many physicians seem unwilling or unable to set aside the substantial amount of time required to prepare a first-rate disability evaluation. Directly related to this is the inability of most older individuals, particularly those who must file for SSDI eligibility, to pay the significant out-of-pocket professional fees that would motivate physicians to devote reasonable time to create top-notch medical reports. This financial aspect should not, however, be overemphasized. A lot of older people have paid a lot of money to buy a lot of physician time to obtain reports that were still quite inadequate.

Probably a more fundamental factor limiting the positive role of some physicians in the disability determination process is their general ignorance and misunderstanding of the workings, content, and purposes of the SSDI statutes and regulations. This may result from a failure of the patient's attorney to properly educate the physician or from an unwillingness on the part of the physician to be educated about these matters. (Of course, the attorney must him- or herself be knowledgeable about the subject and capable of reasonably explaining it to the physician.) The latter explanation is closely linked to a physician's restricted role self-definition that does not consider a working knowledge of government benefit programs to be within its realm. Most physicians simply do not envision filling out bureaucratic forms as a legitimate part of their jobs. Besides seeing it as irrelevant to their true professional calling and disruptive of what they should be doing (making sick people well), most physicians find (and quite justifiably) that the production of government-mandated paperwork is a dull and uninspiring experience.

A major factor impeding positive physician cooperation in some disability cases is the wide divergence in goal orientation between health care professionals and members of the legal community. The attorney is primarily concerned with generating and recording data and opinions that will assist a fact-finder in resolving the precise legal issues defined by the SSDI statutes and regulations. These issues are framed for the purpose of identifying those individuals who should be entitled to receive society's scarce benefits under a particular government program. The physician, on the other hand, has the primary objective of generating data and opinions that can aid in designing and implementing an effective treatment plan for a particular patient. Fulfilling that purpose often entails different methods and results than does an evaluation done strictly to help settle legal questions. Physicians are neither used to nor comfortable with submitting objective findings for others (especially nonphysicians) to consider in arriving at their own ultimate conclusions.

Another serious problem is the significant proportion of physicians who, consciously or unconsciously, erroneously stamp claimants for SSDI benefits with the welfare label and are reluctant to aid and abet what they sense is a social handout. The medical community, at least until quite recently, has been drawn predominantly from the upper socioeconomic strata, and some natural bias on its part against reliance on government-sponsored income maintenance is understandable. Imbued with a firm work ethic, many physicians expect to find rugged individualism embodied in their patients as well. Often, these feelings are benevolent in origin; the physician does not wish to "stigmatize" the patient with the societally abhorrent label of being "disabled" (Firestone, 1997). Physician bias against applicants for public benefits is particularly bothersome when the older individual is forced by financial considerations to be evaluated at a government-operated facility, like a public clinic or military hospital. In such cases, an innate institutional prejudice detrimental to the claimant has sometimes been detected.

Further, some physicians refuse to officially acknowledge a longtime patient's disability out of apprehension that the disability may somehow be attributed to an unacceptable level of medical treatment provided in the past to the patient by the physician. From a perspective of malpractice lawsuit avoidance, most physicians find a healthy clientele (or at least one capable of being made healthy) most desirable.

An additional factor contributing in some instances to physician resistance to taking an active role in disability situations is the anxiety that vigorous advocacy on behalf of the patient may expose the physician to potential prosecution for fraud, a criminal offense for which malpractice liability insurance is not available. Although this fear is groundless, assuming honesty on the physician's part, it nevertheless is real and exerts a powerful negative influence on physician performance in this area. At the same time, however, some physicians report a willingness to exaggerate clinical data to help a patient they think deserving of disability benefits (Zinn & Furutani, 1996).

Besides SSDI, the federal SSA operates another disability program, the Supplemental Security Income for the Aged, Blind and Disabled (SSI—Title 16) program. The operations and medical eligibility criteria of the SSDI and SSI disability programs are essentially identical. The health care professional has a much less important role to play on behalf of older individuals under the latter program than under the former because older individuals who satisfy the financial means test (put more bluntly, are poor enough) automatically qualify for SSI payments on the basis of the objective standard of being 65 years or older, without the need for any showing of functional disability. The disability portion of the SSI program serves mainly the younger population.

A third large disability program is operated by the federal government through the Department of Veterans Affairs (VA), 38 U.S.C. §355.

Veterans having physical or psychiatric diseases or injuries resulting from their military service are eligible to apply for VA disability compensation. Claims for compensation are handled by VA regional offices and submitted to a rating board consisting of a physician and two nonphysician rating specialists. When evaluating a claim, the board determines whether the medical evidence in the veteran's file is sufficient for it to make a rating determination. If not sufficient, the board forwards a request for a medical examination (Form 2507) to a VA medical center. Medical center physicians then perform the necessary examinations and tests and submit medical reports to the rating board. The board then considers the medical report and other available evidence in the veteran's file, including employment history and educational background.

The VA's Schedule for Rating Disabilities is the official guide for converting clinical findings into standard diagnostic codes, covering diseases or injuries and degrees of severity of impairment. Rating specialists convert diagnoses in medical reports to diagnostic codes in the rating schedule and select the appropriate degree of severity from the schedule. Severity is measured in percentages ranging from 0 to 100, in increments of 10%, and 100% means totally disabled.

The prime role of the physician in the disability determination process, as both documenter and advocate, is evident. Legal and ethical responsibility to one's older patients requires the modern physician to accept and respect this important opportunity. The physician must be willing to learn about the disability claims system, both through personal initiative and by listening to the explanations of the patient's attorney. Sufficient time and effort must be allocated to the conduct of disability examinations and the preparation of reports. The physician must strive to provide data, opinions, and advice that are clear, complete, timely, and responsive to the issues involved. Above all, the physician must recognize and strengthen, in this area as well as others, the vital link between the clinical health and the legal and economic well-being of the older patients being served.

DISCRIMINATION AND DISABILITY

American society has made important strides in providing disabled individuals, including older disabled persons, with needed income assistance (e.g., through SSDI), public health insurance (primarily through Medicare and Medicaid), and direct services in the home, community, and institutional settings. We have also enacted laws during the past three decades aimed at eliminating unfair discrimination in access to various types of opportunities against individuals, where that discrimination is based solely on a person's (often an older person's) disability status.

For example, a person suffering from Alzheimer's disease was denied admission to a nursing facility (NF) because the facility felt its staff could not accommodate the behavioral manifestations (e.g., screaming, agitation, and aggressive acting out) of her disease. In a federal lawsuit, the court held that, because the NF was tax-supported, the applicant was protected by the Rehabilitation Act of 1973, 29 U.S.C. §794. Section 504 of the Act protects a person from discrimination in the receipt of services if that person is, with or without "reasonable accommodations" on the part of the service provider, "otherwise qualified" to benefit from the services. Thus, in *Wagner v. Fair Acres Geriatric Center* (1995), the court would excuse the NF's discrimination against the applicant with Alzheimer's disease only if the facility could demonstrate that the accommodations necessary to care for that particular applicant properly would have constituted an undue burden under the circumstances.

In 1990, Congress expanded the impact of the Rehabilitation Act by enacting the Americans With Disabilities Act (ADA), 42 U.S.C. §12101 *et seq.*, which became effective in 1992. Of most relevance to the aged are Titles II and III of the ADA. Title II prohibits discrimination on the basis of disability by state and local government programs, even when those programs receive no federal funds. Such discrimination might take the form of formal or informal barriers in the application process to obtain benefits, including complex application forms, inaccessible application sites, and long waiting times for appointments; reduction in public benefits and services; and intrusions into the disabled person's choices (e.g., about home- and community-based service arrangements [Kapp, 1996d; Sabatino & Litvak, 1996]) and hence independence. Title III of the ADA specifies that no individual shall be subjected to discrimination on the basis of disability in goods, services, facilities, and other advantages in any place of public accommodation or commercial facility (such as a physician's office, hospital, or nursing home).

Just as with the Rehabilitation Act, the ADA defines (and therefore protects) disabled persons as those who (1) have "a physical or mental impairment that substantially limits one or more of the major life activities of such individual," (2) have "a record [history] of such impairment," or (3) are "regarded [by others] as having such an impairment." Clearly, many older individuals fall into one or more of these protected categories and hence will qualify for "reasonable accommodations" (e.g., wheelchair ramps, large-print documents) to allow them to achieve equal opportunities with the nondisabled.

Potential health professional involvement may be essential in several aspects of dealing with legal protections regarding discrimination against older persons on the basis of disability. Among the areas of possible health professional contribution are diagnosis and documentation of the existence and severity of a disability or disabilities qualifying an individual for protection under the ADA; identification of reasonable accommodations that would render the individual able to take part in and benefit from the activity in question; and encouraging and supporting the facilities and other entities with which they are professionally affiliated to willingly and in a timely fashion make structural and operational accommodations necessary to better serve their own older disabled patients/consumers.

Chapter 7

Elder Abuse and Neglect

THE PROBLEM

The prevalence of mistreatment, abuse, and neglect of elderly institutional residents (persons living in nursing facilities (NFs), boarding- and rooming houses, and public mental institutions) has been long documented and widely lamented (Payne & Cikovic, 1995) (see Chapter 9). Elder abuse and neglect as a variety of domestic violence (American Academy of Family Physicians, 1994), on the other hand, has only relatively recently become publicly acknowledged and formally accepted as a matter of interest and concern to health care professionals, social services systems, legal authorities, and society in general (Goldstein, 1995; Gottlich, 1994a; Kleinschmidt, 1997; Lachs & Pillemer, 1995).

Elder abuse and neglect are concepts that are sometimes difficult to apply in practice (Jones, 1994). Generally, they are defined as the frequent but until now largely ignored phenomena of victimization of older persons within the community, in their own or someone else's home, by members of their family or surrogate family. (An adult foster care home would be an example of a surrogate family arrangement [Folkemer, Jensen, Lipson, Stauffer, & Gox-Grage, 1996]). It is the infliction of physical pain or debilitating mental anguish, unreasonable confinement, or willful deprivation by a caretaker of services that are necessary to maintain the mental and physical health of an older person. The mistreatment, sometimes referred to as "battering" in the United States and "Granny bashing" in Great Britain (M. Bradley, 1996), may take almost any form or a combination of many forms (National Center on Elder Abuse, 1994). Forms include physical violence, psychological abuse (e.g., threats), denial of basic human needs (such as withholding nourishment), violation of civil rights (like the right to freely communicate with other persons), excessive use of physical and/or chemical restraints (Kapp, 1995h), medical neglect, financial exploitation (Shiferaw et al., 1994; Wilber, 1990), misuse and abuse of drugs, an unsanitary environment, and destruction of personal property or pets. Elder abuse and neglect may occur as a single incident or as a persistent pattern of behavior. Few professionals who deal regularly with older individuals in the community report no experience with physical abuse, and a much smaller number have no experience with the other categories of abuse and neglect. Abuse and neglect of the aged likely occurs almost as often as child abuse and neglect.

In partial response to this sad situation, state legislatures have created a number of possible intervention mechanisms (Levitt & O'Neill, 1997) intended to alleviate or prevent the elder abuse and neglect problem in particular cases (Neale, Hwalek, Goodrich, & Quinn, 1996; Stiegel, 1995; Tatara, 1995). These protective legal mechanisms include (depending upon the jurisdiction) (1) civil injunctions or protective orders, carrying the sanction of criminal contempt if disobeyed, prohibiting specified harmful actions from happening; (2) temporary or permanent removal of the older individual from the site of abuse or neglect, often accompanied by imposition of guardianship and/or protective services (used in fairly extreme situations); and (3) criminal prosecution, often at the felony level, of the abuser (Polisky, 1995), a course followed in only the most egregious circumstances (Quinn & Tomita, 1997).

These laws are not intended to erode the strength of the family unit but are based on clear socially shared principles that the individual, regardless of family status, has the right to be free from fear of victimization (Byers & Hendricks, 1993). These laws recognize that, although the family is potentially the most nurturing source of long term care for the older person, the family also is too often the source of abuse and neglect (Kapp, 1991b). Several of these state statutes, in addition to authorizing civil protective orders and criminal punishments, appropriate state funds for supportive and rehabilitative services to violent families.

It is essential for health care professionals serving older patients to become aware of their own state's response to the elder abuse and neglect problem. The professional must know which public agencies have been assigned primary responsibility for carrying out preventive, supportive, or remedial activities in this realm, and must develop a satisfactory referral and working relationship with those agencies. As is generally true in dealing with government departments, early identification of particular program personnel who are knowledgeable and sensitive can vastly reduce subsequent frustration and unnecessary expenditure of time and energy. The possible involvement of private social service agencies in one's particular geographic area also should be checked out (Wolf & Pillemer, 1994).

HEALTH CARE PROFESSIONAL'S ROLE

Before the legal system can effectively intervene in an abuse or neglect situation, access to the victim must be secured. It is largely for this reason that health care professionals, particularly nurses (Capezuti, Brush, & Lawson, 1997; Criner, 1994) and emergency department (Lachs et al., 1997) and primary care (American Medical Association, 1992a) physicians, are the ones who most often occupy center stage in the anti–elder abuse and neglect effort. As with most major health care problems of older persons, abuse and neglect demand a multidisciplinary approach (McGuire & Fulmer, 1997). Ideally, a team of practitioners from at least the medical, nursing, social service, mental health (American Psychiatric Association, 1995), clergy, and legal professions should cooperate in taking on responsibility for cases of abuse and neglect. The physician's role in the multidisciplinary management of inadequate care of the older person is multifaceted. It includes: identifying cases of possible abuse and neglect; referring cases for further assessment by nursing, psychiatric, or social service professionals; setting realistic goals for intervention based on prognosis and projected care needs; prescribing medical treatments; certifying the need for long term care placements; and judiciously using the moral and psychological authority traditionally vested in the physician to encourage the older patient and the family in limit-setting and compliance with care plans (American Medical Association, 1992a; Kleinschmidt, 1997; Lachs & Pillemer, 1995). The importance of prevention of abuse and neglect through the recognition of high-risk factors also should be underscored.

Recognition of Signs

Since the vast majority of elder abuse or neglect cases are, in whole or part, physical in nature, the individual's physician—because of professional expertise and a unique, intimate relationship with the patient and often the family—is in the best position to observe, recognize, and report symptoms and signs associated with incidents or patterns of suspected elder abuse or neglect (American Medical Association, 1992a; Jones, 1994; Kleinschmidt, 1997; Lachs & Pillemer, 1995). Physicians who see family members on a regular basis are in a strategic position to detect the atmosphere of violence and thus to assist in preventing a violent outbreak. To accomplish this, however, the physician must learn to (1) recognize the signs and symptoms that may indicate the presence of violence against older persons (Lachs, Berkman, Fulmer, & Horwitz, 1994) and (2) mediate and intervene when necessary. The physician needs to know what can be done for the older victim, for the perpetrator, and for the family as a whole. Humanism, compassion, and respect for people—basic to all health care delivery—are doubly important when dealing with distressed families and their most vulnerable members.

In most cases, some remnant of physical trauma, such as bruises, welts, sprains, or fractures, is evident. These signs are sometimes minor from a treatment standpoint but nonetheless readily identifiable by an alert clinician who knows what to seek out. Victims also tend to request frequent medical attention for conversion symptoms and psychophysiologic reactions such as gastrointestinal disorders, back pain, pelvic pain, choking sensations, and headache. Symptoms often are connected to previous sites of battery.

It is imperative that health care professionals develop and regularly implement in practice clear guidelines for detection of cases of elder abuse and neglect. These guidelines should account for physical indicators and also take into account behavioral observations, in terms of personal interactions between the patient and suspected abuser or neglector. Guidelines for training in case detection are emerging in the literature (Hazzard, 1995; Quinn & Tomita, 1997) and from professional organizations (American Medical Association, 1992a). Many individual health care facilities have developed their own written protocols. Protective services agencies also frequently have written protocols and training materials that are available to practitioners.

Once a case of suspected elder abuse or neglect has been reasonably identified, it is essential that action is taken immediately on the basis of that clinical judgment. In addition to activating therapeutic responsibilities concerning both the individual patient and the family dynamics, the health care professional's recognition of abuse may entail certain legal obligations.

Legislation

Although public and private attitudes toward elder abuse and neglect vary (Moon & Williams, 1993), many victims of elder abuse or neglect are reluctant to voluntarily admit their plight, generally out of feelings of dependency, embarrassment, and fear of abandonment. Friends and relatives, if there even are any besides the wrongdoers, are afraid to become involved. The abusing or neglecting party is interested, of course, in having the acts or omissions go undetected. For these reasons, all states have passed elder abuse and neglect legislation, mandating or at least encouraging certain categories of health care professionals, invariably including physicians, to report to a specified public agency (ordinarily the state or local welfare office, prosecutor, and/or police department) cases of suspected elder abuse or neglect that come to their attention (Kapp, 1995b).

Individual state statutes differ somewhat in their details. Some statutes specify a particular minimum age for the protected population. Other states have mandated reporting of adult abuse generally, unlimited to a particular victim age cohort. Some state statutes (Colorado, Illinois, New Jersey, New York, North Dakota, Pennsylvania, and South Dakota) provide for voluntary rather than mandatory reporting. It is unclear whether employees of the federal Department of Veterans Affairs (VA) are covered by mandatory state reporting statutes; VA staff should seek legal counsel from their institutions. States vary on the specific public agency empowered to receive and investigate reports (Ehrlich & Anetzberger, 1991). In all states, a health care professional making a good faith reporting of reasonable suspicion of elder abuse, whether on a mandatory or voluntary basis, is protected by specific statutory provisions against subsequent legal charges of defamation or breach of patient or family confidentiality. State legislatures continue to debate and enact refinements of their adult abuse and neglect reporting and intervention (e.g., protective services) statutory schemes. Bills also have been introduced and discussed in Congress periodically for the creation of national requirements in this field, but without action at this time. However, the Older Americans Act (OAA) has authorized grant dollars for programs designed to prevent elder abuse, 42 U.S.C. §3030.

The public policy justification for state reporting and intervention statutes is the state *parens patriae* power. This is the inherent authority of society to take measures to protect those individuals who cannot protect themselves from harm. *Parens patriae* is the legal embodiment of the ethical concept of benevolence, or doing good for others.

Various groups and individuals have raised questions concerning the actual effectiveness of mandatory elder abuse reporting requirements. Eric Cassell (1989) has argued that law is a poor source of restraint on the powers of others over the helpless elderly.

Some critics have contended that the legislative response to the political issue of abuse and neglect of older persons has developed without the benefit of any systematic analysis of the theories of causation, study of potential interventions and their risks and benefits, or appreciation of the ethical dilemmas confronting practitioners attempting to respond to these cases and laws (Vaughan & Ingman, 1989). Those making that accusation, as well as other critics, have argued that such legislation is repugnant as a violation of the older individual's fundamental right to autonomy or self-determination because it entails uninvited state intervention into the older person's life. The older victim, according to this view, has the fundamental right to choose to be abused or neglected. Commentators in other democratic nations have pointed out the same legal and policy predicament (Freeman, 1989).

This thesis is unconvincing when applied to the real life circumstances of those dependent and fearful older persons who suffer the indignities and injuries of domestic violence. Elder abuse and neglect legislation is a necessary and reasonable exercise of the *parens patriae* power (T. L. Kramer, 1995; Velick, 1995).

In no way should we minimize the ethical dilemma facing health care professionals as a consequence of laws that mandate or strongly encourage their active participation in forms of governmental intervention that are expressly rejected by an older individual patient (Quinn, 1985). (This struggle between patient autonomy and the societal urge to do good is discussed more fully in Chapter 8). Rather, the health care professional has an ethical (as well as a legal) obligation to assure that the decisions of each older patient have been made without coercion or undue interference and competently. The patient's right to self-determination should not be used as an excuse to ignore ongoing abuse and neglect. The process for working with an unwilling patient, in this context and in many others, involves great skill in persuasion and negotiation. Access and intervention must be carefully finessed with both the older person and the caretaker/abuser, neither of whom may desire help. Successful negotiation is facilitated by emphasizing how the services will resolve unmet needs of the older person while providing both support and continued involvement to the stressed caretaker. Intervention should promote the least restrictive alternative to ongoing abuse and neglect while respecting the rights of the older person to privacy and autonomy. Involuntary interventions like guardianship should be employed only as a last resort (Schmidt, 1995).

As a matter of course, the health care professional must become familiar with the particular reporting provisions currently in effect in the relevant jurisdiction. Since virtually everywhere reporting is explicitly ordered or at least permitted and encouraged under a grant of legal immunity from claims of defamation or breach of confidentiality, the health care professional must develop and integrate into regular practice a systematic means not only of identifying cases of suspected elder abuse and neglect but also of reporting them to the designated public officials.

Besides relying in large measure on health care professionals to call instances of possible elder abuse and neglect to its attention, the legal system also needs medical aid in order to successfully resolve such cases and to devise appropriate protective, supportive, and remedial responses. Medical evidence, especially in the form of documentation in the patient's chart, concerning the extent of the injuries suffered and the physical and mental condition of both the victim and the putative abuser is given great credence by the courts in adjudicating the most beneficial disposition in elder abuse and neglect determinations. The health care professional's role, thus, does not end with identification and reporting.

Experience with health care professional performance in identifying, reporting, and helping to resolve cases of suspected elder abuse and neglect has so far produced a suboptimal record. Frequently blamed is the naive worldview engulfing many physicians and other health care professionals. It simply is difficult for a large number of health care professionals, who come from middle-class backgrounds and embrace middle-class values, to accept and deal with the very real phenomenon of domestic violence directed at older family members (American Academy of Family Physicians, 1994). Many health care professionals lack what one commentator has aptly described as a "realization that [for the elderly] violence often begins at home" (Vaisrub, 1981).

Even among health care professionals who are able to cope with this reality, ignorance of or confusion about legal implications is prevalent (Jones, Veenstra, Seamon, & Krohmer, 1997; Rosenblatt, Cho, & Durance, 1996). Yet there are those who are cognizant of their legal duties but still decline, in large numbers, to become involved in the legal intervention aspects of elder abuse and neglect. This may, in part, be because they are generally uncomfortable with and resistant to legal issues and legal processes, perceiving such matters to be foreign to their healer role and exclusively belonging within the turf of the legal profession. Health care professionals also may shy away from active involvement in cases of elder abuse and neglect for fear of alienating the victim's relatives, who may be perpetrators of or tacit accomplices to the victimization. The health care professional may have a long-standing professional relationship with an abused or neglected person's family, a relationship that the provider is loath to jeopardize by embroiling family members in the legal process.

These factors influencing suboptimal health care professional performance must be consciously confronted and overcome (Hazzard, 1995). Certainly, some duties are owed to a family with whom a health care professional has established a professional relationship. However, it must be kept firmly in mind that the health care professional's primary obligations, of both the legal and ethical sort, are due to the individual patient and to the larger society whose existence and functioning make the realization of individual rights possible. These legal and ethical (T. F. Johnson, 1995) imperatives compel active and effective health care professional involvement in the identification and reporting of cases of suspected elder abuse and neglect, as well as in the processes of protection, support, and rehabilitation of its victims and, where appropriate, its perpetrators (Ohio State Medical Association, 1994). The formation of a durable professional/ patient relationship and a therapeutic alliance with the family are crucial for success in the long-term management of older patients who are receiving inadequate or even harmful care at home.

Chapter 8

Involuntary Commitment, Guardianship, Protective Services, Representative Payees, and Powers of Attorney

INTRODUCTION

Life is a series of decisions waiting to be made. Many of these decisions become complex over time. And for each decision, there must be a decision maker.

Ordinarily, the person who will be most directly affected by a particular decision is the one who makes it. There are times, though, when that individual is not factually and legally capable of making and expressing difficult choices affecting his or her own life. In those instances, the legal system may be called upon to empower one or more other persons to make decisions on behalf of the incapacitated individual. This may be accomplished through a variety of legal devices that vary in terms of their degree of intrusiveness into personal autonomy. These legal mechanisms include involuntary commitment to a public mental institution (or to a private institution that is licensed by the state to accept involuntarily committed patients), involuntary guardianship, adult protective services, representative payees and other money management services, and ordinary and durable powers of attorney.

Factual and legal incapacity to make and express individual decisions is a situation that affects older adults in disproportionate terms. The extent of mental disorders in old age, representing decrements in both intellectual and emotional functioning, is considerable. It is currently estimated that up to 28% (Gatz, 1995) of the older population need mental health services, although the true extent of psychiatric need among older people probably has not been fully documented. Mental illnesses escalate over the course of a life cycle. The increase in incidence is marked, decade by decade, with advancing age.

For some older persons, mental dysfunction may be a carryover from earlier life. For most, though, mental health problems develop later in life as a result of organic brain disorders (primary degenerative disorders or multiinfarct dementia), paranoid disorders, drug reactions, or depression or as the by-product of various physical illnesses. These problems may take the form of cognitive impairment (dementia) in memory, attention, or information processing; emotional lability (psychosis) often manifested as aggression; or pseudodementia (depression).

The disproportionate representation of older persons among those considered incapable of deciding questions for themselves is also a product of the philosophical tension present between the beneficent motives of an altruistic society and our respect for the right of the individual to make personal decisions even if they are "unwise" or "foolish." Society seems somehow unwilling to tolerate in an 80-year-old the same silly decision that we would much more readily condone in a 30- or 40-year old. Thus, an older individual is at a disproportionately high risk of becoming the willing or unwilling "beneficiary" of one of the sorts of legal solutions listed above. The older female is at particular peril, owing to the larger number of women in the total population, the larger percentage of women who live alone, and the traditional legal and social view of women as dependent and unable to manage their own affairs.

Health care professionals serving older patients may be drawn into and treated as essential participants in these legal processes, in a number of different ways. Such involvement is nothing new (Pace & Sullivan-Fowler, 1897/1997). This chapter discusses why and how health care professionals become directly involved in legal matters concerning the decision-making abilities and authority of their older patients.

INVOLUNTARY COMMITMENT

Introduction

Involuntary commitment sometimes is referred to as involuntary institutionalization, involuntary hospitalization, or civil commitment (to distinguish it from the criminal commitment that follows a finding of incompetency to stand trial or a verdict of not guilty by reason of insanity in a criminal proceeding) (Melton, Petrila, Poythres, & Slogogin, 1997). It is one route by which a person may gain entry into a public mental health institution (or a private institution that is licensed by the state to accept and be paid for treating involuntarily committed patients). It is a route that disproportionately (Moak & Fisher, 1991) and often inappropriately affects older persons.

The phenomenon of involuntary institutionalization of older persons has been exacerbated in the past four decades with a rise in the number of patient transfers from nursing facilities (NFs) to mental health institutions, occurring when the NF staff find the older patient "unmanageable" in the NF setting. The behaviors that place the older NF patient at greatest risk for involuntary commitment are hitting, yelling, wandering, smearing excrement, and throwing objects (Moak & Fisher, 1990, 1991). Out of necessity (because they are the placement site of last resort), public mental institutions exhibit a significantly higher tolerance for deviance than does the average NF. Thus, the intended beneficiaries of the much-heralded deinstitutionalization movement of the 1970s (A. B. Johnson, 1990) frequently become the actual victims of the reinstitutionalization and transinstitutionalization reality today.

Also relevant here are federal regulations (discussed in Chapter 9) designed to implement the Nursing Home Quality Reform Act contained in the Omnibus Budget Reconciliation Act (OBRA) of 1987, as amended by OBRA 1990; see §1919(e)(7) of the Social Security Act, 42 U.S.C. §1395r(e)(7). A provision in this law attempts to address a long-standing concern among patient advocates that NFs had not provided sufficient attention and care to the needs of their mentally disabled patients—the complaint that many NFs in effect simply warehoused such individuals without appropriate treatment. This provision requires nursing homes to engage in preadmission screening and annual resident review (PASARR) to assure that individuals whose primary needs concern mental health are not confined in NFs without appropriate treatment. The result has not always meant better mental health treatment in NFs, as the law intends. Instead, the unintended result in some cases has been the refusal of NF admission for, or the involuntary transfer from NFs of, mentally compromised older persons, who end up committed to public mental institutions where, at least theoretically, proper mental health services are available.

Admission

A person also may gain admission to a public mental institution through the process of voluntary hospitalization. Superficially, this represents the free, competent, informed choice of the patient, but the "voluntary" label frequently is misleading. First, a majority of the people presenting themselves for voluntary admission to a public mental institution have severe impairment of mental capacity, likely rendering the giving of truly informed consent difficult if not impossible. Additionally, the "free" nature of the application is suspect when, as often happens, the individual accepts voluntary hospitalization only in response to a threat of involuntary commitment. Finally, it is doubtful whether the material risks and alternatives are often adequately disclosed to a patient applying for admission to a public mental institution.

Thus, for the health care professional serving older patients, the similarities between voluntary and involuntary commitment generally are more important than the distinctions. This was recognized by the U.S. Supreme Court in *Zinermon v. Burch* (1990). In that case, the court ruled that the state of Florida could be sued civilly for permitting an adult person who was later held to be mentally incompetent to admit him/herself "voluntarily" to a public mental institution without first explicitly ascertaining and documenting that the patient possessed sufficient cognitive and emotional capacity to make an autonomous decision about his/her admission (American Psychiatric Association, 1993; Hoge, 1994).

Every state has statutory and constitutional authority (Hermann, 1997; Perlin, 1994) to exercise its inherent police power to protect the general health, safety, welfare, and morals of society by confining in public mental health facilities those individuals who, by reason of mental illness, pose an imminent, serious threat of danger to others. Many jurisdictions require some concrete evidence of this likelihood, in the form of an articulated threat, an overt attempt, or the prior infliction of actual physical harm on another.

Involuntary commitments also may be accomplished in most jurisdictions (Perlin, 1994) under the state's inherent *parens patriae* power, which is the power of society to protect those who cannot protect themselves. Relying upon ethical precepts of benevolence and safeguarding the helpless, the standards ordinarily used to justify the exercise of the *parens patriae* power are danger to oneself or need for care and treatment. In some statutes, the terminology is "gravely disabled." Basing an involuntary commitment on the *parens patriae* rationale requires a determination that the person is mentally incapable of providing for his or her own basic life requirements. Researchers have found that a "need for treatment" criterion correlates with an older and more largely female patient population, whereas a predominant "dangerousness to others" criterion tends to correlate more with commitment of a younger, male-dominated population (Segal, 1989).

The police power theory and the *parens patriae* theory, plus the cited substantive standards they generate, may serve as the basis for an emergency or nonemergency involuntary commitment of an older patient. State laws provide for the short-term forced hospitalization of patients in an emergency situation until a court hearing can be held. The period of time within which the hearing must be commenced varies among states but is invariably limited to a few days. Usually, a physician must sign the emergency commitment certificate, but some states require more than one physician to sign. Some permit other agencies, such as the police or the courts, to initiate the commitments when no physician is available. Psychologists continue to lobby strongly for the power to commit patients in many states. Ordinarily, the substantive criteria that must be met for emergency commitment are identical to those required for court-ordered commitment, namely, those criteria of dangerousness or need mentioned previously.

After the expiration of an emergency commitment, a court of proper jurisdiction can be petitioned for an order of indeterminate commitment. Although this commitment is indeterminate in length, most states require periodic review of its continued factual basis. A petition for indeterminate commitment also may be filed even where there has been no preceding emergency commitment. Depending on state statute, the formal hearing may be conducted in a district, superior, family, or probate court or (in a few jurisdictions) before an administrative board or hearing officer.

A variety of procedural safeguards, mandated by federal or state constitutional due process or equal protection clauses or created by state statute or judicial decision, characterize the civil commitment process (Perlin, 1994). Most states guarantee the individual the right to have a jury decide on the issue of commitment, although in the majority of cases this right is waived or voluntarily given up, and the case is tried instead before a judge sitting as decider of both law and fact. The state has the burden of proof in these situations. The standard of proof is "clear and convincing" evidence (roughly 75 chances out of 100 that the individual is mentally ill and dangerous to self or others or in need of treatment) as a constitutional minimum (*Addington v. Texas,* 1979). Several states, though, have chosen to adopt a "beyond a reasonable doubt" (approximately 90–95 chances out of 100) evidentiary test.

Involuntary commitment does not, as a matter of law, automatically equal a loss of all personal decisional authority for the patient. Put differently, the substantive criteria for commitment are not synonymous with the criteria for a finding of incompetence to make medical or other decisions. Unless a court specifically finds that the patient lacks decisional capacity (discussed below, under "Guardianship"), he or she retains the right to make medical and other choices as a matter of constitutional due process and equal protection and common law informed consent, despite a civil commitment status.

The other side of the coin is that being found in need of a guardianship (see below) does not necessarily mean that a person satisfies the legal criteria for involuntary commitment. In most states, a court-appointed guardian may not "voluntarily" commit a nonconsenting ward to a public mental institution (English, 1996); rather, the guardian must petition the court for involuntary commitment of the ward.

Intrusions by the government into individual freedom must be based on the least restrictive alternative principle under the constitutional due process requirement first set forth by the Supreme Court in *Shelton v. Tucker* (1960). Hence, there has been a limited trend in recent years toward outpatient civil commitment (Torrey & Kaplan, 1995). Under this approach, an individual who is found to satisfy the criteria for commitment may be ordered by the court to comply with an outpatient treatment regimen as a condition of not being placed involuntarily inside a public mental institution (Slobogin, 1994). The outpatient commitment option owes its appeal both to respect for patient autonomy to the maximum feasible extent and to lower costs of care in the community, compared with institutional commitment. Evidence regarding the effectiveness of outpatient civil commitment as a viable alternative to hospitalization is still being collected and analyzed (Munetz, Grande, Kleist, & Peterson, 1996; Swartz et al., 1995).

Some have argued (Spring, 1987) that the same procedural due process safeguards that accompany civil commitment ought to accompany the admission of a person to a NF, on the theory that both situations involve a form of coercive placement. Thus far, this extension of the legal adversary system has not been adopted by courts or legislators, and guardians and other legally authorized substitute decision makers currently have the power to admit a mentally incompetent individual to an NF without specific prior judicial approval (Kapp, 1998d).

Role of the Health Care Professional

The initial role of the health care professional is to help determine whether an involuntary commitment proceeding should be initiated. The health care team, particularly the physician, is responsible for the initial evaluation of the patient's mental capacities and deciding whether the legal criteria for involuntary commitment in that state are met by the particular patient. The health care professional must identify and evaluate less restrictive alternatives to involuntary commitment that are available and are likely to accomplish the objectives of protecting the community and/or protecting and treating the patient. The health care professional must counsel the patient, family, law enforcement officials, and other concerned parties to assure that an involuntary commitment petition is filed only as a last resort after community resources have been explored and ruled out or exhausted.

Once an involuntary commitment action has been initiated against an older person, the role of the health care professional is central. First, as already noted, an emergency commitment petition usually must be accompanied by documentation prepared by a physician or psychologist certifying that the patient meets that state's criteria for commitment. In many jurisdictions, when the petition for court-ordered commitment is filed subsequent to or in lieu of the emergency commitment, it must also include the health care professional's certification of dangerousness or need. The health care professional's involvement in this aspect of the process usually is invoked by family members who are seeking commitment of an older relative or by an NF administrator who is seeking commitment of a troublesome patient. Thus, the health care professional with older patients must be thoroughly conversant with the involuntary commitment standards operating in his or her particular jurisdiction.

Second, the health care professional has a vital contribution to make during the actual prosecution or defense of a commitment proceeding before a judge or jury. This contribution may be coaxed forth either by the party (or parties) attempting commitment or by the patient, depending on the perceived clinical opinion of the health care professional concerning the propriety of commitment. A party in an involuntary commitment trial (ordinarily, the state and family and/or NF administrator are on one side, and the patient is on the other) is virtually precluded from succeeding unless it presents expert medical testimony to bolster its position.

The expert evaluators/witnesses relied upon frequently are specialists in psychiatry. However, another type of health care professional (such as the person's primary care physician, gerontological nurse, psychologist, or social worker), who has had a long-standing relationship with the older individual (and quite possibly with the family), often is in a better position to provide meaningful information to the court concerning the patient's condition, needs, and circumstances than is a new psychiatrist brought in specifically for purposes of the legal proceedings. For this reason, attorneys, judges, and juries generally prefer the live testimony of a litigant's personal health care professionals when such testimony is obtainable. These professionals should work closely with the attorney for the party soliciting their testimony in preparing for the court appearance, particularly to anticipate possible lines of questioning that may be pursued by opposing counsel during cross-examination.

Third, the imposition of an involuntary commitment is never final and unreviewable. The status of one who has been involuntarily committed must be reviewed periodically and the person released if the statutory commitment standards are no longer met. Evidence—in the form of written reports or live testimony given before a judge or hearing board by health care professionals familiar with the older patient—is imperative for a meaningful review of commitment. The individual's health care professionals arguably have a duty, after commitment, to try to rehabilitate the patient. Assuming this clinical endeavor is partially or fully successful, a health care professional's stated assertion verifying the favorable effects of treatment is essential to the physical transfer or discharge of the patient to the least restrictive environment consistent with the individual's needs and the protection of society. The health care professional can be valuable in assisting to identify and secure an adequate community placement at this point.

Problem Areas

Many health care professionals feel psychologically uneasy about participating in the involuntary commitment process and attach low priority to its place in their clinical practices. Dealing with the issues raised by this process and with the types of patients who present them is not especially pleasant or glamorous work. It also is excruciatingly difficult work intellectually, as numerous (but not unanimous; see Mossman, 1994) descriptions in the literature of the unreliability of "scientific" predictions of future dangerousness illustrate (Lidz, Mulvey, & Gardner, 1993). Advocates for older clients facing the threat of involuntary commitment have found fault with the performance of their clients' health care professionals on a number of counts (Kapp, 1982). Many of these criticisms are equally relevant to the discussion of guardianship that appears in the next section.

First, some of the more outspoken advocates accuse health care professionals of improperly colluding with relatives or institutions to have older patients institutionalized when such a disposition is not justified by the facts or the law. In such situations, the commitment action is motivated by some force other than concern for the patient's well-being, like a concern for the convenience or pecuniary gain of the relatives or institutions. The health care professional must keep firmly in mind the primary ethical and legal allegiance owed directly to the patient, an allegiance that may be overridden only when the professional is clearly satisfied that the factual and legal criteria for commitment are present.

Most complaints by patient advocates, however, do not allege purposeful wrongdoing on the health care professional's part. Rather, they center on the professional's ignorance of the applicable legal criteria and standards of proof regarding involuntary commitment and the resultant rendering of opinions in the form of conclusory diagnostic labels rather than as evaluations and explanations of functional capacity. The diagnostic conclusions alone, comprehensible only to medically educated professionals (a fraternity that does not include in its number many practicing attorneys or jurists), are insufficient to adequately answer the legal questions arising in commitment proceedings. Health care professionals must explicitly describe the basis and reasoning underlying their conclusions in order to translate their judgments into useful evidence relevant to the applicable legal criteria and standards.

A further charge is that many health care professionals seem unfamiliar with and uninterested in noninstitutional alternatives for their older patients who are unable to care for themselves totally. Specifically, it is claimed that many health care professionals participate in the placement of older patients in public mental institutions—or more frequently, in NFs—in concert with the individual's attorney, clergyman, or friends, precipitously and without adequate exploration of available community-based options. A number of sources have suggested that much institutionalization of older persons is unwarranted and that health care professional bias is at least partially responsible for this phenomenon. At the least, the health care professional should be well acquainted with the potential adverse clinical consequences of involuntary commitment.

GUARDIANSHIP

Introduction

Every state has enacted statutes that empower the courts to appoint a substitute decision maker with authority to make decisions on behalf of a mentally incompetent ward. (For a list of state statutes, see Table 8.1). As explained below, the terminology for this court-appointed substitute decision maker varies among jurisdictions; the most common term, "guardian," will be employed here.

Guardianship statutes are an example of the state's inherent *parens patriae* power to protect those who cannot take care of themselves in a manner that society believes is appropriate (Hull, Holmes, & Karst, 1990). The origins of some form of guardianship based on the benevolence of the state stretch back as far as 13th-century England and beyond (Neugebauer, 1989).

Most state guardianship statutes are similar in content because they generally are based on the Uniform Probate Code (UPC), Article 5, produced by the National Conference of Commissioners on Uniform State Laws (NCCUSL). At the same time, variations in both the letter of the law and its application exist across the United States (T. F. Johnson, 1990), so knowledge of the specific law in one's own jurisdiction is imperative. These variations have prompted calls for and the introduction of federal legislation compelling states to enact certain minimum procedural protections

TABLE 8.1 State Statutory Authority for Guardianship

Alabama Code §§ 26-1-1 to 9-16
Alaska Stat. §§ 13.26.005 to .410
Arizona Rev. Stat. Ann. §§ 14-5301 to 5607
Arkansas Stat. Ann. §§ 28-65-101 to 67-111
California Prob. Code §§ 1400 to 3803
Colorado Rev. Stat.§§ 15-14-301 to 432
Connecticut Gen. Stat. Ann. §§ 45-70 to 77
Delaware Code Ann.tit. 12 §§ 3701 to 3997
District of Columbia Code Ann. §§ 21-2001 to 2077
Florida Stat. Ann. §§ 744.101 to 747.531 (West)
Georgia Code Ann. §§ 29-2-1 to 8-7
Hawaii Rev. Stat. §§ 560:5-101 to 430
Idaho Code §§ 15-5-101 to 432
Illinois Ann. Stat.ch.110 1/2,para. 11a-1 to 22
Indiana Code Ann. §§ 29-3-1-1 to 15
Iowa Code Ann. §§ 633.566 to .682
Kansas Stat. Ann. §§ 59-3001 to 3038
Kentucky Rev. Stat. Ann. §§ 387.500 to .990
Louisiana Civ. Code Ann. art.389 to 426, La. Code Civ. Proc. Ann. art.4541
    to 4557
Maine Rev. Stat. Ann. tit. 18A, §§ 5-101 to 432
Maryland Est. & Trusts Code Ann. §§ 13-201 to 806
Massachusetts Gen. Laws Ann. ch.201, §§ 1 to 31
Michigan Comp. Laws Ann. §§ 27.5401 to 5461
Minnesota Stat. Ann. §§ 525.539 to .614
Mississippi Code Ann. §§ 93-13-121 to 267
Missouri Ann. Stat. §§ 475.010 to .340
Nebraska Rev. Stat. §§ 30-2617 to 2661
Nevada Rev. Stat. §§ 156.013 to .215
New Hampshire Rev. Stat. Ann. §§ 464-A:1 to :44
New Jersey Stat. Ann. §§ 3B:1-1 to 4:83-12
New Mexico Stat. Ann. §§ 45-5-301 to 432
New York Ment. Hyg. Law §§ 81.01
North Carolina Gen. Stat. §§ 35-A-1101 to 1217
North Dakota Cent. Code §§ 30.1-26-01 to 29-32
Ohio Rev. Code Ann. §§ 2101.01 to .51
Oklahoma Stat. Ann. tit. 30, §§ 1-101 to 5-101 (West)
Oregon Rev. Stat. §§ 126.003 to 126.396
Pennsylvania 20 Pa. Cons. Stat. Ann. §§ 5501 to 5537
Rhode Island Gen. Laws §§ 33-15-1 to 45
South Carolina Code Ann. §§ 62-5-301 to 432
South Dakota Codified Laws Ann. §§ 30-26-1 to 29-52
Tennessee Code Ann. §§ 34-2-101 to 4-213

(continued)

TABLE 8.1 (continued)

Texas Prob. Code Ann. art. 108 to 1300
Utah Code Ann. §§ 75-5-301 to 433
Vermont Stat. Ann. tit. 14, §§ 2671 to 3081
Virginia Code Ann. §§ 37.1-128.01 to 142
Washington Rev. Code Ann. §§ 11.88.005 to .92.190
West Virginia Code §§ 27-11-1 to 44-10A-6
Wisconsin Stat. Ann. §§ 880.01 to .39
Wyoming Stat. §§ 3-1-101 to 4-109

for wards and proposed wards, at least when someone other than a family member is the potential or actual guardian; federal legislation on this point, however, has not been enacted yet.

Another set of problems regarding multiple state laws occurs when a court attempts to impose a guardianship on a ward who has ties to more than one state. In response, some have proposed a uniform guardianship jurisdiction act and a national guardianship registry (Johns, Gottlich, & Carson, 1992).

Like involuntary commitment, guardianship is a legal device that disproportionately affects older persons (Weiler, Helms, & Buckwalter, 1993), especially those residing in institutions (Bulcroft, Kielkopf, & Tripp, 1991). An impressive segment of older persons in the United States have a guardian or its equivalent (Center for Social Gerontology, 1994a). Studies have found that psychiatric consultations regarding mental capacity are requested most often for older patients with organic mental disorders, particularly when the patient's capacity to make health care decisions is called into question because the patient has attempted to refuse treatment (Mahler, Perry, & Miller, 1990).

The number of guardianship petitions filed has increased sharply (Felsenthal, 1994) as standards for involuntary commitment have become more stringent, as families (especially extended families) break down and are less able to provide informal care management for the impaired elder, and as health and human services providers become more concerned about their own legal responsibilities and exposure. Guardianship usually is a somewhat less serious invasion of individual autonomy than is commitment because ordinarily it does not (but sometimes does) entail coerced confinement in a total institution, such as a nursing home (Lamb & Weinberger, 1992, 1993). Guardianship does, however, constitute a major restriction on the fundamental liberties of the older man or woman concerned (Schmidt, 1995), and many of the associated legal problems are similar to those surrounding commitment.

Health care professionals usually employ the terms "capable" or "having capacity" to describe patients who, in the clinician's professional judgment, ought to be permitted to make their own medical (and other) decisions (Stollerman, 1989). The terms "incompetent" or "incompetence" refer to a court's formal ruling on the decision-making status of an individual in the context of a guardianship proceeding (Anderer, 1990).

Every adult person is presumed to be legally competent to make individual decisions in life. This presumption may be declared invalid, and a substitute decision maker may be appointed only upon a sufficient showing that the individual is mentally unable to participate authentically and self-sufficiently in a rational decision-making process. A legal finding of incompetence signifies that a person, because of a lack of capacity to contemplate choices rationally, cannot care adequately for person or property.

Determination of Incapacity/Incompetence

Although this still is an extremely unclear area of the law, several specific criteria for incompetence may be distilled from the medical and legal literature or may be inferred from judicial commentary or statutory enactments or proposals. The UPC (chap. 5, §1-201[7]) and the Uniform Guardianship and Protective Proceedings Act define an "incapacitated person" as one

> who is impaired by reason of mental illness, mental deficiency, physical illness or disability, advanced age, chronic use of drugs, chronic intoxication, or other cause (except minority) to the extent of lacking sufficient understanding or capacity to make or communicate responsible decisions.

In the past decade or so, several states have made substantive changes in their guardianship laws. The newer statutes substitute, in place of traditional definitions of incompetence that rely heavily on labels, a reliance on more objective standards designed to focus on the individual's functional ability to manage personal care or finances on a daily basis—that is, they focus more on the person's ability to meet basic needs rather than on his or her diagnostic "condition" (Wang, Burns, & Hommel, 1990). This fundamental approach recognizes that, precisely because impairments, abilities, and disabilities vary widely within each diagnostic category, assignment of a particular diagnosis does not imply a specific level of impairment.

Literature on the concept of competence to make life decisions (which, incidentally, should not be confused with the concept of insanity, which is concerned with the legal responsibility of an individual for a criminal act that he or she has done) is voluminous and varied. Numerous

constructs of the concept and how it should be assessed have been proposed, both in the United States (Berg, 1996; Janofsky, McCarthy, & Folstein, 1992; Kapp, 1996b; Sabatino, 1996; Tombaugh & McIntyre, 1992) and
abroad (Gunn, 1994; Jones & Keywood, 1996). These proposals are variations, with differing combinations and emphases, on the following basic
questions (Gutheil & Appelbaum, 1991; Roth, Meisel, & Lidz, 1977):

1. Can the person make and express any choices concerning his or her
   life?
2. Are the outcomes of these choices "reasonable"?
3. Are these choices based on "rational," or realistic, reasons?
4. Is the person able to understand the personal implications of the
   choices that are made?
5. Does the person actually understand the implications of those
   choices?

These questions may be broken down into two elements (Beck, 1987).
First, does the individual have the capacity to assimilate the relevant facts,
and second, can the patient appreciate or rationally understand his or her
own situation as it relates to the medical facts?

The items of inquiry suggested by various commentators on the competence issue are interrelated and complementary but by no means synonymous, and the particular item or items upon which the health care
professional principally focuses frequently will determine the clinical
opinion reached and rendered. Put more simply, these questions are distinct, and the one chosen will likely determine the answer given. The more
thoughtful analyses urge that emphasis not be placed on the "objective"
nature or outcome of the specific decision made by the patient (and therefore not on whether the health care professional personally agrees with the
wisdom or disagrees with the folly of that choice) nor on the membership
or categorization of the patient within a specific grouping based solely on
the patient's clinical label (e.g., depression, dementia, mental retardation).
Rather, the determination of capacity ought to be founded on the functional ability of the individual patient and the subjective thought process
actually followed in arriving at a "good" or "bad" decision.

There are profound philosophical considerations at work here. When
we say that someone is mentally incompetent, we are not simply describing
a relative lack of ability. We are also making a moral claim (Cohen, 1996)
that some special regard is due that person, that we ought to treat the person with more care and concern than we give to others, that we ought to do
something about his or her lack of autonomy, or that the lack of autonomy
has implications for what we can reasonably expect of the person (Kaufman, 1995; Reynolds, 1995). To say that a person is legally incompetent

implies that the individual is below some minimum level of capacity and range of opportunity, not simply that the person has less capacity and opportunity than certain other people. Such a statement requires individualized assessment of each potential ward and a resistance of the ageist stereotypes that have sometimes been detected in both medical and judicial (Bulcroft et al., 1991; Johns, 1997) practice.

Role of the Courts

In light of the foregoing discussion, state guardianship statutes contain a two-step definition of competence (Anderer, 1990). In this manner, they parallel involuntary commitment statutes. First, the individual must fall within a particular category such as old age, mental illness, or developmental disability. Second, the individual must be found to be impaired functionally—that is, unable to care appropriately for person or property—as a result of being within that category. Incompetence cannot be equated with the categorical condition (such as advanced years) alone, so the determination of functional, behavioral, or adaptive disability is essential. This requirement is emphasized in those states whose statutes restrict eligibility for guardianship to those who are "gravely disabled" or the equivalent.

A court (designated in various states as the probate court, orphans' court, county count, chancery court, circuit court, surrogate's court, or superior court) appoints a guardian (referred to in a few jurisdictions as a conservator or a "committee," even if only one person is appointed) as substitute decision maker for an incompetent person. That incompetent person for whom a guardian is appointed is a "ward," and the relationship between the guardian and ward is "guardianship."

There has been a strong movement in the past decade and a half toward seriously strengthening the procedural protections available to prospective wards (Tor & Sales, 1994). This trend toward guardianship reform in the direction of patients' rights is intended to prevent involuntary guardianship from being imposed prematurely or inappropriately, to force a consideration of less intrusive alternatives, and to limit the authority and increase the monitoring of guardians. The trend is international in scope (Eekelaar & Pearl, 1989). In some countries (e.g., Great Britain), though, a beneficence model of guardianship still prevails (Barnes, 1992).

In 1987, the Associated Press (AP) conducted and published a series of articles based on a nationwide survey of guardianship practices in the courts. The AP found "a dangerously burdened and troubled system that regularly puts elderly lives in the hands of others with little or no evidence of necessity, then fails to guard against abuse, theft, and neglect." Largely in response to this study (ABA Commissions on the Mentally Disabled and on Legal Problems of the Elderly, 1989), many U.S. jurisdictions amended their guardianship statutes to create or enhance requirements concerning court-appointed counsel with adversarial duties (Pecora, 1990), notice, hearing, personal attendance of the proposed ward at the hearing, standard of proof (varying among states from a preponderance-of-evidence test to a higher standard of clear and convincing evidence to the strictest test: beyond a reasonable doubt), contents of the petition, and more specificity in the court order finding the ward incompetent and appointing the guardian (Hommel, 1996; Wood, Stiegel, Sabatino, & Edelstein, 1993). In a majority of states, statutes allow for the relaxation of normal procedural requirements to permit the appointment of a temporary or emergency guardian when there is an immediate life-threatening situation or when a permanent guardian can no longer serve. At least one court has found a state's emergency guardianship statute to be constitutionally suspect (*Grant v. Johnson*, 1991). Time limits for emergency guardianships vary among the states from 30 days to 6 months.

The guardian who is appointed ordinarily is a private person (relative, friend, attorney) or institution (bank or trust company); approximately 75–85% of all guardians are family members of the ward (Iris, 1988). Many state statutes establish procedures for competent adults to nominate in advance the person they wish to serve as guardian for them in the event that guardianship is ordered, and courts are required to afford strong deference to these preferences. This process of advance nomination of guardianship is related to but distinct from the durable power of attorney concept that is discussed below.

In many cases, though, as the human age span expands and marriage and childbearing patterns change, many older individuals are left without anyone willing to act as a surrogate decision maker (Kapp, 1995i). In response to this unhappy phenomenon, a number of states have devised some form of "public guardianship" system under which a government agency, either directly or through contract with a for-profit or nonprofit organization, functions in the guardian role as a last resort for a ward who has no one else (Siemon, Hurme, & Sabatino, 1993). In many parts of the United States, a number of private corporations, both proprietary and nonprofit, offer their services as guardians directly to the courts; some of these organizations run on fees collected from the wards' estates for their management services, and some of them depend for their operation on private fundraising activities. As a true last resort for a ward who lacks available, willing family and friends in an area where there is neither a public guardianship system nor private guardianship organizations, the judge hearing the guardianship system may be able to cajole a local attorney to take on guardianship responsibilities.

A court may confer different types of powers on a guardian. Plenary power is complete authority over the ward's person and estate, encompassing virtually every element of the ward's life. The plenary guardian may make decisions in three broad areas: (1) disposition of the ward's financial assets and income; (2) where and with whom the ward will reside (including the question of NF placement or the initiation of involuntary commitment proceedings; and (3) granting or withholding of authorization for medical treatment of or biomedical or behavioral research on the ward.

Alternatively, guardianship powers may be restricted to control of the ward's estate. In this event (in many states, termed "conservatorship"), the guardian of the estate (or conservator) may make decisions only about the ward's financial assets—real and personal property—and income (Zimny, Diamond, Mau, Law, & Chung, 1997). The court may also appoint a "guardian ad litem" who has authority to represent the ward only in a particular legal proceeding (Frank, 1993) (e.g., a request for authority to terminate life-sustaining medical intervention; see Chapter 11).

Courts and legislatures traditionally have treated mental competence as a unitary, all-or-nothing concept, even though an older person's functional capacity may wax and wane from time to time and vary widely depending on the kind of choice facing the individual and various environmental factors. In recognition of this clinical reality, all states now allow the consideration and granting of "limited" or "partial" guardianship, in which the court very explicitly delineates the particular and exclusive types of decisions that the ward is incapable of making and over which the guardian may exercise proxy authority, with remaining power residing with the ward (Hurme, 1994). Limited or partial guardianship statutes may be permissive, allowing but not requiring courts to carefully tailor the guardian's powers to the ward's needs, or they may mandate that the powers of the guardian be drawn as narrowly as possible. Even in the absence of specific enabling legislation, state courts have general equity jurisdiction to create limited or partial guardianships *sua sponte* (on their own initiative). One salutary by-product of limited or partial guardianship should be courts doing a better job of documenting and demonstrating with specificity and detail the functional abilities and inabilities of the ward, rather than engaging in the shortcut of vague and conclusory statements in the legal record (Bulcroft et al., 1991). To date, however, courts have not utilized the partial guardianship offer very much (Keith & Wacker, 1992). Some have suggested that modest use of the limited guardianship option by the courts is a good thing, on the theory that too much reliance on limited guardianship could easily lead to inappropriate guardianships being imposed on persons who do not really need this level of protection (Schmidt, 1996).

As discussed in Chapters 3 and 12 (on informed consent and research, respectively), a health care professional relying on the authorization of a limited or partial guardian for medical treatment of or research on a ward must carefully ascertain the exact nature and limits of the powers that the court has conferred on that guardian. In some states, even a plenary guardian may have far less than total prerogative in the medical decision-making sphere, based on specific statutory or judicially imposed restrictions.

Any ward, but especially one for whom a plenary guardian is appointed, suffers a devastating deprivation of decision-making authority. Among numerous other rights, the ward may lose the right to enter into a binding contract, to vote, to hold public office, to marry, to hold a license (such as a motor vehicle driver's license), to execute a will, to hold and dispose of real and personal property, and to sue and be sued in the courts. Consequently, it is important for judges to be flexible in fashioning remedies for incapacitated older persons, choosing from among a variety of reasonable alternatives that have been identified (Center for Social Gerontology, 1994b). The key to linking the person to the appropriate intervention, if any (e.g., some older persons who can make their own decisions may need help to remember to comply with those decisions [Fitten, Coleman, Siembieda, Yu, & Ganzell, 1995]), lies in the comprehensive functional assessment and the role of involved health care professionals (Nolan, 1990), as discussed below.

Motives of Guardians

There are basically two types of motives for initiating judicial appointment of a guardian for another individual. The first type is altruism, a sincere desire to protect and benefit a human being who needs help. Thus, the demand for guardianship often is generated by members of the helping professions, social agencies, and private citizens (relatives or friends) who seek a workable legal method for assuming control over the personal or financial affairs of a disabled individual. Legal advocates for the aged generally acknowledge that many guardianships are sought on the basis of genuinely held beneficent motivations and real patient need. In such cases, after independent investigation has convinced them of the older person's clear incapacity to function at an acceptable level in essential matters and of the integrity of the proposed guardian, even the most zealous advocates rarely oppose the imposition of a guardianship, and often they will work with the guardian in planning for and managing the ward's affairs. In certain cases, the older person's legal representative actually may participate in initiating the guardianship proceeding, although this practice raises certain questions about legal ethics and conflicts of interest (Barnes, Frolik, & Whitman, 1997; Rein, 1998).

The second kind of motivation is more pragmatic; guardianship may be sought for the primary purpose of benefiting a service provider, for example, a health care professional, NF, or hospital. Such providers may use the guardianship structure to definitively establish a party who is responsible for paying for services used by the ward and who is legally capable (in most cases; see earlier notation in this chapter on limitations) of giving binding informed consent for medical treatment. Concern about the legal validity of informed consent and changes in residential placements may increase the incidence of guardianship petitions. Some health care professionals and facilities currently refuse to accept a questionably competent patient without the presence of a legally appointed guardian to guarantee financial reimbursement and treatment permission (Kapp, 1998d). Durable powers of attorney (discussed below) and family consent statutes enacted in over thirty states (see Chapter 11) are responses to the problem of the incapacitated older patient, designed to avoid the need and motivation for invoking the formal guardianship process.

Nonetheless, the desire for assurances of payment and of adequate consent are quite understandable when the proposed ward actually is incapable of rationally making and communicating life-affecting decisions and needs a proxy decision maker to deal with life's vicissitudes. That is not always the case, however. When, for instance, the incompetence determination is requested just so that an unconsenting patient may be involuntarily subjected to medical treatment or research and the functional criteria of incompetence are not clearly present, guardianship deriving from this type of motivation has been criticized as an illegitimate intrusion into personal autonomy (Regan, 1981). In such circumstances, advocates working on behalf of the older patient should be vigorous in opposing the guardianship petition.

The American Bar Association (1989) is on record with

> a guiding principle [that] guardianships should not be used in cases in which, *but for the needs of the third party,* there would be no reason for guardianship. Guardianship should be viewed as a measure of last resort. Thus, there should be sufficient available alternatives so that guardianship will be used only in those cases in which it clearly benefits the ward [emphasis in original].

Most commentators endorse a preference for extrajudicial (i.e., outside the court system) surrogate decision-making arrangements and relegation of formal guardianship proceedings—with their attendant financial, time, and emotional (Winick, 1995) costs—to last-resort status (Center for Social Gerontology, 1996; Herr & Hopkins, 1994; Kapp, 1994c, 1996a).

Even assuming praiseworthy motivation, lack of reasonable, less restrictive alternatives, and guardianship imposition based on a fair and accurate application of facts to law, the preferences of the older ward do not automatically become irrelevant. On the contrary, even though the ward is disempowered to make binding legal decisions, expressed preferences still should be sincerely sought out and respected to the maximum extent feasible (Rein, 1992). When the health care professional's conduct is based on choices signifying both the consent of the guardian and the assent of the ward, the interests of both therapy and individual autonomy are best served.

Role of the Health Care Professional

Health care professionals, particularly the physician, serving older patients will and should be intimately involved in any guardianship activity concerning those patients. The modes of involvement are several.

First, health care professionals are a potentially important source for identifying those older individuals who lack the functional capacity to handle their own affairs and who legitimately need the assistance of a proxy decision-maker. Many such older people, especially those without substantial estates, currently fall between the cracks of the social service system and suffer without basic human protections. The health care professional, because of a unique and intimate relationship with the patient, is in an unparalleled position to recognize and do something about fundamental patient social and legal needs at an early stage. Often, the capacity issue arises for the first time in the context of securing consent for some proposed medical procedure.

As noted in Chapter 7 ("Elder Abuse and Neglect") and in the "Protective Services" portion of this chapter, the states have passed reporting laws that either require or allow physicians, as well as certain other health care professionals, to notify a specified state or county agency whenever they become aware of an individual in need of external intervention. Yet physicians make a disproportionately small percentage of reports of elder abuse and neglect. This limited physician involvement is consistent with the claims of some authors that physicians often superficially overlook certain forms of mental incapacity in older persons (Fitten, Lusky, & Hamann, 1990; Mahler et al., 1990).

However, as noted elsewhere, even when mental impairment is detected in the older patient, the ensuing result usually need not be a guardianship petition. Health care professionals should work with the patient, family, and other involved parties and agencies to identify and explore available alternatives, in terms of substitute decision-making arrangements and community resources, to divert the patient away from the formal judicial system.

Second, once formal guardianship proceedings have been initiated, the health care professional will, as a matter of course, be asked for a medical evaluation of the proposed ward and a professional opinion regarding the necessity of guardianship. This request may emanate from the attorney representing the party seeking guardianship, the patient's attorney, or both. The court also may seek out an expert evaluation on its own initiative. In this regard, although it is normally a physician, particularly a psychiatrist, whose opinion is solicited, the valuable input of other health care professionals should not be overlooked (Melton et al., 1997). Terribly underused, for example, are nurses, whose informational contribution, both directly and through their written treatment notes, should be sought out and carefully taken into account at many points in the guardianship process.

A number of commentators (Coker & Johns, 1994; Hull et al., 1990) have suggested broad input by an array of health and social service providers. This array would bring complementary perspectives to a holistic evaluation both of the patient's abilities and of his or her environment (including the family) that may support or impinge on the patient's capacity to function. Guardianship reform legislation enacted in the past decade in several states encourages and in some cases requires the involvement of professionals in addition to the physician in evaluating the proposed ward's functional capacity (Hommel, 1996). A number of state statutes provide for the appointment of a "visitor," whose role it is to meet the proposed ward and prepare a report for the court that supplements the formal assessment and provides more information about the proposed ward's living situation and about the changes proposed by the petitioner. These developments suggest that functional assessment of an older person for guardianship purposes is likely to become more and more a comprehensive team effort rather than a form-completion exercise by a single physician. Indeed, a comprehensive functional assessment of an older person (Nolan, 1984, 1990) virtually demands the active input of community health nurses, social workers, occupational and physical therapists, mental health workers, and gerontological specialists, in addition to the physician.

Sometimes the health care professional is asked to issue an opinion based exclusively on past contact with and observation of the proposed ward, plus a thorough review of the patient's medical chart. Often, the professional will need to conduct further examinations to establish a firm predicate for a defensible opinion. In either event, there are a multiplicity of separate but interconnected factors that the conscientious health care professional must consider in formulating a recommendation for the most beneficial resolution of the impaired older person's needs (Thomas, 1994).

As a starting point, a comprehensive psychological history and examination of the proposed ward is needed (Gutheil & Appelbaum, 1991). A complete and orderly mental status examination for guardianship purposes should include, minimally, the following elements: (1) an evaluation of the patient's orientation to person, place, time, and situation; (2) a test of recent and remote memory and logical sequencing; (3) an assessment of intellectual capacity, that is, ability to comprehend abstract ideas and to make a reasoned judgment based on that ability; (4) an assessment of mood and affect, noting particularly suicidal ideation; (5) an examination of the content of thought and perception for delusions, illusions, and hallucinations; (6) an inspection of visible behavior, noting agitation and anxiety, as well as appetite, eating habits, and sleeping patterns; and (7) a review of past history for evidence of a psychiatric disturbance that might affect the patient's current judgment. Findings derived from the psychiatric evaluation must be correlated with the previously described functional tests of capacity to understand, assimilate, and utilize information relevant to the specific type of decision facing the patient at the time.

The health care professional also must account for the frequently fluid or transient nature of decisional capacity by considering (1) psychodynamic elements of the patient's personality, (2) the accuracy of the historical information conveyed by the patient, (3) the accuracy and completeness of the information disclosed to the patient, (4) the stability or consistency of the patient's mental status over time (Gottlieb & Reisberg, 1988), and (5) the effect of the setting in which the observations are being made. Communication barriers (e.g., language limitations, lack of education, aphasia, speech disorders) between health care professional and patient must be considered (Goodenough, 1988).

It is advisable for both individual health care professionals and health facilities to devise and follow some form of standardized, reliable protocol that can be used routinely in conducting capacity evaluations (Scogin & Perry, 1986). A direct, explicit process for assessing decision-making capacity generally will be superior in terms of uniformity and objectivity (Goodenough, 1988) to the indirect, ad hoc method that many physicians currently use to form impressions about patient capacity at the bedside (Bulcroft et al., 1991; Fitten et al., 1990; Markson, Kern, Annas, & Glantz, 1994; Marson, Hawkins, McInturff, & Harrell, 1997; Marson, McInturff, Hawkins, Bartolucci, & Harrell, 1997). A variety of assessment instruments exist for examining levels of cognitive functioning in older persons.

At the same time, however, health care professionals conducting capacity assessments on older patients must be careful not to simply

equate the score on a standardized mental status examination with a conclusion about the patient's functional ability to make certain kinds of decisions (Kapp & Mossman, 1996; Tombaugh & McIntyre, 1992). For instance,
the ability of the patient to name the current president or count backward
by 7's may shed little conclusive light on the patient's capacity to understand the consequences of and alternatives to a recommended medical
procedure. A degree of subjectivity in assessing decisional capacity is both
inevitable and not undesirable.

An ideal capacity evaluation would include not only multiple sessions with the patient (Gottlieb & Reisberg, 1988) but also contact with
other persons (friends, relatives, employer, clergy) who know the individual well. This should be done both to obtain accurate and personal data
(e.g., about educational level; see Weiss, Reed, Kligman, & Abyad, 1995))
on which to base an assessment of needs and to ascertain the strength of
the individual's support mechanisms. The effect of testing site should be
considered; there is some evidence that in-home assessment may reveal
the optimal cognitive function of geriatric patients (Ward et al., 1990). The
American Bar Association (1989) is on record in this area: "Whenever possible, proposed wards should be assessed in their usual environment and
with all due consideration given to their privacy and dignity." Other
important possible variables affecting functional test behavior are the use
of alcohol and other drugs, dietary reactions, changes associated with
underlying disease processes, and fatigue and anxiety associated with a
clinic visit or hospital admission (Dellasega, Frank, & Smyer, 1996) and the
concomitant change (leading to disorientation) in ordinary routine.

An interview with the prospective guardian also is highly desirable.
In deciding on the proposed ward's capacity, it is important to consider
and respect the totality of the individual's life experiences and previously
expressed values and preferences and to refrain from placing more of a
burden of proof regarding capacity on the older individual in question
than younger people would put on themselves—that is, from engaging in
an ageist bias (Goodenough, 1988).

Psychiatric consultation can be a highly valuable adjunct in this process
and should be sought freely where available and indicated. The health care
professional should not obtain psychiatric consultation, though, solely to
avoid the necessity of making difficult clinical and ethical judgments by
shifting the burden to the consultant (Perl & Shelp, 1982).

As underscored previously, even when an older individual is believed
to be severely mentally compromised, that belief should not automatically
be assumed synonymous with the need for formal guardianship. The health
care professional's opinion and recommendation should be informed by a
thorough analysis of the availability and desirability of various alternatives
(which may or may not be less restrictive, depending on circumstances) to

the court-ordered imposition of legal guardianship. Assessment of decisional (i.e., functional) capacity ought to occur not in a clinical vacuum but rather as one integral element of the larger process of comprehensive care planning (Hull et al., 1990). What are the relevant community resources, in terms of available social services, that the patient would be willing to accept? Does the person just need some assistance? Is there a "moral equivalent" of guardianship that would suffice in practice? These possible alternatives (most of which are discussed elsewhere) include advance planning through, for example, a durable power of attorney; representative payees; temporary or *ad litem* guardianship; *inter vivos* (while alive) property transfers; insurers or guarantors (for loans, for example); limited bank accounts (including perhaps cosigners, ceiling amounts, or pour-over mechanisms); citizen advocates and aides; and even benign neglect. Also not to be ignored are the adverse clinical consequences that might flow to the patient and family as a result of coerced guardianship (Gutheil & Appelbaum, 1991; Winick, 1995).

Once the health care professional has arrived at an opinion concerning the patient's capabilities and deficiencies, that opinion ordinarily is presented in the form of a written report and/or live testimony in court. There is a growing trend for states to specify by statute, regulation, or court administrative rule the precise form the report must take and the specific content it must include. This trend toward specificity represents an attempt to deal with the prevalent problem of medical reports to the courts in guardianship proceedings that are too vague, sketchy, and conclusory (Hull et al., 1990). Recent legal requirements place a burden on the health care professional to be much more detailed, focused, and discerning in the preparation of reports for judicial consumption (Hommel, 1996). The health care professional should be sure not to release reports to anyone but the patient (or his or her legal counsel) without prior assurance that considerations of confidentiality and privileged information have been addressed and resolved (e.g., under a court order or a statutory grant of immunity).

Ordinarily, the health care professional's live testimony in court is required in addition to any prepared written report. The courts tend to show strong deference toward presumed medical expertise regarding matters such as mental capacity (Krasik, 1989). If the guardianship petition is not seriously contested, there is a real danger that the judge will simply ratify the health care professional's conclusory opinion without any probing of its basis or accuracy (Margolis, 1992). As Pleak and Appelbaum (1985) note, this places a heavy moral responsibility on the health care professional to assure the report's accuracy. They argue that a health care professional who is asked to sign an affidavit or to testify about a patient's incapacity should do so only after a thorough personal examination of the patient, in which the patient's functional capacity for the task in question is directly assessed. These authors convincingly suggest that the clinical basis on which the health care professional infers a patient's incapacity should be stated clearly to permit and perhaps even to stimulate cross-examination (ABA Commission on Legal Problems of the Elderly and Young Lawyers Division, 1990) and judicial review, because the courts ordinarily cannot be depended on to reject inappropriate guardianship petitions.

In a disputed guardianship proceeding, the calling of a medical expert by one side necessitates a similar reliance by the other side. In practice, the medical standard often becomes the primary, if not the sole, basis for adjudicating incompetence. The expert is needed both to present a differing opinion and to assist the requesting attorney in preparing to attack the credibility or opinion of the other party's expert.

Some commentators have called for special geriatric training for experts who testify in guardianship cases (Scogin & Perry, 1986). Although this would represent an ideal, the health care professional who is requested to be an expert witness at least should insist on being sufficiently briefed and prepared by the attorney desiring the testimony in advance of the hearing date. There should be a clear idea of what questions might be asked on both direct and cross-examination. One cannot and should not be expected to take the witness stand "cold." Additionally, as with written reports, there should be assurance that any difficulties with confidentiality or the release of privileged information (see Chapter 4) have been satisfactorily worked out. At a minimum, the health care professional should demand personal delivery of a subpoena before appearing in court to testify for either side. Also, it should be possible to negotiate with the attorney and judge a reasonable time range within which testimony will be taken, so that the court appearance need not be excessively time-consuming and disruptive to scheduling.

An issue that sometimes arises in discussing the role of the health care professional is whether it ever may be proper for the professional himself or herself to serve in the formal capacity of guardian for an incompetent patient under his or her professional care. Opinion on this issue is mixed. Although some argue that the professional should be willing to act as guardian of last resort, especially for older patients with no available, willing family or friends (Wettstein & Roth, 1988), the majority view is that such conduct almost inevitably constitutes a serious conflict of interest and that other alternatives ought to be pursued (Brown & Legal Counsel for the Elderly, 1989). In reality, of course, the health care professional frequently does function as the *de facto* substitute decision maker for an incapacitated elder who has no one else, even in the absence of *de jure* or formal authority (Gillick, 1995b).

Guardian Responsibilities

Once a guardianship has been imposed, the guardian appointed is expected to act in a fiduciary, or trust, manner. This may be fulfilled by acting in a way that is either (1) consistent with the guardian's judgment of the ward's best interests or (2) consistent with previously expressed or implied values and preferences (substituted judgment) of the ward. The substituted-judgment test is more respectful of the older ward's own life experiences and deeply held principles, and this approach now is preferred by most legislatures and courts unless what the patient would choose if competent cannot be ascertained because of insufficient evidence about the patient's values and preferences.

The court retains continuing jurisdiction or power to oversee the guardian's conduct (Parry & Hurme, 1991). Many abuses—physical, emotional, financial—in the fulfillment of guardian responsibilities have been recorded (Iris, 1990). Detection of these abuses has led to widespread calls for better training and postappointment monitoring of guardian performance, especially by the courts (ABA Commission on Legal Problems of the Elderly, 1991; Frolik, 1990; Hurme, 1991) and even proposals for explicit standards of conduct against which guardians should be held accountable (U.S. Congress, House Select Committee on Aging, 1989).

Another area of health professional involvement in the guardianship process—in addition to (a) identification of patients at risk and of alternative ways to help them, (b) patient evaluation, and (c) provision of evidence to the courts—could come into play when the health care professional begins to reasonably suspect that the guardian is neglecting duties and the patient is suffering mistreatment or neglect. This suspicion may stem from personal, physical, or psychological observation of the patient or through other information sources. In such circumstances, the health care professional arguably is obliged, under the inherent professional/patient fiduciary relationship, as well as state statutes mandating the reporting of elder abuse (see Chapter 7), to notify the original court retaining jurisdiction to monitor the guardianship (Fell, 1994) of those suspicions and to assist in their investigation (Kapp, 1994a).

The final sphere in which health care professionals are engaged with the guardianship process concerns termination. Any guardianship may be discontinued when it is no longer needed, and in some states appropriateness must be reviewed at least annually. The successful termination of a guardianship is difficult under any circumstances because the party arguing for termination bears the burden of proving that competence has been restored; this burden is virtually impossible to satisfy without the alliance of health care professionals who are knowledgeable about the specific patient. In theory, the patient has the right to be rehabilitated as much as possible (Barnett, 1978), and the individual's health care professionals should attempt to remove decisional barriers to the extent feasible. Because the professional plays a central role in identifying the causes of the patient's incapacity, an equal role in their remedy or removal should be attempted. Several forms of dementia are reversible through appropriate medication. When clinical and behavioral capacity has been restored, the health care professional's stated opinion to that effect is imperative to achieve a corresponding restoration of the patient's legal decision-making rights.

PROTECTIVE SERVICES

Adult protective services (APS) is a concept that builds directly on the legal mechanism of guardianship, as well as on voluntary transfers of authority (discussed below). Thus, APS can fall into either end of the scale measuring degree of intrusiveness into the life of the older individual. In either event, the health care professional has an important role to play.

In the past two decades, the states have enacted a wide variety of programs under the general rubric of APS. The traditional definition of this concept is a system of preventive and supportive services for older persons living in the community to enable them to maintain independent living and avoid abuse and exploitation (Kapp, 1995d). APS programs are characterized by two elements that can be mixed in an array of ways: the coordinated delivery of services to adults at risk and the actual or potential authority to provide substitute decision making regarding those services.

The services feature consists of an assortment of health, housing, and social services, such as homemaker, house repair, friendly visitors, and meals. Legal and financial management services are also included. Ideally, these services are not just random aids rendered by unrelated agencies; instead, coordination is supposed to be provided by a caseworker/organizer (variously termed case manager, care manager, care coordinator, and the like) who is responsible for assessing an individual's needs and bringing together the available responses. Many state APS statutes mandate that aging or social service agencies undertake both casework coordination and delivery of services.

A number of stimuli have inspired the creation of APS programs (Anetzberger, 1995). Since the early 1970s, some federal funding for these activities has been made available to states through Title 20 of the Social Security Act (Social Services) and Title 3 of the Older Americans Act (OAA). (The sufficient continuation of this funding, of course, is a matter of great uncertainty throughout each budget process.) The trend of the past three decades toward deinstitutionalization of patients from large public mental institutions into often unready communities (Scallet & Robinson, 1991) has provided an ample source of older candidates for APS programs, as has the general rise in the number of people who are very old and at high risk for health, social, economic, environmental, and legal problems. The PASARR requirements imposed by federal law on nursing homes (see Chapter 9) may expand the candidate pool.

The second component of an APS program is authority to intervene on behalf of the client. Ordinarily, the client (if mentally capable) should and will voluntarily grant the helping party permission to help (Kapp, 1983). When the need for a future substitute decision maker is contemplated, a power of attorney (discussed below) may be appropriate. However, if the client refuses offered assistance but continuing intervention appears necessary, the legal system may be invoked to authorize appointment of a substitute decision maker over the client's objections.

Some states with APS programs rely, in the case of recalcitrant clients, on the traditional methods of legal intervention in the lives of older persons, namely, involuntary commitment and guardianship. Legislation has been enacted in many jurisdictions, however, that creates special procedures to secure court orders for various aspects of APS, including institutional placement, emergency interventions when there is imminent danger to the client's safety or health, and entry into an uncooperative client's home. These procedures are either in addition to or in place of the existing guardianship apparatus.

Most of the special procedures that have been established by state legislatures for the issuance of protective services orders bypass many of the protections that have gradually been built into extant guardianship laws. For instance, in many of the special APS statutes, requirements are greatly relaxed in such matters as notice to the client of the filing of the petition, the client's presence at the hearing, and the person's right to counsel. The standard of proof usually is vaguely and cursorily stated, if at all. In practice, the hearing frequently becomes a public agency's *ex parte* (one-sided) presentation of testimony to a sympathetic court that routinely issues protective services orders precisely as requested by the agency.

After a court order is obtained, few limits are imposed on the agencies that provide services. Protective services are so nebulously defined in many statutes that they may encompass virtually any kind of health or social service, including medical care and even property management. Hence, if the court does not expressly limit the services that may be forced on the individual, the agency has a high degree of freedom. A protective services order, therefore, may result in the transfer of the person to a hospital, an

NF, a boarding home, or even a mental hospital. Health care professionals are well advised, as a matter of standard practice, to ascertain carefully the exact nature and scope of a protective services order before ever accepting as legally effective the purported informed consent of a state social service agency offered on behalf of a patient/client.

Moreover, the special APS statutes under discussion here do not impose on the public agency an explicit fiduciary obligation similar to that ordinarily stipulated for a guardian or conservator. The agency is not held by statute, at least in any enforceable manner (Mixson, 1996), to act in the individual's best interests or to determine how the client would choose to act if competent (substituted-judgment test). Rather, the agency's only explicit duty is to provide the services authorized in the court order, more or less in an "arm's length" relationship with the client. Once an order for protective services is issued, the court usually retains no further responsibility toward the client, although the order generally (but not always) is of indefinite duration. The agency need not file periodic reports about the client's status or condition, nor is it ordinarily required to seek regular renewal of the order.

States that have created separate, relaxed procedures to authorize unsolicited intervention, on either an emergency or a continuing basis, also have established standards for identifying candidates for APS, including protective placement. First, a number of categories such as "old age" are listed. Then, certain behavioral disabilities attributable to the person's being a member of that category are described, such as inability to care for oneself properly (self-neglect) or to protect oneself against abuse and exploitation by others. In a few instances, physical impairment alone is considered a sufficient basis for intervention when this condition leads to self-neglect or victimization by others, even when there is no showing of severe mental incapacity.

Some respected commentators have severely criticized APS systems that provide for coerced client participation through the types of special eligibility criteria and abbreviated procedural mechanisms just described (Horstman, 1975; Regan, 1981; Schmidt, 1986). All of the negative arguments raised against the possible abuses of guardianship in the previous section, in terms of peril to the individual's right to self-determination in major life decisions, may be applied *a fortiori* (with even greater logical force) to APS systems that involve still looser eligibility standards and less extensive procedural protections, especially in the area of emergency intervention. It has been suggested that legislatures have been too quick to copy the children's protective services model in devising a scheme for addressing potentially abused or neglected older people (Coleman & Karp, 1989).

Regardless of the validity or invalidity of these criticisms, APS systems are a growing aspect of life for America's older citizens. Health care professionals can enhance the salutary impact of these systems on the lives of the elderly by contributing their expertise in the spheres of (1) identification, (2) providing evidence, (3) exploring voluntary alternatives, and (4) planning and placement.

As alluded to earlier, health care professionals frequently are in a unique and central position to identify initially those older individuals who meet the eligibility criteria for and could benefit significantly from the intervention of an APS program. Notifying a designated local aging or social service agency official of the existence and identity of such patients may be incumbent on the health care professional, depending on that state's reporting statute for elder abuse and neglect. At the least, such notification is permissible without running afoul of confidentiality considerations.

Just as written reports and live courtroom testimony are vigorously sought from health care professionals in guardianship cases, so too are these forms of evidence very important in APS proceedings. The weight of health care professional opinion may be even stronger in the latter situation, where less stringent eligibility criteria and procedural formalities empower the presiding judge with even broader discretion in making findings and fashioning remedies.

As briefly mentioned, it is possible (and highly desirable and common) for APS to be accepted voluntarily by the older person (Kapp, 1983). The mechanisms for achieving this, as well as the health care professional's role in encouraging and facilitating it, are discussed more fully below.

Finally, the potential contribution of health care professionals in service planning and placement activities for nonindependent older persons should not be neglected. The ultimate goal is not the obtaining, in and of itself, of the protective services, whether on a voluntary or an involuntary basis. Rather, the key is to assure the quality and appropriateness of the services actually provided to the older individual. Identification, referral, and testimony should not be the end of health care professional involvement. Social service agencies are not to be utilized as a convenient dumping ground for unwanted elders, and it is just as possible for an older person without personal resources to be harmfully "dumped" into the community as into a nursing home or public mental institution. The older individual is entitled to receive reasonable continuity of care from his or her health care professionals, and these professionals are legally and ethically obligated under the principle of nonabandonment either to directly supply that continuity of care or to ensure its provision by other qualified, willing health care professionals whose services are acceptable to the older person.

REPRESENTATIVE PAYEES

Another way in which society may intervene in the life of an older individual without his or her permission and restrict legal decision-making authority is through the appointment of a substitute payee for a person who is receiving certain regular government benefit payments (Myers, 1989). This substitute check handler is called a fiduciary under the Department of Veterans Affairs (VA) program and a representative payee under the other government programs (Kapp, 1995d).

Participating programs include pension and disability benefits from the VA (38 C.F.R. §§13.1–13.111), Department of Defense (37 U.S.C. §§601–604), Railroad Retirement Board (20 C.F.R. §§266.11–266.13), and Office of Personnel Management (for federal employees' retirement benefits) (5 U.S.C. §8345[e]). Most significant economically in this regard are Old Age, Survivors, and Disability Insurance (OASDI) benefit payments under Title 2 of the Social Security Act (20 C.F.R. §§404.2001–404.2065) and Supplemental Security Income (SSI) benefit payments to the aged, blind, or disabled under Title 16 of the Social Security Act (Social Security Administration, 1996). The representative payee system disproportionately affects older persons.

The secretary or director of the relevant federal agency is given statutory and regulatory authority to appoint a fiduciary or representative payee for persons who are incapable of managing their government benefits in their own best interests. The fiduciary or representative payee receives the beneficiary's government payments directly and is charged with the fiduciary or trust duty of managing those funds for the beneficiary's welfare. The fiduciary or representative payee may be a relative, friend, attorney, or organization. Under provisions in the Omnibus Budget Reconciliation Act of 1990 (OBRA 1990), Public Law No. 101-508, an organization may now charge a monthly fee for performing such services up to the lesser of 10% of the benefit check or $25 (U.S. General Accounting Office, 1992). The American Association of Retired Persons' Legal Counsel for the Elderly division operates a large national representative payee program, and many nonprofit organizations operate for this purpose at the local level.

Some innovative organizations have developed forms of daily money management services that include representative payee functions as an alternative to formal conservator or guardianship (Wilber, 1990). Financial services included under this rubric, for example, are the establishment and maintenance of individual client accounts to receive and safeguard client funds, budgeting and analyzing clients' financial status, negotiating with creditors on balances and payment plans for clients, balancing clients' check registers, determining clients' spending priorities and the investment of surplus funds, preparing a monthly statement of receipts and expenditures, preparing checks for necessary disbursement, and establishing a budget plan.

A licensed health care facility may also serve legally as a representative payee, as may the administrator, owner, or employee of a facility in which the beneficiary lives if the Social Security Administration (SSA) has made a good faith effort to find an alternative payee. Although ethical conflicts may arise (or appear to arise) when a professional caregiver undertakes the representative payee role, some argue that patients who need assistance greatly are without good alternatives and that the benefits outweigh the potential tensions (Brotman & Muller, 1990).

The need for a fiduciary or representative payee may come to an agency's attention in various ways, such as notice that the beneficiary is in a hospital or NF; a call or letter from an interested friend, relative, or health care professional; or the filing of a new claim for mental disability benefits under an applicable program. Once word is received of the beneficiary's alleged incapacity, all federal agencies, with the exception of the SSA, suspend further payments until an agency official or board determines whether the alleged incapacity is true.

An agency's usual procedure is to inquire, through a designated official or board, whether the beneficiary can manage money effectively. The SSA, without regard to legal competence, asks only whether the interest of the beneficiary would be served by the appointment of a substitute. Prior to appointment of a payee, most agencies provide notification to the beneficiary that such an appointment is contemplated; under OBRA 1990, a Social Security beneficiary now has a right to such notice. At that point, the beneficiary is given the opportunity to object and to submit evidence on his or her own behalf.

Once it has been determined that a substitute should be appointed, under OBRA 1990 the SSA has certain responsibilities to investigate the potential fiduciary or representative payee. The SSA is required to obtain documented proof of the prospective payee's identity, conduct a face-to-face interview with the payee applicant if practicable, verify the Social Security number or employer identification number of the payee applicant, and determine whether the payee applicant was ever convicted of a Social Security felony or dismissed as a payee for misuse of funds. Someone who was convicted of a Social Security felony or dismissed as a payee for misuse of funds can be certified as a payee only if SSA determines that such a result would be in the beneficiary's best interest. The beneficiary, under OBRA 1990, has the right to appeal the SSA's determination of the need for a payee and the designation of a particular person to serve as payee.

In reality, the representative payee is subjected only to minimal review and accountability. This is because (1) there are no meaningful statutory or regulatory standards for ascertaining what constitutes being "incapable" of managing one's own benefit payments or whether one's interest would be served by the appointment of a substitute, and (2) there is no opportunity for a full evidentiary hearing prior to the suspension of benefit payments or the appointment of a representative payee; however, the agency that disburses the benefits has the right to monitor the arrangement by requesting a periodic accounting and investigating the veracity of the report. Because of its limited review and accountability safeguards, the entire representative payee system has been subjected to serious criticism. Congress attempted in OBRA 1990 to respond to some of the concerns.

OBRA 1990 tightened up both prior investigation of prospective payees and accountability following appointment. The SSA is required to terminate payments to a payee if it or a court finds that the payee misused the benefit payments. The SSA must maintain a list of those terminated for misuse and provide the list to local field offices. In addition, the SSA is required to maintain an accessible centralized data bank, the master Representative Payee File (57 *Federal Register* 41147, September 9, 1992), with the address and Social Security number of each payee and each person for whom the payee is providing services as a payee. Other changes in the representative payee system mandated by OBRA 1990 included a study of the feasibility and desirability of formulating stricter accounting requirements for all high-risk payees and for more stringent reviews of their accountings. In *Briggs v. Sullivan* (1992), a federal appeals court ruled that the SSA's existing procedures fulfill its statutory and constitutional duties to investigate potential representative payees.

The role of the health care professional in the representative payee process has thus far been quite limited (except, in some cases, for calling a prospective candidate to the attention of the benefit-paying agency). Because the substantive standards are vague and the burden of proof is slight to nonexistent, the sort of documentation and testimony that health care professionals regularly are called on to give during involuntary commitment and guardianship proceedings is unnecessary and almost irrelevant in the representative payee context. Information about the representative payee process is available from the SSA by telephone at 1-800-772-1213.

POWERS OF ATTORNEY

Most of this chapter has focused on the variety of ways in which society possesses the inherent power to intervene in the life of an older individual without that person's acquiescence. It is possible, however, and often desirable, from both a philosophical and a clinical perspective, for many older, partially disabled individuals to voluntarily relinquish certain decision-making powers and to accept needed services willingly.

All APS statutes include a preference for the proposed client's voluntary acceptance of offered services and for coercion through guardianship or special APS procedures only when such acceptance is withheld. Thus, it is a relatively simple process for an older person to willingly accede to the overtures of the initiating public social service agency (Kapp, 1983). In fact, older persons living in the community complain legitimately far more often about the availability of too few, rather than the imposition of too many, services.

Whether or not protective services are needed, for a variety of reasons an older person may be willing to give up some or all decision-making authority, on either a time-limited or a permanent basis (Kapp, 1989). Among these reasons are the avoidance of involuntary guardianship imposition in the future (Alexander, 1990), prevention of future medical situations in which the parties feel hampered in decision making because the patient is mentally disabled and the lines of legal authority are ambiguous, and a desire for the legal empowerment of a capable living advocate to speak for the patient if the patient subsequently becomes unable to speak on his or her own behalf. A legal device that can accomplish these objectives is the power of attorney.

The standard power of attorney is a written agreement, usually with a close relative, attorney, friend, business associate, or financial advisor, authorizing that person (named an "agent" or "attorney-in-fact") to sign documents and conduct transactions on behalf of the person ("principal" or "maker") who delegated away the authority. The principal can delegate as much (e.g., a general delegation) or as little (e.g., specifically delineating what types of decisions the agent may or may not make) power as desired. The principal may end or revoke the arrangement at any time as long as he or she is competent to do so.

The power of attorney in its traditional form has two major drawbacks that render it unsuitable as a method for dealing with medical and financial decision-making authority for older persons on a voluntary basis. First, the person creating the power must, at the time of signing or executing the document, have the mental capacity to make a contract. Should there be any doubt about the individual's capacity at that time, the validity

of the power of attorney is open to legal challenge. If the challenge is successful, any transaction completed under authority of the agreement
might be canceled.

Second, the standard power of attorney authorized by most state laws
ends automatically upon the death or mental incapacity of the person who
assigned it. The underlying theory is that, because a deceased or incapacitated person no longer has the ability to exercise his or her right to revoke
the power of attorney, the law will exercise that right for the principal.
Thus, an older person who establishes a power of attorney to help in managing medical as well as financial and other personal affairs is cut off
peremptorily from such assistance at exactly the moment when assistance
is needed the most.

In an effort to overcome at least this latter deficiency, every state has
enacted legislation authorizing the execution of a *durable* power of attorney (DPA). Although there is some small variation in wording among
jurisdictions, most of the state statutes are based on language adopted by
the NCCUSL, either in section 5-501 of the UPC or in the Uniform Durable
Power of Attorney Act (UDPAA). International models for this legal
device also exist (Farrand, 1989). In contrast to the traditional power of
attorney, the effect of a DPA, when given proper indication by a mentally
capable delegating individual, may endure beyond that individual's subsequent incapacity. A document may state that the decision-making
authority is to transfer from the principal to the agent only upon the happening of some specified event in the future, such as declaration by one
or more physicians that the principal lacks decision-making capacity; this
is called a "springing" DPA. A DPA may be revoked at any point before
incapacity occurs, either expressly or by the principal's action (e.g., tearing
up the document).

The power of attorney, in both its traditional and durable forms, has
been used chiefly for purposes of asset management. However, there is
no reason at common law (judge-made law) why the power may not be
granted for purposes of controlling medical treatment decisions following
onset of mental incapacity. No statutes or decided judicial cases prevent
such use.

To remove any ambiguity about the applicability of the DPA concept
to the realm of medical decision making, almost every state has enacted
legislation that explicitly authorizes the use of this legal device in the medical decisionmaking context (see Table 8.2). The American Medical Association (AMA) adopted and published in 1986 a Model Durable Power of
Attorney Bill. In 1993, NCCUSL approved and recommended for enactment in all states a Uniform Health-Care Decisions Act that includes provisions for conveying a power of attorney specifically for health care.
Some statutes (e.g., those of New York [Swidler, 1988] and Massachusetts

TABLE 8.2   State Health Care Durable Power of Attorney Statutes

Ala. Code §§26-1-2*

Alaska Stat. §§13.26.332 to 13.26.353 (Supp.)

Ariz. Rev. Stat. Ann. §§36-3201 to -3261

Ark. Code Ann. §§28-68-201 to -203*

Cal. Civil Code §§2430 to 2444 and 2500 to 2508 (West Supp.)

Colo. Rev. Stat. §§15-14-501 to -509

Conn. Gen. Stat. §§1-43 to -54a

Del Code Ann., tit. 12, §§4901-4905*

D.C. Code Ann. §§21-2201 to -2213

Fla. Stat. Ann. §§765.101 to .113; 765.201 to -.205; 765.301 to -.310; 765.401

Ga. Code §§31-36-1 to -13

Hawaii Rev. Stat. §551D

Idaho Code §§39-4501 to -4509

Ill. Ann. Stat. ch. 110 1/2, §§804-1 to -11

Ind. Code Ann. §§30-5-1-1 to -10-4

Iowa Code Ann. §§144B.1 to -.12

Kan. Stat. Ann. §§58-625 to -632

Ky. Rev. Stat. §§311.970 to -.986

La. Rev. Stat. Ann. §§40:1299.58..5A(2)(a)

Me. Rev. Stat. Ann. tit. 18-A, §§5-501 to -502

Md. Est. & Trust Code Ann. §§ 13-601 to -603, as interpreted by Attorney General
    Opinions No. 88-046 and 90-044

Mass. Gen. L. ch. 201D

Mich. Comp. Laws, §§700.496

Minn. Stat. §§523.01 to -.25*

Miss. Code Ann. §§41.41-151 to -183

Mo. Ann. Stat. §§404.800 to -.870

Mont. Code Ann. §§50-9-103(4) and 72-5-501 to 502

Neb. L.B. 696

Nev. Rev. Stat. Ann. §§449.800 to -.860

N.H. Rev. Stat. Ann. §§137-J:1 to -J:16

N.J. Stat. Ann. §§26:2h-53 to -78

N.M. Stat. Ann. §§45-5-501 to 502

N.Y. Pub. Health Law §§2980 to 2994

N.C. Gen. Stat. §§32A-15 to -26

N.D. Cent. Stat. §§23-06.5-01 to 18

Ohio Rev. Code Ann. §§1337.11 to -.17

Okla. Stat. Ann. tit. 63, §§3101.1 to .16

Or. Rev. Stat. §§127.505 to -.585

Pa. Stat. Ann. tit. 20, §§5401-5416

R.I. Gen. Laws §§23-4.10-1 to -2

S.C. Code Ann. §§62-5-501 to -504

S.D. Codified Laws Ann. §§59-7-2.1 to -2.8

(continued)

TABLE 8.2 (continued)

Tenn. Code Ann. §§34-6-101 to -214
Tex. Civil Practice & Remedies Code Ann. §§135.001 to -.018
Utah Code Ann. §§75-5-501 to -502*
Vt. Stat. Ann. tit. 14, ch. 121, §§3451 to 3467
Va. Code §§11-9.1 to -9.4 and 37.1-134.4, as interpreted by 1990 Att'y Gen. Ann.
    Rep. 205
Wash. Rev. Code Ann. §11.94.010
W.Va. Code §§16-30a-1 to -20
Wisc. Stat. Ann. §§155.01 to -.80
Wyo. Stat., §§3-5-201 to -214

*Statute does not explicitly mention medical decisions.

[Annas, 1991]) use terminology such as "Health Care Representative,"
"Health Care Agent," or "Health Care Proxy." In addition, a number of
state Living Will or Natural Death statutes (see Chapter 11) expressly
authorize a capable adult to designate a health care agent to make future
treatment decisions in the event of subsequent incapacity, at least concerning the refusal of life-prolonging medical interventions.

The DPA device entails at least two important considerations for
practicing health care professionals who are serving older patients at risk
for mental disability. First, as was noted in the guardianship section of
this chapter, the health care professional must be careful, whenever purported informed consent to medical treatment is offered by a proxy on
behalf of the patient, to accurately ascertain the actual scope of authority
that the proxy is legally empowered to exercise. Hence, when informed
consent for a patient who has or who lacks personal decision-making
capacity is volunteered by another person claiming to possess a power of
attorney, it is incumbent on treating health care professionals to determine carefully the particular nature, extent, and current validity of the
power of attorney arrangement. It is proper and advisable to request
some form of written documentation, a copy of which is placed in the
patient's medical record.

The second consideration goes directly to the heart of the health care
professional's role vis-à-vis an older patient. In all situations, but especially when the patient is older, the health care professional must strive
to avoid functioning only as a technician remedying individual adverse
patient episodes. Rather, the health care professional must become
involved in the totality of the older patient's life, contributing talents as a
supporter, counselor, advocate, and planner. Part of this planning obligation requires the health care professional to encourage and assist the older

patient (and the patient's family) to realize and prepare for the unhappy but very real future contingency of a life in which decisions must be made but in which the patient may be mentally unable to make them. The health care professional should discuss with the older patient and interested family members, compassionately and honestly, this possibility and potential ways to address it (Meier, Gold, et al., 1996; Orentlicher, 1990; Roe, Goldstein, Massey, & Pascoe, 1992). In this way, a large number of agonizing crises may be foreseen and averted before they happen. The health care professional is particularly important in the planning process, both because of the high respect he or she ordinarily is accorded by the older patient and family and because he or she often has intimate contact with the older patient and family at precisely the "teachable moment," such as admission to a nursing home, when a major life event compels the older patient and the family to make serious planning choices and arrangements for the future.

This planning function took on added significance with congressional passage of the Patient Self-Determination Act (PSDA) as part of OBRA 1990. This statute, 42 U.S.C. §§1395cc[a] [1] and 1396a(a), and its implications are discussed more fully in Chapter 11. Among other things, this law requires a health care provider (defined as any hospital, NF, hospice, health maintenance organization, preferred provider organization, or home health agency that receives any federal money) to inquire of the patient or of his or her proxy decision maker, at the time a professional relationship is formed, whether the patient has previously executed an advance directive such as a DPA for health care. For currently competent patients who have not yet executed a directive of this nature, the PSDA requires the provider to offer the patient an opportunity to execute an advance directive at that time (Meier, Fuss, et al., 1996).

Individual health care professionals should discuss with patients and families their own philosophies and practices regarding the use of DPAs (and other advance medical directives; see Chapter 11) for health care. In terms of legal liability, there is express or implied immunity from criminal or civil prosecution for a health care professional who abides by the decision of a proxy who has been validly authorized to exercise power under a DPA. Conversely, a health care professional who disobeys the wishes of a legally authorized health care agent or representative may theoretically be subjected to liability for battery or negligence (Gasner, 1992; Zinberg, 1989), although some courts have restricted such legal actions (*Anderson v. St. Francis–St. George Hospital, Inc.,* 1996). At a minimum, the patient and family have a right to know what they can expect in the future from the health care professionals upon whom they rely, in terms of personal policies on health care planning and decision making.

CONCLUSION

Health care professionals with older clienteles must be familiar with the various mechanisms for substitute decision making outlined in this chapter and their legal, ethical, social, and clinical implications. Health care professionals can contribute greatly to the creation of substitute decision-making arrangements that assure as much as possible continued respect for the individual autonomy and freedom of their older patients while caring for those patients' basic human needs in a thorough and humane manner.

Chapter 9

Medicolegal Problems in Caring for Nursing Home Residents

INTRODUCTION

Most older Americans reside in the community, that is, in their own homes or in those of relatives. Consequently, they receive most of their medical care in community settings and raise and encounter most of their medico-legal problems in community contexts. However, more than 1.5 million people currently live in almost 20,000 nursing homes throughout the United States (Strahan, 1997). The vast majority (90%) of nursing home residents are elderly, and projections from current trends suggest that one of every four persons who reach the age of 65 can expect to spend some portion of his or her life in a nursing home. According to the federal Agency for Health Care Policy and Research (AHCPR), 1 of every 11 Americans who turned 65 in 1990 will spend at least 5 of his or her remaining years of life in a nursing home (Kemper & Murtaugh, 1991). Nursing home residents, who comprise about 5% of the nation's over-age-65 population, present special medico-legal, as well as ethical, challenges to the health care professionals who care for them (Hayley, Cassel, Snyder, & Rudberg, 1996).

The term "nursing home," as employed in this chapter, refers to nursing facilities (NFs) as defined by the federal government in terms of institutions that are eligible to participate in the Medicare and Medicaid programs, 42 C.F.R. part 442. NFs should be distinguished from boarding or rooming homes. Unlike nursing homes, boarding or rooming homes do not provide medical attention. Most boarding home residents are older and totally reliant on Supplemental Security Income (SSI). However, because legal standards for these homes are minimal and enforcement is relatively lax in most states (Hawes, Wildfire, & Lux, 1993), health care rendered to boarding and rooming home residents does not at this time— with a few exceptions (*State v. Warren*, 1990)—ordinarily present the health care professional with the same legal problems that come to light in the nursing home.

NURSING HOME REGULATION

Legal regulation of NFs derives from a variety of sources (National Health Lawyers Association, 1991). We utilize for this purpose state licensure statutes and reimbursement (primarily Medicare and Medicaid) certification requirements and inspection surveys conducted by both state and federal government. NFs seek voluntary forms of accreditation from private agencies such as the Joint Commission on Accreditation of Healthcare Organizations (JCAHO), whose guidelines frequently are relied on by courts as legally enforceable industry standards. Voluntary professional standards of practice also help guide appropriate conduct (American College of Health Care Administrators, 1987). Internal and external utilization review (UR) and quality assurance (QA) mechanisms have proliferated. Several criminal prosecutions against NFs and their staffs have emerged in the past few years. There is the professional liability or malpractice claim, involving an individual lawsuit brought by or for an individual NF resident against one or a combination of institutional or individual providers (Felsenthal, 1995; Spitzer-Resnick & Krajcinovic, 1995). In addition to civil lawsuits predicated on intentional (e.g., assault and battery) or unintentional (i.e., negligent) tortious behavior, NFs also face the possibility of legal claims based on allegations that they violated provisions of their contract, explicit or implied, with the resident (Armour, 1994).

This chapter does not pretend to act as a comprehensive survey of nursing home law or as a complete guide to risk management (Weinberg, 1998). Instead, this chapter concentrates on a few issues of critical importance to physicians and other health care professionals practicing within NFs. However, in light of the pervasive influence of the federal regulatory environment on the entire enterprise of NF resident care and the role of long-term care professionals and the dynamic nature of that environment, some specifics on NF regulation are provided as background.

The federal government has set mandatory standards since the early 1970s for NFs that wish to participate in the Medicare and Medicaid programs. Enforcement of these standards is accomplished through regular survey and certification by a state administrative agency (usually the state health department) that has been designated for that purpose by contract between specific states and the federal government. The federal Health Care Financing Administration (HCFA) provides the state survey agency with interpretive guidelines (compiled in the *Medicaid State Operations Manual*) and a survey form for use during NF surveys. Frequently, state surveys examine NFs for compliance with both the federal certification standards and state licensure requirements at the same time. Violation of federal standards may lead to decertification of the NF from participation in Medicare or Medicaid financing, and failure to satisfy state requirements may result in serious penalties (Crotts & Martinez, 1996) such as delicensure or intermediate sanctions, including civil fines, restrictions on admissions, or receivership. Violations of federal and state statutory and regulatory standards also may be introduced into evidence in civil tort actions (Edelman, 1990). Inspection reports are widely available to the public at Social Security offices and elsewhere. Not infrequently, the local press actually publishes survey results.

A final rule allowing HCFA to confer "deemed status" on a private accrediting organization (i.e., to treat that organization's approval of an NF as sufficient to satisfy Medicare/Medicaid certification standards for NF certification purposes) was published on November 23, 1993, 58 *Federal Register* 61837–61843. To date, no private accrediting organization has applied for deemed status in this context.

As part of the Omnibus Budget Reconciliation Act of 1987 (OBRA 87), Public Law 100-203, Congress enacted the Nursing Home Quality Reform Act, codified at 42 U.S.C. §§1395i-3(a)–(h) and 1396r(a)–(h). This statute is modeled on many of the recommendations made in a 1986 Institute of Medicine report that Congress had directed HFCA to commission. Passage of the 1987 legislation represented the impatience of Congress (and indirectly, of the courts) with what they perceived as the inadequate regulation of NFs by the Department of Health and Human Services (DHHS). The 1987 statute amended the Social Security Act, Titles 18 (Medicare) and 19 (Medicaid), to require substantial upgrading in NF quality and enforcement in several areas (Marek, Rantz, Fagin, & Krejci, 1996). To implement this legislation, HCFA published "final" regulations (with a public comment period) on February 2, 1989, in 54 *Federal Register* 5316, codified at 42 C.F.R. chapter 4, subchapter C, part 483. These regulations became effective on October 1, 1990. Additional "final" regulations were published on September 26, 1991, at 56 *Federal Register* 48826. Among the most significant requirements imposed by these regulations are those relating to the following:

- Ensuring resident privacy and decisional rights regarding accommodations, medical treatment, personal care, visits, written and telephone communications, and meetings with others.
- Maintaining confidentiality of personal and clinical records.
- Guaranteeing facility access and visitation rights to persons of the resident's choosing.
- Requiring issuance of notice of rights at the time of admission.

- Implementing admissions policy requirements (Kapp, 1998d; Knepper, 1996).
- Ensuring proper use of physical restraints and psychoactive drugs (see below).
- Protecting resident funds being managed by a facility.
- Ensuring transfer and discharge rights and issuing related notices.
- Requiring a minimum amount of nursing and social work coverage.
- Requiring comprehensive resident assessments and individualized care plans in accordance with those assessments (Fries et al., 1997; Hawes et al., 1997; Phillips et al., 1997).
- Requiring training and competency evaluations of nurses' aides.
- Requiring state prescreening of all prospective NF admittees and prohibiting admission of individuals with mental illness or mental retardation unless they specifically need NF services. This is referred to as the PASARR requirement, for preadmission screening and annual resident review (Eichmann, Griffin, Lyons, Larson, & Finkel, 1992; Pepper & Rubenstein, 1994).

A final and long-awaited (Robbins, 1994) rule pertaining to the survey, certification, and enforcement process of the government vis-à-vis NFs was published on November 10, 1994, at 59 *Federal Register*, 56116–56251, codified at 42 C.F.R. Part 401. On November 30, 1992, DHHS published a final rule on preadmission screening and annual resident review (PASARR), 57 *Federal Register* 56450–56514; part of this rule was abrogated when Congress passed Public Law 104-315 in 1996, repealing the requirement for annual resident review. On November 12, 1992, DHHS published a final rule on permissible charges against the personal funds of residents whose care is financed by Medicare or Medicaid, 57 *Federal Register* 53572–53587.

Receipt of federal funds brings NFs within the purview of the Rehabilitation Act of 1973. Section 504 of that federal statute prohibits programs receiving federal dollars from discriminating in the delivery of their services on the basis of an applicant's handicap. The 1990 Americans With Disabilities Act (ADA), Public Law 101-336, codified at 42 U.S.C. §§12101 through 12213, extended that prohibition even further into the private sector (Gottlich, 1994b; Schneider, 1997). Under these laws, for example, an NF's denial of admission to a prospective resident solely because the applicant has acquired immune deficiency syndrome (AIDS) or a positive HIV test would be highly suspect.

In addition to federal requirements tied to Medicare and Medicaid, regulation of NFs by individual states under their respective licensure authority is extensive, with specific requirements often exceeding those set on the federal level, especially regarding resident rights (Hyman, 1989).

NFs also are heavily regulated under state and local fire and building codes and similar business-related safety provisions. In their role as employer, NFs fall within state, federal, and local labor law requirements.

ACCESS TO MEDICAL CARE

As a general proposition, most older NF residents suffer from a variety of acute and chronic physical and mental ailments that regularly require the attention of health care professionals (Besdine, Rubenstein, & Cassel, 1994; Evans et al., 1995; Ouslander, 1997; Ouslander, Osterweil, & Morley, 1996). It is, after all, the characterization of NFs as primarily health care facilities—having, for example, an organized infection control program— that sets them apart from other types of housing arrangements and that entitles them to participate in certain public and private health care financing programs. Many of those who enter an NF never return again to the community.

Role of the Physician

Federal regulations limit admissions to NFs to those persons who have been referred directly by their personal physicians; put differently, one needs a physician's referral in order to gain admission to an NF. Medical need for the placement is frequently documented by the physician through use of a needs-assessment form supplied by the NF. In addition, the NF itself is required to perform a comprehensive assessment of the new resident, using HCFA's Long Term Care Resident Assessment Instrument (RAI), in accordance with a minimum data set (MDS) established by the federal government, 42 C.F.R. §483.20(b). Most individuals and their families make the major decision about NF entrance only after extensive consultation with the individual's private physician. It is imperative that the physician be factually prepared to provide informative consultation in this regard.

Health care professionals, most notably physicians, sometimes provide less than optimal care to their older patients who happen to reside in NFs (Keay & Taler, 1992). Deficiencies in the quality and quantity of medical services made available to NF residents may entail potentially significant legal ramifications.

The level of physician involvement in the continuing care of NF residents has long been a matter of public scrutiny and criticism (Katz, Karuza, Kolassa, & Hutson, 1997; U.S. Congress, Senate Committee on Aging, 1975). There is evidence that the average level of care of older persons in general (Kapp, 1998a) and of NF residents in particular often is not up to the same high standards available to patients in other age groups and other treatment locations. This is particularly true in the area of mental health services, where, paradoxically, the need may be greatest (Borson, Loebel, Kitchell, Domoto, & Hyde, 1997; Lombardo, Fogel, Robinson, & Weiss, 1996). Physicians often attempt to avoid visiting their patients once they have entered an NF and, when a visit is made, may rush through their examination and treatment.

Role of the Medical Director

The overall daily health care of most NF residents is left to health care professionals other than the personal physician who served the resident prior to NF entrance. These long-term caregivers may include registered or licensed practical nurses, nurse's aides, and social workers. These professionals may vary widely in extent of experience, training, and skill.

Beyond these individuals, federal Medicare and Medicaid regulations require that every NF employ, on at least a consultant basis, a licensed physician to function in the position of medical director, 42 C.F.R. §483.75(k). The Medical Director is responsible, according to the NF regulations, for the overall coordination of the medical care in the NF to ensure the adequacy and appropriateness of the medical services provided to patients (Ouslander & Tangalos, 1995). The NF should have a written contract with its medical director, explicitly spelling out respective responsibilities and expectations. One specific duty of the medical director in fulfilling his or her obligations is to delineate the responsibilities of attending physicians. In practice, though, much of the responsibility for the ordinary medical care of the NF's residents actually falls on the shoulders of the medical director. He or she generally functions as the equivalent of the primary care physician for many of the residents of the employing NF. In addition, the medical director serves a central role as explainer of information to surveyors during the NF's certification process. Most medical directors are quite competent health care professionals and belong to their own professional association, the American Medical Directors Association (AMDA). AMDA operates a Certified Medical Director (CMD) credentialing process.

There are, however, some troubling aspects to a system that in essence permits a physician who has held a professional relationship with an individual and perhaps with that individual's family for a lengthy period of time to unilaterally abdicate personal involvement and responsibility once the patient has entered an NF (Coons & Reichel, 1988). First, regardless of how highly qualified and experienced he or she may be, the medical director does not have the benefit of knowing all of the relevant historical and social factors about the resident to which the individual's own long-standing physician should be privy. Beyond that, the law does not require that the medical director be employed full time by the NF or that outside medical practice be restricted at all. Many NFs hire medical directors on a part-time consultant basis, and the actual care given is sometimes not much more than perfunctory (Elon, 1993; Zimmer, Watson, & Levenson, 1993).

Legal and Ethical Obligations of the Physician

A physician who has entered into and sustained a professional relationship with a patient, assists that patient to gain admittance to an NF and then, in effect, ignores responsibility for the continued medical care of that now-institutionalized individual runs a risk of incurring potential legal liability under the long-recognized common law theory of abandonment. Under traditional legal principles, a physician is free to unilaterally (i.e., by himself or herself) terminate a professional relationship with a patient for any reason. However, the courts have established certain continuing obligations and conditions that restrict the time and manner surrounding the breaking up of a relationship at the physician's instigation. Violating those obligations and conditions may subject the physician to the possibility of a successful lawsuit for abandoning the patient (Annas, 1989).

Thus, if a physician ceases caring for a former patient upon the latter's becoming an NF resident or renders care that is so infrequent or cursory that it might just as well not be given at all, and if the NF resident has not voluntarily and knowingly agreed to a termination of the professional relationship, the physician must fulfill certain legal duties in order to protect against potential liability for abandonment. The underlying theory is that patients who are in need of medical care should not suddenly be left "high and dry" without adequate access to appropriate services. Consequently, certain duties are incumbent upon the physician to prevent that situation from happening when the physician terminates the professional relationship with a previous patient who has become institutionalized.

First, if the physician intends to terminate the relationship, he or she should clearly and unambiguously notify the NF resident of that intention, preferably both orally and in writing. If the resident is not mentally competent to make treatment decisions, notice should be supplied to the resident's proxy decision maker—usually the family or court-appointed guardian. The physician also should notify the NF, preferably without any statement of reasons (because of possible defamation considerations), through the medical director. The NF resident has a right, under federal Medicare and Medicaid regulations, common law precepts, and JCAHO Standards for Long Term Care Facilities, to be fully informed about the identity of the physician who is principally responsible for his or her care.

Failure to properly notify the resident of an intended relationship termination may lull the resident into a false sense of security and thus impede
efforts to secure necessary medical attention from a different physician. If
the resident suffers an injury because of such a delay, liability of the original physician may result.

Second, assuming proper notice of termination has been given, the terminating physician is still obliged to make "reasonable" efforts to assist the
former patient to obtain appropriate continuing care. This duty ordinarily
will be satisfied by referring the patient to another competent physician
who is acceptable to the patient and who agrees to accept the patient. What
efforts in this regard are "reasonably" required will necessarily depend on
the unique facts of the case under consideration, but factors to be taken into
account include such things as (1) the immediacy, seriousness, and kind of
medical attention required by the patient; (2) the availability of another
qualified physician to replace the one who is withdrawing; and (3) personal
characteristics that might tend to make the patient a desirable or an undesirable addition to someone else's medical practice. If a physician seeks to
fulfill this obligation by referring the former patient to the NF's medical
director, reasonable effort must be invested to ascertain that the medical
director has sufficient training and skill to deal competently with the medical problems of the particular resident and that in fact competent care is
likely to be delivered.

Finally, if a competent referral has been accomplished and accepted
by all concerned parties, the previous physician must reasonably cooperate with the new physician to assure continuity of care for the patient.
Such cooperation generally takes the form, when requested by the new
physician and authorized by the patient (see Chapter 4), of supplying
copies of relevant clinical records and otherwise sharing information concerning earlier care that might be useful in future decision making. This
requirement certainly would apply with full force in the case of an NF resident who is forced to change physicians involuntarily.

It is most desirable that the legal issue of abandonment remain more
academic than real as applied to NF patients. That is, ideally, a physician
who has enjoyed a professional relationship of substantial duration with a
patient in the community should continue to supply care, even after the
patient has entered an NF, in as conscientious and complete a manner as
before. The resident's personal physician should promptly furnish the NF
with clinical findings, diagnoses, and orders and be available (either personally or through a competent substitute that he or she designates and
the patient approves) in times of resident need. Further, the patient's
physician and certainly the NF's medical director should reject the pure
medical model of NF care in favor of accepting responsibility for contributing to the psychosocial as well as medical needs of the patient. The

physician's cooperation and coordination with the activities of other health care professionals within the NF should be considered an integral element of the acceptable standard of care that the physician owes the patient (Vladeck, 1996b).

This ideal, however, is not always achieved in actual practice. Chapter 13 discusses several elements impinging on the optimal delivery of physicians' services to the elderly, including the ageism phenomenon, the "YAVIS" syndrome, the hectic pace of medical practice, and the limited financial resources of older health care consumers. These factors apply with even greater force to the NF population. NF patients often are perceived by physicians, albeit inaccurately, as always depressing, uninteresting, and hopeless. Serving NF patients also can be logistically taxing and financially relatively unrewarding. The clear signal from sources of third-party payment that physician services acquire a lower economic value when provided in NFs evokes a professional response of less effort exerted on behalf of NF residents.

NFs are troubled by physician abrogation of responsibility concerning their institutionalized patients. NFs realize that the medical director often is an imperfect substitute for a personal physician who has dealt with the patient and family for years. Additionally, federal Medicare and Medicaid regulations place upon the NF the burden of ensuring the creation of a comprehensive plan of medical treatment, 42 C.F.R. §483.20(d), and the conduct of regular physician examinations for each patient for whom Medicare and/or Medicaid reimbursement is sought. For NFs, each patient must be seen physically by a physician every 30 days during the first 90 days in the facility and at least every 90 days thereafter. Under HCFA regulations, physicians may delegate every other required visit to a nurse practitioner or physician's assistant. Under Public Law 101-239, Medicare reimbursement is available for nurse practitioner visits to NF residents.

In the final analysis, it is the NF that is responsible for accomplishing compliance with regulations requiring routine physician visits and for otherwise ensuring the availability of appropriate medical care in times of resident need. This responsibility exists despite the independent contractor (as opposed to employee) status of the patient's personal physician. Penalties for not properly fulfilling this duty could include decertification of the NF from eligibility for Medicare and Medicaid payment or withholding of some portion of payment otherwise due, as well as potential negligence liability to the individual patient who is harmed by the NF's shortcomings. Understandably, strains have developed between NFs that are concerned with patient well-being and with their own legal liability, on one hand, and physicians who have admitted individuals to the NF and have then in essence abandoned them, on the other. Many NFs have developed various forms of affiliation agreements and arrangements that aim to improve the system for defining, monitoring, and controlling the conduct of physicians who desire admitting privileges.

In contrast to the loose arrangements that are widely prevalent today, every NF should seriously consider forming a formal, organized medical staff, analogous to the model found in acute care hospitals. The medical staff should be organized and function according to specific, written internal bylaws. Bylaw provisions should include at least a description of the medical staff organization; a statement of attending physician qualifications; fair procedures and standards for granting, withdrawing, suspending, or limiting privileges; a schedule for staff meetings; medical records requirements; methods for securing emergency medical services when the attending physician is unavailable; a process for dealing with written and oral orders; a statement of qualifications for allied health professionals with medical staff privileges; and quality control mechanisms.

Support for the medical staff bylaws and their rigorous enforcement must be fostered among potential and existing members of an NF's medical staff. Besides relying on feelings of institutional and professional pride and a sincere concern for patient welfare, the NF should remind health professionals on its staff that, under the legal theories of joint undertaking, negligent referral, and borrowed servant, there may be circumstances in which they can be held legally liable for the negligence of their errant professional colleagues (King, 1986).

All initial applications for medical staff privileges should be thoroughly investigated. This should include verification of all academic degrees, professional licenses, specialty board certifications, other institutional affiliations (past and present), and personal references.

The periodic privilege renewal process should include a meaningful peer review of the physician's continued competence and the quality of recent patient care provided by the applicant. Relevant data concerning lawsuits or potential lawsuits should be considered as one part of that review. As a related element of peer review, each physician should be encouraged to report, through the NF's QA and risk management (Weinberg, 1998) systems, without fear of reprisal, observations of poor patient care in the NF.

Under the federal Health Care Quality Improvement Act of 1986, each NF is required to send information to a central National Practitioner Data Bank (NPDB), operated by the DHHS, regarding adverse actions involving members of the medical staff. Reportable adverse actions include such events as a suspension or revocation of clinical privileges or paying money on the physician's behalf as the result of a malpractice claim. An NF also is obligated to access the NPDB to study the dossier on any physician applying for privileging or reprivileging with the NF.

As a general proposition, NF patients should be permitted and encouraged to select their own personal physician, assuming their choice is willing to assume or continue that role. However, the NF has both the right and the duty to regulate medical privileges in furtherance of patient welfare, as long as fair procedures and reasonable standards are utilized.

It is incumbent upon physicians who admit individuals to NFs to understand both their own legal and ethical responsibilities and those of the NF to which their patients are admitted. Private physicians, NF administrators, and medical directors must work together to ensure that their separate and mutual duties are carried out to the ultimate betterment of the patient (Fortinsky & Raff, 1995–96). When the NF already has a policy in effect regarding its expectations and requirements concerning admitting physicians, the admitting physician should be aware of that policy, scrupulously obey it, and offer to assist in amending portions that are unreasonable or otherwise ill-advised. The physician also should encourage his or her students and peers to act similarly regarding their own NF patients. If the NF to which the physician sends patients has not yet formulated and adopted a policy in this area, the physician practicing in the community should become heavily involved in the design of this policy so that it will reflect his or her legitimate needs and concerns while at the same time adequately protecting the rights of patients.

INSTITUTIONAL ABUSE

The physical and mental abuse suffered by residents of some NFs has been well documented. Although important improvements have been realized as a result of government regulation, industry sensitivity, and vigorous consumer advocacy, NF-induced deprivation of basic rights is still a fact of life for a number of older Americans (Marks, 1996).

In the Violent Crime Control and Law Enforcement Act of 1994, Public Law 103-222, the U.S. Attorney General was directed to "develop guidelines for the adoption of appropriate safeguards by care providers and by States for protecting children, the elderly, or individuals with disabilities from abuse . . . and to address the availability, cost, timeliness, and effectiveness of criminal history background checks." Several states have reacted by codifying mandatory criminal background checks of care providers in NFs (California, Florida, Idaho, Illinois, Kentucky, Louisiana, Maryland, New Jersey, Nevada, Ohio, Oregon, Pennsylvania, Rhode Island, Texas, Vermont, and Washington, as of mid-1996). The implementing regulations of the Nursing Home Reform Act of 1987, at 42 C.F.R. §483.156, mandate that "the state must establish and maintain a registry of nurse aides that meets the requirements of this section. . . . The registry must include as a minimum . . . information on any finding by the State survey agency of abuse, neglect, or misappropriation of property by the individual." An NF is no longer able to credibly claim ignorance of the past history of prospective employees.

Health care professionals serving the older NF resident, especially the individual's personal physician, can be of invaluable assistance in the identification, investigation, and proof of patterns or instances of resident abuse. This is especially true when such abuse is readily detectable during physical examination and treatment. The health care professional also may help to resolve complaints before they escalate into litigation (e.g., *Beverly Enterprises-Florida, Inc. v. Spilman,* 1995) by acting as a credible communicator or mediator between the allegedly abused resident and the NF administration and by producing illuminating medical records upon which some informal accommodation may be based.

The role of the health care professional, particularly of the physician, in initially detecting abuse of older persons is discussed at some length in Chapter 7. While I deal there with elder abuse occurring in community settings, most of the same clinical principles apply here, although the location and circumstances of the physical examination will be different. Additionally, the statute in effect in one's own jurisdiction concerning the mandatory or permissive reporting of cases of suspected elder abuse to identified public health authorities (also discussed in Chapter 7) should be consulted to determine its applicability to NF residents. Most states have enacted specific obligations for reporting NF resident abuse. When they are found applicable, these reporting statutes should be carefully adhered to by health care professionals who observe evidence of covered forms of abuse.

Health care professionals also can be instrumental during the investigatory stage of an alleged abuse claim. For example, NF ombudsmen, who are created and authorized by a combination of the federal Older Americans Act (OAA) and state elder program legislation to advocate on behalf of the rights of NF residents (Kahana, 1994), frequently utilize medical records to delve into and, it is hoped, resolve resident complaints before any formal legal process has been instigated. Failing an informal resolution, medical records and reports are essential investigatory and preparatory implements for the attorney who is representing a resident in a potential or actual civil lawsuit (Hemp, 1994) alleging medically ascertainable abuse. Every NF should have in place a formal system for investigating internally any possible incidents involving the abuse of a resident.

Likewise, proof presented to the trier of fact (judge or jury) by the examining and treating physician or other health care professional, relating clinical observations and impressions about the resident, is virtually imperative at the evidentiary stage of a formal abuse claim. This proof may be presented either through live testimony or a sworn, recorded deposition. It is almost impossible to succeed in pressing an abuse claim without active health care professional cooperation.

For these reasons, health care professionals must be cognizant of and alert to manifestations of possible abuse suffered by NF residents under their care. Statutory reporting requirements must be observed. Participation in the investigatory, negotiating, and evidentiary stages of alleged abuse complaint resolution must be undertaken willingly and with candor and completeness. The health care professional can also be a valuable change agent during the remedial phase (i.e., the implementation part) following formal or informal resolution of the problem.

Finally, the central role of the medical director in preventing or stemming patterns or instances of resident abuse in the NF should not be overlooked. As the health care professional upon whom the burden of providing primary care often falls, this person could be an important liaison to the community (including, where necessary, the ombudsman, resident advocate, and legal community) and an enthusiastic community advocate within the facility.

TRANSFER TRAUMA

"Transfer trauma" refers to the serious physical and emotional difficulties that older, chronically ill individuals may suffer as a direct result of forced relocation from the community to an institution, from one institution to another, from an institution to the community, or from one place to another within the same institution. By "forced" relocation, I refer to a change that takes place over the objection of the affected resident, as contrasted with, for example, room changes initiated by residents themselves (Everard, Rowles, & High, 1994).

An NF resident may, as a practical matter, be at risk of an involuntary transfer for any of a variety of reasons, although this practice probably is lessening. The reasons might include (1) financial considerations (i.e., the private-pay resident has depleted personal financial resources and the NF refuses to accept or retain Medicaid beneficiaries, has already exceeded its self-imposed quota of them, or keeps its Medicaid residents separate from its private-pay population in a *de facto* "Medicaid Wing"); (2) administrative convenience (for instance, a resident's medical condition and needs change, and the NF segregates residents according to type of diagnosis and treatment requirements); or (3) retaliation against a particularly troublesome resident (in response, for example, to the resident's publicly airing a complaint about conditions in the NF).

Such transfers occur periodically despite provisions in the federal Medicare and Medicaid regulations (and similar provisions in the NF statutes and regulations of states and in JCAHO standards) limiting legitimate grounds for resident transfers to the following: (1) situations in which the resident agrees to the proposed transfer; (2) medical necessity (e.g., the patient requires acute care that can be provided only in a hospital environment); (3) failure of the resident to pay the NF for services provided; or (4) the resident's "welfare or that of other patients." The residents' rights section of the federal (and most state) regulations also requires the NF to give the resident advance notice before any transfer, except in emergency situations (Knepper, 1996).

The "medical necessity" exception to the general legal prohibition against forced relocations deserves special attention (e.g., *In the Matter of the Involuntary Discharge or Transfer of J.S. by Hall*, 1994). The medical-necessity provision encompasses situations in which the government-mandated UR process determines that, for a resident whose care is being financed by Medicare, Medicaid, or another third-party payer, NF-level care is no longer medically necessary or appropriate. The U.S. Supreme Court has ruled that an NF's decision to discharge or transfer a Medicaid resident to a lower level of care, based upon a UR committee judgment and without prior notice to the resident, does not violate the resident's constitutional right to due process (*Blum v. Yaretsky*, 1982). The Court found that the UR committee's decisions to transfer or discharge residents "ultimately turn on medical judgments made by private parties according to professional standards." The Court referred to the fact that physicians in these situations act in accordance with the ethics established within their own professional groups.

Federal regulations provide that UR decisions in the NF have to be based on the primary judgment of the resident's attending physician, who alone has firsthand, accurate knowledge of the resident's needs. It is the job of the health care professional, especially the attending physician, involved in the care of a resident to ensure that UR personnel are fully informed of and pushed to seriously consider all aspects of that resident's case, including the likely adverse physical, emotional, and social ramifications of an involuntary transfer. If a resident exerts the right to demand a hearing to challenge a UR finding, the health care professional should be prepared to testify. Health care professionals who are themselves part of a UR process are responsible for conscientiously ensuring that they become fully informed of and seriously consider this full range of relevant factors. Only then can the UR process properly serve its important and legitimate QA function.

Although social science researchers have debated in scholarly journals the reality and extent of the transfer trauma phenomenon, a number of attorneys have relied upon this concept in challenging attempted involuntary transfers (Keville, 1993). Legal advocates unsuccessfully attempted to have the U.S. Supreme Court accept transfer trauma as the basis for holding that NF residents possess a constitutional right to challenge a state agency's decision to terminate a substandard NF from participation in the Medicaid program (*O'Bannon v. Town Court*, 1980). Instead, the Court's 7-to-1 decision held the residents' Fourteenth Amendment substantive due process liberty interests in this situation to be insubstantial either because the transfer trauma effect had not been conclusively proved by medical evidence or, if transfer trauma did exist, its deleterious results were only incidentally or indirectly caused by the government's action in decertifying the NF.

The *Town Court* case did not, despite the fears of some, mean that transfer trauma as an argument in the judicial forum was dead. On the contrary, the door was left open, at least by implication, for health care professionals to join with legal advocates in compiling and presenting data that the courts would accept as conclusive proof of transfer trauma in particular cases. At the least, the transfer trauma argument may be used, when supported by sufficient health care professional testimony about the probable effects of forced relocation on a particular resident, to prevent the NF itself from initiating the transfer.

Despite the efforts of all involved to prevent involuntary transfers from occurring, there nonetheless are times when it becomes unavoidable. This may happen, for example, when an NF goes out of business and ceases to operate. In such situations, health care professionals must work together in the vital (and legally required) process of discharge planning to attempt to accomplish a transfer process and placement that will minimize any adverse effects of the forced relocation on the individual resident. Although discharge planning is primarily the legal responsibility of the NF (Murtaugh, 1994), all health care professionals involved in the care of its residents should actively cooperate in this effort to maximize the likelihood of success and to guard against any allegations of abandonment at this point.

DRUG PRESCRIPTION

Most NF residents take a lot of drugs, particularly antipsychotic medications, which act on the central nervous system to diminish emotional response to external and internal stimuli. This phenomenon has been widely attributed to the large number of individuals who, in the past three decades, have been "deinstitutionalized" from large state mental hospitals into private NFs, either directly or with one or more intermediary stops.

There are legitimate clinical indications for the prescription of these drugs to enhance resident well-being (Everitt & Avorn, 1986). It even has been proposed that NF residents may possess a federal constitutional entitlement to adequate treatment that would include, for some, the right to have antipsychotic drugs prescribed for them (Barnett, 1978).

There is substantial evidence, however, that drugs, especially of the antipsychotic variety, are still sometimes unnecessarily and inappropriately prescribed for NF residents (Avorn & Gurwitz, 1995; Beers et al., 1992). "Polypharmacy" is recognized as a major problem in geriatrics in general and in NFs specifically. It is primarily the legal and ethical responsibility of the resident's attending physician, or of the NF's medical director if an attending physician is not to be found, to prescribe medications properly and to monitor their sometimes severe toxic side effects. Some states also permit nurses to prescribe drugs, ordinarily under physician supervision.

Chapter 3 deals extensively with the subject of informed consent to medical diagnosis or treatment. The informed consent legal doctrine and its ethical foundations apply with full force to the situation of proposed drug therapy for NF residents. Besides common law principles, the right of a competent NF resident to give either informed consent or refusal to a proposed course of treatment, including prescribed medications, is amply supported by federal Medicare and Medicaid regulations, 42 C.F.R. §483.10(b)(4), state NF codes, and the JCAHO. In addition, drug prescribing is regulated by the federal Food and Drug Administration (FDA), which requires special labeling of pharmaceuticals to include information pertinent to their proper use by older persons, 62 *Federal Register* 45313–45326 (August 27, 1997).

MENTAL CAPACITY AND INFORMED CONSENT IN THE NURSING HOME

The key problem frequently encountered by health care professionals in attempting to apply the informed consent doctrine to the NF environment is difficulty in accurately ascertaining the level of decisional capacity of the individual resident who is consenting to or refusing proffered treatment. Unfortunately, the mechanical "capacimeter" that supplies objective numerical readings on this patient dimension is a device that has yet to be invented (Kapp & Mossman, 1996). Chapters 3 and 8 describe some of the guidelines and criteria that have been suggested for use in reaching decisional capacity determinations.

The institutionalized elderly suffer disproportionately from organic brain syndrome and other types of maladies that may contribute to some degree of mental disability. Over half of NF residents have symptoms of mental illness. When a formal court adjudication of incompetency has been rendered and a guardian appointed as substitute decision maker (see Chapter 8), the health care professional should deal directly with that guardian to obtain informed consent, while still taking into account any expressed feelings or reactions of the resident regarding treatment.

For many NF residents, however, mental functional ability may be highly problematic even though no formal guardianship proceedings have been initiated. This situation is most likely when the resident lacks interested family members and has little in the way of assets or income beyond a monthly SSI check. Statistically, it is precisely the poor elderly without interested family members who are most likely to enter an NF.

Capacity assessment is presently an extremely murky area, in which decision making depends on largely unguided clinical judgment exercised in individual cases (Kapp, 1996b). Although, as a pragmatic matter, this is an area in which the likelihood of health care professionals incurring legal liability historically has been very slight, the theoretical possibility of a successful battery or negligence lawsuit for erroneous treatment or non-treatment certainly is real. This possibility has led some to make the unduly cumbersome and unnecessarily broad (Kapp, 1996a) suggestion that guardianship proceedings be initiated in all situations of questionably competent NF residents or applicants.

One alternative for dealing with the "unbefriended" situation of incapacitated residents without family or significant others would be the creation of internal administrative systems by individual NFs for processing important decisions in a timely manner that accounts for both the resident's needs and his or her preferences (to the extent the latter can be ascertained). Geriatrician Muriel Gillick (1995b) has proposed such an approach, although one leading consumer advocate (Freeman, 1995) has expressed unease at the conflict-of-interest implications of an internal decision-making system. A California statute allows a decisionally incapacitated NF resident to receive medical treatment after a physician has determined that resident's incapacity to give informed consent to such treatment and an interdisciplinary review team has found the treatment to be medially appropriate (Cal. Health and Safety Code §1418.8); this statute has survived a challenge based on constitutional objections (*Rains v. Belshe*, 1995).

Another idea that has been proposed as a possible way of avoiding or at least mitigating the dilemma of the incapacitated NF resident without a legal guardian is a more extensive use of the durable power of attorney (DPA). This device is discussed in Chapter 8. NFs may not require, although many appropriately encourage, decisionally capable residents to select a decision-making agent in advance to guard against the contingency of subsequent incapacity. It is the person who functions as the gatekeeper to NF services (generally, the individual's personal physician) who has contact with the resident at the optimum "teachable moment" (i.e., when the resident has an immediate, serious need that makes the resident amenable to listening to the speaker's message) and who therefore is most favorably situated to encourage the resident to plan ahead through designation of a proxy via a DPA. As discussed in Chapter 11, the Patient Self-Determination Act (PSDA), passed by Congress in 1990, requires each NF to inquire about advance directives at the time of the resident's admission to the NF (Walker & Blechner, 1995–96).

An interesting, emerging set of issues revolves around many NFs' increasing reluctance or even unwillingness to admit as residents in the first place individuals whose legal status is unclear because of murky mental capacity and the absence of explicitly designated decision-making surrogates. Many NF admission directors are uneasy about accepting new residents unless the resident or a surrogate has clear legal authority to voluntarily consent to admission. This reluctance is due to fear about potential legal (including regulatory) liability. It may cause excessively long hospital stays while the legal details concerning decision-making authority are being resolved. Delays in placement may expose prospective NF residents to unnecessary medical risks in the hospital and can financially penalize hospitals that are paid according to a prospective payment system (PPS) (Kapp, 1998d).

PHYSICAL/MECHANICAL RESTRAINTS

The practice of using physical or mechanical restraints on residents has been ubiquitous in American NFs. Defined in the "Interpretive Guidelines" to the current federal NF regulations as "any manual method or physical or mechanical device, material, or equipment attached or adjacent to the resident's body that the individual cannot remove easily which restricts freedom of movement or normal access to one's body," physical restraints have been a regular part of the institutional long-term care scene in the United States for hundreds of years (Evans & Strumpf, 1989).

The last decade has produced a growing professional and public realization that the use of physical restraints in NFs in many instances is unnecessary, improper, and even abusive. A strong movement has developed, led by certain segments of the NF industry itself, government regulators on both the federal and state levels, and resident advocacy groups to bring about a greatly reduced reliance on the use of physical restraints in NFs (American Geriatrics Society, 1991; C. C. Williams & Finch, 1997).

The proper and improper use of physical restraints within NFs is a matter of direct, explicit regulation by the federal government and by each of the individual states. On the federal level, important changes in this regard were contained in OBRA 1987's Nursing Home Quality Reform Act, discussed earlier, and implementing regulations published February 2, 1989, and February 5, 1992. The federal rule provides that "the resident has the right to be free from any physical restraints imposed or psychoactive drug administered for purposes of discipline or convenience, and not required to treat the resident's medical symptoms" (42 C.F.R. §483.13[a]). The OBRA 87 statute itself goes even further:

> Restraints may only be imposed to ensure the physical safety of the resident or other residents, and only upon the written order of a physician that specifies the duration and the circumstances under which the restraints are to be used (except in emergency circumstances which are to be specified by the secretary [of DHHS] until such an order could reasonably be obtained) (Public Law 100-203, §§4201(c) (1)(A)(ii) (Medicare) and 4211(c)(1)(A)(ii) (Medicaid)).

HCFA's "Interpretive Guidelines" to its regulations, which guide state surveyors in evaluating the compliance of NFs with the federal requirements, contain several pertinent provisions:

> [Physical restraints include] [a]ny manual method or physical or mechanical device, material, or equipment attached or adjacent to the resident's body that the individual cannot move easily which restricts free movement or normal access to one's body. Leg restraints, arm restraints, hand mitts, soft ties or vests, wheelchair safety bars, and Geri-chairs are physical restraints.

Bed rails (siderails) have not been included in this list, but the "misuse of bed rails"—for example, to prevent the resident from voluntarily getting out of bed—is listed in the HCFA "Interpretive Guidelines" as an accident hazard. Lawsuits based on injuries to a resident for whom bed rails have been raised, occurring in the course of the resident attempting to get out of bed (Parker & Miles, 1997), will be very difficult for the NF to defend against in the face of this regulatory forewarning:

> Discipline is any action taken by the facility for the express purpose of punishing or penalizing residents.
> Convenience is any action taken by the facility to control resident behavior or maintain residents with the least amount of effort by the facility or its staff and not in the resident's best interest. . . .
> Less restrictive measures than restraints, such as pillows, pads, removable lap trays coupled with appropriate exercise, are often effective in achieving proper body position, balance, alignment, and preventing contractures. A facility must have evidence of consultation with

appropriate health professionals, such as occupational or physical therapists in the use of less restrictive supportive devices *prior to* using physical restraints as defined in this guideline for such purposes.

If after a trial of less restrictive measures, the facility decides that
a physical restraint would enable and promote greater functional
independence, then the use of the restraining device must first be
explained to the resident, family member, or legal representative, and
if the resident, family member, or legal representative agrees to this
treatment alternative, then the restraining device may be used for the
specific periods for which the restraint has been determined to be an
enabler.

If there are medical symptoms which are life threatening (such as
dehydration, electrolyte imbalance, urinary blockage) then a restraint
may be used temporarily to provide necessary life-saving treatment.
Physical restraints may be used for *brief* periods to allow medical treatment to proceed, if there is documented evidence of resident or legal
representative approval of the treatment.

HCFA encourages state surveyors to take an aggressive stance in
enforcing statutory and regulatory requirements concerning the use of
physical restraints. This stance is consciously intended to be consistent with
the resident outcome orientation characterizing the NF survey process
under OBRA 87, as exemplified by the requirements that all NFs administer a comprehensive assessment for each resident based on a national uniform MDS and "[t]hat each resident must receive and the facility must
provide the necessary care and services to attain and maintain the highest
practicable physical or mental and psycho-social well-being in accordance
with the comprehensive assessment and plan of care." State surveyors also
receive pressure from the Long Term Care Ombudsman network (Harris-
Wehling, Feasley, & Estes, 1995) established under the OAA to enforce
strictly the OBRA requirements on physical restraints.

In addition to federal regulation by HCFA tied to an NF's participation in Medicare and Medicaid, providers also should be aware of potential liability connected to regulation by the FDA. Under FDA regulations,
21 C.F.R. §880.6760[a], "[a] protective restraint is a device, usually a wrist-
let, anklet, or other type of strap, that is intended for medical purposes and
that limits a patient's movements to the extent necessary for treatment,
examination, or protection of the patient."

These devices used to be specifically exempted from FDA pre-
market notification requirements; this exemption was revoked effective
September 3, 1996, 21 C.F.R. §880.6760. The FDA actively maintains complaint files concerning such devices, and the information collected in
these complaint files is available to the general public, including plaintiffs' attorneys, under the federal Freedom of Information Act (FOIA), 5
U.S.C. §552.

Under the Safe Medical Devices Act (SMDA), 21 U.S.C. §360, effective 1991, and its implementing regulations, 21 C.F.R. Part 803, NFs (as well as hospitals, ambulatory surgical facilities, and outpatient treatment facilities) are obligated to report certain incidents to the FDA on Form 3500A within 10 working days. A Medical Device Report (MDR) must be submitted whenever the "user facility" receives or otherwise becomes aware of information from any source that reasonably suggests that a device may have caused or contributed to either (a) the death of a patient or employee of the facility or (b) serious injury to a patient or facility employee. "Caused or contributed" includes problems that arise because of device failure, malfunction, improper or inadequate design, manufacture defects, mislabeling, or (particularly relevant in the restraint context) user (e.g., NF) error. "Serious injury" means an illness or injury that (a) is life-threatening, (b) results in permanent impairment of a body function or permanent damage to a body structure, or (c) necessitates medical or surgical intervention to preclude permanent impairment of a body function or permanent damage to a body structure. If previous problems involving the use of specific devices have been made a matter of public record but an NF nonetheless persists in utilizing those devices on residents, and if injuries occur for which compensation is sought, the NF's obligation to justify the use of the restraining device in the face of information it had or should have had about its hazards will be difficult to satisfy.

Besides applicable federal provisions, virtually every state guarantees NF residents the right to be free from excessive physical restraints as part of the state's Resident Bill of Rights. These state provisions are in accord with both the spirit and the letter of the federal requirements.

Contrary to popular belief in some provider circles, governmental provisions limiting the permissible use of physical restraints do not automatically increase the potential negligence or malpractice exposure of NFs based on resident falls or wandering. In fact, the exact opposite is true (Kapp, 1992a; S. H. Johnson, 1990).

Of those relatively few negligence lawsuits that have been brought against NFs based on resident falls or wandering in which the resident was unrestrained, many have resulted in judgments for the defendant, absolving it of any blame for failure to restrain. A typical court opinion held that "[a] nursing home is not the insurer of the safety of its patients. The standard of care imposed upon a nursing home is that of reasonable care considering the patient's known mental and physical condition."

In addition, the courts in most of these cases have held that the NF's compliance with applicable federal and state regulations regarding the safeguarding of resident welfare satisfied the tort standard of care, even if resident injury unfortunately happened. The tendency toward judicial deference to regulatory standards as defining minimum acceptable conduct for tort litigation purposes takes on added importance in light of the Nursing Home Quality Reform Act and its implementing regulations, cited above, and relevant state statutes and regulations.

Further, even in those cases in which NFs or their personnel have been found liable for injuries associated with resident falls and wandering in the absence of restraints, no lawsuit has been successful against a NF *solely* for failure to restrain a resident. Prevailing NF plaintiffs in nonrestraint cases have had to prove by a preponderance of evidence the presence of one or more other elements of negligence or deviation from the professionally acceptable standard of care, such as improper assessment of the resident's needs; a failure to monitor the resident's condition and supervise his or her care adequately, especially if the resident's ability to function physically and mentally is substantially impaired by the administration of sedative drugs; inadequate documentation concerning resident care; failure to respond to the fall or wandering in a timely and professionally acceptable manner; staff conduct that placed the unrestrained resident in jeopardy in the first place; or failure to provide needed, reasonable services to the resident. Reacting to this line of cases solely by increasing the utilization of physical restraints would not repair the deficiencies that have led to liability.

Importantly, even if finding an NF liable when restraints were not used, the courts have consistently emphasized that the NF could have fulfilled its responsibilities acceptably by implementing means of monitoring and supervising residents other than imposing restraints. In other words, no court has held that restraining a resident is the only or best way an NF can satisfy its obligation of due care. This line of cases thus haltingly approves the use of restraints but by no means compels or even prefers it. In several of these cases, NFs actually had implemented appropriate alternatives to the use of restraints, such as purchasing and installing alarm systems, but those systems were not working properly (either because they had broken down or they had intentionally been turned off by staff) at the time of the resident injury.

Even in nonrestraint cases in which plaintiffs have prevailed, the size of judgments or settlements ordinarily has been modest. The courts have disfavored the awarding of punitive damages in these legal actions.

Notably, in cases holding NFs liable for resident injuries happening in the absence of restraints, the defendant NFs generally had not been complying with relevant federal or state statutory and regulatory requirements regarding minimum precautions for resident safety at the time of the injury. In light of the federal Nursing Home Quality Reform Act and its implementing regulations and corresponding state statutes and regulations on this subject, it will be quite unlikely for a court in the future to impose liability on an NF that is in compliance with legislative and regulatory requirements and limitations concerning the imposition of restraints, even when resident injury occurs.

Not only is apprehension of potential legal liability that is based solely on the failure to impose restraints the product of seriously skewed perceptions on the part of most NF professionals, but any legal exposure associated with failure to restrain residents is substantially outweighed by the legal risks attached to the improper application of physical restraints. As illuminated by a review of both the clinical literature and legal case law, mounting data show that physical restraints used in the name of defensive medicine not only may fail to be defensive but actually may be counterproductive.

Numerous epidemiological studies conducted over a long period of time demonstrate that the chance of morbid outcomes, including injurious falls, increases significantly with the prolonged use of mechanical (as well as chemical) restraints. Residents get injured—sometimes fatally—while becoming agitated and trying to escape from their restraints (e.g., by trying to climb over siderails to get out of bed), while strangling and suffocating or otherwise losing control because of improperly applied restraints (for instance, Posey vests being put on the resident backward) or because of staff failure to monitor and adjust restraints at regular, timely intervals. The range of potential physical and psychological (Mion, Frengley, Jakovcic, & Marino, 1989) problems associated with restraint use, especially over a prolonged period, is very broad.

Bad clinical outcomes, particularly if unexpected by the resident or family, are the most reliable leading indicator of eventual lawsuit initiation. Additionally, the rate of serious resident injury falls (over two thirds of falls in NFs are not associated with serious injuries) does not increase appreciably in situations where restraints have not been imposed. Put differently, unrestrained residents do not tend to suffer more serious falls than do restrained residents with similar characteristics.

Thus, cases holding providers liable in the absence of NF restraints are far eclipsed in number and in size of damages by legal judgments and settlements made on the basis of inappropriate ordering of restraints, failure to monitor and correct their adverse effects on the resident, or errors in the mechanical application of the restraint. Claims in the latter category (i.e., misused restraints) have been filed on theories of both negligence, or unintentional deviation from acceptable professional standards, and battery, which is defined as an intentional unconsented-to invasion of the resident's personal integrity.

In addition to civil liability as a potential consequence of excessively utilizing physical restraints, NFs cannot rule out the possibility of criminal prosecution in especially outrageous circumstances. Criminal prosecutions charging NF corporations and specific staff members with negligent homicide for the deaths of residents by vest strangulation have been brought in several states. Further, in some states, inappropriate restraint use is classified as a form of criminal elder abuse, implicating both substantial penalties for the perpetrators and the question of mandatory abuse reporting requirements for observers. The violation of mandatory reporting requirements carries its own criminal ramifications.

For all of these reasons, physical restraint minimization in NFs is imperative. NFs must develop and carry out policies and procedures to comply with all applicable criminal, regulatory, and common law requirements in this regard (Braun & Lipson, 1993; Zusman, 1997). Less restrictive alternatives to the use of restraints, including both environmental and administrative changes in the NF, must be explored fully and explained to staff (Dunbar, Neufeld, Libow, Cohen, & Foley, 1997), residents, and families. There are numerous successful models of restraint reduction to emulate (Dunbar, Neufeld, White, & Libow, 1996; Neufeld & Dunbar, 1997).

CHEMICAL RESTRAINTS

As the use of physical restraints is reduced, NFs are not able simply to substitute psychoactive medications as an alternative means of attempted behavior control. OBRA 87 and its implementing regulations impose substantial limitations on the prerogative of physicians to order and NFs to administer mind-altering drugs to residents.

Specifically, as noted earlier, 42 C.F.R. §483.13(a) assures each NF resident "the right to be free from any . . . psychoactive drug administered for the purposes of discipline or convenience, and not required to treat the resident's medical symptoms." Additionally, 42 C.F.R. §483.25(l)(1) states that each resident's drug regimen must be free from unnecessary drugs, and 42 C.F.R. §483.25(l)(2) provides that a resident for whom antipsychotics have not been used previously may be given them only to treat a specific condition. Residents getting antipsychotic drugs must receive gradual dose reductions or drug holidays.

OBRA 87 has had a demonstrably significant impact on antipsychotic drug use in NFs (Borson & Doane, 1997; Garrard, Chen, & Dowd, 1995; Lantz, Giambanco, & Buckalter, 1996; Semla, Palla, Poddig, & Brauner, 1994). Reductions in both physical and chemical restraints have taken place at the same time (Siegler et al., 1997). Moreover, a decrease in the prescription and administration of antipsychotics has been associated with improved outcomes and no discernible adverse effects (Thapa, Meador, Gideon, Fought, & Ray, 1994; Shorr, Fought, & Ray, 1994). Among other things, reducing the use of psychotropic agents has reduced the number of resident falls and fall-related injuries (Cooper, 1994, 1997).

NFs, if they have not already done so, need to develop and implement careful policies and procedures on this matter, including the exploration of reasonable, less restrictive alternatives before powerful psychoactive drugs are prescribed. Education of facility staff, both nursing and medical, is imperative.

MORE SUBACUTE NATURE OF THE NF POPULATION

Various cost containment efforts, such as the Medicare prospective payment system (PPS) through diagnosis-related groups (DRGs), focus on reduction in length and intensity of patient stays in acute care hospitals. These efforts produce ripple effects on NFs. Specifically, some older patients are being discharged from hospitals "quicker and sicker" than they would have been in the past. Frequently, these patients enter NFs for relatively short periods to receive subacute medical care and rehabilitation services to bridge the gap between the hospital and a safe return to home. These individuals generally require a higher intensity of health-related services from the NF (Swan, de la Torre, & Steinhart, 1990) than do traditional long term NF residents for whom goals may be more modest and custodial in nature. NFs today must take the "quicker and sicker" factor into consideration in the hiring, training, and assignment of staff, the assessment and treatment of individual residents, and periodic reevaluation of general facility orientation and operations.

CONCLUSION

Older persons who reside in NFs present many interesting medicolegal challenges for the health care professionals who serve them there. These professionals must remember that the NF resident generally deserves the same rights as are guaranteed to persons residing in the community (Kane et al., 1997) and may additionally be entitled to claim certain other rights by virtue of placement in the NF. Both generic and specific resident rights entail particular duties of which health care professionals must be fully knowledgeable.

Chapter 10

Legal Considerations in Home Health Care

Most older people who have problems requiring long-term care services strongly prefer to remain in their own homes and receive those services in that setting, rather than to move into an institution or facility. Largely in response to this overwhelming consensus, as well as to economic factors such as anticipated savings by avoiding or delaying nursing facility (NF) placement, the home care industry in the United States has burgeoned in size and complexity over the past couple of decades.

A broad range of different services fall within the general rubric of home care. Health-related services entail medical, skilled nursing, home health aide, physical therapy, occupational therapy, respiratory therapy, and similar activities taking place within the patient's home. These services usually are delivered through the auspices of a formal home health agency (HHA) and by private physicians working in collaboration with HHA staff (Brickner, Kellogg, Lechich, Lipsman, & Scharer, 1996). Many older persons require, either instead of home health services or in addition to them, personal care (e.g., bathing and dressing), homemaker services (e.g., cooking and cleaning), and/or case management; these services may be provided through HHAs or by individual independent providers (Kapp, 1996d). Although personal and homemaker services affect millions of older persons and substantial amounts of money, in this chapter, I concentrate primarily on the health-related aspects of home care.

Home care providers may be organized, from a legal and financial perspective, in a variety of different ways. In terms of ownership, a home care agency may be either (1) public or governmental, (2) private nonprofit, or (3) proprietary or for-profit (investor-owned). Private nonprofit agencies are those that are owned and operated by a private group, such as a religious, fraternal, or community organization, but without stockholders or investors who expect to be paid financial dividends out of profits generated by the agency. These types of agencies are sometimes termed "charitable" or "voluntary."

Private nonprofit and proprietary HHAs may operate either independently or as part of a corporate chain. In the first situation, the agency usually is incorporated as an entity that exists legally and financially on its own; whereas in the latter, a large corporation may own and run (or hire a management firm to run) several different HHAs under one organizational and financial umbrella. In addition, HHAs that are owned and operated by a hospital or NF have become increasingly common. Such an affiliation may result from the parent institutions either developing its own HHA or purchasing an existing one.

Regardless of ownership status, most HHAs enter into a variety of legal and financial arrangements with other health and human service providers (e.g., hospitals, durable medical equipment suppliers, NFs, and employment agencies) pertaining to the recruitment and servicing of clients. These arrangements may be informal (unwritten) but often are formal (written); they include contracts and subcontracts for services or products, as well as joint ventures. Many other kinds of organizational arrangements may exist between an HHA and other corporations simultaneously.

In a joint venture, an HHA and another corporation, such as a hospital, agree to work together for the purpose of attracting and serving home care clients. A joint venture may take the form of a general or limited partnership or a new corporation.

An HHA also may have relationships with health maintenance organizations (HMOs). In return for a prospectively paid single premium, an HMO promises to provide comprehensive health care, which in many HMO contracts includes home care, to its members. An HMO may satisfy this obligation either by owning and operating its own HHA or by contracting with an existing one to provide services to HMO members in return for payments (based on either a capitation or a fee-for-service formula) from the HMO.

An HHA also may enter into relationships with preferred provider organizations or arrangements (PPOs/PPAs). Although the variety of specific forms it may take is virtually infinite, essentially a PPO/PPA is an agreement by a group of providers to serve a defined group of clients, such as the employees of a large corporation, at a reduced rate. In return, the organization with control over that group of consumers (for instance, a large corporation that provides health care coverage for its employees, retirees, and their dependents) creates economic incentives for members of the consumer group to use the "preferred" providers. Slightly more extreme in terms of the economic incentives created are exclusive provider organizations (EPOs). By joining with PPOs/PPAs or EPOs, an HHA may, by agreeing to charge reduced rates, secure a defined segment of the potential patient market.

A detailed analysis of these different organizational forms and their legal ramifications is beyond the scope of this book. Suffice it to say here that an HHA should retain competent legal counsel to assist it in considering, negotiating, and executing any advantageous arrangements with other provider agencies (McAdams, 1997). Specific questions that HHA staff and directors should pose to legal counsel about any contemplated agreement include those relating to tax implications, resulting locus of organizational control (including managerial control over patient care staff), payment maximization considerations, legal liability exposure, and additional regulatory compliance requirements.

REGULATORY ISSUES

HHAs and their staffs, regardless of their specific organizational structure, are held legally accountable under a panoply of federal and state statutes and regulations and the case law that has interpreted them.

Licensure

Traditionally, licensure of both individual and organizational health care providers has been a matter of state responsibility. Presently, at least 41 jurisdictions require the licensure of HHAs by the state. Most state licensure statutes follow the federal Medicare Conditions of Participation (COP) regulations (discussed below) on home care, although several states have enacted more stringent provisions. Many statutory schemes delineate a bill of rights for home care clients.

Because licensure in those jurisdictions that have chosen to step into this area is required as the basic permission of government for an agency to conduct home care activities, licensure is applicable regardless of an agency's source(s) of funding. The state has the power to force an HHA to cease activity altogether (i.e., to permanently revoke or temporarily suspend a license) in instances of serious violation of important licensure standards, especially when client safety is compromised. Many states also have the authority under their licensure acts to impose intermediate sanctions, such as civil money fines, injunctions, criminal penalties, conditional licensure, a ban on new patients, or receivership.

In addition to the approximately 41 statutes that license the HHA directly, there exist in every state statutes that regulate individual health care professionals (such as physicians, nurses, psychologists, social workers, and physical and occupational therapists) regardless of their employment setting. The HHA must ensure that the health care professionals it employs directly or for whose services it contracts possess legally appropriate credentials, including individual professional licensure. Tasks must be assigned in conformity to licensure restrictions. The HHA must keep abreast of any limitations placed on the permissible service activities of individual health care professionals by state licensure statutes, implementing state regulations (ordinarily published by the state health or social service department) or state Attorney General interpretations of state law.

Medicare and Medicaid Certification

Under the Balanced Budget Act (BBA) of 1997, Public Law 105-33, home care continues to be a covered service under Parts A and B of Medicare (see Chapter 5). Reflecting a solid medical or noncustodial model, Medicare payment is made only if the following four conditions are met: (a) the care needed includes part-time or intermittent skilled nursing services, physical therapy, or speech therapy; (b) the patient is confined to home; (c) the physician certifies that home health care is needed; and (d) the agency providing the care is certified for quality purposes by Medicare.

In 1995 there were more than 8,700 Medicare-certified HHAs in the United States (Welch, Wennberg, & Welch, 1996). Under the Omnibus Budget Reconciliation Act (OBRA) of 1980, Public Law 96-499, Medicare certification status is open to nonprofit and proprietary HHAs both in states that license such agencies and in states that do not. Services provided by these HHAs to over 3.9 million Medicare-eligible patients in 1996 exceeded $17.7 billion.

Current federal quality standards for Medicare-participating HHAs are found in OBRA 1987, Public Law 100-203, Title IV, subpart B, as implemented in 42 C.F.R., part 484, and surveyor *Home Health Certification Process and Interpretive Guidelines* released by the Department of Health and Human Services (DHHS) on March 21, 1991. Slightly revised final regulations were published on July 18, 1991, at 56 *Federal Register* 32967–32975. The surveyor guidelines place emphasis on surveyor home visits as a basis for evaluating the quality of services, as opposed to the former almost exclusive reliance on review of documentation, a practice that had been criticized harshly. Other important sources of information about federal regulation are the Health Care Financing Administration's (HCFA's) *State Operations Manual* and its *Medicare Home Health Agency Coverage Manual*. Whether or not an HHA is in compliance with federal requirements is determined through inspections conducted by the state-designated Medicare survey agency, usually the state health department.

OBRA 87 made a number of significant changes in the COP for HHAs wishing to receive Medicare funding. Most notable are the enumeration of an extensive list of consumer rights, strict criteria for training and competency of home health aides, and requirements that the HHA operate and provide services in compliance with all applicable federal, state, and local laws and with accepted professional standards and principles that apply to professionals providing items and services in such an HHA.

Section 4022 of OBRA 87 sets forth new requirements relating to state surveys of HHAs. Most important, state survey agencies are required to conduct their surveys on a surprise, no-prior-notice basis. Section 4023, relating to enforcement, required DHHS to establish a range of intermediate sanctions short of dismissal from the Medicare program that could be imposed on HHAs found to be out of compliance with specific parts of the COP. These federal intermediate sanctions include civil money penalties, the suspension of Medicare payments, and temporary receivership. Section 4025 required the states, as a condition of receiving federal matching funds for their Medicaid programs, to set up, for clients receiving services from Medicare- or Medicaid-certified HHAs, a toll-free hotline and investigative unit for complaints about the quality of home care services being received.

The HCFA published a proposed rule to revise the home health Medicare COP on March 10, 1997, at 62 *Federal Register* 11005. The proposed requirements focus on the actual care delivered to patients by HHAs and the outcomes of that care, reflect an interdisciplinary view of patient care, allow HHAs greater flexibility in meeting quality standards, and eliminate some procedural mandates. Public comments on these proposals were being considered by the HCFA as this chapter was written.

Another regulatory issue tied to Medicare reimbursement for services is utilization review (UR). For a number of years, the necessity and appropriateness (and to a lesser extent the quality) of institutional health care services has been subject to a UR process, with payment denied for services deemed inappropriate or unnecessary. A 1986 federal statute amending section 1156 of the Social Security Act required the extension of Peer Review Organization (PRO) review to home care settings for compliance with "professionally recognized standards of care." PROs initially were required to review home care services only in circumstances when a patient was readmitted to a hospital in less that 31 days from the date of the hospital discharge. Currently, PRO investigations also are undertaken when beneficiary complaints, received by fiscal intermediaries and HCFA regional offices and directed to the PRO, concern the quality or quantity of care or access to services.

The Medicaid program (see Chapter 5) also provides some coverage for home care services on a financial means-tested eligibility basis. Home-delivered services reimbursable under Medicaid include nursing services provided by an HHA or registered nurse; medical supplies, equipment, and appliances; and physical therapy, occupational therapy, speech pathology, and audiology services provided by a licensed practitioner. A number of states expand public funding for home care services, especially those provided by homemakers and home health aides. This expansion is financed in one of two ways: (1) with a Medicaid Home and Community-Based Waiver that allows Medicaid dollars (which are partially derived from the federal government) to be used for supportive, rather than purely medical, services (Melden, 1995); or (2) with state money separately appropriated for this purpose through line item legislation. Section 440.70 of 42 C.F.R. specifies that HHAs participating in the Medicaid program must meet Medicare COP. Home care consumers and their families also pay for home health services out of private funds when eligibility for public funding is not available or when cost sharing is imposed.

Regulation of Business Aspects

In addition to regulation aimed at patient care standards, a panoply of federal and state laws regulate many of the business aspects of home care delivery. HHAs must comply with all pertinent state health planning and certificate-of-need laws before creating or expanding services. The federal Medicare-Medicaid Antifraud and Abuse Amendments of 1977 and Medicare and Medicaid Patient and Program Protection Act of 1987, Public Law 100-93, prohibit any form of kickback, rebate, or unfair inducement for health care referrals of patients whose care is paid for by public funding programs. The Sherman Antitrust Act and the Robinson-Patman Price Discrimination Act, Public Law 74-692, regulate methods of economic competition among home care providers.

VOLUNTARY ACCREDITATION

In addition to the public, or governmental, mandatory forms of regulation just discussed, there exist a variety of private, voluntary forms of accreditation by nongovernmental organizations in the home care arena. Although such accreditation is not obligatory (it often is considered a form of self-regulation) in the same way that compliance with governmental regulations is legally required, there may be strong incentives—in terms of prestige, competition for patients and staff, and affiliations with other organizations—encouraging HHAs to achieve voluntary accreditation.

The most significant private organization currently involved in accrediting home care programs is the Joint Commission on Accreditation of Healthcare Organizations (JCAHO). Standards contained in JCAHO's

Accreditation Manual for Home Care (1999) apply to both hospital-based and freestanding HHAs.

The JCAHO's on-site survey process includes an in-depth review of an HHA's management and delivery of care to individuals in their place of residence. Included in this survey process are staff and management interviews, home visits and interviews with patients or their caregivers, home care record documentation review, and a review of the HHA's clinical and administrative policies, including quality assurance (QA) activities, governing body bylaws, financial policies and statements, and promotional materials.

In more than half the states, JCAHO accreditation automatically qualifies an HHA for state licensure. In those states, JCAHO inspection reports concerning a particular HHA are available to the public under the state's Freedom of Information Act. Since September 28, 1993, HCFA has considered JCAHO's standards and survey process to be consistent with Medicare and Medicaid requirements for HHAs. This means that HHAs can be deemed Medicare-certified by achieving JCAHO accreditation (JCAHO, 1995), 58 *Federal Register* 35007–35017 (June 30, 1993).

Several other private organizations also engage in aspects of voluntary home care accreditation. Skilled nursing services delivered in the home are accredited by the National League of Nursing's Community Health Accreditation Program (CHAP) under its "Standards of Excellence." CHAP accreditation was given deemed status in 1992, 57 *Federal Register* 22773 (May 29, 1992). The National Homecaring Council (NHCC), under the auspices of the Foundation for Hospice and Home Care, accredits and approves homemaker and home health aide services. Additionally, the American Nurses Association (ANA) has published standards developed by a task force of home care and nursing associations for home health nursing practice, the American Association for Continuity of Care (AACC) has published a Code of Professional Ethics, and the National Association for Home Care (NAHC) has developed a Model Home Care Bill of Rights. Home care providers should become familiar with each of these forms of voluntary professional standards.

LEGAL LIABILITY TO THE PATIENT

Relatively few civil lawsuits have been filed to date by or on behalf of patients against HHAs or individual home care professionals. However, those engaged in the provision of home care services to older persons ought to be aware of the potential liability risks associated with their activities (Brake, 1997).

Factors Influencing Potential Litigation

A number of social, economic, and technical factors combine to place home health providers at unique risk for potential litigation and civil liability. These factors relate to special characteristics regarding the nature of home health services, service settings, personnel, and payment.

For one thing, as the degree of technology associated with home care becomes increasingly complex (Arras, 1995), the opportunities for things to go disastrously wrong grow as well. Examples of new technologies that are commonly used today outside the acute care setting and in the patient's own home include continuous ambulatory peritoneal dialysis (CAPD), phototherapy and apnea monitoring for newborns, programmable infusion pumps for pain control, computerized information and emergency call transmission, and home intravenous (IV) and intraarterial treatments. Intravenous infusion treatment includes hydration and fluid nutritional maintenance, blood products, and complex antibiotic, antifungal, and chemotherapy products, among others.

Such high-tech home care services often mean greater physician involvement (AMA, 1992b) than did traditional home care services. In many instances, HHA personnel must maintain an increased and extended level of contact with the physician managing the patient's treatment. The need to provide accurate, detailed, complete information to the physician, often through telephone conversation, places a high degree of pressure on an HHA and its staff.

The permeation of home health services with high technology, combined with powerful economic incentives to keep older patients out of hospitals or to shorten their hospitalizations as much as possible, frequently results in a high sickness or acuity level within the home care patient population. Sicker home care patients demanding more intense and time-consuming attention increase the level of risk for unfavorable outcomes.

Although home care patients may be sicker than was previously the case, they frequently have higher consumer expectations regarding the availability and quality of their care. The demands of families are growing as well, including demands regarding training and preparation of family members to assist in and frequently to bear the brunt of patient care (AMA Council on Scientific Affairs, 1993a; Kapp, 1995c, 1995e, 1995f).

Unique personnel challenges increase the possible liability exposure of home care providers. As the variety and number of personnel required by HHAs rapidly expand, so too does the reliance by many HHAs on independent contractors (see below). Further, the diffusion of home care services through a wide array of sites, combined with delivery of services by a wide array of individuals, presents special management information, monitoring, coordination, and supervision difficulties for HHAs. These factors can make it more problematic to control legal risks.

Contractual Liability

One source of potential liability of HHAs to patients is based on breach or violation of contract. Contractual liability may occur under several legal theories.

An HHA may be held to have made express or implied promises to patients in the form of claims about quality or price of services contained in the HHA's advertising or marketing materials. Promises placed in promotional brochures, for instance, may be introduced in evidence to establish that an agency undertook a specific duty. Hence, the exercise of prudence in marketing efforts is essential as a risk management strategy.

An HHA also may be held liable for failure to fulfill promises made directly to clients (or their surrogates), either orally or in the form of written admission and service contracts. Such written contracts should be drafted carefully, with the assistance of knowledgeable legal counsel, and explained fully to the prospective patient (or surrogate), using these documents as an opportunity for meaningful client education. The guiding principle must be avoidance of any promise whose carrying out the HHA cannot control or for whose violation the HHA is not willing to be held answerable.

Negligence

Practical considerations limit the threat of tort or negligence liability for home care providers. (Many of these factors apply with equal force to the NF context; see Chapter 9). Several factors keep in close check the amount of money that an older home care patient might recover from his or her provider.

Because the vast majority of older home care patients already are out of the compensated job market, it would be difficult for a plaintiff to prove substantial future lost income as a result of a negligently caused injury. With the home care patient already disabled, establishing that the provider's substandard care directly or proximately caused injury to the patient usually is a hard evidentiary hurdle to surmount. Noneconomic or general damages for pain and suffering would be limited to compensation only for the few projected remaining years of life. These factors reduce the economic incentive for a patient to pursue a legal claim and for a lawyer working on a contingency fee basis to become involved.

Additionally, Medicaid recipients are discouraged from bringing civil claims because any ultimate recovery would become assets that would jeopardize their continued Medicaid eligibility; thus, the benefit of the lawsuit would accrue to the state rather than to the injured patient. Further, frail, debilitated home care consumers are unlikely to have the physical or mental wherewithal to vigorously stick with a claim that may take several years to resolve in the courts. Finally, even if a claim against a home care provider is filed by or on behalf of a patient, there are a number of defenses that may be interposed successfully to shield the provider against liability.

Nonetheless, the possibility of tort liability for professional negligence or malpractice (i.e., for unintentional errors or omissions leading to the occurrence of foreseeable and preventable harms) looms as one important legal mechanism for controlling the quality of services delivered by an HHA to its patients and for compensating patients who are injured as a result of the HHA's professional malpractice. For a plaintiff to succeed with a negligence claim against an HHA, each of four essential elements must be proved by a preponderance of the evidence: (1) a duty owed, defined by the applicable standard of care; (2) a violation or breach of that duty; (3) damage or harm; and (4) a direct or causal connection between the violation of duty and the resulting injury.

Once an HHA accepts a patient, it is obligated to provide care in a reasonable manner. As home care becomes a more sophisticated enterprise, providers' responsibilities increase because the standard of care rises to reflect the improved state of the art of acceptable practice. In deciding upon the appropriate standard of care for the reasonable or prudent provider, judges and juries typically seek out guidance from one or more of several sources of evidence.

Expert witnesses are qualified by education and experience to shed light on the relevant issues through testimony about, among other things, the current standard practice in the field. Federal and state regulations set forth public expectations about appropriate provider conduct. In some jurisdictions, violation of government requirements establishes *negligence per se*, that is, proof by itself that negligence has taken place (*Roach v. Kelly Health Care, Inc.*, 1987). In other jurisdictions, government requirements count as only one piece of evidence on the legal standard of care for tort liability purposes, to be considered along with other evidentiary sources such as the present industry consensus or usual practice. Voluntary standards of private, nongovernmental professional or trade associations help create a presumption about what the legal standard of care should be. The HHA's internal policies and procedures help define reasonable expectations on the part of patients about the quality of their care.

Under the theories of personal, vicarious, and corporate liability, an HHA and its staff may be exposed to liability for negligence to patients. Because the HHA performs, or fails to perform, its functions through the actions (or inactions) of its staff, the enterprise of selecting, monitoring, and supervising professional and paraprofessional staff represents one of the major liability danger zones in home care. The most frequently cited complaint about home care is failure of the HHA to properly supervise staff, particularly home health aides.

Staff Supervision

The courts have held HHAs liable for deficiencies in training, credentialing, supervising, and delegating responsibility among staff members. Although control over staff may be more difficult in the geographically dispersed home care situation than in an institutional environment, and recruitment of sufficient qualified staff may be frustrating or worse (Feldman, 1994), legal standards of care ordinarily are not relaxed to reflect the practical operational challenges borne by most home care providers.

An HHA's responsibilities regarding staff screening, supervision, monitoring, and assignment (including reassignment if necessary) are imposed by common law tort principles, state licensure statutes, and federal Medicare law. For instance, over 15 states require, as a condition of agency licensure, criminal background checks of individuals who may be employed as home care workers (U.S. General Accounting Office, 1996a). On the federal level, HCFA in 1994 published a regulation specifying home health aide supervision and duty requirements, 42 C.F.R. §484.36. In addition, JCAHO home health standards bear directly on this subject. At a minimum, the HHA must do the following: (a) properly screen staff, both for legal authority (e.g., professional licensure) and actual skills; (b) properly train staff, in terms of a pertinent knowledge base, techniques, attitudes, and dress and shoe codes; (c) assign tasks based only on demonstrated abilities; (d) monitor staff performance, both clinically and administratively, using agency policies and procedures as a guide; and (e) take corrective action, such as reassignment, suspension, or termination, where staff performance demands such action.

Communication Problems

Another important negligence risk in the home care situation is the possibility of patient injury caused by inadequate communication of treatment-related information among agency staff or between the HHA and other providers who are involved in the care of the same patient.

Each HHA must devise, implement, and monitor an effective system for communication of information necessary for client care for all staff, both within and outside the agency, who are involved in the client's care (keeping in mind confidentiality considerations). The communication system within the HHA and between the HHA and independent contractors (see below) should be concerned with background information and treatment plans from the referral source, physician orders (admitting, standing, and special treatment orders), and unanticipated changes in client condition that compel rapid action. The HHA's communication system must be timely and accurate in transmitting information to the party(ies) (e.g., the physician or nurse) who is/are authorized to give or carry out orders. Periodic spot audits of the HHA's communication system are advisable.

An HHA also may be held legally accountable for negligence in failing to communicate properly with its patients, when patient damage results. The HHA's responsibility to communicate with the patient (or surrogate) in the context of obtaining informed consent for various interventions has been discussed in depth in Chapter 3. However, the HHA's ongoing communication duties go well beyond the relatively narrow parameters of the informed consent doctrine. For instance, when the home care nurse neglects to provide adequate, clear instructions to the patient regarding the taking of medication and the medication is taken improperly, resulting in an overdose, a court may find the HHA liable for negligence in its communications responsibilities.

The whole area of client and family teaching and training is replete with potential problems (Kapp, 1995c), not the least of which is ensuring that instructions are presented in an accurate, consistent way. Among the factors impinging on staff attempts to educate the patient and family are shortness of time, different learning styles and paces of patient or family, a patient or family without motivation to learn, and past negative experiences of the patient or family. The HHA can reduce the effect of these constraints on the teaching/learning process by providing training information in a variety of formats, including workbooks, checklists, and audiovisual tapes.

Regardless of the method, all patient and family training should be documented carefully, along with their ability to understand and to demonstrate satisfactorily what they have absorbed. This is especially important in the case of complex equipment. Documentation of the teaching process and the progress of the patient or family caregiver in learning how to use the equipment is recommended. A safety checklist should be left in the home for the HHA staff or caregiver to complete regularly, to ensure that essential safety checks have been conducted and recorded.

An HHA's communications obligations grow out of common law tort principles predicated on the agency/patient relationship and are also based on requirements in federal and state law and voluntary standards to keep the patient fully informed about his or her condition and care.

HHAs should develop and implement written policies and procedures for carrying out these responsibilities and should conduct regular in-service training sessions to ensure compliance by staff.

Products Liability

Modern home care increasingly relies on the use of complex, sophisticated medical equipment. HHAs frequently supervise the use of oxygen, suction machines, home ventilators, pacemaker communication devices, alternating pressure mattresses, apnea monitors, electric beds, orthopedic devices, and hyperalimentation and chemotherapy mechanisms, among many others.

A variety of problems can occur with the use of medical equipment (even assuming the equipment has been prescribed properly in the first place) that can result in legal risk if the patient is injured. The machinery may fail to function properly as a result of a defect in the equipment itself. The machinery may be manufactured properly but installed incorrectly. Even when correctly manufactured and installed, equipment may malfunction when a home care professional or paraprofessional uses it improperly, either because of lack of knowledge and skill or because of carelessness in the particular instance. Finally, in the home care setting the equipment may malfunction because the patient or family caregiver uses it improperly, either through sloppiness or because of inadequate training by the HHA. In any of these situations, the consequences for the patient who depends on the equipment may be dire, and litigation may ensue.

For legal purposes, the HHA is considered to act both as a professional service provider and as the seller of a product. The sufficiency of its professional services is determined according to a negligence standard, that is, whether those services were of a quality that would be acceptable to other reasonable, prudent HHAs. In its role as a seller (or rental agent) of a piece of equipment, the HHA is evaluated according to a different (from malpractice or professional negligence) standard, namely, according to principles of products liability. Under products liability law, the seller of a product is legally liable for injuries caused to the purchaser if the product malfunctions due to inherent defects, even if the seller was not personally at fault. The manufacturer of the equipment and other companies in the chain of supply also may be held accountable without fault. Beyond liability as a seller for inherent defects, the HHA may be held responsible under a negligence standard for its errors and omissions in operating or installing the equipment or in training the patient or caregiver to use it.

For these reasons, HHAs must make sure that equipment is properly installed and operates correctly. The HHA must write, implement, and monitor policies and procedures for preventing equipment failure and providing backup support. Many HHAs supply clients with generators, battery rechargers, and backup systems for electricity-dependent equipment.

All equipment should be inspected initially and regularly thereafter for proper function and condition, with these precautions documented. There should be a clear, written delineation of responsibilities among equipment suppliers along the entire equipment supply chain regarding warranty, maintenance, emergency repair, backup systems, and round-the-clock availability. The JCAHO has established standards for the selection, inspection, monitoring, and use of medical equipment in the patient's home, as well as for the training of staff, patients, and caregivers. It is likely that courts will adopt these industry standards as the minimum level of performance that home care consumers are entitled to expect.

Often, when the HHA obtains equipment for the patient's home use through the manufacturer or an independent supplier, the manufacturer or supplier is the most knowledgeable party concerning that specific piece of equipment. Generally, state home care licensure statutes and regulations require that teaching about the use of that equipment be conducted by licensed professionals, such as a nurse or physical therapist who works for the HHA. Licensure provisions ordinarily preclude HHAs from delegating away teaching responsibility from themselves to the manufacturer or supplier because these entities are not licensed as HHAs and do not regularly employ professional staff with appropriate licensure credentials. As a realistic matter, however, an HHA should include representatives from the manufacturer or supplier in its teaching activities for the patient and/or caregiver. Contracts between the HHA and independent contractors from whom it purchases medical equipment should include stipulations obligating the manufacturer or supplier to assist HHA staff in patient and caregiver training concerning equipment provided.

Relations with Independent Agencies and Contractors

HHAs rely heavily on independent agencies and practitioners to supply them with certain workers who provide services to clients. The primary HHA faces potential liability under the doctrine of apparent or ostensible agency when the patient (or surrogate) reasonably believed, because of the HHA's conduct, that the independent contractor was acting on behalf of the HHA. In addition to exposure under apparent or ostensible agency principles, an HHA also faces liability directly, under the principles of corporate responsibility, for negligence as an agency in the selection of independent contractors and the monitoring of their performance. The primary HHA is obligated to exercise due care, according to industry standards, in its selection and monitoring of independent contractors. Industry standards in this regard are contained in most state HHA licensure acts, in federal Medicare and Medicaid regulations, and in JCAHO home care standards.

A provision that an HHA ought to consider negotiating and including in its contracts with outside agencies is an indemnification, or "hold harmless," clause. That clause spells out the respective rights and responsibilities of the parties in the event of a lawsuit brought by or on behalf of a patient. A release of liability contained in a contract between the primary HHA and the independent contractor or supplier may not be legally valid if it purports to limit a party's responsibility for its own negligence, especially if the parties hold unequal bargaining power. However, each party may agree to be responsible only for its own acts and omissions, in return for the other party's similar promise. In other words, a vendor or seller may promise to "hold harmless" the primary HHA for any injury caused by the vendor's negligence, as distinguished from the primary HHA's negligence; if, in such a case, the primary HHA were ordered to compensate the patient for a negligently caused injury, the vendor would be obligated to indemnify or pay back to the primary HHA the amount that the HHA had been forced to pay the patient.

Acceptance, Transfer, and Discharge of Clients

An HHA's legal duties to each patient grow out of the professional relationship that is formed between the two parties. Hence, one of the most fundamental issues the HHA confronts is whether to enter into a professional relationship with a particular individual in the first place; a related question is when an ongoing relationship with a patient may be terminated (Popovich et al., 1996).

Federal regulations require that an HHA accept patients only when there exists a reasonable expectation that the patient's medical, nursing, and social needs can be met adequately by the HHA in the patient's residence. The Americans With Disabilities Act (ADA) (see Chapter 6) prohibits discrimination in the provision of services on the basis of a potential patient's disability, when "reasonable accommodations" by the provider would render the patient able to benefit from the services sought. JCAHO home care standards provide detailed criteria for the admission, acceptance of referrals, initial assessment process, and acceptance or refusal of patients.

Although the HHA may place great weight on the recommendation of a referring physician or facility, it may not legally delegate its duty to perform an adequate assessment and to make the ultimate decision concerning admission of a new patient. New referrals must be evaluated carefully to ensure that the patient is medically stable or that predictable instability, as in the case of a dying patient, can be managed; that there is a desire for home care; that the home environment is safe and suitable for the delivery of care; that the needs of the patient can be met safely and effectively by the HHA; and that satisfactory financial arrangements can be made.

Often a predischarge hospital visit and a home assessment visit are necessary during the initial evaluation. Problems—particularly regarding the lack or adequacy of a family caregiver who will act in the absence of the paid home care provider—should be discussed with the physician and the patient (or the patient's surrogate) and carefully documented.

Information about patient education and informed consent should be communicated to the patient (or surrogate), both orally and in writing, at or prior to admission. Patients should be instructed about their options and other available resources and services. Realistic patient, family, and physician expectations should be fostered by carefully explaining the scope and limitations of the agency's services.

The other side of the coin is determining under what circumstances an HHA may transfer or discharge a patient for whom it has been caring. Because patients may suffer adverse physical and mental reactions (akin to "transfer trauma") as a result of such changes in status, care in making and implementing these decisions is needed. In accepting a patient for care, an HHA generally becomes, in effect, a case manager for that patient (at least insofar as home care–related services are concerned). In terminating a relationship, the HHA must be careful to avoid abandoning the patient—that is, leaving the patient who continues to need home care services in the lurch without adequate access to a competent, acceptable source of care.

A patient may be discharged to an equivalent or more appropriate setting but may not merely be dropped. To avoid liability for patient abandonment or dumping, the HHA must develop and implement a satisfactory discharge planning program. JCAHO standards for home care provide specific guidelines for the transfer and discharge of patients.

The process of planning the patient's eventual discharge from the HHA cannot begin too early. Ideally, discharge planning should begin immediately at the initial assessment visit, to help identify the goals of home care, what post–home care services will be needed, and how best to obtain them. Patients and families who have been kept involved in the discharge planning process all along the way are much less likely to feel abandoned when the relationship is terminated. Patients and families must be informed about other funding sources, community and social services, and further alternatives once they are no longer in need of or eligible for home care. It is important to document all discharge planning efforts and alternatives suggested.

Miscellaneous Areas of Liability Exposure

Chapter 7 explicates the problem of elder abuse and its legal ramifications. An HHA may be held criminally (*Caretenders, Inc. v. Commonwealth*, 1991) and civilly liable for patient abuse or neglect committed by its staff.

Additionally, HHAs must have clear, written policies and procedures regarding the detection and reporting by staff of suspected patient abuse or neglect by caregivers or others in the home. Failure to comply with mandatory reporting requirements may subject the HHA and individual staff members involved to criminal prosecution. In addition, the HHA could face possible civil litigation brought by or on behalf of an abused or neglected patient, on the theory that a timely report to adult protective services (APS) could have prevented or mitigated some of the later abuse or neglect. It is important to remember that mandated reporting of suspected abuse does not depend on the patient's permission and must occur even over the patient's objection.

The legal definitions of abuse and neglect are not much help in delineating circumstances under which intervention by the home care provider and the state is both justified and required (Kapp, 1995h). Home care providers are privy to private family conflicts and have the responsibility to sort out conflicts that represent abuse and neglect from those that are merely the normal arguments and hassles of family life. Home care personnel may identify with the stress experienced by a family in cases of abuse and neglect, which can result in a reluctance to report the incident to public authorities. A distinction, therefore, is necessary between deliberate abuse and unintentional harm to vulnerable older persons. The home care provider may find itself increasingly involved in identifying unintentional harms to patients and working with the family to develop better coping methods and providing alternative services and support.

Another potential source of liability in home care stems from the unauthorized release of patient information. The legal requirements of confidentiality, as well as its limited exceptions, are discussed in Chapter 4 and are fully applicable to health-related services delivered in the home care setting.

Defenses to Liability Claims

Several different kinds of legal defenses are available to counter a claim of negligence that might be brought against home care providers. One type of defense is procedural, such as the expiration of the applicable statute of limitations. Another category of defense would be denial of one or more of the plaintiff's essential elements of proof, namely, the duty or standard of care; deviation from that duty, or fault; injury or damage; and proximate causation.

In home care settings, as noted earlier, it may be especially difficult for patients to establish the element of causation, because the defendant may be able to argue persuasively that fault by the patient or caregiver was just as likely as improper conduct by the HHA to have brought about the patient's injury. Under the contributory negligence defense, a defendant is not legally liable, despite negligence, if the plaintiff was at fault too and the injury was caused at least in part by the plaintiff's error. Thus, if an HHA improperly installs a device in the home, but the caregiver makes the situation worse by using the equipment in an improper manner, in a contributory negligence jurisdiction the HHA would be relieved of any responsibility. Many states have moved to a comparative negligence standard, in which the complete defense afforded by the contributory negligence rule is replaced by a rule that relieves negligent defendants of responsibility only to the extent or degree that the plaintiff's own fault contributed to his or her injury.

An HHA might also argue the defense of assumption of risk in opposition to a negligence claim. Under the assumption of risk principle, a defendant is relieved of responsibility if the plaintiff voluntarily assumed a known risk that materialized and caused injury. Thus, for instance, if a patient is told that he or she may suffer a negative reaction to a specific drug and such a reaction does occur, the patient cannot blame the HHA for the happening of the risk that the patient voluntarily and knowingly assumed.

Documentation

In Chapter 4 and elsewhere, I emphasize the importance of complete, timely, accurate documentation of patient care. Adequate patient records are essential not only for liability prevention and claims defense but also for licensure, certification, and reimbursement purposes. Federal and state law set minimum requirements for record keeping, and JCAHO home care standards contain an entire chapter on the subject.

Special documentation challenges arise in home care because the supervision of care often is at a distance, two or more providers may share responsibility for a patient's care, physician orders regularly are obtained by telephone, environmental factors and interventions by family members must be taken into account, and many of the personnel are either independent contractors or employed part-time. Specific areas in which special documentation efforts must be exerted by the HHA include admission assessments; informed consent; verbal orders; emergency responses, including notifying the physician of patient instability; and charting of ongoing stable conditions as well as any unusual developments.

Risk Management Strategies

Many HHAs have always engaged in some risk-management activities, mainly through their financial offices, such as safety programs, insurance coverage, asset management, and corporate configuration to reduce legal exposure. Today, however, the home care industry is too large and complex to do risk management on a piecemeal, ad hoc basis in the face of a precarious legal climate. HHAs need to implement comprehensive, formal risk management systems designed to reduce legal (and thus financial) exposure resulting from injuries to patients (American Society for Healthcare Risk Management, 1995).

A full discussion of the structure and operation of a risk management system (Rozovsky & Rozovsky, 1993) is beyond the scope of this book. At the least, liability insurance coverage or a funded self-insurance program, as well as extensive staff education, should be included. Written HHA policies and procedures are imperative for a variety of topics. In addition, an occurrence- or incident-reporting and follow-up system is an essential building block of risk management. Incident reports are written, contemporaneous records of events that function to (1) inform management so that it can identify trends and take preventive or corrective action and (2) inform legal counsel so that he or she can evaluate particular risks and prepare to prevent or defend a lawsuit. There are several strategies for protecting confidentiality of incident reports under attorney-client privilege and the attorney–work product doctrine.

There is another important component of risk management in home care, where supervision is so diffuse and care and supplies often are provided on a contractual basis. This is a system giving patients and families the chance to provide feedback directly to management about their perceptions of the quality of services received. These perceptions—particularly when negative—should be investigated and acted upon by HHA management to head off or mitigate potential problems and to maintain good relations generally with patients and their families. In the final analysis, maintaining good relations with those to whom the agency owes a duty— and thus those who might qualify as possible plaintiffs in a malpractice lawsuit—represents the most effective risk management strategy of all.

A further strategy with risk management implications is the creation of an ethics committee. Ethics committees may be developed and/or trained ethics consultants retained to assist HHAs to foresee and prepare for a wide array of management challenges (Kapp, 1995f). An ethics committee is a formal, multidisciplinary group composed of representatives from both within and outside an HHA who bring to the table a variety of relevant perspectives and areas of expertise. The actual composition, structure, and operation of an ethics committee are matters to be decided upon at the level of the particular HHA. Similarly, the HHA must decide which of the following functions its own ethics committee will pursue: policy formulation and review; staff, patient, family, and public education; concurrent case review; and/or retrospective case review. An HHA may opt to sponsor its own ethics committee or to pool resources with other HHAs in a regional effort.

If an ethics committee is assigned to concurrent case review, it may operate either in an advisory capacity or merely as a forum for the expression of various viewpoints. Virtually no ethics committees are authorized to render binding decisions for an HHA or institution, although in a few cases courts have cited ethics committee recommendations in support of upholding the propriety of provider conduct. While ethical analysis ought to be the focus of activity for this type of committee, positive risk management by-products are inevitable. Moreover, the establishment of some regular process (of which an ethics committee is one example) for resolving ethical problems regarding patient care is now part of the JCAHO's accreditation standards for HHAs.

END-OF-LIFE ISSUES

People died at home 40 years ago, and few members of the public or the health professions gave that natural phenomenon much thought. As the technological capabilities of modern medicine have advanced, however, the locus of life's conclusion has changed for many to institutional settings.

Ironically, we are now in the process of coming full circle. Today's technology enables us to medically treat many patients at home who earlier would have needed to receive treatment in the hospital. At the same time, an increasing number of people wish to and believe they can exercise personal control over that technology better in the home setting than as inpatients in a health care institution.

The advent of high-tech home care for dying persons raises special legal concerns, as home moves from a place where treatment decisions made elsewhere are carried out to a site where decision making itself happens (Kapp, 1995g). For example, by 1998, statutes had been enacted in at least 32 states to ensure that terminally ill persons at home are not resuscitated against their will by emergency medical services (EMS) teams. Legal concerns pertinent to end of life decision making are addressed in Chapter 11.

ASSISTED LIVING

In response to a broad public demand for more "homelike" long-term care alternatives for older persons whose deficits and needs for help with activities of daily living (ADLs) exceed those usually managed in private homes but who desperately desire to avoid NF placement, a burgeoning assisted living industry has emerged (R. A. Kane & Wilson, 1993). In 1997, the Assisted Living Federation of America (ALFA) estimated that as many as 40,000 assisted living facilities (ALFs) were caring for up to 1 million residents. Precise numbers of facilities and residents are difficult to obtain because there is no generally accepted definition of assisted living and no systematic means of counting those facilities.

Although there is no agreed-upon, standardized definition, assisted living has come to be understood as a residential setting where access to limited, delineated 24-hour health, social, and personal care services are available and personal autonomy provides a philosophical framework for decision making. It is a departure from the more medicalized, institutional model characterizing NFs (K. B. Wilson, 1995). ALFs attempt to create an environment that feels more residential than institutional.

Current state regulation of ALFs is very inconsistent (Mollica & Snow, 1996). Costs ordinarily are borne out of pocket by the consumer. A variety of consumer protection and quality-of-care concerns need substantial clarification and refinement (U.S. General Accounting Office, 1997a).

Essential to the success of this developing service/residential model is commitment by service providers and consumers (and their families) to the underlying paradigm of homelike individual autonomy and self-determination rather than the traditional institutional care watchword of safety and protection as the highest priority. Under the autonomy paradigm, individuals are presumed to be adults who are capable of formulating, expressing, and acting upon their own values and preferences regarding both major life decisions and smaller but nonetheless important choices arising in everyday life (Kapp, 1997c).

Tension between the traditional safety/protection model, on the one hand, and the autonomy paradigm, on the other, will present some difficult legal issues as the assisted living movement proliferates and matures. In specific cases, this tension may best be mediated through a process of negotiated or managed risk in which the respective expectations, rights, and responsibilities of all involved parties are determined and explicitly delineated prospectively (Gordon, 1997; Kapp & Wilson, 1995).

Chapter 11

Medicolegal Issues at the End of Life

INTRODUCTION

Death is a natural process and a uniquely personal experience (Holstein, 1997; Nuland, 1994). Most people, if pressed to categorize them, would probably term the major controversies surrounding death ethical rather than medical or legal. These controversies are of long standing (Emanuel, 1994) but are intensified today by the development and proliferation of sophisticated, expensive medical technologies that are capable of maintaining some semblance of human life almost indefinitely (R. S. Kane, 1996). In the overwhelming majority of situations in which decisions must be made about the initiation, continuation, withdrawal, or withholding of life-sustaining medical treatments (LSMTs) for a critically ill patient, a resolution is reached and implemented on the basis of a process of discussion and negotiation (Faulkner, 1998; Johnston, Pfeifer, & End-of-Life Study Group, 1998; Miller, Coe, & Hyers, 1992) involving the patient (where able to participate), family or significant others, physician, other members of the health care team, and perhaps some form of institutional ethics committee (IEC) (discussed below). In most of these situations, decisions quite properly are made and carried out without asking for the intervention of the courts (Hanson, Danis, Mutran, & Keenan, 1994; Kapp, 1996/97; Prendergast & Luce, 1997).

In some cases, however, the informal, extrajudicial decision-making process breaks down, and the parties go to court to initiate a judicial ruling. Judges are asked to decide these questions, not because they have any special expertise or wisdom but because it is perceived that only they can provide health care professionals with civil and criminal immunity for their actions. In seeking this immunity, legal considerations quickly transcend ethical and medical judgments (Annas, 1978). Most state courts that have become embroiled in LSMT issues have indicated in their opinions that such decisions are inherently private and medical in nature and therefore best resolved without judicial intervention. Generally, courts have considered judicial intervention appropriate only as a matter of last resort, when there are irreconcilable differences among the participants.

Nevertheless, some LSMT cases have ended up in court. A body of case law has evolved over the past two decades since the famous Karen Quinlan (In re Quinlan, 1976) decision in New Jersey. The various courts that have confronted these issues have achieved a high degree of consensus on the major points, although there remains diversity among jurisdictions on some secondary questions. LSMT cases ending up in court are relatively small in number, considering that the American Hospital Association in its *amicus curiae* (friend of the court) brief in the Cruzan case (discussed below) asserted that 70% of the 1.3 million Americans who die in health care institutions each year die after a decision to forgo medical treatment has been made. Few trial court judges have the opportunity to hear an LSMT dispute, and those who deal with such cases rarely have heard more than one. Nonetheless, these well-publicized cases exert an enormous intimidating influence on modern medical practice and the rights of patients and families within the health care system (Kapp, 1997b). Thus, it is important that the general boundaries or parameters for LSMT decision making set by the courts, as well as by legislatures, be understood by those who have to render professional services within those legal limits.

Death, of course, is not a subject limited to the elderly. Men and women of all ages die every day. It is an undeniable fact of life, however, that proximity to one's mortal end increases with each day that one lives. Six percent of Medicare enrollees die annually (Webster & Berdes, 1990). Thus, no treatment of geriatrics would be adequate without some attention paid to legal issues confronting the health care professional caring for older patients who have entered the process of dying. My treatment of this subject within this chapter is sketchy at best; for a more detailed analysis of "right to die" or "death with dignity" questions, the reader is referred to the numerous references cited here and other information sources listed in the Appendix.

LIMITING MEDICAL TREATMENT

Competent Patients

There is virtually universal agreement today that a decisionally capable adult patient has a right to make personal medical treatment decisions, including the right to accept or refuse even LSMT (American College of Physicians, 1998). Based on the ethical principle of autonomy or self-determination, the competent patient's right to choose has several firm legal underpinnings (Meisel, 1995).

A significant number of judicial opinions base this prerogative on the right to privacy that has been read into the Bill of Rights of the federal Constitution. In *Cruzan v. Director of Missouri Department of Health* (1990), one of only two "right to die" cases decided by the U.S. Supreme Court, eight Supreme Court Justices held that a competent patient's right to make LSMT choices is guaranteed as a liberty interest falling within the Due Process clause of the Fourteenth Amendment of the U.S. Constitution. Other courts have additionally relied on the respective state constitutions and state statutes and regulations. In addition, the common law principle of respect for bodily integrity that undergirds the doctrine of informed consent (see Chapter 3) extends and applies with full force to LSMT decisions. Under any of these theories, it is now universally accepted that a competent patient need not be terminally ill (i.e., imminently dying) for the right to choose to be relevant and that there is no meaningful legal distinction between withholding LSMT, on one hand, and withdrawing it, on the other.

The patient's right to reject LSMT is not absolute and thus conceivably can be defeated in certain situations. But it is considered a fundamental right and hence can be overruled only when society has a compelling interest (an extremely vital need) that can be fulfilled only if medical intervention is forced on the unwilling patient. The five compelling societal (state) interests that have been mentioned by various courts as potential justifications for overriding the patient's wishes in particular fact situations are as follows: (1) preventing suicide, (2) preserving life, (3) protecting innocent third parties, (4) maintaining the ethical integrity of the health professions, and (5) maintaining institutional order. These societal interests have had far more theoretical than practical impact as justifications for overriding patient self-determination in actual litigated cases. Put differently, except for a few cases noted under "protecting innocent third parties" (statement 3, below), courts have not actually relied on these stated factors to order medical treatment over the express, voluntary, informed objections of a competent adult patient. These purported societal interests are especially weak in the case of a critically ill older person. Each of these interests is mentioned here briefly.

1. Suicide is dealt with later in this chapter. Suffice it to say here that suicide is not involved in cases of refusal of LSMT, because suicide by definition occurs only when the patient himself or herself intentionally attempts to bring about death through his or her own affirmative actions (Quill, Lo, & Brock, 1997).

2. Courts have declined to rely on the preservation-of-life rationale to overrule the voluntary, informed decision of a mentally capable adult. The preservation-of-life rationale carries very little weight if the patient is

seriously debilitated and successful return to a normal, meaningful quality of life if treated is remote.

3. The courts have acknowledged a compelling societal need to protect innocent third parties (invariably minor or otherwise dependent children) from suffering unnecessary material or psychological harm. This interest has led, in a few cases, to judicially enforced medical treatment, although even here the courts are reluctant to intervene unless the threat of harm to the children is serious, the prognosis for the patient without intervention is dire, and the prognosis for the patient with medical treatment is for a full recovery to a normal, productive life. It is quite improbable that the natural death of an aged, critically ill individual would threaten to create any new ward of the state.

4. Society has a compelling interest in safeguarding the ethical integrity of the health professions, which is furthered by ensuring that members of those professions are not required legally to engage in conduct that is fundamentally and diametrically contrary to the deep-seated normative principles of their professions (Loftus, 1990; Miles, Singer, & Siegler, 1989). For an aged, critically ill patient, the withholding or withdrawal of aggressive medical intervention does not pose a significant problem in this respect, as such conduct under those circumstances would be fully consistent with the prevailing modern precepts of the health care professions. Among the professional organizations and groups of commentators who have officially endorsed the LSMT decisional rights of a competent adult are the American College of Physicians (ACP) (1998), American College of Chest Physicians, Society of Critical Care Medicine (1992), AMA Council on Ethical and Judicial Affairs (1992), and American Academy of Hospice and Palliative Medicine (1997).

5. The maintenance-of-institutional-order rationale has been cited by a few judges in forcing food on hunger-striking prisoners. It is conceivable that this theory could be interpolated to medical care in other types of institutions, such as nursing facilities (NFs) or public mental hospitals, but such an extension seems far-fetched and most unlikely.

In most cases involving older, severely debilitated patients, their competent nontreatment decision and its inevitable consequence—death—should be respected as proper and even good. Such respect may be viewed as one—although the most gripping—aspect of the professional/patient relationship. This does not mean that the health care professional must or should stand meekly by when an older patient refuses LSMT that the professional feels is clinically indicated and in the patient's best interests. Several courses of action are available and appropriate in the latter situation.

First, the health care professional should be satisfied that the patient's refusal is voluntary, competent, and informed and should reject any decision that fails to meet these three requirements. Consultation, including psychiatric consultation (Sullivan & Youngner, 1994), should be freely sought, and the clinical basis for the professional's ultimate judgment regarding the refusal's validity or invalidity should be thoroughly and objectively documented in the patient's medical record. When the refusal of clinically indicated, appropriate treatment is felt to be involuntary, incompetent, (e.g., unduly determined by clinical depression [Ganzini, Lee, Heintz, Bloom, & Fenn, 1994; Lee & Ganzini, 1992, 1994]), or misinformed or uninformed, the health care professional should seriously consider initiating court review and determination of the legal legitimacy of the patient's decision, with the possible result of the judicial appointment of a substitute or proxy decision maker. Alternatives to formal guardianship (see Chapter 8) should first be explored to protect the patient.

Second, if the health care professional considers the proffered medical intervention to be both necessary and proper for a particular patient, he or she is not only authorized but obligated to use maximum persuasive powers, short of coercion, to try to influence the patient to reverse field (see Chapter 3). The professional should also involve the patient's family in the decision-making process to the extent that the patient permits and should try to exploit (in the positive sense) the family's persuasive capabilities.

There is no magic formula to automatically guide the health care professional in deciding how hard or how far to push the patient and family before acceding to their refusal of treatment or when to initiate or refrain from initiating formal judicial or other third-party involvement. The following are some factors that the health care professional might consider in formulating his or her conduct in these difficult situations (Asch, Hansen-Flaschen, & Lanken, 1995; Fried, Stein, O'Sullivan, Brock, & Novack, 1993; Jackson & Youngner, 1979):

1. Is the refusal based on whim or on deeply held and thoughtfully considered conviction, such as (but not limited to) religious belief?
2. What is the patient's realistic prognosis, with and without the disputed treatment, in terms of life, health, and pain and suffering?
3. How will the refusal of treatment (or the forcing of treatment) affect significant others in the patient's life?
4. Are the views of the patient and family in conflict or conformity with each other?
5. What are the views of other members of the health care team, and what positive or negative effects would respecting the patient's refusal of care have on the team, particularly those team members who have the most responsibility for daily, hands-on patient contact?
6. What financial, emotional, and physical costs are anticipated with and without the treatment in question?

7. Because most deaths (about 80% in the United States) and therefore most decisions about LSMT occur in hospitals and NFs, what is the effect of a institution's structure, rules, and character—its ethos—on the quality and product of decision making?
8. What is the patient's age, which may be relevant in assessing the life experience and accumulated values that inform and guide the patient's decision?

Acceptance of the patient's rejection of aggressive therapy should not translate into total neglect of that patient. Palliative measures—aggressive remediation of discomfort—for the critically ill patient need to be provided even when the life itself is not being prolonged (American Geriatrics Society, 1995a; Byock, 1997). In Great Britain, for example, heroin is widely used as a painkiller for terminal cancer patients. In the United States, the use of pain-relieving drugs that are likely to hasten death is legally permissible as long as the primary reason for their ordering and administration is to relieve intractable pain and that reason is amply documented in the patient's medical record. The patient and family often may need more clinical and psychological support from health care professionals after they have made their nontreatment decision than during the decision-making agony itself (Quill, 1996). The health care professional's goal should be to maintain the intactness and integrity of the person in the face of severe, increasing sickness and a deteriorating body. Any aspect of personhood—emotional, social, physical, familial, or private—may provide the locus of intervention (Cassell, 1991).

Additionally, it should be borne in mind that ordinarily there are several degrees of treatment or nontreatment that may be chosen or rejected. To recognize the competent patient's right to autonomous choice in matters concerning the treatment of the patient's own body, the health care professional must provide information about all available medically and legally acceptable options, not just information sufficient to choose between accepting or rejecting a single proposed intervention. Most patients do not have enough medical knowledge to foresee the consequences of refusing treatment on a selective basis; it is this information that the health care professional must supply. The patient's right to information about risks and outcomes—in clinical, emotional, economic, and legal terms—of alternative kinds of refusal is crucial in making a genuinely informed decision (Cohodes, 1995; Silverman, McDowell, Musa, Rodriguez, & Martin, 1997).

Incompetent Patients

A more perplexing legal and ethical dilemma is presented when the critically ill patient is mentally or physically incapable of making and expressing rational decisions regarding the initiation or continuation of LSMT. Several thousand Americans exist in persistent or permanent vegetative states (PVS) at any point in time, and millions of older persons have significant cognitive dysfunction.

For a long time, the customary practice regarding such patients has been for the health care team to confer and negotiate (Molloy, Clarnette, Braun, Eisemann, & Sneiderman, 1991) with and generally to defer to the wishes of the patient's available family members and additional significant others. The rationale for this deference is the presumption, first, that families are most likely to know what decisions the patient would make personally if he or she were decisionally capable at present and, second, that families ordinarily act honestly in the best interests of their loved ones. The former decision standard is termed "substituted judgment," and the latter is referred to as the "best interests" test.

In the vast majority of circumstances, the traditional extralegal decision-making process works well on behalf of the incapacitated patient, without any legal repercussions. Nonetheless, a body of case law has partially evolved in this area based on requests by contentious or anxious family members or health care providers to have the courts intervene into what is usually a private matter. In addition, many state legislatures also have developed relevant public policy. An examination of case law and state statutes reveals guidelines for (1) identifying appropriate surrogate decision makers for an incapacitated patient and (2) identifying appropriate substantive decision-making criteria for use by the surrogate.

Our examination must begin with the Supreme Court's 1990 *Cruzan* decision, which, although leaving many questions unresolved (Hafemeister, 1990), delineated the general legal environment for this branch of medical decision making. *Cruzan* involved a woman in her early 20s who was tragically injured in an automobile accident. Within a short period of time following her accident, Nancy Cruzan was placed in a long-term care facility owned and operated by the state of Missouri. She existed in a PVS and was kept alive by artificial feeding and hydration tubes. After several years in that status, Nancy's parents, with whom she had always enjoyed a very close relationship, requested that the feeding tubes be removed, with the inevitable result of their daughter's death. This request was refused by the attending physician and the facility on the grounds that the public policy of Missouri was a strong interest in the preservation of life, an interest that could be overcome in the case of a cognitively incapacitated patient only when there was "clear and convincing" evidence that the patient would want to forgo LSMT.

Nancy Cruzan's parents initiated a lawsuit to obtain authority to order removal of her feeding tubes. Eventually, this case made its way to the U.S. Supreme Court as the Court's first attempt to deal with the right-to-die question. Although the immediate result of the Court's 1990 decision was to deny the Cruzan family the power to order removal of Nancy's feeding tubes, the decision had several implications of great importance in setting the legal parameters for future medical decision making in LSMT situations.

First, as noted above, the Court almost unanimously ruled that, were Nancy Cruzan mentally and physically capable at the time of making and expressing her own voluntary and informed treatment choices, those choices would govern her care as a matter of her liberty rights as protected by the Fourteenth Amendment of the federal Constitution. Second, if Nancy, prior to her accident (i.e., while still decisionally capable), had clearly expressed her future treatment wishes in the event of subsequent incapacity, those expressed wishes would be entitled to respect. The patient could have (but in this case had not) accomplished this by creating an advance directive such as a living will or a durable power of attorney (DPA).

Third, the Court drew no distinction, for the decisionally incapable as well as the decisionally capable, between "terminal" illness and "nonterminal" illness. The decisional rights guaranteed to an incapacitated patient through one acting on his or her behalf were not made to depend on proof that the patient's death was imminent. Put differently, *Cruzan* is in accordance with the weight of previous judicial opinion that there exists no valid legal or ethical distinction between omission (i.e., withholding LSMT in the first place) and commission (i.e., withdrawing intervention that was already being provided) for the decisionally incapable patient. This ruling should dispel the still too common mythology that, once an LSMT has been started, it cannot thereafter be discontinued.

Fourth, the Court in *Cruzan* held that, for decisionally incapacitated patients like Nancy, it is constitutionally permissible for each particular state to establish its own public policy and standard of proof to protect incapacitated patients against medical neglect. The Court therefore upheld Missouri's policy and its state court decision that there had not been presented "clear and convincing" evidence that Nancy would want to forgo LSMT in her circumstances. However, and of vital importance, the Supreme Court left the door open for other states to adopt their own policies and standards of proof, including (a) policies embodying a less emphatic, more qualified state interest in preserving life regardless of its quality and (b) standards of proof based on a less stringent "preponderance of the evidence" (i.e., 51%) test.

In fact, only a few states require "clear and convincing" evidence of the incapacitated patient's wishes before they will allow proxy decision makers to authorize withholding or withdrawal of LSMT. This standard creates a heavy burden of proof for families who purport to represent the values of the patient (Lo, Rouse, & Dornbrand, 1990). In those states, absent straightforward, unambiguous, specific, repeated written or (perhaps) oral statements by the patient while still decisionally capable regarding the choice to forgo LSMT in certain scenarios, health care providers must err on the side of preserving life regardless of its present or future anticipated quality.

Other states have adopted legislation and/or judicial decisions that are more favorable to deferring to family prerogatives concerning the nontreatment of critically ill, decisionally incapacitated patients without advance directives. Readers are strongly advised, here as with other issues covered in this book, to consult the law of their own jurisdiction because there is variation from state to state, especially on certain technical procedural requirements. On the whole, however, the strong trend is for states to permit families of decisionally incapacitated patients who have not executed advance directives to authorize withholding or withdrawal of LSMT on a substituted judgment or, if necessary, a best-interests basis.

Under substituted judgment, the proxy decision maker is expected to act in accordance with what would be the patient's own autonomous preferences if the patient currently could make and express those preferences (B. D. White, Siegler, Singer, & Iserson, 1991). The legal preference is to rely on patient choices that have been straightforwardly, unambiguously, and repeatedly stated by the patient while able to make and express autonomous decisions. When such evidence is unavailable, however, most states permit and indeed encourage family decision making on the basis of whatever reasonable inferences about the patient's preferences may be drawn by piecing together the patient's prior informal statements and life decisions.

Substituted judgment for incapacitated patients has been criticized by some commentators as artificial or "invented consent" and too speculative on which to predicate the abatement of LSMT (Dresser, 1990; Dresser & Robertson, 1989; Ellman, 1989). In this view, substituted judgment does not account for the fact that an individual's interests change radically once that person has become decisionally incapacitated; upon decisional incapacity, one is literally no longer the "same person" as before (Dresser, 1994). According to most of these critics, LSMT should always proceed at full pace for decisionally incapacitated, vulnerable patients who failed to leave detailed, specific, explicit instructions prior to their incapacity (Bopp & Avila, 1991). The substituted judgment concept has been broadly defended, however, by others as often the best we can do to support some semblance of autonomy for patients who have lost decisional capacity (Welch, 1989).

When even inferential evidence of the patient's substituted judgment is absent, the strongly prevailing legal weight is to defer to the family's opinion about the course of care that will most likely promote the patient's best interests, as those interests would be viewed from the patient's perspective (*Harvard Law Review* Staff, 1990). Although some would argue that aggressive LSMT is always in any patient's best interests (Bopp & Avila, 1991), the much more widely held position is that a patient's quality of life may be so hopelessly diminished that the burdens of treatment outweigh any benefits and hence that death is an acceptable and perhaps preferable objective alternative. In fact, some have urged that the current approach, in which continued medical intervention is presumed and the advocate of withholding or withdrawing must overcome that presumption, be replaced at least for PVS patients by a presumption of nontreatment with a shifting of the responsibility of proof to the advocate of more intervention (Angell, 1994). The idea of weighing respective burdens and benefits, both broadly construed, has largely replaced earlier, confusing language about "ordinary" and "extraordinary" or "heroic" treatments.

Most states promote deference to the dominant role of the family in cases of LSMT decision making for incapacitated patients without advance directives (ADs) because of a presumption that the family is in a superior position to know, directly or inferentially, what the patient would want done or at least to make a good, loving judgment about the patient's best interests (Gerety, Chiodo, Kanten, Tuley, & Cornell, 1993). Although deference to family decisions has been a long tradition in medical practice (Luce, 1990) and (on the extremely rare occasions that it has been questioned) judicial opinions (Areen, 1987; E. B. Krasik, 1987), a majority of states have now formalized this deference by enacting what have been generically termed "family consent" statutes (Menikoff, Sachs, & Siegler, 1992). These statutes codify standard practice by explicitly authorizing the relatives (in an order of priority specified in the statute but ordinarily starting with the spouse) of an incapacitated patient without an AD to make LSMT decisions, at least within certain parameters. This trend is consistent with, and several state statutes are based largely on, the recommendations of the Uniform Health-Care Decisions Act (National Conference of Commissioners on Uniform State Laws, 1993).

Even in the absence of specific authorizing legislation, the traditional practice of "bumbling through" with unofficial but honest and conscientious next of kin usually has served the patient's best interests well and without causing negative legal repercussions to health care providers (Hesse, 1995). As one realistic physician has observed,

> Ethicists and lawyers advise designating the surrogate with a formal durable power of attorney for health care. Doing so, however, is rarely needed unless the best surrogate is contentious, or the care is to be given in a state where only formal designations are likely to be honored. (Lynn, 1997)

Health care professionals should encourage and enable family members or significant others to exercise their appropriate surrogate decision-making roles (American Geriatrics Society, 1995a). At the same time, the health care professional has both a legal and an ethical responsibility to identify serious conflicts of interest when the family member(s) is/are deviating from the patient's substituted judgment and best interests in order to further the family member's own agenda (Kapp, 1994a). In such rare but real situations, the presumption in favor of family decision making is rebutted, and the health care professional may have to confront the family and possibly involve an IEC (discussed below), ombudsman program, or (in extreme situations) the court to assure that the vulnerable patient is protected from unnecessary harm.

The health care professional also may need to invoke external assistance when challenged by a situation in which individual family members sharply and strongly disagree among themselves about the proper course of action and counseling and education are ineffective in reconciling the family's internal dispute. If courts must become involved in what are ordinarily private matters because of irreconcilable family differences or an obvious, serious conflict of interest between the normal decision maker and the patient, the courts are better suited to choosing a more appropriate surrogate than to making the decisions themselves about patient care (Lo et al., 1990; Parry, 1990); in only an extremely small number of cases have judges themselves actually made or ratified the LSMT decision itself or held that judges ought to be involved routinely in such direct decision making.

Foods and Fluids

One of the more controversial ethical issues surrounding LSMT decisions has concerned the status of artificial means of nutrition and hydration for the patient who is unable to eat by mouth (Ackerman, 1996; Sheiman, 1996). Some argue that nutritional sustenance, regardless of its form or mechanism, is so fundamental that it should never be denied to any person (M. J. Cox, 1998), but the overwhelming weight of ethical commentary, professional opinion, and legal authority has been in the other direction. The better view is that artificial feeding and hydration is not obligatory except where the benefits are likely to exceed the burdens imposed. The courts consistently have held that artificial means of nutrition and hydration are forms of medical intervention, that the material thus provided is more accurately characterized as a drug rather than a food, and that the same circumstances and principles that would justify the withholding or withdrawal of other kinds of LSMTs (e.g., mechanical ventilators) also justify the forgoing of artificial nutrition and hydration.

This legal proposition was reiterated by the Supreme Court in *Cruzan;* no legal or ethical distinction whatsoever was drawn between the feeding tubes that were keeping Nancy alive and other forms of medical intervention that could have been removed in appropriate circumstances. Justice O'Connor wrote:

> Artificial feeding cannot readily be distinguished from other forms of medical treatment. . . . Whether or not the techniques used to pass food and water into the patient's alimentary tract are termed "medical treatment" it is clear they all involve some degree of intrusiveness and restraint.

Any remaining confusion in this area results from a number of state living will and DPOA statutes that, on their faces, purport to limit narrowly the power of patients or their proxies to authorize the withholding or withdrawal of life-sustaining artificial feeding and hydration. These statutory provisions, attempting to draw a distinction between artificial sustenance, on one hand, and other LSMT, on the other, run counter to judicial holdings and are probably unconstitutional (Kapp, 1992b). Until these restrictive provisions are invalidated by the courts or repealed by state legislatures, health care professionals working in jurisdictions having such provisions must proceed cautiously and consult with legal counsel about specific situations involving the possible forgoing of artificial nutrition and hydration.

As is true for any other form of medical intervention, health care professionals should encourage and facilitate the active participation of the patient, if capable of participating, and/or the family in decision making regarding the use of feeding and hydration tubes (Ouslander, Tymchuk, & Krynski, 1993). This requires a balanced factual presentation of potential benefits, burdens, and limitations in patients with severe irreversible illnesses (Mitchell, Kiely, & Lipsitz, 1997). It should be explained that feeding tubes frequently are associated with the use of restraints to keep the patient from pulling out the tubes (Quill, 1989; Morrison, Meier, & Cassel, 1996).

Within the health care community, there are substantial differences in practices and attitudes concerning artificial feeding and hydration. Health care institutions must formulate, implement, and make available clear, written policies concerning their own practices and philosophy regarding artificial nutrition and hydration (Meyers & Grodin, 1991; Rabeneck, McCullough, & Wray, 1997). Among numerous other things, these policies ought to address situations of patient/family refusal of medically indicated feeding tube placement (DeChicco, Trew, & Seidner, 1997). Tube feeding policies should be included as part of the institutional protocol development process that is discussed later in this chapter. Policies should be consistent with guidelines developed by relevant professional societies (A.S.P.E.N. Board of Directors, 1997) and the Joint Commission on Accreditation of Healthcare Organizations (JCAHO).

ADVANCE HEALTH CARE PLANNING

Over the past 25 years, a great deal of attention has been focused on advance or prospective health care planning as a way for individuals to maintain some degree of control over their future medical treatment even if they become physically or mentally incapable of making and expressing autonomous choices at the time that the treatment must be contemplated (Cantor, 1993; Emanuel, 1993; King, 1996; Miles, Koepp, & Weber, 1996). Advance health care planning has also been touted as a way to avoid court entanglements in LSMT decision making, conserve scarce financial resources in a manner consistent with patient autonomy, and reduce families' feelings of burden (Jacobson et al., 1996). The Supreme Court's decision in *Cruzan*, strongly implying that Nancy could have controlled her medical destiny and spared her family the turmoil of litigation if, while decisionally capable, she had thought ahead and clearly documented her particular future treatment preferences, gave additional impetus and urgency to the concept of advance planning.

Currently, there are two main legal mechanisms available for prospective health care planning. One is the proxy directive, ordinarily in the form of a DPOA, which names a proxy or agent who is authorized to make future medical decisions on behalf of the individual delegating the authority (the "principal" or "maker") in the event of the latter's subsequent decisional incapacity. Many commentators and health care professionals favor the proxy directive because it empowers a living, breathing human advocate who can speak for the patient at the critical juncture and with whom the health care team can communicate and interact in the patient's stead (Mower & Baraff, 1993). Every state has enacted a DPOA statute, and many have enacted explicit legislation on the use of this device specifically for health care purposes. For example, a month after the Supreme Court issued its *Cruzan* decision, the New York legislature passed the New York Health Care Agents and Proxies Law (T. E. Miller, 1990; Rouse, 1990). The concept of the DPOA is discussed in detail in Chapter 8.

Living Wills

The second legal device presently available for advance health care planning is the instruction directive, usually referred to as a living will, health care declaration, or natural death declaration. This form of instruction was devised in 1969 by the Euthanasia Education Council, known subsequently as Concern for Dying and now merged with the Society for the Right to Die into Choice in Dying. The living will document was intended to be "a simple, reasonable statement of the belief in the right of the dying to die and not be kept alive by artificial and heroic measures." Within 6 years of its appearance, more than a half million copies had been distributed, frequently by religious organizations and senior citizen groups.

A variety of different formulations of the living will document have since appeared (Hoffmann, Zimmerman, & Tompkins, 1996). Many of these formulations, including a number based on particular state statutes, follow the model of the Uniform Health Care Decisions Act (National Conference of Commissioners on Uniform State Laws, 1993). An elaborate matrix form for combining value preferences with quite specific instructions regarding specific interventions in specific situations has been packaged by Ezekiel Emanual and Linda Emanuel and distributed by the American Medical Association as a comprehensive Medical Directive (Emanuel & Emanuel, 1989). Persons sometimes write out a living will in their own words. Some health care facilities have developed their own institutional advance care planning forms (Bradley, Blechner, Walker, & Wetle, 1997).

Health care professionals should consult the law in their own jurisdictions regarding procedural formalities for living wills. Prodded by the aggressive lobbying efforts of important civic and professional organizations, as well as by the arguments of respected scholars (Bok, 1976), states began to consider legislation seriously in the late 1970s that would specifically authorize the execution of and provide for the enforcement of living wills. California led the way in 1976. The President's Commission (1983) endorsed such legislation in the early 1980s. Significant endorsements have continued (Cantor, 1992). As of 1998, 48 states had enacted some version of living will or natural death legislation.

Although the specifics vary from state to state, the common theme of natural death legislation is endorsement of a patient's right, while still decisionally capable (Bradley et al., 1997; Kapp, 1994b; Silberfeld, Nash, & Singer, 1993), to sign a written directive concerning the patient's wishes about the use of LSMT in the event of subsequent serious illness and decisional incapacity. Such a directive (misnamed a living will, since it has nothing to do with distribution of property and deals with dying rather than living) frees the health care professionals and treatment facility from potential civil or criminal liability for withholding or withdrawing treatment under the specified conditions. Just as is true for the DPOA, the legal force of the living will goes into effect when the patient, after executing the document, becomes incapable of making LSMT decisions.

Even in the couple of states that have not yet adopted comprehensive natural death legislation, many individuals (especially older persons) have signed written documents that purport to be living wills anyway. Voluntary organizations have been instrumental in encouraging this planning activity. Since the *Cruzan* decision appears to have given constitutional status to an individual's liberty right to plan ahead for future decisional incapacity by documenting future LSMT preferences, advance instruction directives that accurately reflect the voluntary, informed choice of a then-competent patient ought to carry the same weight as would a document executed in a state with living will legislation.

As a practical matter, it is quite possible for the intent of a living will to be subverted (Bowers, 1996). State statutes in essence provide that, if a living will has been properly created, the attending physician must either follow its directions or refer the patient and family to a different physician who will obey it. At the least, the attending physician is admonished against interfering with such a transfer. Such a statutory provision, however, does not assure compliance with the stated instructions (SUPPORT Principal Investigators, 1995; Robb, 1997).

The attending physician may simply be unaware that the patient, at some earlier point in life, signed a living will; getting the document to accompany the patient is a difficult logistical challenge (Ghusn, Teasdale, & Jordan, 1997; Morrison, Olson, Mertz, & Meier, 1995) that has attracted a good deal of attention and innovation. The federal Patient Self-Determination Act (PSDA), discussed below, is supposed to help address this problem. The physician may thwart the effectiveness of a living will by refusing to confirm clinically that a triggering factual circumstance, such as terminal illness or PVS, has occurred. Further, even if a physician refused outright to comply with the applicable directions of a living will or to refer the patient elsewhere, it would be unusual for the patient or family to possess the physical, emotional, and financial ability to initiate legal action to compel compliance or to hold the physician liable after the fact for noncompliance.

The key thus lies with the good faith and ethical integrity of the health care professionals involved, particularly the attending physician. It is in their own legal and ethical best interests, as well as the self-determination interests of their patients, for health care professionals and the institutions in which they practice to be aware of advance planning devices and to maximize their effectiveness (Hammes & Rooney, 1998).

It may be unrealistic to expect the majority of citizens to document formally their future LSMT preferences (R. F. Johnson, Baranowski-Birkmeier, & O'Donnell, 1995). Studies indicate, however, that many patients, including older persons, are willing and even anxious to discuss

and document their future LSMT preferences in a timely and nonthreatening setting (Reilly, Magnussen, Ross, Ash, Papa, & Wagner, 1994; Joos,
Reuler, Powell, & Hickam, 1993), but they seldom initiate such communication with their physicians; the patient generally looks to the professional
to take the lead (Johnston, Pfeifer, & McNutt, 1995; Cox & Sachs, 1994;
Emanuel, Barry, Stoeckle, Ettelson, & Emanuel, 1991). However, physician
performance in facilitating timely discussion and documentation of patient
values and future LSMT choices often has been less than exemplary, for a
variety of psychological, organizational, and professional socializational
reasons (Sachs, Stocking, & Miles, 1992; Morrison, Morrison, & Glickman,
1994; Sulmasy, Song, Marx, & Mitchell, 1996). It is imperative for the medical profession to learn to overcome existing communication barriers and to
improve substantially in this respect. Not incidentally, changes in public
policy that enhanced financial reimbursement for physician time spent in
conversing with patients about LSMT matters might be quite salutary
(Emanuel, 1995; Murphy, 1990), although monetary payment will not take
the place of special training and sensitivity. Physicians ought to be especially sensitive to pertinent cultural, ethnic (Eleazer et al., 1996), socioeconomic (Hanson & Rodgman, 1996), and religious (Grodin, 1993) factors
that might influence a particular patient's attitude toward end-of-life medical interventions.

A number of strategies for enhancing physician/patient discussions
about advance health care planning and for encouraging patients to
complete formal ADs have been tested and found useful (Sachs, 1994b).
Examples of such strategies include computer reminders for physicians
(Dexter et al., 1998), providing institutional education and feedback for
physicians (Reilly et al., 1995; Markson, Fanale, Steel, Kern, & Annas, 1994)
and other professional personnel (Barnett & Pierson, 1994), structured discussions with patients and follow-up mailings (Richter et al., 1995), alter-
ing the timing of advance planning discussions (Cugliari, Miller, & Sobal,
1995), distributing informational booklets to patients (Rubin, Strull, Fialkow, Weiss, & Lo, 1994), and letting patients choose from among a selection of forms (Reinders & Singer, 1994). Direct, face-to-face discussions
between patients and nonphysician health care providers, such as social
workers, also have demonstrated promise for effectively encouraging
advance health care planning by patients (Mezey, Mitty, Rappaport, &
Ramsey, 1997). It has been suggested that hospitals appoint standing committees to encourage both patients to execute ADs and physicians to pay
close attention to their patients' wishes regarding medical care at the end
of life (Gross, 1998).

The physician should endeavor to determine whether a patient, especially one who is older, has signed a valid advance directive; the PSDA
should assist here. Ideally, the physician should have discussed this matter

with the patient, been integrally involved in the patient's decision to execute or not execute such a directive, and placed a copy of the completed
form in the patient's permanent medical record long before critical illness
and decisional incapacity (i.e., a crisis) erupts (Loewy, 1998; Gillick, 1995a).
To avoid confusion caused by ambiguous wording in the document itself,
the physician should discuss with the decisionally capable patient the
patient's understanding and the intent (Jacobson et al., 1994) of the words
of the AD (Malloy, Wigton, Meeske, & Tape, 1992). Absent that opportunity, the physician should attempt to reconstruct and clarify the patient's
understanding and intent from relatives and close friends familiar with the
patient's values and desires (Emanuel, Barry, Emanuel, & Stoeckle, 1994),
although projecting patients' preferences accurately is often precarious
(Reilly, Teasdale, & McCullough, 1994). The physician must be candid in
determining when the conditions contemplated by the patient in signing
the document have materialized. A physician who does not intend, for
religious or other personal reasons, to honor an AD should notify the
patient of his or her intent and the underlying reasons as early in the relationship as possible.

   While ADs hold substantial promise for promoting valuable ethical,
legal, and clinical goals (Emanuel, Emanuel, Stoeckle, Hummel, & Barry,
1994; Fins, 1997), their impact in assuring autonomous, authentic medical
decisions and results will necessarily remain limited (Block, 1993; Larson
& Eaton, 1997; Jacobson et al., 1996; Schonwetter, Walker, Solomon,
Indurkhya, & Robinson, 1996; Teno, Licks, et al., 1997; Teno, Lynn, et al.,
1997; Terry & Zweig, 1994; Tonelli, 1996; Virmani, Schneiderman, &
Kaplan, 1994). Concern with documentation of future treatment preferences should not usurp the place of trying, whether or not the efforts are
formally enshrined in writing, to continuously improve the current pattern of end-of-life practice through better, more comprehensive physician/
patient communication (Loewy & Carlson, 1994). Put differently, advance
care planning should be conceptualized as a process of developing a valid
expression of wishes rather than a single consultation event or the signing
of a statutory piece of paper (Ackerman, 1997; Emanuel, Danis, Pearlman,
& Singer, 1995).

INSTITUTIONAL POLICIES AND PROCEDURES

Health care institutions are supposed to lay out their philosophies and
practices concerning LSMT decision making, with or without the presence
of ADs, in the form of written policies and procedures. Such written protocols have been urged as a way to enhance patient autonomy by providing timely information—hence, more meaningful choice—to patients and

their families, to serve the patient's best interests as viewed from the patient's perspective, to facilitate a more harmonious and less stressful decision-making process, and to reduce provider anxiety about potential criminal or civil liability for withholding or withdrawing LSMT.

These rationales undergirded Congress's enactment of the PSDA as sections 4206 and 4751 of the Omnibus Budget Reconciliation Act (OBRA) of 1990 (Public Law 101-508), codified at 42 U.S.C. §§1395cc(a)(1) and 1396a(a). Effective since 1991 and demonstrating decidedly limited impact thus far (Teno, Branco, et al., 1997), this federal law requires all Medicare and Medicaid provider organizations (specifically defined as hospitals, skilled NFs, home health agencies, hospices, health maintenance organizations, and preferred provider organizations) to

- Provide written information to patients at the time of an admission concerning "an individual's right under State law (whether statutory or as recognized by the courts of the State) to make decisions concerning . . . medical care, including the right to accept or refuse medical or surgical treatment and the right to formulate advance directives."
- Maintain written policies and procedures with respect to ADs and to inform patients of the policies.
- Document in the individual's medical record whether or not the individual has executed an AD. Under §4641 of the Balanced Budget Act (BBA), Public Law 105-33, this information must be displayed in a "prominent" part of the patient's medical record.
- Ensure compliance with the requirements of state law respecting ADs.
- Provide (individually or with others) for education of staff and the community on issues concerning ADs.

The law also requires providers "not to condition the provision of care or otherwise discriminate against an individual based on whether or not the individual has executed an advance directive." The statute imposes an obligation on the states to develop a description of state law. Specifically, it requires

> that the State, acting through a State agency, association, or other private nonprofit entity, develop a written description of the law of the State (whether statutory or as recognized by the courts of the State) concerning advance directives that would be distributed by providers or organizations.

Finally, the law requires the Department of Health and Human Services (DHHS) to undertake a public education campaign. This entails developing or approving national educational materials, assisting states in developing state-specific documents, and mailing information to Social Security recipients.

Health care providers who do not have in place adequate written policies and procedures should develop them expeditiously, and those with current protocols must review and, if necessary, revise them. A number of excellent models exist to assist providers in this endeavor, although ultimately each set of policies and procedures must be tailored to the individual mission and ethos of the provider, rather than copied from a "cookbook." Providers additionally must develop or enhance their informational and educational activities for patients, families, staff (including employed and affiliated physicians), volunteers, and the community. Management must assure that institutional protocols are being implemented conscientiously and effectively, ideally accomplishing the spirit as well as the letter of the PSDA's requirements. The commitment and cooperation of attending physicians are the key to meaningful implementation of the PSDA, as opposed to merely formalistic, ritualistic compliance with the legal dictates as an administrative paper-shuffling exercise (M. L. White & Fletcher, 1991).

More and better educational experiences and materials must also be developed and disseminated for attorneys and risk managers who advise health care providers. Sometimes provider behavior that is counterproductive to both patient autonomy and provider legal protection is the result of erroneous guidance by uninformed legal and risk-management counselors (Kapp, 1997b). The PSDA provides the occasion for accurate, realistic edification of the bestowers, as well as the beneficiaries, of legal and risk management counsel (White & Fletcher, 1991).

The development of written institutional protocols regarding LSMT and advance directives may reduce the ethical and legal dilemmas that often occur when the wishes of the patient or family, especially concerning a decision to forgo LSMT, conflict with provider values. Health care institutions stand for certain principles, as reflected in their mission statements, and those principles should be part of the provider's dialogue with potential patients and their families so that informed choices may be made before a crisis unfolds, and arguments and/or patient transfers can be avoided.

Although the PSDA does not apply specifically to physicians' private offices, it in no way precludes or is intended to discourage discussions about future patient medical treatment wishes from being conducted in the primary care setting. Indeed, it is preferable that such conversations occur in these relatively nonthreatening settings rather than during admission to a health care institution at a time of crisis.

In 1998, Congress considered a bill to create the Advance Planning and Compassionate Care Act, S. 1345. This legislation would have expanded and enhanced the requirements of the PSDA, and will be reintroduced in 1999.

"DO NOT" ORDERS

Many health care facilities, both acute (Jayes, Zimmerman, Wagner, Draper, & Knaus, 1993) and long-term (Finucane & Leal-Mora, 1997; Kane & Burns, 1997; Zweig, 1997), have developed and implemented written protocols regarding prospective physician orders to withhold the initiation of particular kinds of LSMTs in the future under specified circumstances. Such "do not" orders are a form of advance health care planning. Although this section focuses on "do not" orders in health care facilities, policies and procedures for withholding LSMT in the home are also important (Kapp, 1995f). Over half the states have passed statutes explicitly authorizing do-not-resuscitate (DNR) orders outside of institutions (Parri, 1996), professional associations have developed policy statements to deal with resuscitation attempts in the field (American College of Emergency Physicians, 1996; Delbridge, Fosnocht, Garrison, & Auble, 1996), and individual agencies have adopted implementation strategies for these situations (Sosna, Christopher, Pesto, Morando, & Stoddard, 1994).

The most prevalent kind of "do not" order in health care facilities and homes is the order not to initiate cardiopulmonary resuscitation (CPR) for a particular patient in the event of cardiopulmonary arrest; this is variously termed a DNR order, an order not to resuscitate (ONTR), an order to not attempt resuscitation, or a no-code order. Professional organizations have for many years urged institutions to create formal DNR policies; JCAHO has required accredited hospitals to have such a policy since 1988; and New York was the first state to legislatively mandate DNR policies in health care facilities (DeBuono, 1997; McClung & Kamer, 1990; Pollack, 1996). The PSDA requires each Medicare and Medicaid provider to adopt a policy on this subject, to notify potential patients or their proxies of their policy's contents, and to educate staff and the community appropriately.

There is a broad social and professional consensus regarding the propriety of withholding the initiation of CPR from certain patients (American Heart Association, Emergency Cardiac Care Committee and Subcommittees, 1992; American Nurses Association, 1992; Choice in Dying, 1995). Criteria for DNR orders are consistent with criteria for forgoing other types of medical interventions when the patient, either as a decisionally capable individual or through substituted judgment, makes the choice (Finucane, 1996; Hakim et al., 1996; Rosenfeld et al., 1996) or the surrogate believes that the disproportionate balance between likely burdens and benefits renders the intervention not in the patient's best interests. There is substantial agreement that judicial involvement is superfluous and undesirable (*Murphy v. Wheeler*, 1993) except in extreme cases (*In re Austwick*, 1995) and indeed that one of the primary goals of prospective planning is to obviate such involvement (Ebell, 1994; Kapp, 1996/97).

The policies and procedures developed, revised, or expanded by health care providers under the PSDA must include other kinds of prospective orders in addition to the DNR. Resuscitation is not the only medical intervention about which decisions may and often should be made in advance of the triggering event. For instance, for patients in a long-term care setting, advance planning about transfer to a hospital under certain foreseeable circumstances may be especially essential (Tresch, Sims, Duthie, Goldstein, & Lane, 1991), and a do-not-hospitalize (DNH) order entered by the physician prospectively may enhance patient autonomy and obviate a lot of turmoil and burden for the family and the health care team. The doctrine of informed consent applies with full force to interfacility transfers (Jablonski, Mosley, & Byrd, 1991).

Institutional policies should clearly delineate which do-not orders will be permitted, under what circumstances or criteria, and according to what procedural guidelines (Doyal & Wilsher, 1993; Heffner, Barbieri, & Casey, 1996; Mittelberger et al., 1993). Ideally, these policies will incorporate the spirit (e.g., autonomy, dignity, quality of life) as well as the legal formalities of patient and family participation in prospective decision making (Brunetti, Weiss, Studenski, & Clipp, 1990; Zweig, 1997). Institutional policies in this area must work against the common *de facto* variations that occur in practice, consciously or not, in the use of DNR orders based on socioeconomic and other patient characteristics unrelated to medical prognosis or patient choice (Jayes et al., 1996; Shepardson et al., 1997; Wenger, Pearson, Desmond, Harrison, et al., 1995). The provider must regularly monitor staff behavior to ensure that its policies are being carried out faithfully (e.g., not in the form of "show" or "slow" codes (Gazelle, 1998)) and without undue incident (Swig et al., 1996).

Orders should be documented and communicated among members of the health care team explicitly and unambiguously (e.g., does a DNR order refer to both basic and advanced cardiac life support?) to avoid future confusion and erroneous performance in the midst of a crisis (Walker, Schonwetter, Kramer, & Robinson, 1995; Wenger, Pearson, Desmond, Brook, & Kahn, 1995). Careful, detailed documentation and communication, particularly in the case of DNR orders, should address and avoid the twin dangers of both overinterpretation (i.e., inappropriately depriving the patient of potentially beneficial interventions other than CPR or of palliative or comfort measures that are always appropriate) and underinterpretation (i.e., inflicting other futile and burdensome interventions on the patient because they are not CPR) (Lo, 1991). Do-not orders should be incorporated into the comprehensive care plan for the patient, rather than treated as a separate subject.

Communication with the patient and/or family is essential regarding prospective decisions to withhold particular interventions (Prendergast & Raffin, 1996). Decisions about CPR and other LSMTs must be individualized (Health Care Financing Administration, 1996). Facts must be presented sensitively and tactfully but honestly and realistically (Diem, Lantos, & Tulsky, 1996; Florin, 1994; Ghusn, Teasdale, & Skelly, 1995; Karetzky, Zubair, & Parikh, 1995; McIntyre, 1993a; D. L. Miller, Gorbien, Simbartl, & Jahnigen, 1993; Sorum, 1995; Tulsky, Chesney, & Lo, 1995, 1996; Zweig, 1996). It is best when discussions can begin early, outside a crisis atmosphere. As indicated by a couple of cases (*Payne v. Marion General Hospital,* 1990; *Wendland v. Sparks,* 1998), entering and acting upon DNR or other do-not orders without the informed consent of the patient or authorized surrogate decision maker may be problematic if the withheld intervention can be shown to have been potentially beneficial to the patient—that is, if there really was a choice to make. To ease the discussion psychologically, in terms of relieving feelings of guilt from the family's shoulders, the physician may want to present the situation less as a set of viable options from which to choose and more as one requiring patient or family permission to follow the one course of conduct that is clinically and ethically indicated.

A number of studies indicate that most patients and families are willing, even anxious, to engage in serious prospective discussions about withholding medical interventions and that the vast majority cope well with such conversations (Murphy et al., 1994; Phillips et al., 1996; Schonwetter, Walker, Kramer, & Robinson, 1993; Stolman, Gregory, Dunn, & Levine, 1990). However, the performance of physicians in initiating such discussions has lagged generally behind this patient/family interest, and do-not orders often get entered and carried out absent adequate interaction (Paris, Carrion, Meditch, Capello, & Mulvihill, 1993). Conversely, physicians' failure to understand and/or honor patients' wishes may result in unwanted, excessive resuscitation attempts (Teno et al., 1995). Health care professionals, particularly physicians, must work to overcome some of the barriers that have impeded this form of communication (Tulsky et al., 1995, 1996). Institutional protocols and educational efforts mandated by the PSDA are intended to have a positive influence in this regard. All communication conducted with patients and families, including decisions made or ratified by the patient or family, must be documented thoroughly in the medical record.

Patients and families should have explained to them that prospective decisions to withhold specific interventions are subject to ongoing review and revision if the clinical circumstances change. If, for example, the patient's condition changes either positively or negatively, so that the balance between likely benefits and burdens of intervention is altered, a do-not order can be revised. Documentation in the patient's chart should reflect this continual process of review and, where appropriate, revision.

An important ongoing debate rages over the legal and ethical obligation of the health care team, particularly the physician, even to raise with the patient or family the possibility of medical interventions that, in the health care team's professional judgment, would be futile or nonbeneficial for the patient. Put differently, if the health care team believes that CPR, for example, for a particular patient has a negligible chance for success, is there a duty nonetheless to present a choice to the patient or family—that is, to ask for their consent prior to entering a DNR order—or may the physician enter such an order unilaterally? This specific issue has not been squarely presented to the courts yet, and hence there is no definitive legal precedent. Statutory law has not addressed this issue either. Institutional protocols and community education activities undertaken in compliance with the PSDA should address this subject (Schoenenberger, von Planta, & von Planta, 1994) and notify potential patients and families concerning the provider's philosophy on this point. Sufficient documentation regarding the patient's condition and the futility (and therefore absence of a meaningful choice) regarding specific medical interventions should be present. The subject of medical futility and its legal implications is discussed further, below.

INSTITUTIONAL ETHICS COMMITTEES

One mechanism that a growing number of health care organizations, including home health agencies (HHAs) and NFs (Hoffmann, Boyle, & Levenson, 1995), have put into place since the mid-1970s to assist in dealing with difficult legal and ethical questions surrounding LSMT (and sometimes other kinds of medical) decisions is the IEC, also referred to as a bioethics committee. There is no single model for the composition and operation of an IEC, but the general idea is to create a multidisciplinary, interdisciplinary body bringing together a broad array of expertise, experience, and philosophical perspectives (including that of the community and/or consumer) that is proactively (Dowdy, Robertson, & Bander, 1998) available to the health care provider and its staff in ethical matters (Spicker, 1998).

An IEC can be involved in any combination of policy-making, educational, or individual case consultation activities concerning ethical aspects of patient care (Robertson, 1991). IECs are especially useful in helping providers to satisfy the policy-making and staff and community education requirements of the PSDA. Regarding case consultation, an IEC may be involved concurrently or retrospectively. IECs ordinarily offer advice, rather than binding holdings, to the involved parties. IECs differ significantly over operational issues surrounding who may and who must bring a case before the IEC and under what circumstances (Gramelspacher, 1991).

Despite the potential benefits of IEC development and implementation for many health care providers, a host of legal, ethical, and administrative questions arise whose answers either depend on particular state law or, more likely, have not yet been determined. Most basically, what is the relationship between the IEC's ethics focus and its potential risk management role, and how can (should?) a provider prevent the latter role from totally dominating the former? Should the institutional risk manager and/or attorney be a member of the IEC, and if so, what role should that person play to prevent institutional interests from overwhelming the patient's interests when there is a tension between the two? What record-keeping and reporting practices are advisable if a provider is anxious about the legal issues of possible discoverability and testimonial privilege for IEC records and reports? Structurally, should the IEC be a committee of the medical staff or of the governing board? What are the confidentiality considerations, in the sense of IEC access to patient records with and without patient or family permission? What weight do and should courts give IEC recommendations (R. F. Wilson, 1998)? Thus far, courts have shown great respect for IECs as sources of guidance. No court has imposed any legal liability on an IEC or on any health care provider who acted under an IEC's advice, but the question of potential liability for IEC-related activity is one that continues to bother members and sponsoring providers nonetheless.

Individual providers must take into account their own unique situations in deciding upon the value of an IEC for them. If an IEC exists or there is a decision to create one, each facility must deal with the operational questions just posed in terms of individual strengths and needs, experiences, resources, and state law. Providers may want to experiment with different structural forms, including regional networks or Ethics Consultation Services (Orr, Morton, de Leon, & Fals, 1996), where individual IECs are not practical. Regardless of structure, extensive educational efforts regarding the role of the IEC or ethics consultation service should be aimed at patients, families, and the larger community served. IEC members must receive education regarding the ethical issues they are likely to confront, as well as about special considerations relevant to older patients and their families.

LEGAL LIABILITY FOR DECISIONS
TO WITHHOLD OR WITHDRAW LSMT

One of the problems that characterizes this practice area and that, to a significant extent, has impeded good decision making and desirable conduct regarding medical care near the end of life is the existence of a deepseated, pervasive, free-floating anxiety on the part of many health care providers about incurring potential criminal or civil liability as a result of withholding or withdrawing LSMT (Kapp, 1997b). End-of-life decision making frequently is "influenced more by considerations of risk management than by those of patient care" (Quill, 1992).

There is a strong consensus among knowledgeable observers that these fears are grossly exaggerated and unrealistic. As legal scholar Alan Meisel (1996) has noted,

> As small as the proportion of appealed cases is, the proportion of deaths from foregoing life-sustaining treatment that is litigated is also very small. Somewhere between 0.2% and 0.5% have been litigated at all, and between 37 and 55 in 10 million have been litigated to the point of yielding an appellate decision.

Much of the legal anxiety influencing inappropriate medical treatment for critically ill and dying patients is fueled by misunderstanding and misinterpretation. For example, legal experts interviewed by the U.S. General Accounting Office (1995) indicated that, when an individual's wishes are clear, difficulties in getting requests to withhold or withdraw artificial nutrition and hydration honored typically arise from confusion about the legal ramifications, rather than because any legal impediment actually exists. By early 1998, a dozen state legislatures had enacted "Intractable Pain Statutes" providing criminal, civil, and disciplinary immunity for physicians engaged in justifiable, aggressive pain management practices using opioids.

Nonetheless, however weak the factual foundations, the anxieties felt by physicians and other health care providers about potential criminal, civil, and/or regulatory liabilities are real and palpable influences on the quality and humanity of medical care actually provided to vulnerable older patients. Adverse effects may take the form of overtreatment (e.g., inappropriate resuscitation attempts or artificial feeding) (Ely, Peters, Zweight, Elder, & Schneider, 1992), undertreatment (e.g., insufficient pain control), and impaired communications with patients and families. The problem exists even for physicians who understand intellectually that their own legal exposure is minimal when their conduct is medically and ethically proper. The very fact that physician conduct in this most delicate of areas could conceivably be questioned in a legal context is enough to skew behavior. Physician Jack McCue (1995) most assuredly is correct when he urges that "[t]he exaggerated fears of liability risks that pressure physicians and nurses to withhold palliative treatment or continue futile therapy in patients near the end of life must be addressed in a forthright fashion."

As usual, the most realistic and effective risk management in this realm lies not in reflexive resort to the courts or a cowardly refusal to respect patient and family wishes. Rather, the emphasis ought to be on conducting timely (Lynn, Teno, & Harrell, 1995) and open conversations with patients and families regarding current and future treatment preferences (Hanson, Danis, & Garrett, 1997), as well as scrupulous documentation of such conversations.

PHYSICIAN-ASSISTED DEATH

Fear of potential criminal or civil liability is a much more realistic and relevant concern when the issue is not the withholding or withdrawal of LSMT from a seriously ill patient so that nature can take its course, but rather the provider's engaging in some active intervention for the purpose and with the result of hastening the patient's death. Current U.S. law is unambiguous in its condemnation, particularly through state homicide statutes, of health care providers engaging in active (voluntary, positive) euthanasia (i.e., actively and intentionally doing something like administering a lethal injection to hasten the death of a patient without that patient's permission). In addition, almost all states explicitly legislatively condemn physician-assisted suicide (i.e., actively helping a patient to purposely take his or her own life), through either a specific statute on the subject or judicial interpretations of their general homicide statutes (Tarnow, 1996).

In 1997, the U.S. Supreme Court unanimously upheld the validity of state laws making it criminal for physicians or other health care professionals (Asch, 1996; Asch & DeKay, 1997) to assist a patient to commit suicide. In these decisions (*Vacco v. Quill*, 1997; *Washington v. Glucksberg*, 1997), the Court rejected the notion of any constitutional right to physician-assisted suicide (Annas, 1997).

Legislatures, courts, professional organizations (American Academy of Neurology, 1998; American Medical Directors Association, 1997), and most commentators thus far have consistently distinguished between abating medical treatment, on the one hand, and assisted suicide and active euthanasia, on the other, with the latter categories being legally out of bounds (L. J. Harris, 1997) and widely considered to be inferior approaches to alleviating the problem of patient suffering, compared with the provision of competent, aggressive palliative care (Bretscher & Crea-gan, 1997; Cohn, Forlini, & Lynn, 1997; Quill, Meier, Block, & Billings, 1998). Indeed, some commentators argue that the Supreme Court's rejec-tion of a constitutional right to assisted suicide actually amounted to endorsement of a constitutional right to palliative care (Burt, 1997), while others assert that failure to provide adequate palliative care ought to be punishable through medical malpractice litigation and professional dis-ciplinary proceedings (Tucker, 1998).

Although the Constitution does not require it, the door is open legally for particular states to choose, as a matter of their own respective public policies and politics, to decriminalize physician-assisted suicide or even active euthanasia (Churchill & King, 1997; E. J. Emanuel, 1998; Gostin, 1997). In Oregon, voters in 1997 passed (for the second time [Annas, 1994a]) a referendum (Measure 16) on a Death With Dignity Act per-mitting physician-assisted suicide under certain strictly constrained cir-cumstances, Or. Rev. Stat. §§127.800–.897. Based upon the pragmatic experience (S. M. Wolf, 1998) in that state (Goodwin, 1997; Josefson, 1998; Tolle, 1998), as well as close scrutiny of medical practice in the Nether-lands (where physician-assisted death is illegal but not prosecuted [Onwuteaka-Philipsen, Muller, van der Wal, van Eijk, & Ribbe, 1997], other jurisdictions may follow similar paths in the coming years. A shift from criminalization to regulation of certain forms of physician-assisted death will pose vexing ethical and practical challenges to physicians and the organizations that advise them (Haley & Lee, 1998; Heilig, Brody, Mar-cus, Shavelson, & Sussman, 1997).

HOSPICE CARE

For a growing number and variety (Luchins, Hanrahan, & Murphy, 1997; National Hospice Organization, 1996; Volicer, 1997) of terminally ill patients in the United States, care is being provided through hospices. Hospice care focuses on providing palliative and supportive services to the patient and family rather than aggressive medical intervention (Lattanzi-Licht, Mahoney, & Miller, 1998; McCue, 1995). *Hospice* originally was a medieval name for a way station for pilgrims and travelers, where they could be re-plenished, refreshed, and cared for; today, the term refers to an organized program of care for people going through life's last station (AMA Council on Scientific Affairs, 1996). The whole family is considered the unit of care, and the care extends through the mourning process. Emphasis is placed on symptom control and preparation and support before and after death, full-scope health services being provided by an organized interdisciplinary team on a 24-hour-a-day, 7-day-a-week basis regardless of the patient's physical location. Hospices originated in England and slowly came to the United States over the past three decades.

Hospice organization may take a number of different forms (Volicer & Hurley, 1998): (1) home care programs, which may be affiliated with a hospital or other health care facility; (2) freestanding hospice facilities that provide inpatient services; (3) freestanding hospice facilities affiliated with hospitals or health professions schools; (4) hospice units within a hospital, which may range from several beds to an entire ward or floor; and (5) hospice teams working inside a hospital or nursing facility (Keay & Schonwetter, 1998).

The growing hospice movement poses several potential legal implications. First, individual health care professionals bear the same sorts of potential legal liability that they would in any model of health care delivery, in terms of informed consent and acceptable standards of care. In addition, hospice organizations themselves encounter many of the same types of legal issues that have concerned other institutional health care providers for years, such as health planning requirements, licensure, accreditation, and, closely tied to licensure and accreditation, fiscal reimbursement regulations.

Hospices in Europe and the United States traditionally have been funded mainly by religious organizations or private foundations, but as hospices continue to spread in numbers and scope of services, third-party public and private insurance payments must be more actively pursued. Medicare coverage for hospice services delivered outside the confines of the acute care hospital to terminally ill patients over 65 years is available. Under the BBA of 1997, Public Law 105-33, the Medicare hospice benefit now includes any items or services that are listed in the individual's plan of care and for which payment may otherwise be made under the Medicare program. There are two 90-day hospice benefit periods, followed by an unlimited number of 60-day periods. A physician must certify that the patient is terminally ill at the start of the initial 90-day benefit period. Then, at the beginning of each 60-day period, an appropriate medical professional must recertify that the beneficiary is terminally ill.

In addition to the formal legal requirements that a hospice must satisfy, the National Hospice Organization (NHO), a voluntary association in Washington, DC, has adopted standards for hospice programs. Developed by a group of hospice professionals representing the various disciplines utilized in hospice care, these standards and their underlying principles cover the following components: (1) program administration, (2) unit of care (patient/family), (3) symptom control, (4) quality assurance, (5) records, (6) continuity of care, (7) personnel, (8) bereavement care, and (9) physical plant. The Hospice Association of America has developed and disseminated a Code of Ethics and a Hospice Patient's Bill of Rights for its members.

Further, JCAHO conducts a hospice accreditation service, including standards and surveys. "Deemed" status for these services, under which programs accredited by JCAHO would be recognized as meeting the government's eligibility requirements for Medicare reimbursement, is a possibility in the future.

A hospice must never be used by health care professionals as a convenient dumping ground to avoid the legal, ethical, emotional, and clinical problems encountered in caring for terminally ill persons in hospital or NF settings. The health care professional should be aware of the hospice movement, both in general and in terms of particular community resources, and should appreciate its potential advantages in caring for certain terminally ill patients (Harrold & Lynn, 1998). The current legal and accreditation status of the specific hospice(s) with which they are associated should also be known to health care professionals.

DEMANDS FOR FUTILE MEDICAL CARE

A new kind of "right to die" dilemma has emerged on the scene in the past decade (Fins, 1994). This is the problem of patients or their families demanding that health care professionals provide them with forms of LSMT that, in the opinion of the health care professionals, are "futile" or "nonbeneficial." Such demands for aggressive medical interventions occur often, even in the face of dismal survival and quality-of-life prospects (Levinsky, 1996; O'Brien et al., 1997) and may create a clash at the bedside between patient autonomy (asserted personally or through a proxy) and the professional's own conscience (Daar, 1993). Some have suggested that this clash may be avoided or softened if the issue is characterized as one of "appropriateness" of specific treatments (Prendergast, 1995; Sharpe & Faden, 1996). Additionally, although they are not the same thing, the concepts of futility and economic waste overlap considerably; wasteful treatment offends the ethical notion of distributive or social justice/fairness (Luce, 1994). In the same vein, the concept of futility must not be used as a ploy to justify health care rationing in disguise (Jecker & Schneiderman, 1992; Lantos, 1994).

A number of commentators have argued cogently that, whereas the patient's right to autonomy in medical decision making, whether exercised personally or through a surrogate, allows for the informed refusal of LSMT, it should not extend to demands for pointless interventions (Layson & McConnell, 1996). In the latter situation, the argument goes, there really is no choice to make, and the health care professional is under no ethical duty to respond affirmatively to the patient's or family's unreasonable demands (Layson & McConnell, 1996; Society of Critical Care

Medicine, 1997). In fact, the argument is made, acceding to requests for nonbeneficial treatment would constitute the practice of poor medicine and violate the health care provider's ethical precepts of beneficence and nonmaleficence (Brody, 1994; Paris, Schreiber, Statter, Arensman, & Siegler, 1993).

Others caution that determining the futility of a particular form of LSMT for a patient in advance depends upon how one conceptualizes the issue. Physiological futility refers to interventions that will have no plausible effect on a disease, (e.g., resuscitation attempts in situations where survival is unprecedented) (Marsden, Ng, Dalziel, & Cobbe, 1995). Quantitative futility refers to therapies that are extremely unlikely to work; there is active debate about who determines when an outcome is so rare that a therapy is quantitatively futile and what value ought to be assigned to small but measurable effects (Ebell, 1995; Jecker & Pearlman, 1992; McCrary, Swanson, Youngner, Perkins, & Winslade, 1994). Qualitative futility refers to situations where proposed life-sustaining medical treatments would do nothing to improve—and might even diminish—the patient's overall quality of life (Schneiderman, Jecker, & Jonsen, 1996).

The problem is complicated by the phenomenon of medical uncertainty and the inevitability of value judgments intruding (Lo, 1991; Scofield, 1991; Waisel & Truog, 1995). For example, there is well-documented age bias in how physicians make many critical treatment decisions (Kapp, 1998a) that may reflect subjective assessments that old age equals medical futility, regardless of the unique patient's own actual life expectancy, ability to tolerate interventions, and quality of life. Additionally, it is important for health care professionals to consider potential psychological and other intangible benefits in addition to physiological success in judging an intervention's futility. Under the most extreme—arguably even cruel (Smith, 1995)—version of this view, the physician has a moral responsibility to provide, and third parties have a duty to pay for, virtually any medical treatment demanded by the patient or proxy (Veatch, 1994). The National Right to Life Committee has developed and distributes a Will to Live form intended to allow individuals to prospectively demand maximal medical intervention as a matter of advance planning for eventual incapacity.

The issue of whether a health care professional has a legal obligation to effectuate a patient's or family's demand for LSMT that the professional believes to be futile (in the most complete sense) is unclear at the present time. This is despite the venerable legal maxim, *lex neminem cogit ad vana seu inutilia peragenda!*—"the law compels no one to do vain or useless things!"—and the AMA's opinion (AMA Council on Ethical and Judicial Affairs, 1997) that physicians "are not ethically obligated to deliver care that, in their best professional judgment, will not have a reasonable chance of benefiting their patients. Patients should not be given treatments simply because they demand them." Treatment decisions and conflict resolution at present must take place in the context of a lack of judicial consensus (Johnson, Gibbons, Goldner, Wiener, & Eton, 1997; Wendland v. Sparks, 1998). Especially uncertain is the potential relevance of the Americans With Disabilities Act (ADA) to physicians' treatment decisions predicated on the futility concept (P. G. Peters, 1997).

Consequently, providers overwhelmingly (but not unanimously [Asch, Hansen-Flaschen, & Lanken, 1995]) tend to take the perceived path of least resistance and provide the intervention demanded (Luce, 1990). Using CPR as their focus, Marsh and Staver (1991) argue persuasively that a physician has no legal duty to provide or even to discuss a futile intervention. However, actual case law in what one set of commentators has termed the "right to live" area (Middleditch & Trotter, 1997) is still quite sparse. In one of the few published judicial decisions on this topic (*In re Conservatorship of Wanglie*, 1991), a trial court in Minnesota denied a hospital's request to appoint an independent guardian to evaluate the benefits versus the futility of continuing a respirator for an 86-year-old patient in a PVS of more than a year's duration; instead, the court appointed as guardian the patient's husband, who insisted on the respirator's continuation as long as the patient remained alive in any condition (Angell, 1991; Miles, 1991). The patient died 3 days after the court's ruling anyway, making an appeal moot and leaving a legal precedent that, although not dealing directly with the futility issue, may have the effect of frightening health care providers into submission to family requests, regardless of how unreasonable they are clinically and ethically.

The futility issue is one with enormous financial (Halevy, Neal, & Brody, 1996; Murphy & Finucane, 1993; Teno et al., 1994), ethical, and legal implications. Legislative, judicial, and/or professional organizational guidance is needed desperately (Murphy, 1994), although the reluctance of elected representatives and the courts to wade into this thicket is understandable (Cranford, 1994; Mason & Mulligan, 1996). Formal clinical practice guidelines might eventually play a role in this sphere (L. J. White, 1994). Health care institutions, acting singularly or collectively (Halevy & Brody, 1996), should consider the development and adoption of their own explicit policies to guide their medical and nursing staffs in this area.

Until some definitive guidance (Curtis, Park, Krone, & Pearlman, 1995) is provided, health care professionals should act carefully in defining benefit in its broadest sense and erring on the side of the patient and family as the best evaluators of whether LSMT is worthwhile (Alpers & Lo, 1995; Truog, Brett, & Frader, 1992). When in doubt, the health care provider probably should presume that the patient would want an intervention whose benefits are uncertain (McIntyre, 1993a). At the same time, though, health care providers should be aggressive in explaining to the patient and/or family their point of view concerning an intervention's futility (Dunn & Levinson, 1996; Tong, 1995), using information and reason to guide them to a responsible choice (Doukas & McCullough, 1996); few (albeit some) patients and families are likely to persist in insisting upon truly burdensome, nonbeneficial medical assaults if they trust the physician (Caplan, 1996; Lantos, 1994; Youngner, 1995). Additionally, some providers will need to have the courage to challenge a patient or family through the legal process so that legal precedent can evolve and clarify respective rights and obligations (Cantor, 1996; Lloyd, 1996).

DEFINITIONS OF DEATH

For most of our history, cessation of cardiorespiratory functioning has served quite adequately as a definition of death for all purposes. The usefulness of this definition has been seriously impaired in recent years, however, as amazing advances in biomedical technology have made it possible to sustain cardiopulmonary functioning artificially in certain individuals almost indefinitely. Thus, we have been forced to search for a revised definition of death that is comprehensive (legal, ethical, and clinical) and that responds to the following questions: (1) when is a person dead, so that there is no doubt that LSMT can be withheld or withdrawn, and (2) when is a person dead, so that organs may be removed from his or her body and transplanted into a living human being?

Most of the legal reform attention of the past 30 years has focused on some version of irreversible cessation of brain function as a definition capable of meeting today's legal, ethical, and clinical needs, either as a substitute for or as a supplement to the traditional cardiorespiratory definition. In this vein, the American Bar Association (ABA) proposed a model brain death statute in 1974; the National Conference of Commissioners on Uniform State Laws (NCCUSL) proposed a different version (the Uniform Brain Death Act) in 1978; and the AMA proposed its own model in 1979. Prior to 1981, half the states had adopted some form of brain death definition by statute, and several more jurisdictions had done so through judicial decision.

In 1981, a presidential commission issued a comprehensive report (President's Commission, 1981) analyzing this subject and recommending that state legislatures adopt a Uniform Determination of Death Act (UDDA), stating: "Any individual who has sustained either (1) irreversible cessation of circulatory and respiratory functions, or (2) irreversible cessation of all functions of the entire brain, including the brain stem, is dead." This proposal was warmly received generally and won the quick endorsement of the

ABA, AMA, and NCCUSL. Virtually all the states have adopted the Uniform Determination of Death Act either by statute or judicial decision.

Some have criticized the prevailing brain death definition for its failure to address the Quinlan or Cruzan situations, that is, a person who will never again regain cognition or sapience (upper brain function) but who still possesses some degree of primitive reflex (lower brain) function. These critics suggest that irreversible cessation of all consciousness and cognition alone ought to justify defining and declaring a (former) person as dead (Devettere, 1990; Truog & Fackler, 1992; Veatch, 1993). Additionally, despite widespread modern legal consensus on the definition of death, there still remains some unfortunate confusion about the criteria embodied in the brain death definition (Charlton, 1996; Halevy & Brody, 1993; Hughes & McGuire, 1997; Taylor, 1997). There also are some religious objections to the concept of brain death (Fins, 1995); and in New Jersey, physicians must consider a patient's religious beliefs before making a declaration of death and removing life-sustaining medical interventions, N.J. Stat. Ann. 26:6A-5. Nonetheless, the strongly prevailing view is that, notwithstanding any conceptual or practical problems with the "whole brain" standard for brain death, it is preferable to the two main alternatives, namely, (1) a return to the traditional heart/lung formulation alone and (2) upper brain cessation alone (Bernat, 1998).

The President's Commission (1981) emphasized its recognition that, whereas establishing the standards for defining death is a proper function of the legal system, determining the clinical criteria or tests to be used in applying those legal standards to any particular patient is a matter best left to the medical profession:

> In light of the challenges that have been mounted to any professional prerogative in establishing the standards for determining that a human being has died, it may seem surprising that the traditional role of physicians in *applying* the standards has not been challenged. The difference in the task probably explains the lack of controversy in the latter situation. Application of an agreed-upon standard is a matter for technical expertise, and it is not doubted that competent physicians (among others) possess the necessary proficiency in diagnosis.

Following this reasoning, the Uniform Determination of Death Act states that "[a] determination of death must be made in accordance with accepted medical standards." All extant state statutes on this subject concur with this approach.

In 1968, an Ad Hoc Committee of the Harvard Medical School to Examine the Definition of Brain Death published a report defining "irreversible coma" as a criterion for death. The Harvard criteria soon became widely recognized and accepted. The so-called Harvard Test argued that a permanently nonfunctioning brain could be accurately diagnosed on the basis of four factors:

1. Unreceptivity and unresponsivity, meaning a total unawareness of inner need and externally applied stimuli regardless of the painful nature of the stimuli.
2. No spontaneous movements nor spontaneous breathing. When a person is on a mechanical ventilator, this criteria can be established by turning off the machine for 3 minutes and observing whether there is an effort to breathe spontaneously.
3. No reflexes and the absence of elicitable reflexes—pupils fixed and dilated, no ocular movement, no blinking, swallowing, yawning, or vocalization.
4. Flat electroencephalograms (EEGs), taken twice within at least a 24-hour intervening period, that are coincident with the absence of hypothermia and central nervous system depressants, such as barbiturates, and that are taken with an EEG machine that is functioning and utilized properly. The EEG criterion was recommended by the committee as a confirmatory rather than a mandatory test.

As an appendix to the 1981 report of the President's Commission, a panel of Medical Consultants on the Diagnosis of Death analyzed and updated the Harvard criteria in light of advances in medical knowledge and technology. The panel's report (Medical Consultants, 1981) is an important source of information for health care professionals on the clinical criteria for the determination of death. The state of the art in this realm continues to evolve along with the rest of medicine (American Academy of Neurology, 1995; Williams & Suarez, 1997).

Once a patient meets the legal criteria, the health care professional is obligated to make a declaration of death. Once the criteria are met, there also is an obligation to respect a family's request to discontinue any LSMT and to release the body, or else liability for emotional distress may be imposed (*Strachan v. JFK Memorial Hospital*, 1988).

CERTIFICATION OF DEATH AND AUTOPSIES

Upon a patient's death, the attending physician ordinarily is responsible for filling out the medical portion of the death certificate. Physicians and other health care professionals should be familiar with the requirements of their own state's vital records statute. They also should be knowledgeable about appropriate techniques for filling out death certificates accurately and helpfully (Huffman, 1997; Magrane, Gilliland, & King,

1997; Messite & Stellman, 1996). Properly completed death certificates provide information that is vital to public health and that also can be useful as a risk management tool in defending against claims of substandard medical treatment (Klatt & Noguchi, 1989). The Autopsy Committee of the College of American Pathologists (CAP) has developed a model protocol for writing cause-of-death statements for deaths due to natural causes (Hanzlick, 1996).

In certain circumstances, the attending physician is required by statute to report the circumstances of a patient's death to a local public official. This official is either a coroner or a medical examiner, depending on the public death-investigation system in place in the particular jurisdiction (Hanzlick & Combs, 1998). This public official then determines what steps, including an autopsy, are appropriate to investigate the deceased's death. When a case is within the jurisdiction of the coroner or medical examiner, the deceased's family may not prevent the public investigation from proceeding; the family's consent for autopsy or other measures is not legally necessary. Nevertheless, because this may be a particularly anxiety-provoking event for the family, it is helpful for the attending physician to convey that the autopsy is an operative procedure performed by a skilled professional to determine the final diagnosis and, when possible, the cause of death.

State statutes differ in detail concerning when an attending physician is mandated to report a patient's death to the coroner or medical examiner. Physicians should be aware of the specific items in their own jurisdiction's mandatory death-reporting statute. As a basic rule of thumb, when in doubt, the death should be reported so that discretion may be exercised at the level of the public official rather than by the individual private practitioner. Standard grounds for mandatory death reporting include the following: (a) There is a reasonable belief of criminal activity, (b) there is a reasonable belief that the death was violent in nature, (c) the death occurred by casualty (accident), (d) the death was an apparent suicide, (e) the individual died suddenly when in apparent good health, and (f) the death occurred in any suspicious or unusual manner. Many states also have mandatory reporting provisions encompassing such situations as (a) death occurring within 24 hours of hospital admission, (b) death related to occupation, and (c) death of a patient not recently attended by a physician. Once a coroner or medical examiner has conducted an autopsy, some states treat the results as an easily accessible public record, whereas other states prevent the public from obtaining the resulting information.

There are cases in which referral to the coroner or medical examiner is not legally mandated, but the attending physician may recommend that a hospital autopsy be performed. This desire may be motivated by family, clinical, institutional, educational, research, or public health considerations (Pellegrino, 1996). An autopsy also may be advisable to clarify legal concerns involving civil responsibility for wrongful death, worker's compensation, estate (probate) questions, and insurance claims. By dispelling family suspicions about improper medical care of the deceased, the autopsy can be a valuable risk management device for the health care team. Further, it is legitimate for the attending physician to communicate that a postmortem examination is an important ingredient in his or her and many others' continuing professional education. The benefits of an autopsy may be especially great in the case of older persons (Galanos, Gardner, & Riddick, 1989).

In situations in which referral to the coroner or medical examiner is not required by statute, an autopsy may be performed only upon receipt of valid informed consent. Anyone who alters the deceased's body without consent may be held liable civilly to the survivors and sometimes even prosecuted criminally. For this reason, it is as important to obtain a properly given informed consent for autopsy as it is to obtain consent for any medical intervention with a live patient (see Chapter 3). State statutes enumerate who is legally authorized to consent to an autopsy; because the statutes may vary, physicians should become well acquainted with the specific priority order of potential consenters in their own jurisdiction. Many families are willing to grant autopsy permission if physicians can overcome psychological barriers to broaching the subject with them. Consent also may be obtained for partial autopsies; many families, for instance, allow brain autopsies to be done to confirm a diagnosis of Alzheimer's disease.

Most state statutes permit an individual, while alive and mentally capable, to give prospective voluntary, informed consent to the performance of an autopsy upon his or her body after death. Although, of course, the sensitivity of this subject to the patient cannot be overstated, it is something that the attending physician should seriously consider discussing with terminally ill patients in a factual but compassionate manner. The patient's right to know about and consent to an autopsy should not be ignored summarily.

Family members have a legal right to access to information derived through an autopsy. Postmortem findings should be discussed with them honestly, in a timely manner, and in understandable language.

ORGAN DONATION

As major scientific advances in the area of human organ transplantation have taken place in recent years, the shortage of available, usable organs from competent, willing donors has gathered national and international attention on a public and professional (medical, legal, and ethical) level.

The dilemma is exacerbated by the fact that many types of human organs, to be successfully transplanted, can be obtained only from a deceased donor and only within a very short time span following the death. Indeed, the Institute of Medicine (IoM; 1997b) recently recommended that the inadequate supply of donor organs could be eased somewhat by using organs from people whose hearts have stopped but who have not yet been declared dead; this idea has been promoted by some for almost a decade (Cho, Terasaki, Cecka, & Gjertson, 1998; Youngner & Arnold, 1993). There is general consensus that there are more than enough deaths in the United States annually to provide a surplus of organs if there were a satisfactory method of bringing all cadavers into the pool of donors (U.S. General Accounting Office, 1993). Society thus has an important stake in finding ways to improve donor recruitment. In 1984, Congress passed Public Law 98-507, 42 U.S.C. §273, the National Organ Transplant Act, which established a nonprofit Organ Procurement and Transplantation Network; the federal government in 1987 awarded the contract for this network to United Network for Organ Sharing (UNOS).

In 1968, NCCUSL proposed the Uniform Anatomical Gift Act (UAGA). Its purpose was to standardize and simplify state laws on donation of all cadaveric tissues and organs. By 1970, this Act had been adopted in all 50 states and the District of Columbia, and its purpose has been largely achieved.

Under the adopted state statutes, the wishes of a mentally capable adult donor are binding after death and cannot be vetoed by family members or others. The legal instrument is a simple wallet-size card that requires the signatures of the donor and two adult witnesses. Many states have placed the donor card format on the back of each motor vehicle driver's license as a convenience to encourage organ gifts. Unfortunately, hospitals and physicians refuse to harvest organs without the family's permission, even though the patient personally gave consent and the law clearly does not require family permission (Jardin, 1990). As physician John Luce (1990) has noted, "Although there are good reasons to honor patients' previously expressed desires to donate organs despite surrogates' wishes to the contrary, most physicians find it difficult to do so." At the same time, if the patient did not document his or her wishes in advance, while capable, the family's decision does and should rule (Klassen & Klassen, 1996) and the health care provider may not coerce organ donation by, for example, refusing to release the corpse (Annas, 1988).

Health care professionals, particularly physicians, can and should play a vital role in improving organ donor recruitment, both through public education efforts and by discussing the possibilities with individual patients (Peters, Kittur, McGaw, First, & Nelson, 1996; Simonoff, Arnold, Caplan, Virnig, & Seltzer, 1995). Under 42 U.S.C. §1320b-8, each state was required to enact legislation that forces hospitals participating in the Medicare or Medicaid financing programs to establish "routine request" or "routine inquiry" policies. Under these policies, the hospital must have a system for asking relatives of most patients who die for permission to harvest organs. There is some room for physician discretion when the patient would be excluded from being a donor on medical grounds, such as having organs that were destroyed or diseased.

Because the physician is involved in the care and family consultation of the dying patient, a thorough understanding of the medical and legal aspects of organ donation is essential. Through closer cooperation between physicians and their patients, plus better education of the public, more individuals would be able to benefit from transplantation of cadaveric donor organs.

Although this topic is pertinent to patients of all ages, physician encouragement may be especially apt—and may be most warmly received—in the case of patients who realize that they are approaching the end of their life span. Although the majority of cadaveric donors are less than 50 years old, organs from an older individual of healthy physiology are also useful (Waltzer, 1983). Age limits ordinarily are not set for donations of cornea, skin, and bone (as opposed to internal organs). Even for internal organs, the age criterion keeps rising as the focus sets more firmly on the function of the organ rather than the years accumulated by the donor (Darby, Stein, Grenvik, & Stuart, 1989).

CONCLUSION

We have available today forms of medical intervention for older persons that were undreamed of only a few years ago; the possibilities of medicine have expanded enormously, even since the first two editions of this book were written. The central questions have become, which of these interventions should be used and when? The ending of life presents wrenching clinical, ethical, financial (Gillick, 1994), and legal challenges. For health care professionals who care for older patients during this process, it is imperative that these four aspects of this inevitable dilemma be dealt with effectively and humanely, for the benefit of patient, family, professional, and society alike (Institute of Medicine, 1997a).

Chapter 12
Research with Older Human Subjects

IMPORTANCE OF CLINICAL GERIATRIC RESEARCH

"Research means a systematic investigation designed to develop or contribute to generalizable knowledge," 45 C.F.R. §46.102(e). It is different from medical practice, which consists of interventions that are designed solely to enhance the well-being of an individual patient and that have a reasonable expectation of success.

It is appropriate and important for investigators from the social and behavioral sciences, from the health services and policy arena (Brett & Grodin, 1991), and from basic sciences and clinical medicine (Sachs & Cassel, 1990) to conduct research activities on a broad array of geriatric issues. It is, in fact, essential for extensive high-quality research to be done if the lives of older citizens are to be significantly enhanced in the years to come (USDHHS, 1995).

In many circumstances, particularly in clinical investigations, worthwhile research primarily intended to benefit older persons as a group demands that the human subjects taking part in the protocols be themselves drawn from the ranks of the older community. Research on the aging process and diseases that accompany old age could become unapproachable in many cases without the conduct of investigatory procedures on older persons themselves. In some situations, there simply are not acceptable substitutes for older human subjects. One prominent example of this category of research involves investigations into senile dementia of the Alzheimer's type (SDAT). This is a devastating affliction with a vastly disproportionate impact on the aged (and their families and treating health care professionals), and it is not realistic to expect any real developments in ameliorating this condition without the active cooperation of large numbers of personally afflicted older human subjects (Dresser, 1996;

Sachs & Cohen, 1997). Similarly, new knowledge on drugs and the elderly compels human-subjects research (Avorn, 1990).

A serious quandary is thus presented for health care professionals who either (1) are themselves engaged in clinical geriatric research or (2) treat as patients older individuals who are solicited to become human subjects. How best should we balance the private rights of the older individual against the researchers' contemplated potential future benefits to the aged as a group? Health care institutions within which human-subjects research is going to be conducted should develop and implement clear, written policies and procedures governing the conduct of such research and the rights and responsibilities of respective parties (Berg, 1996; Keyserlingk, Glass, Kogan, & Gauthier, 1995). This chapter first describes the basic legal principles that generally govern biomedical and behavioral research using human subjects in the United States. This general treatment is followed by a look at some specific considerations that arise when the human subjects to be utilized happen to be older.

Even for health care practitioners who are neither actively engaged in clinical investigation nor caring for patients who are solicited to become human subjects, a rudimentary understanding of the legal and ethical environment surrounding the conduct of human-subjects research will be valuable. Since every practitioner is in one way or another a utilizer of the fruits of earlier research, some appreciation of how available research results and consequent changes in clinical practice came to pass is essential to optimal, responsible, up-to-date patient care.

GENERAL LEGAL REQUIREMENTS

The Development of Governmental Regulation

The historical underpinnings leading up to the current status of government regulation of biomedical research involving human subjects in the United States have been amply chronicled elsewhere (Rothman, 1991). Beginning with the Nuremberg Code, adopted in 1947 for use in Nazi war crimes trials in which defendant physicians tried to justify their inhumane treatment of human beings under the guise of scientific experimentation (Annas & Grodin, 1992; Lifton, 1986; Pellegrino, 1997), the proper conduct of human experimentation has been formalized into over 30 different international guidelines and ethical codes since World War II (Brody, 1998). In 1993, the Council for International Organizations of Medical Sciences issued revised _International Ethical Guidelines for Biomedical Research Involving Human Subjects._

Implicitly or explicitly, these guidelines and ethical codes all emphasize the concept of informed consent (Kapp, 1995a) (see Chapter 3) and draw on the following principles: (1) The subject must have volunteered on the basis of having had all of the information necessary for his or her decision to be an informed one; (2) the subject should be allowed to withdraw from the research at any time without negative repercussions; (3) all unnecessary risks (risks being defined to include not only invasive physical procedures but also matters of confidentiality and social and psychological jeopardy) should be eliminated, and if feasible, computer and animal studies should precede those on humans; (4) the benefits of the research to the subject or to society, preferably to both, should outweigh the risks to the subject; and (5) research should be conducted only by qualified researchers.

In the United States, federal government involvement in the regulation of biomedical research began in 1966. Officials at the Public Health Service (PHS), the branch of what was then the Department of Health, Education, and Welfare (DHEW, now Health and Human Services, DHHS) providing the majority of federal funding for extramural research, became concerned about the increasing frequency with which human subjects were being used. Formulation of a formal PHS policy was initiated, and resulting guidelines were eventually released in May 1969. These guidelines served as a model for the development of a department-wide DHEW policy announced in April 1971. DHEW's guide (USDHEW, 1971) retained the institutional review process initiated by PHS; that is, the administrative review machinery was adjusted to cope with the rising tide of research being conducted with human subjects by switching from the prior centrally conducted, grant-by-grant review procedure to an individual institutional responsibility for compliance with ethical standards. The DHEW publication also included more specific requirements for obtaining informed consent than did the PHS guidelines.

In 1974, these DHEW policy guidelines were translated into enforceable law through publication of regulations in the *Federal Register*. These regulations formalized the institutional review boards (IRBs) by withholding DHEW financial research support from institutions unless they had established an organizational review committee that was reviewed and approved by DHEW. It became incumbent upon these internal review committees to provide both general and special assurances of subject protection, as well as documentation of informed consent.

The next significant step was enactment of Public Law 93-348 by Congress on July 12, 1974. This law, commonly known as the National Research Act, established the National Commission for the Protection of Human Subjects in Biomedical and Behavioral Research (the Belmont

Commission). This 11-member body with a 2-year lease on life was charged by Congress to (1) conduct a comprehensive study to identify the basic ethical principles that should underlie the conduct of biomedical and behavioral research involving human subjects and (2) recommend to the secretary of DHEW research guidelines and administrative actions for the implementation of those guidelines. The accelerating public concern with the protection of subjects thought to be at special risk can be seen in Congress's specific charge to the commission to investigate the ethics of (1) research with children, (2) research with prisoners in correctional institutions, (3) research on the institutionalized mentally infirm (delineated as those "mentally retarded, emotionally disturbed, psychotic, or senile" persons who reside as patients in a health care institution), (4) research involving living fetuses, and (5) psychosurgery. After extensive hearings, meetings, and deliberations, the commission issued a series of reports and recommendations between 1975 and 1977.

Although the commission concentrated in particular on the ethics of experimenting on certain identified subgroups of the population, it also studied the overall question of how research subjects in general can best be protected from harmful research practices. The commission followed the basic thrust of earlier federal pronouncements by recommending (1) that all research involving human subjects conducted at an institution that receives federal funding be reviewed by an IRB before it is begun and (2) that there be prior informed consent by the subject involved.

Final regulations resulting from these recommendations were not issued until the January 26, 1981, _Federal Register_. These regulations became legally effective on July 27, 1981, and are codified at 45 C.F.R., part 46.

The federal regulations originally applied on their face only to research involving human subjects that was conducted by the DHHS itself or funded in whole or in part by the department. However, most institutions conducting research have voluntarily agreed to apply the federal regulations to all of their research protocols, regardless of funding source for a particular study. Additionally, other federal agencies have adopted a Common Rule for human subjects protection in any research protocol that they sponsor, 45 C.F.R., part 46, subpart A.

Specifically excluded from coverage by regulatory exemption is most research involving normal educational practices or use of educational tests, research involving survey or interview procedures, research involving the observation of public behavior, and research "involving the collection or study of existing data, documents, records, pathological specimens, or diagnostic specimens, if these sources are publicly available or if the information is recorded by the investigator in such a manner that subjects cannot be identified." Moreover, the secretary of DHHS may waive application of the regulations to specific research or classes of research that would otherwise be covered.

Much has been happening lately in the ethics of human-subjects research generally. For example, 1997 marked the 50th anniversary of an international tribunal declaring the Nuremberg Code to be the standard by which German physicians should be judged for their involvement in horrific experiments on concentration camp inmates during the Holocaust (Shuster, 1997). In October 1995, the President's Advisory Committee on Human Radiation Experiments reported that, between 1944 and 1974, the U.S. government sponsored several thousand human radiation experiments. It further found that government officials and investigators were blameworthy for not having had policies and practices in place to protect the rights and interests of human subjects who were used in research from which those subjects could not possibly derive any direct, personal medical benefit. This advisory committee recommended that a mechanism be established to provide for continuing interpretation and application in an open and public forum of ethics rules and principles for the conduct of human subjects research, and identified guidelines for research with adults of questionable competence as one policy issue (among others) needing public resolution.

On October 3, 1995, President Clinton created, through Executive Order No. 12975, published at 60 *Federal Register* 52063, the National Bioethics Advisory Commission (NBAC), with one of its enumerated key functions the identification of principles to govern the ethical conduct of human-subjects research. As of late 1998, this commission was actively considering a proposal to create a new, independent federal government office to regulate the protection of human subjects in federally financed research. In fiscal year 1997, the National Institutes of Health (NIH) (including the National Institute on Aging [NIA]) joined with the federal Departments of Energy and Veterans Affairs in issuing a Request for Applications for original research proposals in the area of "Informed Consent in Research Involving Human Participants." In the U.S. Senate, John Glenn (Ohio) introduced in the 105th Congress the Human Research Subject Protections Act, S. 193, which would, among its other provisions, have made violation of rules established to protect research subjects a criminal offense. Congress did not vote on this bill.

Institutional Review Boards

Research to which the federal Common Rule regulations apply must be reviewed and approved by an IRB and must be subject to continuing IRB review. IRB approval is necessary initially and at least annually thereafter.

An IRB must have at least five members of varying backgrounds; at least one must be from a nonscientific area, and at least one must be from outside the institution. However, if the research involves "no more than minimal risk" or "minor changes in previously approved research," then approval—but not disapproval—can be given through an expedited review procedure under which "the review may be carried out by the IRB chairperson or by one or more experienced reviewers designated by the chairperson from among members of the IRB." Minimal risk is defined as not greater than "those ordinarily encountered in daily life or during the performance of routine physical or psychological examinations or tests." It specifically includes such things as collection of hair, nail clippings, excreta, and external secretions; recordings of data from adult subjects, using noninvasive procedures; and the study of existing data, documents, records, and pathological and diagnostic specimens.

In order to approve research, the IRB must determine that each of the following requirements is satisfied:

1. Physical and psychological risks to subjects are minimized.
2. Physical and psychological risks to subjects are reasonable in relation to anticipated benefits to those subjects and to the importance of the general knowledge that may reasonably be expected to result.
3. Selection of subjects is equitable.
4. Informed consent will be sought.
5. Informed consent will be appropriately documented.
6. Where appropriate, the research plan makes adequate provisions for monitoring the data collected to ensure the safety of subjects.
7. Where appropriate, there are adequate provisions to protect the privacy of subjects and maintain the confidentiality of data (see Chapter 4).

No human subjects may be involved in research unless legally effective informed consent has been obtained and "only under circumstances that provide the prospective subject . . . sufficient opportunity to consider whether or not to participate and that minimize the possibility of coercion or undue influence."

The regulatory provisions for informed consent in research are basically a codification and an extension of the common law that was developed in the therapeutic setting (see Chapter 3). At an operational level, important distinctions between the nature and purpose of research and clinical practice affect the characteristics of informed consent applicable to either of these two realms. At a more basic level, though, there is much more similarity than difference because the fundamental purpose of informed consent is the same in research, therapy, or in any other health care context (Levine, 1983).

Specifically, informed consent for research requires that the prospective subject must be provided with

1. A statement that the study involves research, an explanation of the purposes of the research and the expected duration of the subject's participation, a description of the procedures to be followed, and identification of any experimental procedures.
2. A description of any reasonably foreseeable risks or discomforts to the subject.
3. A description of any benefits to the subject or to others that may reasonably be expected from the research.
4. A disclosure of appropriate alternative procedures or courses of treatment, if any, that might be advantageous to the subject.
5. A statement describing the extent, if any, to which confidentiality of records identifying the subject will be maintained.
6. An explanation for research involving more than minimal risk, as to whether any compensation and any medical treatments are available if injury occurs and, if so, what they consist of or where further information may be obtained.
7. An explanation of whom to contact for answers to pertinent questions about the research and research subjects' rights and whom to contact in the event of a research-related injury to the subject.
8. A statement that participation is voluntary, refusal to participate will involve no penalty or loss of benefits to which the subject is otherwise entitled, and the subject may discontinue participation at any time without penalty or loss of benefits to which the subject is otherwise entitled.

An IRB may "approve a consent procedure that does not include, or which alters, some or all of the elements of informed consent . . . or waive the requirement to obtain informed consent" when the waiver or alteration "will not adversely affect the rights and welfare of the subjects" or when the research involves "no more than minimal risk" or "could not practicably be carried out without the waiver or alteration."

In October 1996, DHHS issued regulations creating a special exception allowing an IRB to waive the usual informed consent requirements in the case of certain research involving emergency interventions, 61 *Federal Register* 51498–51533 (Wichman & Sandler, 1997). Waiver is permissible when the potential subject's life is in jeopardy, standard therapy is likely to be ineffective, and obtaining timely informed consent would be impossible.

Some commentators have tried to draw a parallel between such situations and those involving seriously demented patients who cannot personally give informed consent but who desperately need the development of more efficacious interventions (Karlawish & Sachs, 1997).

One area in which the research regulations go beyond common law is the requirement that informed consent be documented, either by the signing of a written consent form embodying the elements of informed consent listed above or with a " 'short form' written consent document stating the elements of informed consent required . . . have been presented orally to the subject or the subject's legally authorized representative. When this method is used, there shall be a witness to the oral presentation." An IRB may waive the requirement of a signed consent form for research that "presents no more than minimal risk of harm to subjects and involves no procedures for which consent is normally required outside of the research context" or if "the only record linking the subject and the research would be the consent document and the principal risk would be potential harm resulting from a breach of confidentiality."

Some states also have passed laws concerning conditions for human experimentation in situations not covered by federal regulations; such laws also require some manner of prior review and supervision. State statutory treatment of informed consent to human experimentation runs the gamut from comprehensive, specific coverage of the issue to general treatment in informed consent statutes. A few states have enacted legislation that specifically addresses informed consent in the research context, enumerating particular elements of information that must be communicated to the prospective human subject. Some state statutes expressly require informed consent to human-subjects research, without specifying in detail the exact elements of information disclosure. Some states have created legislation concerning human experimentation as part of general patients' rights laws. Other statutes address research on human subjects in miscellaneous provisions, such as regulation of cancer interventions. The majority of states have not dealt specifically with informed consent to human experimentation but instead have passed general informed consent statutes (see Chapter 3) that govern in the absence of more explicit law. Some state laws focus on research involving particular drugs, such as controlled substances or marijuana. It is essential for health care professionals to be familiar with any particular requirements of their own jurisdictions.

Although health care professionals have an ethical duty to safeguard the integrity of older individuals, there are also important practical reasons for knowing and complying with legal requirements in this area. One important function of the formal process is to protect investigators and other professionals who comply strictly with its provisions from subsequent claims of legal liability. Strict compliance, of course, should not result in an emphasis of form over substance. The first step in meeting one's legal and ethical obligations is to establish contact with the appropriate IRB. Every research-conducting institution or company subject to the federal guidelines must either (1) adopt and submit to DHHS an "assurance" that establishes an IRB and describes review and implementation procedures or (2) contract with an approved IRB for review of protocols. The assurance document, plus the IRB's own rules and regulations, should provide guidance for the investigator or clinician. In any research project, however, it is the investigator who bears the primary legal and administrative responsibility and who must inform the institution if human subjects are involved in the research design—in which case the proposal must come before the IRB.

SPECIAL CONSIDERATIONS
FOR OLDER SUBJECTS

A number of guidelines have been promulgated recently attempting to address ethical facets of the research enterprise pertaining specifically to cognitively impaired potential subjects. These various proposed guidelines respond to the fact that the federal government has never followed through with tangible action—proposed rules published at 43 *Federal Register* 53,954 were never made final—on the 1978 recommendation of the Belmont Commission that, at least for individuals institutionalized as mentally disabled, there be promulgated distinct regulations governing human-subjects research (Levine, 1996). Neither has action been taken in response to recommendations emanating from an NIA-sponsored study group that convened a decade and a half ago to discuss the use of demented persons in research (Melnick & Dubler, 1985; Melnick, Dubler, Weisbard, & Butler, 1984). In November 1998, NBAC issued a report endorsing specific regulations in this sphere.

Along with other groups, the national Alzheimer's Association recently has called "upon state and federal authorities to clarify existing laws and regulations as they relate to research on people with cognitive impairments." Among the organizations that have developed and adopted relevant research guidelines during the past several years are the Alzheimer's Association (1997), American College of Physicians (1989), NIH Clinical Center (1986), Council for International Organizations of Medical Sciences (in collaboration with the World Health Organization) (1993), Council of Europe (de Wachter, 1997), and the British Medical Research Council (Medical Research Council Working Party, 1991). The American Psychiatric Association has organized a work group for the purpose of formulating ethical guidelines for psychiatric researchers dealing with the decisionally impaired (Appelbaum, 1996). A number of individual scholars also have weighed in with comprehensive policy proposals in the area (Dresser, 1996; High, Whitehouse, Post, & Berg, 1994; Keyserlingk et al., 1995).

While some commentators lament that no consensus or uniform approach to the ethical conundrums raised by conducting research with severely cognitively impaired human subjects have yet been achieved (DeRenzo, 1994) and that government pronouncements are fairly non-committal, the various sets of guidelines promulgated thus far share certain common threads. In essence, they tend to develop various sliding scales of permissibility and protections based on a categorization of research protocols in terms of (a) degree of risk (minimal versus greater than minimal) to the subject (Glass & Speyer-Ofenberg, 1996) and (b) potential for direct, tangible benefit to the subject personally. More specifically, the main research categories addressed by the various promulgated guidelines fit into four quadrants: (1) research in which there is potential therapeutic benefit for the subject and no more than minimal risk, (2) research in which there is potential therapeutic benefit for the subject but more than minimal risk, (3) research in which there is no expected therapeutic benefit for the subject personally and no more than minimal risk, and (4) research in which there is no expected therapeutic benefit for the subject and more than minimal risk.

In a broad sense, neither the ethical principles nor the dilemmas in research with older adults differ on the basis of chronological age alone from the principles and dilemmas associated with any biomedical, behavioral, or social science research with any age group (Sachs & Cassel, 1990). Therefore, in principle, it makes sense to treat older subjects according to the same ethical considerations and legal restrictions that apply to a person of any age. Certainly, there is no clear consensus that special ethical principles and legal rules are needed to respond to the moral dilemmas raised by biomedical or behavioral research in the aged.

There have been several arguments made against singling out older persons for special treatment. It might be impossible to define adequately who should be included within such a class and, moreover, what would be needed to protect the persons so classified, because they represent such a diverse range of people. The existence of wide variations in intellectual or physiological impairment or lack of it among older persons makes any general requirements inappropriate for specific individuals. To separate out the aged as a special group incapable of caring for its own members would only further stigmatize them. Finally, special provisions for research with older subjects might inhibit rather than enhance the ability of researchers to seek answers to serious problems that disproportionately affect older persons, such as senile dementia (Hirschfeld, Winslade & Krause, 1997).

The desirable resolution is to utilize the prevailing standards of competence, knowledge, and voluntariness but to test for these elements with inquiries that are appropriate and relevant to the specific patient or subject, regardless of age. Thus, although there often is a clustering of physiological and affective changes as one ages, the aging processes must be considered only when pertinent and not necessarily in all aspects for all older patients.

The real problem arises when older individuals have, as they often do, other characteristics (besides chronological years) that render them especially vulnerable to abuse as research subjects. Some persons are also poor, impaired, institutionalized, and/or without family or significant others, in addition to being older. Such a combination of factors has led to serious abuse of the elderly in the past (*Hyman v. Jewish Chronic Disease Hospital,* 1965). Many older persons also have weak formal educational backgrounds, which may impair their comprehension of information. The task for the clinical investigator or health care professional serving geriatric patients is to examine the circumstances of each potential human subject to determine whether one or a combination of those other characteristics impedes the ability of the older person to offer voluntary, competent, informed consent to participation in the research protocol.

Several factors potentially jeopardize the voluntary nature of an older subject's consent to research involvement, which is the first essential element of legally effective consent. First, today's older people are products of an earlier era, an era of greater public acceptance of and deference to authority and authority figures. The questioning and challenging of authority that contemporary younger people take for granted is a very modern phenomenon. Many older citizens do not share the healthy skepticism, especially toward the uses and practices of science, that guides many of their younger counterparts. The reluctance of an older person to offend authority—represented by the clinical investigator (who may also be the treating caregiver) seeking informed consent pursuant to the research design—may be the deciding factor in his or her agreeing to comply, rather than more positive motivations of inquisitiveness, altruism, or anticipation of benefit.

Additionally, consent to research participation is frequently sought from older potential subjects in environments or atmospheres that have inherent elements of coerciveness. Older nursing facility (NF) or other institutional residents make a particularly attractive "captive population" for researchers. These individuals run an increased risk of vulnerability because they are so heavily dependent on their caregivers, especially their health care professionals, for fulfillment of many of their most basic daily physical, emotional, and social needs. This extreme dependence on assistance, in the face of a previous lifetime of independence, ordinarily tends to encourage passivity and willingness to comply with instructions and threatens the psychological ability of the older person to say no to a figure of authority whom the older person needs and, generally, respects. The coercive aspect of dependency in old age may be subtle and may vary appreciably among individuals, but it is a force that those involved in obtaining consent within dependency-breeding settings must acknowledge.

Another factor contributing to potential vulnerability is the fact that many older persons are alone in this world, without the support of interested, involved family or friends. Studies have shown that older individuals without family ties are much more likely to volunteer for research than are those with such ties (Berkowitz, 1978). The disproportionate participation of the "unbefriended" may merely reflect a greater willingness to volunteer when the volunteer is not connected to others. But it is also likely that the absence of family or other confidants removes an invaluable forum for consideration of the risks involved. Absence of this forum could also mean, to an isolated individual, that any weighing of the risks is a futile gesture because no one would care about his or her decision anyway.

It also is possible that an aged subject, stricken with depression, may consent in the hope of gaining some measure of respect from those surrounding him or her. Another older and depressed subject may consent out of indifference to whether he or she lives or dies (Elliott, 1997). Perhaps, as well, the promise of improved living conditions, better food, or just more personal attention may induce consent from a vulnerable older person (Kaye, Lawton, & Kaye, 1990).

Although old age, when combined with other factors mentioned, may induce subject cooperation on less than a fully voluntary basis, the opposite result may ensue instead. That is, some older persons may react to researchers' proposals overcautiously and may refuse at a disproportionate rate. Richard Ratzan (1982) has offered some possible explanations for this type of reaction. First, for older persons, comfort often supersedes risk as a decisive element in medical decision making. For the institutionalized aged, constantly surrounded by inevitable death, the goal is often optimal comfort—not maximum life—and this preference is perfectly logical and appropriate for some elderly. A second reason is that, whereas older persons without family are more likely to volunteer for research, older persons who have active families may be unduly influenced and overprotected against research participation by excessively apprehensive and guilt-plagued relatives. An older person may feel some sense of duty to relatives that compels refusal to permit research. Researchers should involve family members thoroughly in consent conversations, if this is consistent with the subject's wishes regarding confidentiality, to gain family understanding and commitment and thus to avoid being undercut by them later. A third explanation for disproportionate rejection centers on the paternalism practiced by many personal health professionals serving older patients. Particularly the private physician, Ratzan argues, often convinces the older patient and family to avoid research participation out of a sincere but overblown sense of protectionism.

A second essential element of effective consent for research participation that may be jeopardized in older subjects is that of mental competence. The legal principles applicable in research are the same as those applicable in therapeutic situations involving other adult patients (see Chapter 3). Cognitive and emotional impairments that are often a natural concomitant of the aging process raise questions but do not automatically disqualify the individual from making choices (Weintraub, 1984). Neither does residence in a nursing or mental health facility. Each prospective research subject requires a careful individual assessment of functional capacity to engage in rational decision making—that is, an evaluation of both comprehension and the quality of reasoning (Sachs et al., 1994).

Both the researcher and the direct caregiving health care professional should realize that personal idiosyncratic and cultural biases play a role in making the acquisition of informed consent among older persons especially complex. The elderly bring to the decision-making process lifelong-developed goals and values. Also, the timing of consent is particularly important because competency often tends to wax and wane more dramatically among older persons. Additionally, innumerable gradations of capacity inevitably are present in clinical geriatric practice (Kapp & Mossman, 1996).

All of these factors can make research on older persons problematic. They present the most serious difficulty when the research itself is directly concerned with some aspect of mental dysfunction, such as Alzheimer's disease or other forms of senile dementia. In such catch-22 situations, effective research virtually compels the participation of subjects suffering from a degree of mental impairment that may prejudice their personal capacity to consent (Popp & Moore, 1994).

The third mandatory element of effective consent, disclosure of adequate information, also presents important considerations when the prospective subjects are older. Some believe that the mere suggestion of research involvement to an older person may in itself engender a high degree of anxiety that seriously interferes with the individual's capacity to process and comprehend the information that is being communicated. In this view, the presence of a formal, written consent form to be signed may heighten this incapacitating sense of apprehension. Further, the investigator's way of framing the risks of an experiment can diminish or enhance the cautiousness of older subjects. In no event can known material information (i.e., information that might make a difference) purposely be withheld from a subject in the research context under a justification of therapeutic privilege or exception (see Chapter 3), because that doctrine, by definition, is limited to therapeutic interventions.

Several suggestions have been put forward to address the issues of voluntariness, competence, and understanding when older human-subject research is contemplated, especially in the NF setting (Sachs, Rhymes, & Cassel, 1993). Some contributors to this discussion have urged IRBs to involve various sorts of independent third parties to assist in and oversee consent negotiations in situations involving especially vulnerable population groups such as the cognitively impaired aged. Extant federal regulations already give IRBs the "authority to observe or have a third party observe the consent process," 45 C.F.R. §46.109(e). This third-party concept has been discussed under the titles of "auditor," "advocate," neutral person" (Levine, 1986), and "risk advisor" (Ratzan, 1982). The National Alliance for the Mentally Ill (NAMI) has adopted as a core principle that "[t]he determination of competence shall be made by someone other than the principal investigator or others involved in the research" (Flynn, 1997).

Taking this approach to its logical extreme, based on his stated distrust of both self-interested researchers and institution-protecting IRBs, attorney Philip Bein (1991) has called for creation of a new administrative program in which independent advocates employed by the DHHS's Office of Inspector General would determine the decision-making status of prospective research subjects and assist the families of incapacitated persons in the process of deciding whether or not to enroll their relatives in specific protocols. In the absence of this administrative structure, Bein argues for prior judicial approval of every instance of research participation involving a person currently unable to consent on his own behalf. A notably less cynical (not to mention less bureaucratic) approach has been practiced at the Clinical Center of the NIH, where the subject's noninvestigator attending physician directs the process for determining the level of impairment and decision-making capacity (Fletcher, Dommel, & Cowell, 1985).

A leading group of Canadian scholars has concluded that, as a general rule, assessment and monitoring of the prospective subject's decisional capacity should be conducted by the research team in collaboration with family members (Keyserlingk et al., 1995). This model recognizes four exceptions when it is appropriate for an IRB to mandate the involvement of a consent assessor/monitor independent of the research project: (a) the project staff lack the necessary skills to assess or monitor the capacity of prospective subjects; (b) the investigator or IRB perceives a particularly strong danger of conflict of interest; (c) a previously capable prospective subject had executed an advance directive concerning research, but the person's wishes under the circumstances require interpretation; and (d) the research protocol's interventions entail more than minimal risk and do not hold out the prospect of direct benefit for the individual subjects.

The IRB would appear to be the best instrument for assuring the voluntariness of consent to geriatric research, particularly if its members are attuned to the special considerations that affect older subje[.] ιs (Kapp, 1998b). Properly functioning, the IRB can perform the multipιe roles of (1) protecting vulnerable older persons from abuse while not overly shielding them, (2) advocating in favor of elderly research participation in appropriate protocols, and (3) monitoring the consent process in operation. Some have suggested that this latter function be assigned to a separate, independent "consent auditor" (Schwartz, 1981), whose job would be to assess the subject's actual understanding of the information communicated.

On this question of voluntariness, the clinical investigator and the individual's personal health care professionals must keep firmly in mind the distinction between research and therapy (Levine, 1983). Although the health care professional has both the right and the duty to seriously attempt to persuade a patient to accept medically indicated treatment (i.e., medical intervention that is expected and intended to yield a direct therapeutic benefit to that particular patient), there exists neither the right nor the duty to seriously pressure an individual to participate in a research project that is not expected or intended to benefit that individual directly.

Because an incompetent person cannot supply legally effective consent for research participation, any more than for therapeutic intervention, it is imperative that the investigator know clearly whether the legal power to consent to research participation lies with the potential subject or with some surrogate decision maker.

A determination that a prospective human subject is not capable of making and expressing a legally and ethically valid decision regarding research participation in no way dispenses with the usual requirement of informed consent. Instead, it means that any legitimate consent for participation must come from a surrogate who makes choices on behalf of the incapacitated person. Current federal regulations supply little guidance in this matter, beyond requiring that "[i]nformed consent will be sought from each prospective subject or the subject's legally authorized representative" under state law, 45 C.F.R. §111(a)(4). Only a few states have enacted statutes explicitly giving designated relatives the legal authority to consent to research participation on behalf of a decisionally incapacitated relative.

Important international guidelines are similarly vague, stating that "[f]or all biomedical research involving human subjects, the investigator must obtain the informed consent of the prospective subject or, in the case of an individual who is not capable of giving informed consent, the proxy consent of a properly authorized representative" (Council for International Organizations of Medical Sciences, 1993).

According to survey responses from IRB officials, a majority of IRBs allow a family member or friend to give consent for the research participation of a demented person, although two thirds of this group limit surrogate decision makers to relatives (LeBlang & Kirchner, 1996). NAMI endorses a preference for family members as ordinarily the most appropriate surrogates in the research situation (Flynn, 1997). A minority of IRBs appear to interpret the meaning of "legally authorized representative" restrictively, limiting recognition to court-appointed guardians, designated health care agents under a written durable power of attorney (DPA), a health care surrogate empowered under express state statute, or a combination of these individuals (LeBlang & Kirchner, 1996).

Once the individual's functional mental abilities have become problematic, the only definite legal resolution is judicial appointment of a guardian for the incompetent ward (see Chapter 8). However, attorney Rebecca Dresser and neurologist Peter Whitehouse (1997) have argued convincingly against the need for or effectiveness of formal legal proceedings as a routine way to protect incapable subjects:

> The legal guardianship inquiry is insufficiently focused to provide an adequate forum for addressing issues raised by particular research projects. We believe the delays and financial costs of formal proceedings are not justified because better alternatives are available for ensuring appropriate protection for prospective subjects with cognitive impairment.

Philosopher Dallas High and colleagues (1994) are in accord, although they add, "However, family members may be disqualified as surrogates for a variety of reasons, including lack of capacity, unavailability, or inattention to the subject's well-being." As a practical matter, requiring court appointment of a guardian as a formal prerequisite for research participation—with its attendant expense, time, general hassle, and difficulties in identifying a willing and suitable person to be appointed—probably would preclude the conduct of much research relying on cognitively impaired research subjects in the future. As an alternative, IRBs might require facilities in which research is to be conducted to emulate the model in place at the NIH Clinical Center: an extensive internal system of oversight and consultation that swings into action once the appointment of a surrogate decision maker has been authorized by the IRB (Candilis, Wesley, & Wichman, 1993).

Recent landmark litigation illustrates how excessive insistence on the formalities of proxy consent may sow the seeds of potential devastation for the effective future conduct of human-subjects research on mental impairment (Capron, 1997). The most noteworthy case grows out of 1990 regulations issued by the New York State Office of Mental Health, which were designed to respect the autonomy of psychiatric inpatients in state-operated or -licensed facilities to make decisions about participation in research while protecting patients whose capacity to consent may be impaired. Under these regulations, patients who lack adequate capacity to give valid consent on their own could be included in research with the consent of a specified legally authorized surrogate. Surrogate consent could be given only if (1) the facility's IRB determined that the research could not be done without the participation of incapable subjects and (2) the study was (a) considered likely to produce knowledge of overriding therapeutic importance for persons with the subject's condition or (b) it had the possibility of directly benefiting the particular subject. In all cases involving more than minimal risk, the approval of the subject's treatment team would have been required as well, 14 NYCRR §527.10 (Delano & Zucker, 1994).

Despite this panoply of protections, the regulations were challenged for their failure to comply with New York Public Health Law Article 24-A, which was adopted in 1975 following public reaction to experiments performed in the 1960s and early 1970s on mentally impaired persons in New York. In April 1995, the trial court issued an order invalidating the regulations for the procedural reason that they had been issued by the mental health commissioner instead of the health commissioner. On December 5, 1996, New York's highest court upheld the decision below, *T.D. v. New York State Office of Mental Health.* In addition, the Court of Appeals, anticipating that the state might attempt to cure the procedural defects and reissue the regulations in compliance with proper administrative requirements, held that even if the regulations were lawfully promulgated they would violate potential research subjects' rights regarding bodily integrity under both the common law and the due process clauses of the state and federal constitutions.

This judicial opinion was urged by a herd of self-appointed health consumer advocates (interestingly, none of them concentrate on representing the interests of older persons). It effectively prohibits the conduct of biomedical and behavioral research, regardless of funding source, using any human subject who cannot personally give contemporaneous consent to his or her own participation. The court's decision is limited on its face to inpatients in facilities either owned or licensed by the New York Office of Mental Health. Nevertheless, the *T.D.* ruling has generated enormous attention nationally, with expansion—in terms of how researchers and health care providers are interpreting and applying it in practice—to other jurisdictions and settings (including NFs) already being reported anecdotally. Further expansion of this case's impact is quite reasonably foreseeable.

Even when incompetence has been adjudicated and a proxy appointment has been made, the investigator must inquire about any express or inherent limitations on the decision-making authority of the guardian that might interfere with the proxy's legal power to volunteer the ward for research. If proxy consent to research participation is being relied on, the investigator has the ethical, if not the legal, responsibility to inquire whether the choice made for the older subject is consistent with that subject's own previous values and preferences.

In terms of the decision-making standards or tests to be employed by a surrogate on behalf of a demented potential subject, a mail survey of IRBs found that about half the respondents permitted surrogates to use either the best-interests or substituted-judgment (i.e., what the subject would personally choose if currently decisionally capable) tests (LeBlang & Kirchner, 1996). Assorted other IRBs indicated that they either require one test or the other or have no formal policy on this point. Respect for the idea of including the perspective of the subject as much as feasible leads many IRBs to require the subject's assent, as well as the surrogate's legally necessary consent, before enrollment in a study may occur (Sachs et al., 1994). This requirement in effect gives the potential subject absolute veto power.

There is no reason that the DPA device that is discussed in Chapter 8 for therapeutic situations should not be extended to the research context as a means of allowing the potential future research subject to personally select his or her own surrogate decision maker in the event that subsequent incapacity should occur. This document would name someone else to act as a proxy with delegated authority to continue or discontinue the subject's participation in the study even as the decisional capacity of the actual subject falls below the minimum level needed for valid choice (Dukoff & Sunderland, 1997). This approach arguably has the advantage of identifying and empowering a living, breathing, capable advocate to weigh shifting risks and benefits on a continuing, dynamic basis. Thus, the problem of the incompetent subject may be foreseen and prepared for in advance by the formal designation of another who ordinarily should be trusted to act in the older person's best interests (Kapp, 1994c; Sachs, 1994a). Empowerment of a proxy to make legally effective decisions in this regard should be combined with respect for the subject's right—even when exercised incompetently—to withdraw from a study by actively manifesting (e.g., by unambiguous forms of noncooperation) any objection to continued participation.

It also should be remembered that many important geriatric studies using simple chart reviews or aggregate statistics remain to be done. These studies do not require the active participation of actual human subjects. In such chart or statistical studies, the legal and ethical difficulties found in obtaining informed consent from questionably competent older persons for more invasive research are minimized, although recent state legislation and proposed federal legislation may seriously threaten investigators' ability to easily conduct medical records research (Melton, 1997). Additionally, much worthwhile geriatric research using simple surveys is needed. Although requiring the subject's informed consent, the legal and ethical problems in such survey research usually are less serious than arise in more intrusive, risky medical interventions.

In terms of the informed element of consent, the investigator may have to take special steps in communicating with older potential subjects to address their particular needs and characteristics. Modification of the manner of asking for consent from older individuals may include an extra effort on the investigator's part to reduce bureaucratic jargon and technical scientific terminology to a level more understandable to lay individuals. Special attention should be paid to the readability of written consent forms. Calculation and presentation of risks in comprehensible terms is vital to alleviating some of the anxieties that may lead older individuals to react overcautiously to research proposals. Because the physical deterioration that often accompanies aging may lead to a decrease in hearing ability and vision, researchers providing information to a subject who is hearing-impaired will have to speak loudly, and those presenting information to one who is visually impaired should not depend on the fine print of the written consent form. In such circumstances, including one of the subject's relatives or friends in the communications process is especially advisable.

It has been suggested that acceptance of oral consent be considered sufficient for older subjects who are made unnecessarily and unduly anxious by the prospect of affixing their signatures to formal documents and who decline participation solely for that reason (Makarushka & McDonald, 1979). At present, however, this is not an acceptable legal alternative except in those limited situations, enumerated earlier, involving IRB waiver of standard procedure.

In the context of human-subjects research whose topic is cognitive impairment, surely one of the most significant issues for continuing IRB oversight is the ongoing validity of informed consent, originally given by a subject when decisionally capable, as the protocol proceeds over a lengthy period of time. The capacity of an individual with a cognitive impairment may either remain relatively constant, fluctuate, or steadily, inexorably deteriorate (Glass & Somerville, 1991). A person who is capable of comprehending the nature of a specific research protocol at the beginning of the process (the time when informed consent typically is sought, provided, and documented) may not be able to comprehend and manipulate material information at later points during the research process.

Changes in capacity may occur as a result of the natural history of the individual's underlying medical ailment and/or the study intervention itself.

A number of commentators advocate the popularization of advance instruction directives for research participation (Keyserlingk et al., 1995), analogous to the living wills that are executed widely by currently capable persons in an attempt to prospectively control the future use of life-sustaining medical interventions (see Chapter 11). Even if such directives turn out to be useful in enrolling a person in a study in the first instance, though, how does the continued participation by a now-incapacitated subject square with the law's guaranty, at 45 C.F.R. §46.116(a)(8), of a right to withdraw from any protocol at any time without penalty or reprisal? How could the right to withdraw be exerted and by whom?

Another possible intervention by the IRB might be to appoint and assign some sort of third-party monitor, mentioned earlier in the context of initial protocol approval, to be involved on an ongoing basis throughout the conduct of a longitudinal protocol. This monitor or "research intermediary" (Reiser & Knudson, 1993) could be authorized to terminate a particular subject's participation—or to end the entire protocol early—in the event that an unacceptable risk/benefit ratio develops (i.e., that the principle of equipoise is out of kilter [Karlawish, 1997; Karlawish & Lantos, 1997]) or there is a clear manifestation of a subject's desire (even if incompetently formulated) to withdraw. Since the monitor is not selected by the subject, this approach is less consistent than the DPA with facilitating the subject's own autonomy. Accordingly, it should be limited—if utilized at all—to situations in which no DPA or other valid proxy directive was timely executed by a previously capable, prospectively thinking human subject.

CONCLUSION

I have attempted in this chapter to point out some of the unique and interesting legal and ethical challenges that the older research population presents to both clinical investigators and caregiving health care professionals. It is imperative to protect from exploitation those older individuals who are vulnerable due to a combination of advanced years and mental or physical impairment, institutionalization, or psychological isolation. I have endeavored to offer some insights into how such protection might reasonably be accomplished.

It is essential at the same time, however, that neither the individual investigator, the older person's health care professionals (including the personal physician), nor society as a whole (through the enactment of laws) (DeRenzo, 1997) commit the mistake of excessive paternalism toward the older potential research subject. There are many dangers, both philosophical and practical, of adverse consequences stemming from over-protectionism.

Philosophically speaking, unduly inhibiting the ability of older persons to consent to research involvement arguably deprives them of a measure of decision-making autonomy and unfairly stigmatizes them as not worthy of full self-determination. This affront to their right to control their own participation may come at the same time that other intrusions into their autonomy are materializing in their lives, such as the loss of individual prerogative that necessarily accompanies entry into an NF.

On the more tangible level, there are both direct and indirect detriments that the older individual might suffer as a consequence of being deprived of the opportunity to consent to research participation. Because many research protocols pose at least the possibility of a therapeutic benefit for the particular participants, one who is prohibited from participating is automatically deprived of this chance. Although the likelihood of direct benefit is commonly more theoretical than concrete, the older person should be as free as possible to weigh the known odds him- or herself and to take a chance if desired. The therapeutic possibility for an intervention that is being tested is especially significant when no other proven treatment is available to alleviate the ailment of the subject/patient. Secondary benefits of research participation that are lost through excessive paternalism include contact with others, more attention from caregivers (including health care professionals), a break from routine, and the psychological satisfaction of contributing to knowledge that may have practical value to others. Finally, overzealous attempts to protect the aged as a group would tend to inhibit research with great eventual potential value to precisely the population cohort being shielded.

Clinical investigators and treating health care professionals must protect vulnerable older persons while assessing and respecting each older person as an individual. More research probably has to be done on the process itself (i.e., conducting research on older, cognitively impaired persons) before we can assess accurately the desirability of various specific strategies (Appelbaum, 1997b; Sachs & Cassel, 1990). I have discussed here the legal parameters that now guide conduct in this area. Within those broad parameters, though, the capacities of external overseers are limited; it is the researcher's and treater's own sense of ethics that will ultimately determine the well-being of the older research subject and the future of geriatric research. Realistically, "[n]o practical level of oversight can guaranty that each researcher will protect subjects with complete integrity" (U.S. General Accounting Office, 1996b). The operationalization of these ethical principles is itself a proper subject for further research in the future.

Chapter 13

Legal Services to Older Persons: Physician/Attorney Cooperation

INTRODUCTION

As the previous chapters have amply illustrated, it is frequently impossible to separate the health care of the aged from their legal (as well as ethical, financial, and public policy) needs. Some problems require the involvement of both the legal and health care systems for their favorable resolution. When this occurs, and the legal and health aspects of an older individual's problems become intertwined, the person becomes both a health care professional's patient and a lawyer's client on the same matter(s). Such cases may be characterized as medicolegal.

Besides those provided by privately practicing attorneys retained directly by older persons or their surrogates, legal services are available from a variety of other sources. These sources include *pro bono* (donated) services by the private bar; legal aid offices funded through the federal Legal Services Corporation, Title 3 of the Older Americans Act (OAA), state appropriations, or local charitable contributions; and frequently, law school clinical programs. Information on reduced or nonfee legal services for older persons generally may be obtained from one's local bar association, long-term care ombudsman's office, legal aid office, or Area Agency on Aging. Information on private *pro bono* services is available from the American Bar Association Commission on Legal Problems of the Elderly (see Appendix).

Not only is the subject matter of the problems encountered by older persons medicolegal. The relationship between the different professionals who are attempting to serve the needs of their joint older patient/client also must be medicolegal. That is, when dealing with an older patient/ client who presents a situation that incorporates both medical and legal considerations requiring the assistance of professionals skilled in each of those realms, both the health care professional and the representing attorney are called upon to cooperate with each other to resolve the problem or problems that brought their common patient/client to their respective practices. In that event, members of the different professions must work as partners instead of adversaries in order to ensure the well-being of the total older person.

Although no litigated case has yet specifically raised this issue, it might be contended that the existence of the health care professional/ patient relationship imposes upon the professional an ethically grounded and legally enforceable duty to assist the older patient's attorney. This duty would be especially strong if the health care professional has knowledge and expertise concerning the patient's health status that would be relevant to the resolution of a legal claim. Failure to cooperate in such a matter, it is arguable, leaves the individual in the lurch and should render the health care professional civilly liable under the common law wrong of abandonment.

What has just been said applies with particular force to the proper role of the physician. There is the potential and a strong need for physicians of all specialties and particularly those engaged in the delivery of primary care to become actively involved in an interdisciplinary professional team approach to patient care so as to benefit the total well-being of older individuals. This need is especially pressing with reference to legal advocacy on behalf of older persons. Legal representation of older clients could regularly benefit from physician cooperation in the preparation, prosecution, or defense of claims and in the rendering of planning and advice designed to prevent legal problems from arising in the future. In many cases, even minimally adequate representation is jeopardized or rendered impossible if such cooperation is absent. The ideal role of the physician as interdisciplinary team partner is a vital one.

The physician usually is entitled to financial compensation for time spent in providing medicolegal services, such as review of medical records, providing an affidavit, or giving sworn testimony at a deposition or trial. This right to compensation is waived in some circumstances. Although there exists no set fee schedule for such services, a fair rule of thumb is that a physician's charge for medicolegal services should be roughly equivalent to a charge for spending a comparable amount of time in providing clinical care. In other words, it seems appropriate that the physician neither suffer financially nor secure a windfall by cooperating in and contributing to the resolution of a patient's legal problem.

PROBLEMS IN PERFORMANCE

Unfortunately, it seems that a wide chasm frequently exists between the actual and ideal roles of the physician as a member of the professional team concerned with assisting older individuals to fully realize the legal rights and entitlements that society has sought to afford them. Put less delicately, the performance level of physicians in this regard is sometimes lacking in sufficient quality and commitment. In certain circumstances, physicians actually may create or contribute to older individuals' legal problems, rather than aiding in their resolution. This may come about through such practices as collusion with unscrupulous relatives or nursing facility (NF) operators in having older patients unnecessarily or prematurely found incompetent and/or institutionalized or overly sedating or restraining older patients for the management convenience of others. In the vast majority of cases, however, physician noncooperation is a passive, rather than an active, phenomenon.

The fundamental nature of the attorney/physician impasse may be characterized as communication and information exchange failures. The main problems may seem at first blush rather mundane, but in reality they are at the very heart of the legal service provider's ability to provide competent (let alone ultimately successful) legal counsel and representation to older clients. Shortcomings in this category include (a) physician failure to respond, in a timely fashion or at all, to attorney telephone calls or correspondence; (b) physician failure to provide attorneys with requested medical reports that are complete, conclusive, and relevant to the issue(s) the physician was asked to address (follow-up requests for the correction or supplementation of deficient medical reports ordinarily meet with an even colder physician shoulder than do original requests); and (c) resistance to or refusal of requests for the patient-authorized release of medical records to the attorney.

The other major negative aspect of physician performance in this sphere is closely related to the first and centers around physician attitudes. In many cases, physicians are reluctant and, in a certain proportion of cases, are outwardly hostile about becoming professionally involved with lawyers or the legal system through performance of medicolegal evaluations, rendering medicolegal reports about older patients, and especially giving oral testimony (and potential submission to cross-examination) before any judicial or administrative tribunal. Exacerbating these attitudinal difficulties is the seeming resistance of some physicians to being educated by their older patients' legal representatives about either the legal system, legal issues confronting their older patients, or the appropriate respective roles of medical and legal professionals in addressing those issues.

IMPEDIMENTS TO COOPERATION

A number of factors have been suggested as possible partial explanations for the communication and attitudinal difficulties that block achievement of optimal physician performance as members of the total professional team concerned with aiding older adults to fully realize their legal entitlements. These impeding factors fall into essentially two classifications: (1) those that are associated with the advanced age of the patient/client and (2) those that would be present regardless of the patient/client's age. Identifying and weighing these factors is essential to any effort to improve the quality and commitment of physician participation in the resolution of medicolegal issues confronting older patients.

The most important reason underlying frequent ineffectiveness of physicians as patient advocates is the still too prevalent tendency evidenced by a large portion of the medical community to minimize relating to the older population in any, even a purely medical, context. There is strong evidence that the average level of care of the elderly, particularly for those in long-term care institutions, is not up to the same high standards available to patients in other age groups (Kapp, 1998a). According to a Harvard Medical School study of New York State hospital care, patients over age 65 were twice as likely to be iatrogenically injured as those between 16 and 44 years (Weiler et al., 1993). Physicians as a whole spend less time examining and treating older patients than patients who are younger. The prejudice against the aged, commonly referred to as "ageism" (Butler, 1975), has several sources as applied to the practice of medicine. The average age of patients in a physician's practice (in every area except pediatrics) increases 5 years for every 10 years that the physician ages. According to a former president of the American Medical Directors Association, an organization of NF medical directors, "Age frightens physicians. They imagine themselves in that age range." Tied to this negative identification is the personally depressing outlook still held by most physicians that the ailments of the aged are chronic and eventually fatal, so active treatment is largely a waste of time and resources. As one physician has observed, in a statement just as true almost a quarter of a century after originally made, most of his colleagues tend to view chronic care, particularly of the aged, as

> . . . boring, tedious, uninteresting and unproductive. Since chronic conditions are by nature irreversible (though nonetheless treatable), doctors tend to view them with despair and even nihilism. There is almost a Peter Pan sense that medicine should be immediately gratifying and not spoiled by situations which defy the doctor's ability to "make it all better." (Butler, 1975)

There are other explanations offered for the medical profession's preference for younger patients, a preference that has been cynically dubbed "the YAVIS syndrome" (an acronym for young, attractive, verbal, intelligent, and successful) (Dickman, 1979). One explanation prominently suggested is the dearth in most medical school curricula of sufficient learning experiences in geriatrics and gerontology. This deficiency has included a failure to convey to medical students the necessary special understanding of the impact of social, economic, and legal conditions on older persons.

Another frequently cited potential explanation for the widespread ageism-in-medicine phenomenon is the filled schedules and hectic pace of practice that most physicians maintain, from a combination of necessity and choice. Examining and treating an older patient quite often requires more professional time and patience than does processing someone younger through the physician's office. The older patient can be slower, more difficult, and more demanding to work with, impairing the efficiency of the physician's business operations. This is an especially vexing challenge in the modern age of managed care.

Closely related to the topic of time is that of finances. Primary treatment and care of older patients is not an especially lucrative area of practice, compared with serving other kinds of patients. In fee-for-service settings, the type of chronic, maintenance care generally required by older patients does not generate medical fees of the same magnitude as the acute care, with its emphasis on procedures, more frequently needed by younger populations. In managed care arrangements, with their strict cost controls, the added time that proper geriatric care requires can impair efficiency in a way that places the physician at personal financial risk. Additionally, Medicare and Medicaid, upon which most older patients rely, limit fee supplementation opportunities. Moreover, the 1996 federal Health Insurance Portability and Accountability Act (HIPAA) provides that if a physician accepts cash payment for services rendered to a Medicare-eligible patient in lieu of billing the government for those services, even when the patient requests or is satisfied with this arrangement, that physician is then precluded from collecting Medicare payments for services provided to *any* patient for the following 2 years. The physician must rely on a public third-party reimbursement system that often (quite correctly) is perceived as inadequate in amount and untimely in payment, particularly when care is rendered in an NF setting. This system therefore acts as a real practical disincentive to serving older persons medically.

One factor contributing to insufficient primary care attention to the aged is the overeagerness on the part of many primary care physicians to transfer, rather than just refer, older patients with any semblance of a psychiatric symptom to a psychiatrist or other mental health caregiver. Psychiatric and psychological consultations may be extremely helpful in caring for older patients; however, the primary care physician should not be too precipitous in relinquishing involvement altogether, as most older patients have basic medical maladies that can best be medically evaluated and treated by primary care physicians.

The lack of enthusiastic cooperation by some physicians on behalf of the rights of older clients/patients also may be traced to the overly deferential posture in which many older adults hold their physicians. As a result of their cultural upbringing, most members of today's older generation are conditioned to treat authority figures with great respect and even awe. Many older clients/patients are afraid or reluctant to "bother" or "intrude upon" the time and energies of their personal physician with requests pertaining to matters such as filling out legally required forms, writing letters, talking on the telephone, or testifying in judicial proceedings. This reluctance to invoke physician involvement in "nonmedical" matters is especially pronounced when a long-term, hierarchical doctor/patient relationship has developed—exactly the type of situation in which the physician would have the most to offer the older person's legal representative in terms of relevant data and opinions. Deference to one's own physician is particularly strong in older females, who have been trained to react passively and defer to authority in many situations.

Finally, and paradoxically, it is precisely when the older individual needs the cooperation of his or her personal physician the most that the patient may be most reluctant to ask for it. Excessive deference to the physician not only may result in the older patient/client personally refraining from imposing upon the physician to become involved in the patient/client's affairs but also may take the form of explicit or implicit client instructions to the attorney to avoid making demands upon the physician that the client feels are too intrusive and disrespectful.

An additional consideration contributing to the failure of physicians as a whole to undertake a more activist role in advocating on behalf of their older patients' legal rights is the great extent to which the physician deals with surrogates purporting to represent the older patient, rather than with the patient directly. A surrogate, often a relative but sometimes a nonrelated guardian or friend, who claims to act for the older patient and in that patient's best interests may come between the doctor and patient and divert communication and interpersonal contact from the physician away from the patient and toward the surrogate. Such a surrogate may (but does not inevitably) steer the physician away from positive cooperation with the older patient's attorney (if the patient is even permitted to have an attorney in the first place). This is most likely when the respective interests of the patient and the surrogate are inconsistent with each other or in clear conflict.

On the other hand, much of the time the interests of the patient and surrogate are fully in concert. In such cases, the surrogate will encourage and facilitate physician/attorney collaboration.

So far, discussion has focused on considerations unique to older patient/client populations. There do exist, however, factors that would impede a productive physician/lawyer working relationship regardless of the characteristics of the particular patient/client involved. These types of problems apply both generically and to the specific case of the older person in need of medicolegal assistance.

One of these factors is the manner in which physicians ordinarily delineate their own professional role and goals. They generally define their jobs and their product, and therefore what others may reasonably expect from them, according to a narrow medical model. They surely do not envision assisting in the legal representation of patients as an important element of what the physician does for a living or sets out to achieve. The average physician would describe his or her proper role and goal strictly as defining and developing a course of diagnosis and therapy that the physician feels to be in the best medical interest of the patient under the circumstances. Against such a job and product description, the attorney seeking to engage physician assistance in preparing forms and testimony for administrative or judicial consumption understandably faces an uphill battle.

When physicians do think of the law as relevant to their professional conduct, the connotation is almost invariably negative (Kapp, 1998c). The attitude of most physicians is that the law and the legal system serve primarily to prescribe or proscribe medical conduct, often interfering with good clinical judgment and restricting the delivery of what is believed to be good, ethical patient care. Most physician contact with the law and with lawyers unfortunately has been antagonistic in nature. The chief legal concern in the doctor/patient relationship has been with methods through which the physician can avoid liability, not on how the patient's legal and ethical interests may best be advocated.

Each of the factors mentioned, operating separately and in concert, contribute to the overall suboptimal history of physician performance as members of the interdisciplinary team responsible for promoting the legal welfare of their older patients. What steps can reasonably be attempted to address this urgent situation? Deficiencies in attorney/physician relationships, in which the well-being of the older client/patient suffers, are too deep-seated and long-standing to be solved overnight. Nevertheless, several proposals for improvement are offered here, briefly but enthusiastically.

PROPOSALS FOR IMPROVEMENT

I consciously have refrained in this book from proposing vast socially oriented schemes entailing such initiatives as greatly increased public spending for legal and medical services for the aged, the creation of new government agencies to coordinate physician/attorney activities in this realm, or broader mandatory reporting requirements in cases of suspected elder abuse. I do not endorse global suggestions in this vein as necessarily effective or desirable. In any event, a worthy, comprehensive discussion of governmentally induced changes in the legal and health care delivery systems as they affect older persons is a subject best left for another forum at another time. I concentrate here instead on a few practical ideas that actual health care professionals will be able to realistically consider, accept, and implement to enhance the quality of lives of those older patients whom they serve daily in their professional practices.

First and most fundamentally, physicians must possess and exhibit a high degree of compassion and empathy for the vicissitudes—medical, legal, and combined—sometimes encountered by their older patients. What is needed is not a paternalistic, noblesse oblige attitude but rather a sincere emotional identification. This psychological commitment must be accompanied by a thoughtful reexamination and redefinition of the health care professional's basic aims or goals in rendering services to older patients. Instead of invariably and indomitably striving for and expecting to achieve a miraculous scientific cure, breakthrough, or remission in every clinical experience, the physician in many cases must come to realize and emphasize instead the palliative, caring, supportive purposes of medical intervention, the quality-of-life-enhancing opportunities that challenge the physician who is caring for a patient of advanced years. The zero-sum ideology of medicine, in which there is clear victory or defeat, must be put aside in favor of a much broader spirit of compassionate sustenance as a valid role of medicine.

Just as the health care professional's basic aims or goals in rendering services to older patients must be reexamined, so too must the appropriate role of the health care professional himself or herself be carefully reevaluated. A more encompassing vision of the physician as member of the interdisciplinary professional team responsible for assuring the well-being of older individuals, including prominently their legal and social welfare, must be accepted enthusiastically. The earlier self-perception of the physician as detached, objective scientist is part of a bygone era, if it ever was an accurate or desirable description. The physician must understand and agree that actively cooperating with an older patient's attorney in the preparation, prosecution, or defense of a legal claim involving that patient is a proper and necessary aspect of sensitive and complete medical practice.

Physicians must learn to overcome the inevitable pragmatic pressures and constraints of time and finances. They must cultivate a skill for and interest in listening to the lessons of older patients and their social service and legal representatives and learning from them about a patient's legally related needs and the physician's potential contribution to answering them. The physician must develop habits of timely, responsive, and full replies to written and oral queries from older patients' attorneys, establishing contact and asking questions and making suggestions where attorney requests are ambiguous or unduly burdensome. Perhaps most significantly, it is important for the physician to exert a sincere effort to alert and inform his or her older patient clientele and their legal advocates of the physician's sensitivity to the panoply of legal entanglements potentially in the offing for older patients. The physician must show readiness to positively participate in the successful resolution of those challenges.

Assuming the desirability of these proposals, how then, as a realistic matter, can they be affirmatively promoted? The answer, of course, is multifaceted, but I heartily endorse the central notion that one valuable strategy to address deficiencies in physician performance is through reform of the medical education process, on both the pre- and post-M.D. or D.O. levels.

It is imperative, in the first instance, that a core geriatrics and gerontology curriculum be more fully integrated into our medical and other health professions schools. Beyond that, it is essential that this curriculum incorporate attention to the psychosocial and cultural components of aging, as well as the physical and mental maladies of patients. Medical education must encompass courses in geriatrics that aim for a detailed understanding of community services, how they operate, and how they influence the patient's and family's ability to function.

A thoughtfully devised and enthusiastically implemented medical educational experience in legal issues relating to older persons should enjoy the visible and vocal support of the medical school's administration and clinical faculty. Such an endeavor can help in accomplishing the objectives of broadening physicians' role perceptions and forcing physicians to appreciate the contribution of other professions, including but not limited to the law, in serving the total well-being of the aged. (This discussion presumes, of course, that law schools must do their job to prepare graduates who are capable of devising and implementing appropriate learning experiences concerning the legal rights of older citizens.)

Specific coursework, some of it with a central focus on legal issues and some of it integrating legal issues into existing clinical rotations, is needed. Continuing medical education (CME) conferences also must include an emphasis on these issues for the benefit of active practitioners.

We must write, publish, and read more comprehensive yet comprehensible textbooks, designed with health professions students, teachers, and clinicians foremost in mind, that explicate legal issues facing the aged and how they impact on the real-world practice of medicine.

Above all, health care students, teachers, and practitioners must conscientiously strive to continue learning and relearning about these vital matters. The tools and mechanisms for education are only as effective as students would have them be. In the final analysis, the quality of the attorney/physician partnership continues to depend most clearly upon the quality of the respective partners.

Appendix
Information Sources

Alzheimer's Disease and Related Disorders Association, Inc., 919 North Michigan Avenue, Chicago, IL 60611-1676, *phone* 312-335-8700, *E-mail* info@alz.org, *web* www.alz.org/

American Association of Homes and Services for the Aging, 901 E Street, NW, Suite 500, Washington, DC 20004-2011, *phone* 202-783-2242, *web* www.aahsa.org

American Association of Retired Persons, 601 E Street, NW, Washington, DC 20049, *phone* 202-434-2277, *web* www.aarp.org

American Bar Association, Commission on Legal Problems of the Elderly, 740 15th Street, NW, Washington, DC 20005-1022, *phone* 202-662-8690, *E-mail* abaelderly @abanet.org *web* www.abanet.org/elderly

American Bar Association, Commission on Mental and Physical Disability Law, 740 15th Street, NW, Washington, DC 20005-1022, *phone* 202-662-1570, *web* www.abanet.org/disability/

American College of Legal Medicine, 611 East Wells Street, Milwaukee, WI 53202, *phone* 800-433-9137 and 414-276-1881, *E-mail* info@aclm.org, *web* www.aclm.org

American Geriatrics Society, 770 Lexington Avenue, Suite 300, New York, NY 10021, *phone* 212-308-1414, *E-mail* info.amger@americangeriatrics.org, *web* www.americangeriatrics.org

American Health Care Association, 1201 L Street, NW, Washington, DC 20005, *phone* 202-842-4444, *web* www.ahca.org

American Health Lawyers Association, 1120 Connecticut Avenue, NW, Suite 950, Washington, DC 20036-3902, *phone* 202-833-1100, *E-mail* info@healthlawyers.org, *web* www.healthlawyers.org

American Medical Association, 515 North State Street, Chicago, IL 60610, *phone* 312-464-5000 and 800-621-8335, *web* www.ama-assn.org

American Medical Directors Association, 10480 Little Patuxent Parkway, Suite 760, Columbia, MD 21044, *phone* 410-740-9743, 410-995-1240, and 301-596-5774, *web* www.amda.com

American Society on Aging, 833 Market Street, Suite 511, San Francisco, CA 94103-1824, *phone* 415-974-9600, *E-mail* info@asa.asaging.org, *web* www.asaging.org

American Society of Law, Medicine and Ethics, 765 Commonwealth Avenue, 16th Floor, Suite 1634, Boston, MA 02215, *phone* 617-262-4990, *E-mail* aslme@bu.edu, *web* www.aslme.org

American Society for Healthcare Risk Management, American Hospital Association, One North Franklin, Chicago, IL 60606, *phone* 312-422-3980, *E-mail* LMangan.1@aha.org, *web* www.ashrm.org

Americans for Better Care of the Dying, 2175 K Street, NW, Suite 820, Washington, DC 20037-1803, *phone* 202-530-9864, *E-mail* caring@erols.com, *web* www.abcd-caring.com

Center on Disability and Health, 1522 K Street, NW, Suite 800, Washington, DC 20005, *phone* 202-842-4408

Center for Health Care Law, National Association for Home Care, 228 7th Street, SE, Washington, DC 20003, *phone* 202-547-5262

Center to Improve Care of the Dying, George Washington University, 2175 K Street, NW, Suite 820, Washington, DC 20037, *phone* 202-467-2222, *E-mail* cicd@gwis2.circ.gwu.edu, *web* www.gwu.edu/~cicd

Center for Social Gerontology, 2307 Shelby Avenue, Ann Arbor, MI 48103-3895, *phone* 734-665-1126, *web* www.tcsg.org

Choice in Dying, Inc., 475 Riverside Drive, Room 1852, New York, NY 10015, *phone* 212-870-2003, *web* www.choices.org

Gerontological Society of America, 1030 15th Street, Washington, DC 20005, *phone* 202-842-1275, *E-mail* geron@geron.org, *web* www.geron.org

Hastings Center, Route 9D, Garrison, NY 10524-5555, *phone* 914-424-4040, *E-mail* thehastingscenter.org

Internet and E-Mail Resources on Aging: An Online Directory, *web* www.aoa.dhhs.gov/aoa/pages/jpostlst.html

Joint Commission on Accreditation of Healthcare Organizations, One Renaissance Boulevard, Oakbrook Terrace, IL 60181, *phone* 630-792-5000, *web* www.jcaho.org

Legal Counsel for the Elderly, 601 E Street, NW, Washington, DC 20049, *phone* 202-434-2170

Legal Services Corporation, 750 1st Street, NE, 10th Floor, Washington, DC 20002, *phone* 202-336-8800, *web* www.lsc.gov

National Academy on Aging, 1275 K Street, NW, Suite 350, Washington, DC 20005-4006, *phone* 202-408-3375, *E-mail* geron.geron.org, *web* www.geron.org

National Academy of Elder Law Attorneys, 1604 N. Country Club Road, Tucson, AZ 85716, *phone* 520-881-4005, *E-mail* info@naela.com, *web* www.naela.org

National Aging Resource Center on Elder Abuse, 810 First Street, NE, Suite 500, Washington, DC 20002-4205, *phone* 202-682-2470, *web* www.gwjapan.com/NCEA

National Association of Area Agencies on Aging, 1112 16th Street, NW, Suite 100, Washington, DC 20036-4823, *phone* 202-296-8130 (phone for Eldercare Locator 800-677-1116), *web* www.aoa.dhhs.gov

National Center on Elder Abuse, 810 First Street, NE, Suite 500, Washington, DC 20002-4267, *phone* 202-682-2470, *web* www.gwjapan.com/NCEA

National Citizens Coalition for Nursing Home Reform, 1424 16th Street, NW, Suite 202, Washington, DC 20036, *phone* 202-332-2275, *E-mail* NCCNHR1@erls.com, *web* www.NCCNHR.org

National Conference of Commissioners on Uniform State Laws, 211 E. Ontario Street, Suite 1300, Chicago, IL 60611, *phone* 312-915-0195, *E-mail* NCCUSL @NCCUSL.org, *web* www.NCCUSL.org

National Council on the Aging, Inc., 409 Third Street, SW, Suite 200, Washington, DC 20024, *phone* 202-479-1200, *E-mail* info@NCOA.org, *web* www.NCOA.org

National Hospice Organization, 1901 N. Moore Street, Suite 901, Arlington, VA 22209, *phone* 703-243-5900, *web* www.NHO.org

National Legal Center for the Medically Dependent and Disabled, 7 South 6th Street, Suite 208, Terre Haute, IN 47807, *phone* 812-238-0769, *E-mail* tmarzen @aol.com

National Reference Center for Bioethics Literature, Kennedy Institute of Ethics, Georgetown University, Box 571212, Washington, DC 20057-1212, *phone* 202-687-3885 and 800-MED-ETHX, *E-mail* medethx@gunet.georgetown .eduNational, *web* www.gu*web*.georgetown.edu//nrcbl/

National Senior Citizens Law Center, 1815 H Street, NW, Washington, DC 20006, *phone* 202-289-6976, *web* www.nsclc.org/

Older Women's League, Office of Legal Counsel, 666 11th Street, NW, Suite 700, Washington, DC 20001, *phone* 202-783-6686

Public Responsibility in Medicine and Research, 15 Court Square, Suite 340, Boston, MA 02108, *phone* 617-367-4992

U.S. Administration on Aging, Department of Health and Human Services, 330 Independence Avenue, SW, Room 4760, Washington, DC 20201, *phone* 202-619-0556, *E-mail* aoainfo@ban-gate.uoa.dhhs.gov, *web* www.aoa.gov/

U.S. Health Care Financing Administration, Department of Health and Human Services, 200 Independence Avenue, SW, Suite 314G, Humphrey Building, Washington, DC 20201, *phone* 410-966-6784, *web* www.hcfa.gov

U.S. National Institute on Aging, Public Information Office, Bethesda, MD 20892, 800-222-2225, *web* www.nih.gov/nia/

U.S. Senate Special Committee on Aging, Dirksen Senate Office Building, Room G31, Washington, DC 20510-6400, *phone* 202-224-5364, *E-mail* mailbox@aging .senate.gov, *web* www.senate.gov\~aging

World Institute on Disability, 510 16th Street, Suite 100, Oakland, CA 94612, 510-763-4100, *E-mail* wid@wid.org, *web* www.wid.org

References

Ackerman, T. F. (1996). The moral implications of medical uncertainty: Tube feeding demented patients. *Journal of the American Geriatrics Society, 44*(10), 1265–1267.

Ackerman, T. F. (1997). Forsaking the spirit for the letter of the law: Advance directives in nursing homes. *Journal of the American Geriatrics Society, 45*(1), 114–116.

Adamson, T. E., Tschann, J. M., Gullion, D. S., & Oppenberg, A. A. (1989). Physician communication skills and malpractice claims: A complex relationship. *Western Journal of Medicine, 150*(3), 356–360.

Addington v. Texas, 99 S.Ct. 1804 (1979).

Adelsward, V., & Sachs, L. (1996). The meaning of 6.8: Numeracy and normality in health information talks. *Social Science and Medicine, 43*(8), 1179–1187.

Ad Hoc Committee of the Harvard Medical School to Examine the Definition of Brain Death. (1968). A definition of irreversible coma. *Journal of the American Medical Association, 205*(6), 337–340.

Ainslie, N., & Beisecker, A. E. (1994). Changes in decisions by elderly persons based on treatment description. *Archives of Internal Medicine, 154*(19), 2225–2233.

Alexander, G. J. (1990). Avoiding guardianship. *Journal of Elder Abuse and Neglect, 2*(3/4), 163–175.

Alpers, A., & Lo, B. (1995). When is CPR futile? *Journal of the American Medical Association, 273*(2), 156–158.

Altman, S. H., Reinhardt, U., & Shactman, D. (1997). *Policy options for reforming the Medicare program: Papers from the Princeton Conference on Medicare reform.* Princeton, NJ: Robert Wood Johnson Foundation.

Alzheimer's Association. (1997). *Position statement: Ethical issues in dementia research.* Chicago: Author.

American Academy of Family Physicians. (1994). Family violence: An AAFP white paper. *American Family Physician, 50*(8), 1636–1646.

American Academy of Hospice and Palliative Medicine. (1997). *Comprehensive end-of-life care and physician-assisted suicide.* Chicago: Author.

American Academy of Neurology, Ethics and Humanities Subcommittee. (1998). Assisted suicide, euthanasia, and the neurologist. *Neurology, 50*(3), 596–598.

American Academy of Neurology, Quality Standards Subcommittee. (1995). Practice parameters for determining brain death in adults. *Neurology, 45*(5), 1012–1014.

American Association of Retired Persons (AARP). (1996). *A profile of older Americans: 1995.* Washington, DC: Author.

American Bar Association, Commission on Legal Problems of the Elderly. (1995). *Medicaid estate recovery: Picking the bones of the poor?* Washington, DC: ABA.

American Bar Association, Commission on Legal Problems of the Elderly and Commission on the Mentally Disabled and the National Judicial College. (1991). *Court-related needs of the elderly and persons with disabilities: A blueprint.* Washington, DC: Author.

American Bar Association, Commission on Legal Problems of the Elderly and Young Lawyers Division, Committee on the Delivery of Legal Services to the Elderly. (1990). *Guardianship of the elderly: A primer for attorneys.* Washington, DC: Author.

American Bar Association, Commissions on the Mentally Disabled and on Legal Problems of the Elderly. (1989). *Guardianship: An agenda for reform—recommendations of the National Guardianship symposium and policy of the American Bar Association.* Washington, DC: Author.

American College of Emergency Physicians. (1996). "Do not attempt resuscitation" directives in the out-of-hospital setting. *Annals of Emergency Medicine, 27*(5), 684.

American College of Health Care Administrators. (1987). Standards of practice for long-term care administrators. *Journal of Long-Term Care Administration, 15*(1), 11–12.

American College of Physicians. (1989). Cognitively impaired subjects. *Annals of Internal Medicine, 111*(10), 843–848.

American College of Physicians. (1998). Ethics manual (4th ed.). *Annals of Internal Medicine, 128*(7), 576–594.

American Geriatrics Society. (1991). *Clinical practice statement: The use of restraints.* New York: Author.

American Geriatrics Society, Ethics Committee. (1995a). The care of dying patients. *Journal of the American Geriatrics Society, 43*(5), 577–578.

American Geriatrics Society, Ethics Committee. (1995b). *Making treatment decisions for incapacitated elderly without advance directives.* New York: Author.

American Heart Association, Emergency Cardiac Care Committee and Subcommittees. (1992). Guidelines for cardiopulmonary resuscitation and emergency cardiac care. *Journal of the American Medical Association, 268*(16), 2171–2295.

American Medical Association. (1991). *Medicolegal forms with legal analysis.* Chicago: Author.

American Medical Association. (1992a). *Diagnostic and treatment guidelines on elder abuse and neglect.* Chicago: Author.

American Medical Association. (1992b). *Physicians and home care: Guidelines for the medical management of the home care patient.* Chicago: Author.

American Medical Association. (1993). *Guides to the evaluation of permanent impairment* (4th ed.). Chicago: Author.

American Medical Association, Council on Ethical and Judicial Affairs. (1991). Guidelines for the appropriate use of do-not-resuscitate orders. *Journal of the American Medical Association, 265*(14), 1868–1871.

American Medical Association, Council on Ethical and Judicial Affairs. (1992). Decisions near the end of life. *Journal of the American Medical Association, 267*(16), 2229–2233.

American Medical Association, Council on Ethical and Judicial Affairs. (1997). *Code of medical ethics: Current opinions with annotations.* Chicago: Author.

American Medical Association, Council on Scientific Affairs. (1993a). Physicians and family caregivers: A model for partnership. *Journal of the American Medical Association, 269*(10), 1282–1284.

American Medical Association, Council on Scientific Affairs. (1993b). Users and uses of patient records. *Archives of Family Medicine, 2*(6), 678–681.

American Medical Association, Council on Scientific Affairs. (1996). Good care of the dying patient. *Journal of the American Medical Association, 275*(6), 474–478.

American Medical Directors Association. (1997). Care at the end of life. *Annals of Long-Term Care, 5*(2), 11.

American Nurses Association. (1992). *Position statement on nursing care and do-not-resuscitate decisions.* Washington, DC: Author.

American Psychiatric Association. (1993). *Task force report 34: Consent to voluntary hospitalization.* Washington, DC: Author.

American Psychiatric Association. (1995). Position statement on elder abuse, neglect, and exploitation. *American Journal of Psychiatry, 152*(5), 820.

American Psychiatric Association. (1997). Practice guideline for the treatment of patients with Alzheimer's disease and other dementias of late life. *American Journal of Psychiatry, 154*(5) (Supplement 1-39).

American Society for Healthcare Risk Management. (1995). *Mapping your risk management course in home health care.* Chicago: American Hospital Association.

Anderer, S. J. (1990). Determining competency in guardianship proceedings. In N. A. Coleman, E. C. Lichtenstein, & J. W. Parry (Eds.). *Determining competency in guardianship proceedings.* Washington, DC: American Bar Association, Division of Public Services.

Anderson v. St. Francis–St. George Hospital, Inc., 77 Ohio St.3d 82, 671 N.E.2d 225 (1996).

Anetzberger, G. J. (1995). Protective services and long-term care. In Z. Harel & R. E. Dunkle (Eds.). *Matching people with services in long-term care.* New York: Springer Publishing Company.

Angell, M. (1991). The case of Helga Wanglie: A new kind of right to die case. *New England Journal of Medicine, 325*(7), 511–512.

Angell, M. (1994). After Quinlan: The dilemma of the persistent vegetative state. *New England Journal of Medicine, 330*(21), 1524–1525.

Angell, M. (1997). Fixing Medicare. *New England Journal of Medicine, 337*(3), 192–195.

Annas, G. J. (1978). The incompetent's right to die: The case of Joseph Saikewicz. *Hastings Center Report, 8*(1), 21–23.

Annas, G. J. (1988). Brain death and organ donation: You can have one without the other. *Hastings Center Report, 18*(3), 28–30.

Annas, G. J. (1989). *The rights of patients* (2nd ed.). Carbondale: Southern Illinois University Press.

Annas, G. J. (1991). The health care proxy and the living will. *New England Journal of Medicine, 324*(17), 1210–1213.

Annas, G. J. (1994a). Death by prescription—the Oregon initiative. *New England Journal of Medicine, 331*(18), 1240–1243.

Annas, G. J. (1994b). Informed consent, cancer, and truth in prognosis. *New England Journal of Medicine, 330*(3), 223–225.

Annas, G. J. (1997). The bell tolls for a constitutional right to physician-assisted suicide. *New England Journal of Medicine, 337*(15), 1098–1103.

Annas, G. J., & Grodin, M. A. (Eds.) (1992). *The Nazi doctors and the Nuremberg code: Human rights in human experimentation.* New York: Oxford University Press.

Appelbaum, P. S. (1996). Drug-free research in schizophrenia: An overview of the controversy. *IRB: Review of Human Subjects Research, 18*(1), 1–5.

Appelbaum, P. S. (1997a). Informed consent to psychotherapy: Recent developments. *Psychiatric Services, 48*(4), 445–446.

Appelbaum, P. S. (1997b). Rethinking the conduct of psychiatric research. *Archives of General Psychiatry, 54*(2), 117–120.

Appelbaum, P. S., Lidz, C. W., & Meisel, A. (1987). *Informed consent: Legal theory and clinical practice.* New York: Oxford University Press.

Areen, J. (1987). The legal status of consent obtained from families of adult patients to withhold or withdraw treatment. *Journal of the American Medical Association, 258*(2), 229–235.

Armour, M. (1994). A nursing home's good faith duty "to" care: Redefining a fragile relationship using the law of contract. *Saint Louis University Law Journal, 39*(1), 217–336.

Arras, J. D. (Ed.). (1995). *Bringing the hospital home: Ethical and social implications of high-tech home care.* Baltimore: Johns Hopkins University Press.

Asch, D. A. (1996). The role of critical care nurses in euthanasia and assisted suicide. *New England Journal of Medicine, 334*, 1374–1379.

Asch, D. A., & DeKay, M. L. (1997). Euthanasia among U.S. critical care nurses: Practices, attitudes, and social and professional correlates. *Medical Care, 35*, 890–900.

Asch, D. A., Hansen-Flaschen, J., & Lanken, P. N. (1995). Decisions to limit or continue life-sustaining treatment by critical care physicians in the United States: Conflicts between physicians' practices and patients' wishes. *American Journal of Respiratory and Critical Care Medicine, 151*(2), 288–292.

Asch, D. A., & Ubel, P. A. (1997). Rationing by any other name. *New England Journal of Medicine, 336*, 1668–1671.

A.S.P.E.N. (American Society for Parenteral and Enteral Nutrition) Board of Directors. (1997). Standards for nutrition support for adult residents of long-term care facilities. *Nutrition in Clinical Practice, 12*(6), 284–293.

Atchley, R. C. (1994). *Social forces and aging* (7th ed.). Belmont, CA: Wadsworth.

Avorn, J. (1990). The elderly and drug policy: Coming of age. *Health Affairs, 9*(3), 6–19.

Avorn, J., & Gurwitz, J. H. (1995). Drug use in the nursing home. *Annals of Internal Medicine, 123*(3), 195–204.

Barnes, A. P. (1992). Beyond guardianship reform: A reevaluation of autonomy and beneficence for a system of principled decision-making in long term care. *Emory Law Journal, 41,* 633–760.

Barnes, A., Frolik, L. A., & Whitman, R. (1997). *Counseling older clients.* Philadelphia: American Law Institute–American Bar Association Publications.

Barnett, C. (1978). Treatment rights of mentally ill nursing home residents. *University of Pennsylvania Law Review, 126,* 578–629.

Barnett, C. W., & Pierson, D. A. (1994). Advance directives: Implementing a program that works. *Nursing Management, 25*(10), 58–65.

Barry, M. J., Fowler, F. J., Jr., Mulley, A. G., Jr., Henderson, J. V., Jr., & Wennberg, J. E. (1995). Patient reactions to a program designed to facilitate patient participation in treatment decisions for benign prostatic hyperplasia. *Medical Care, 33,* 771–782.

Bates, D. W. (1997). Quality, costs, privacy and electronic medical data. *Journal of Law, Medicine and Ethics, 25*(2&3), 111–112.

Battin, M. (1983). The least worst death. *Hastings Center Report, 13*(2), 13–16.

Beck, J. C. (1987). Right to refuse antipsychotic medication: Psychiatric assessment and legal decisionmaking. *Mental and Physical Disability Law Reporter, 11*(5), 368–372.

Beers, M. H., Ouslander, J. G., Fingold, S. F., Morgenstern, H., Reuben, D. B., Rogers, W., Zeffren, M. J., & Beck, J. C. (1992). Inappropriate medication prescribing in skilled-nursing facilities. *Annals of Internal Medicine, 117,* 684–689.

Bein, P. M. (1991). Surrogate consent and the incompetent experimental subject. *Food, Drug and Cosmetic Law Journal, 46,* 739–771.

Beisecker, A. E. (1988). Aging and the desire for information and input in medical decisions: Patient consumerism in medical encounters. *Gerontologist, 28,* 330–335.

Beisecker, A. E. (1994). Attitudes of oncologists, oncology nurses, and patients from a women's clinic regarding medical decision making for older and younger breast cancer patients. *Gerontologist, 34,* 505–512.

Bennett, C. L., Greenfield, S., Aranow, H., Ganz, P., Vogelzand, N. J., & Elashoff, R. M. (1991). Patterns of care related to age of men with prostate cancer. *Cancer, 67,* 2633–2641.

Benson, J., & Britten, N. (1996). Respecting the autonomy of cancer patients when talking with their families: Qualitative analysis of semistructured interviews with patients. *British Medical Journal, 313,* 729–731.

Berg, J. W. (1996). Legal and ethical complexities of consent with cognitively impaired research subjects. *Journal of Law, Medicine and Ethics, 24,* 18–35.

Berg, J. W., Appelbaum, P. S., & Grisso, T. (1996). Constructing competence: Formulating standards of legal competence to make medical decisions. *Rutgers Law Review, 48*(2), 345–396.

Berkowitz, S. (1978). Informed consent, research, and the elderly. *Gerontologist, 18,* 237.

Bernard v. Char, 79 Haw. 362, 903 P.2d 667 (1995).

Bernat, J. L. (1998). A defense of the whole-brain concept of death. *Hastings Center Report, 28*(2), 14–23.

Berry, R. M. (1997). The genetic revolution and the physician's duty of confidentiality: The role of the old Hippocratic virtues in the regulation of the new genetic intimacy. *Journal of Legal Medicine, 18,* 401–441.

Besdine, R. W., Rubenstein, L. Z., & Cassel, C. (1994). Nursing home residents need physicians' services. *Annals of Internal Medicine, 120,* 616–618.

Beverly Enterprises–Florida, Inc. v. Spilman (1995). 661 So.2d 867 (Fla. App.5).

Binstock, R. H., & Post, S. G. (Eds.). (1991). *Too old for health care? Controversies in medicine, law, economics, and ethics.* Baltimore: Johns Hopkins University Press.

Block, A. J. (1993). Living wills are overrated. *Chest, 104,* 1645–1646.

Blum v. Yaretsky, 457 U.S. 991 (1982).

Blumstein, J. F. (1981). Rationing medical resources: A constitutional, legal, and policy analysis. *Texas Law Review, 59,* 1345–1400.

Bodnar, J. C. (1994). Are older Americans dangerously driving into the sunset? *Washington University Law Quarterly, 72,* 1709–1740.

Bok, S. (1976). Personal directions for care at the end of life. *New England Journal of Medicine, 295*(7), 367–369.

Bonnie, R. J. (1997). Research with cognitively impaired subjects: Unfinished business in the regulation of human research. *Archives of General Psychiatry, 54*(2), 105–111.

Bonnie, R. J., & Monahan, J. (Eds.). (1997). *Mental disorder, work disability, and the law.* Chicago: University of Chicago Press.

Bopp, J., Jr., & Avila, D. (1991). The sirens' lure of invented consent: A critique of autonomy-based surrogate decisionmaking for legally-incapacitated older persons. *Hastings Law Journal, 42,* 779–815.

Borson, S., & Doane, K. (1997). The impact of OBRA-87 on psychotropic drug prescribing in skilled nursing facilities. *Psychiatric Services, 48,* 1289–1296.

Borson, S., Loebel, P., Kitchell, M., Domoto, S., & Hyde, T. (1997). Psychiatric assessments of nursing home residents under OBRA-87: Should PASARR be reformed? *Journal of the American Geriatrics Society, 45,* 1173–1181.

Bowers, V. J. (1996). Advance directives: Peace of mind or false security? *Stetson Law Review, 26,* 677–723.

Boyd, K., Teres, D., Rapoport, J., & Lemeshow, S. (1996). The relationship between age and the use of DNR orders in critical care patients: Evidence for age discrimination. *Archives of Internal Medicine, 156,* 1821–1826.

Braddock, C. H., Fihn, S. D., Levinson, W., Jonsen, A. R., & Pearlman, R. A. (1997). How doctors and patients discuss routine clinical decisions: Informed decision making in the outpatient setting. *Journal of General Internal Medicine, 12*(6), 339–345.

Bradley, E. H., Blechner, B. B., Walker, L. C., & Wetle, T. T. (1997). Institutional efforts to promote advance care planning in nursing homes: Challenges and opportunities. *Journal of Law, Medicine and Ethics, 25*(2&3), 150–159.

Bradley, E. H., Walker, L., Blechner, B., & Wetle, T. (1997). Assessing capacity to participate in discussions of advance directives in nursing homes: Findings from a study of the Patient Self Determination Act. *Journal of the American Geriatrics Society, 45*(1), 79–83.

Bradley, M. (1996). Elder abuse. *British Medical Journal, 313,* 548–550.

Brahams, D. (1992). Informed consent when an investigation is interrupted. *Lancet, 339,* 51–52.

Brake, B. K. (1997). Legal aspects of home health care. In J. S. Spratt, R. L. Hawley, & R. E. Hoye (Eds.), *Home health care: Principles and practices.* Delray Beach, FL: GR/St. Lucie Press.

Braun, J. V., & Lipson, S. (1993). *Toward a restraint-free environment.* Baltimore: Health Professions Press.

Bretscher, M. E., & Creagan, E. T. (1997). Understanding suffering: What palliative medicine teaches us. *Mayo Clinic Proceedings, 72*(8), 785–787.

Brett, A., & Grodin, M. (1991). Ethical aspects of human experimentation in health services research. *Journal of the American Medical Association, 265,* 1854–1857.

Brickner, P. W., Kellogg, F. R., Lechich, A. J., Lipsman, R., & Scharer, L. K. (Eds.). (1996). *Geriatric home health care: The collaboration of physicians, nurses, and social workers.* New York: Springer Publishing Company.

Briggs v. Sullivan, 954 F.2d 534 (9 Cir., 1992).

Brody, B. A. (1998). *The ethics of biomedical research: An international perspective.* New York: Oxford University Press.

Brody, H. (1994). The physician's role in determining futility. *Journal of the American Geriatrics Society, 42*(8), 875–878.

Brooten, K. (1982). What a malpractice attorney looks for in medical records. *Physician's Management, 22,* 36.

Brotman, A. W., & Muller, J. J. (1990). The therapist as representative payee. *Hospital and Community Psychiatry, 41*(2), 167–171.

Brown, R., & Legal Counsel for the Elderly. (1989). *The rights of older persons* (2nd ed.). Carbondale: Southern Illinois University Press.

Brunetti, L. L., Weiss, M. J., Studenski, S. A., & Clipp, E. C. (1990). Cardiopulmonary resuscitation policies and practices: A statewide nursing home study. *Archives of Internal Medicine, 150*(1), 121–126.

Brushwood, D. B. (1997). The pharmacist's duty under OBRA-90 standards. *Journal of Legal Medicine, 18*(4), 475–519.

Buckman, R. (1996). Talking to patients about cancer. *British Medical Journal, 313,* 699–700.

Bulcroft, K., Kielkopf, M. R., & Tripp, K. (1991). Elderly wards and their legal guardians: Analysis of county probate records in Ohio and Washington. *Gerontologist, 31*(2), 156–164.

Burnum, J. F. (1989). The misinformation era: The fall of the medical record. *Annals of Internal Medicine, 110*(6), 482–484.

Burt, R. A. (1997). The Supreme Court speaks: Not assisted suicide but a constitutional right to palliative care. *New England Journal of Medicine, 337,* 1234–1236.

Butler, R. N. (1975). *Why survive? Being old in America.* New York: Harper and Row.

Byers, B., & Hendricks, J. E. (Eds.). (1993). *Adult protective services: Research and practice.* Springfield, IL: Charles C. Thomas.

Byock, I. (1997). *Dying well: The prospect for growth at the end of life.* New York: Riverhead Books.

Cabral, J. D. Y. (1997). Poor physician penmanship. *Journal of the American Medical Association, 278,* 1116–1117.

Callahan, D. (1987). *Setting limits: Medical goals in an aging society*. New York: Simon & Schuster.

Calman, K. C. (1996). Cancer: Science and society and the communication of risk. *British Medical Journal, 313*, 799–802.

Candilis, P. J., Wesley, R. W., & Wichman, A. (1993). A survey of researchers using a consent policy for cognitively impaired human research subjects. *IRB: Review of Human Subjects Research, 15*(6), 1–4.

Cantor, N. L. (1992). Prospective autonomy: On the limits of shaping one's post-competence medical fate. *Journal of Contemporary Health Law and Policy, 8*(1), 13–48.

Cantor, N. L. (1993). *Advance directives and the pursuit of death with dignity*. Bloomington: Indiana University Press.

Cantor, N. L. (1996). Can healthcare providers obtain judicial intervention against surrogates who demand "medically inappropriate" life support for incompetent patients? *Critical Care Medicine, 24*, 883–887.

Capezuti, E., Brush, B. L., & Lawson, W. T., III. (1997). Reporting elder mistreatment. *Journal of Gerontological Nursing, 23*(7), 24–32.

Caplan, A. L. (1996). Odds and ends: Trust and the debate over medical futility. *Annals of Internal Medicine, 125*(8), 688–689.

Capron, A. M. (1995). Abandoning a waning life. *Hastings Center Report, 25*(4), 24–26.

Capron, A. M. (1997). Incapacitated research. *Hastings Center Report, 27*(2), 25–27.

Caretenders, Inc. v. Commonwealth, 821 S.W.2d 83 (Ky. Supreme Ct., 1991).

Carr v. Strode, 79 Haw. 475, 904 P.2d 489 (1995).

Cassell, E. J. (1989). Abuse of the elderly: Misuses of power. *New York State Journal of Medicine, 89*(3), 159–162.

Cassell, E. J. (1991). *The nature of suffering and the goals of medicine*. New York: Oxford University Press.

Center for Social Gerontology. (1994a). *National study of guardianship systems: Findings and recommendations*. Ann Arbor, MI: Author.

Center for Social Gerontology. (1994b). *National study of guardianship systems: Implications for judicial education*. Ann Arbor, MI: Author.

Center for Social Gerontology. (1996). *Adult guardianship mediation manual*. Ann Arbor, MI: Author.

Chapman, A. R. (Ed.). (1997). *Health care and information ethics: Protecting fundamental human rights*. Kansas City, MO: Sheed & Ward.

Charles, C., Gafni, A., & Whelan, T. (1997). Shared decision-making in the medical encounter: What does it mean? (Or it takes at least two to tango). *Social Science and Medicine, 44*, 681–692.

Charlton, R. (1996). Diagnosing death. *British Medical Journal, 313*, 956–957.

Cho, Y. W., Terasaki, P. I., Cecka, J. M., & Gjertson, D. W. (1998). Transplantation of kidneys from donors whose hearts have stopped beating. *New England Journal of Medicine, 338*(4), 221–225.

Choice in Dying. (1995). *Cardiopulmonary resuscitation, do-not-resuscitate orders and end-of-life decisions*. New York: Author.

Churchill, L. R., & King, N. M. P. (1997). Physician assisted suicide, euthanasia, or withdrawal of treatment. *British Medical Journal, 315*, 137–138.

Cobbs v. Grant, 502 P.2d 1, 104 Cal.Rptr. 505 (1972).

Cohen, E. S. (1996). Resolving ethical dilemmas arising from diminished decision-making capacity of the elderly. In M. Smyer, K. W. Schaie, & M. B. Kapp (Eds.), *Older adults' decision-making and the law.* New York: Springer Publishing Company.

Cohn, F., Forlini, J. H., & Lynn, J. (1997). *The advocate's guide to better end-of-life care: Physician-assisted suicide and other important issues.* Washington, DC: Americans for Better Care of the Dying.

Cohodes, D. R. (1995). Through the looking glass: Decision making and chemotherapy. *Health Affairs, 14*(4), 203–208.

Coker, L. H., & Johns, A. F. (1994). Guardianship for elders: Process and issues. *Journal of Gerontological Nursing, 20*(12), 25–32.

Col, N., Finale, J. E., & Kronholm, P. (1990). The role of medication noncompliance and adverse drug reactions in hospitalizations of the elderly. *Archives of Internal Medicine, 150,* 841–845.

Coleman, N., & Karp, N. (1989). Recent state and federal developments in protective services and elder abuse. *Journal of Elder Abuse and Neglect, 1*(3), 51–63.

Coons, D. H., & Reichel, W. (1988). Improving the quality of life in nursing homes. *American Family Physician, 37*(2), 241–248.

Cooper, J. W. (1994). Falls and fractures in nursing home patients receiving psychotropic drugs. *International Journal of Geriatric Psychiatry, 9,* 975–980.

Cooper, J. W. (1997). Consultant pharmacist fall risk assessment and reduction within the nursing facility. *Consultant Pharmacist, 12,* 1294–1304.

Council for International Organizations of Medical Sciences. (1993). *International ethical guidelines for biomedical research involving human subjects.* Geneva, Switzerland: Author.

Cox, D. M., & Sachs, G. A. (1994). Advance directives and the Patient Self-Determination Act. *Clinics in Geriatric Medicine, 10*(3), 431–443.

Cox, M. J. (1998). A compassionate response toward providing nutrition and hydration in vulnerable populations. *Journal of Gerontological Nursing, 24*(2), 8–13.

Cranford, R. E. (1994). Medical futility: Transforming a clinical concept into legal and social policies. *Journal of the American Geriatrics Society, 42,* 894–898.

Criner, J. A. (1994). The nurse's role in preventing abuse of elderly patients. *Rehabilitation Nursing, 19*(5), 277–280, 297.

Crotts, T. J., & Martinez, D. A. (1996). The nursing home residents' rights act: A good idea gone bad! *Stetson Law Review, 26*(2), 599–615.

Cruzan v. Director, Missouri Department of Health, 109 S. Ct. 3240 (1990).

Cugliari, A. M., Miller, T., & Sobal, J. (1995). Factors promoting completion of advance directives in the hospital. *Archives of Internal Medicine, 155,* 1893–1898.

Curtis, J. R., Park, D. R., Krone, M. R., & Pearlman, R. A. (1995). Use of the medical futility rationale in do-not-attempt-resuscitation orders. *Journal of the American Medical Association, 273*(2), 124–128.

Daar, J. F. (1993). A clash at the bedside: Patient autonomy v. a physician's professional conscience. *Hastings Law Journal, 44,* 1241–1289.

Daniels, N. (1988). *Am I my parents' keeper? An essay on justice between the young and the old.* New York: Oxford University Press.

Darby, J. M., Stein, K., Grenvik, A., & Stuart, S. A. (1989). Approach to management of the heartbeating brain dead organ donor. *Journal of the American Medical Association, 261,* 2222–2228.

Daum v. SpineCare Medical Group, 52 Cal.App.4th 1285, 61 Cal.Rptr.2d 260 (1997).

Deber, R. B., Kraetschmer, N., & Irvine, J. (1996). What role do patients wish to play in treatment decision making? *Archives of Internal Medicine, 156,* 1414–1420.

DeBuono, B. A. (1997). New York's DNR law does not require futile resuscitation [Letter to the editor]. *Archives of Internal Medicine, 157,* 467–468.

DeChicco, R., Trew, A., & Seidner, D. L. (1997). What to do when the patient refuses a feeding tube. *Nutrition in Clinical Practice, 12*(5), 228–230.

Degner, L. F., Kristjanson, L. J., Bowman, D., Sloan, J. A., Carriere, K. C., O'Neil, J., Bilodeau, B., Watson, P., & Mueller, B. (1997). Information needs and decisional preferences in women with breast cancer. *Journal of the American Medical Association, 277,* 1485–1492.

Delano, S. J., & Zucker, J. L. (1994). Protecting mental health research subjects without prohibiting progress. *Hospital and Community Psychiatry, 45,* 601–603.

DeLaughter v. Lawrence County Hospital, 601 So.2d 818 (Miss., 1992).

Delbridge, T. R., Fosnocht, D. E., Garrison, H. G., & Auble, T. E. (1996). Field termination of unsuccessful out-of-hospital cardiac arrest resuscitation: Acceptance by family members. *Annals of Emergency Medicine, 27,* 649–654.

DeLew, N. (1995). The first 30 years of Medicare and Medicaid. *Journal of the American Medical Association, 274*(3), 262–267.

Dellasega, C., Frank, L., & Smyer, M. (1996). Medical decision-making capacity in elderly hospitalized patients. *Journal of Ethics, Law, and Aging, 2*(2), 65–74.

Denton v. Superior Court of Arizona. (1997).

DeRenzo, E. G. (1994). Surrogate decision making for severely cognitively impaired research subjects: The continuing debate. *Cambridge Quarterly of Healthcare Ethics, 3,* 539–548.

DeRenzo, E. G. (1997). Decisionally impaired persons in research: Refining the proposed refinements. *Journal of Law, Medicine and Ethics, 25*(2/3), 139–149.

Devettere, R. J. (1990). Neocortical death and human death. *Law, Medicine and Health Care, 18*(1&2), 96–104.

de Wachter, M. A. M. (1997). The European convention in bioethics. *Hastings Center Report, 27*(1), 13–23.

Dexter, P. R., Wolinsky, F. D., Gramelspacher, G. P., Zhou, X. H., Eckert, G. J., Waisburd, M., & Tierney, W. M. (1998). Effectiveness of computer-generated reminders for increasing discussions about advance directives and completion of advance directive forms. *Annals of Internal Medicine, 128*(2), 102–110.

Dickerson, D. A. (1995). A doctor's duty to disclose life expectancy information to terminally ill patients. *Cleveland State Law Review, 43,* 319–350.

Dickman, I. (1979). Ageism—discrimination against older people (Public Affairs Pamphlet No. 575). New York: Public Affairs Committee.

Diem, S. J. (1997). How and when should physicians discuss clinical decisions with patients? *Journal of General Internal Medicine, 12*(6), 397–398.

Diem, S. J., Lantos, J. D., & Tulsky, J. A. (1996). Cardiopulmonary resuscitation on television: Miracles and misinformation. *New England Journal of Medicine, 334,* 1578–1582.

Donnelly, W. J., & Brauner, D. J. (1992). Why SOAP is bad for the medical record. *Archives of Internal Medicine, 152,* 481–484.

Doukas, D. J., & McCullough, L. B. (1996). A preventive ethics approach to counseling patients about clinical futility in the primary care setting. *Archives of Family Medicine, 5*(10), 589–592.

Dowdy, M. D., Robertson, C., & Bander, J. A. (1998). A study of proactive ethics consultation for critically and terminally ill patients with extended lengths of stay. *Critical Care Medicine, 26*(2), 252–259.

Doyal, L., & Wilsher, D. (1993). Withholding cardiopulmonary resuscitation: Proposals for formal guidelines. *British Medical Journal, 306,* 1593–1596.

Dresser, R. (1990). Relitigating life and death. *Ohio State Law Journal, 51*(2), 425–437.

Dresser, R. (1994). Missing persons: Legal perceptions of incompetent patients. *Rutgers Law Review, 46,* 609–719.

Dresser, R. (1996). Mentally disabled research subjects. *Journal of the American Medical Association, 276,* 67–72.

Dresser, R., & Robertson, J. (1989). Quality of life and non-treatment decisions for incompetent patients: A critique of the orthodox approach. *Law, Medicine and Health Care, 17*(3), 234–244.

Dresser, R., & Whitehouse, P. (1997). Emergency research and research involving subjects with cognitive impairment: Ethical connections and contrasts. *Journal of the American Geriatrics Society, 45,* 521–523.

Drickamer, M. A., & Lachs, M. S. (1992). Should patients with Alzheimer's disease be told their diagnosis? *New England Journal of Medicine, 326,* 947–951.

Dubler, N. N. (1990). Legal issues. In W. B. Abrams & R. Berkow (Eds.), *The Merck manual of geriatrics.* Rahway, NJ: Merck Sharp & Dohme Research Laboratories.

Duensing v. Southwest Texas Methodist Hospital, SA 87 CA 1119 (W.D. Texas).

Dukoff, R., & Sunderland, T. (1997). Durable power of attorney and informed consent with Alzheimer's disease patients: A clinical study. *American Journal of Psychiatry, 154,* 1070–1075.

Dunbar, J. M., Neufeld, R. R., Libow, L. S., Cohen, C. E., & Foley, W. J. (1997). Taking charge: The role of nursing administrators in removing restraints. *Journal of the Occupational Nursing Association, 27*(3), 42–48.

Dunbar, J. M., Neufeld, R. R., White, H. C., & Libow, L. S. (1996). Retrain, don't restrain: The educational intervention of the national nursing home restraint removal project. *Gerontologist, 36,* 539–542.

Dunn, P. M., & Levinson, W. (1996). Discussing futility with patients and families. *Journal of General Internal Medicine, 11*(11), 689–693.

Dzielak, R. J. (1995). Physicians lose the tug of war to pull the plug: The debate about continued futile care. *John Marshall Law Review, 28,* 733–767.

Ebell, M. H. (1994). Practical guidelines for do-not-resuscitate orders. *American Family Physician, 50,* 1293–1299.

Ebell, M. H. (1995). When everything is too much: Quantitative approaches to the issue of futility. *Archives of Family Medicine, 4*(4), 352–356.

Edelman, T. (1990). The nursing home reform law: Issues for litigation. *Clearing-house Review, 24,* 545–553.

Eekelaar, J., & Pearl, D. (Eds.). (1989). *An aging world: Dilemmas and challenges for law and social policy.* Oxford: Clarendon Press.

Ehrlich, P., & Anetzberger, G. (1991). Survey of state public health departments on procedures for reporting elder abuse. *Public Health Reports, 106*(2), 151–154.

Eichmann, M. A., Griffin, B. P., Lyons, J. S., Larson, D. B., & Finkel, S. (1992). An estimation of the impact of OBRA-87 on nursing home care in the United States. *Hospital and Community Psychiatry, 43*(8), 781–789.

Eleazer, G. P., Hornung, C. A., Egbert, C. B., Egbert, J. R., Eng, C., Hedgepeth, J., McCann, R., Strothers, H., Sapir, M., Wei, M., & Wilson, M. (1996). The relationship between ethnicity and advance directives in a frail older population. *Journal of the American Geriatrics Society, 44,* 938–943.

Elliott, C. (1997). Caring about risks: Are severely depressed patients competent to consent to research? *Archives of General Psychiatry, 54*(2), 113–116.

Ellman, I. M. (1989). *Cruzan v. Harmon* and the dangerous claim that others can exercise an incompetent patient's right to die. *Jurimetrics Journal, 29*(4), 389–401.

Elon, R. (1993). The nursing home medical director role in transition. *Journal of the American Geriatrics Society, 41*(2), 131–135.

Ely, J. W., Peters, P. G., Jr., Zweig, S., Elder, N., & Schneider, F. D. (1992). The physician's decision to use tube feedings: The role of the family, the living will, and the *Cruzan* decision. *Journal of the American Geriatrics Society, 40*(5), 471–475.

Emanuel, E. J. (1994). Euthanasia: Historical, ethical, and empiric perspectives. *Archives of Internal Medicine, 154,* 1890–1901.

Emanuel, E. J. (1998). The future of euthanasia and physician-assisted suicide: Beyond rights talk to informed public policy. *Minnesota Law Review, 82,* 983–1014.

Emanuel, L. (1993). Advance directives: What have we learned so far? *Journal of Clinical Ethics, 4*(1), 8–16.

Emanuel, L. L. (1995). Structured advance planning: Is it finally time for physician action and reimbursement? *Journal of the American Medical Association, 274,* 501–503.

Emanuel, L. L., Barry, M. J., Emanuel, E. J., & Stoeckle, J. D. (1994). Advance directives: Can patients' stated treatment choices be used to infer unstated choices? *Medical Care, 32*(2), 95–105.

Emanuel, L. L., Barry, M. J., Stoeckle, J. D., Ettelson, L. M., & Emanuel, E. J. (1991). Advance directives for medical care: A case for greater use. *New England Journal of Medicine, 324,* 889–895.

Emanuel, L. L., Danis, M., Pearlman, R. A., & Singer, P. A. (1995). Advance care planning as a process: Structuring the discussions in practice. *Journal of the American Geriatrics Society, 43,* 440–446.

Emanuel, L. L., & Emanuel, E. J. (1989). The medical directive: A new comprehensive advance care document. *Journal of the American Medical Association, 261,* 3288–3293.

Emanuel, L. L., Emanuel, E. J., Stoeckle, J. D., Hummel, L. R., & Barry, M. J. (1994). Advance directives: Stability of patients' treatment choices. *Archives of Internal Medicine, 154,* 209–217.

Ende, J., Kazis, L., Ash, A., & Moskowitz, M. A. (1989). Measuring patients' desire for autonomy: Decision making and information-seeking preferences among medical patients. *Journal of General Internal Medicine, 4*(1), 23–30.

English, D. M. (1996). The authority of a guardian to commit an adult ward. *Mental and Physical Disability Law Reporter, 20,* 584–587.

Evans, J. M., Chutka, D. S., Fleming, K. C., Tangalos, E. G., Vittone, J., & Heathman, J. H. (1995). Medical care of nursing home residents. *Mayo Clinic Proceedings, 70,* 694–702.

Evans, L. K., & Strumpf, N. E. (1989). Tying down the elderly: A review of the literature on physical restraint. *Journal of the American Geriatrics Society, 37,* 65–74.

Everard, K., Rowles, G. D., & High, D. M. (1994). Nursing home room changes: Toward a decision-making model. *Gerontologist, 34,* 520–527.

Everitt, D. E., & Avorn, J. (1986). Drug prescribing for the elderly. *Archives of Internal Medicine, 146,* 2393–2396.

Faden, R. R., & Beauchamp, T. (1986). *A history and theory of informed consent.* New York: Oxford University Press.

Farrand, J. T. (1989). Enduring powers of attorney. In J. Eekelaar & D. Pearl (Eds.). *An aging world: Dilemmas and challenges for law and social policy.* Oxford: Clarendon Press.

Faulkner, A. (1998). Communication with patients, families, and other professionals. *British Medical Journal, 316,* 130–132.

Feegel, J. R. (1998). Liability of health care entities for negligent care. In S. S. Sanbar, A. Gibofsky, M. H. Firestone, & T. R. LeBlang (Eds.), *Legal Medicine* (4th ed.). St. Louis: C. V. Mosby.

Feldman, P. H. (Guest Editor). (1994). Theme issue: Frontline workers in long-term care. *Generations, 18*(3), 3–86.

Fell, N. (1994). Guardianship and the elderly: Oversight not overlooked. *University of Toledo Law Review, 25*(1), 189–213.

Felsenthal, E. (1994, May 20). Judges find themselves acting as doctors in Alzheimer's cases. *Wall Street Journal,* p. B1.

Felsenthal, E. (1995, Sept. 5). Jury awards rise for improper care of elderly. *Wall Street Journal,* p. B1.

Ficke v. Evangelical Health Systems, 285 Ill.App.3d 886, 674 N.E.2d 888 (1996).

Fins, J. J. (1994). Futility in clinical practice: Report on a Congress of Clinical Societies. *Journal of the American Geriatrics Society, 42,* 861–865.

Fins, J. J. (1995). Across the divide: Religious objections to brain death. *Journal of Religion and Health, 34*(1), 33–39.

Fins, J. J. (1997). Advance directives and SUPPORT. *Journal of the American Medical Association, 45,* 519–520.

Finucane, T. E. (1996). Choosing resuscitation late in life: Problems with the paradigm. *American Journal of Medicine, 100*(2), 126–127.

Finucane, T. E., & Leal-Mora, D. (1997). From Jezebel to a dead man walking: Attempting resuscitation in long-term care. *Journal of the American Geriatrics Society, 45,* 245–246.

Firestone, A. J. (1997). A doctor's dilemma: Is a diagnosis disabling or enabling? *Archives of Internal Medicine, 157,* 491–492.

Fitten, L. J., Coleman, L., Siembieda, D. W., Yu, M., & Ganzell, S. (1995). Assessment of capacity to comply with medication regimens in older patients. *Journal of the American Geriatrics Society, 43,* 361–367.

Fitten, L. J., Lusky, R., & Hamann, C. (1990). Assessing treatment decision-making capacity in elderly nursing home residents. *Journal of the American Geriatrics Society, 38,* 1097–1104.

Flamm, M. B. (1998). Medical malpractice and the physician defendant. In S. S. Sanbar, A. Gibofsky, M. H. Firestone, & T. R. LeBlang (Eds.), *Legal Medicine* (4th ed.). St. Louis: C. V. Mosby.

Fletcher, J. C., Dommel, F. W., Jr., & Cowell, D. D. (1985). Consent to research with impaired human subjects. *IRB: Review of Human Subjects Research, 7*(6), 1–6.

Flood, A. B., Wennberg, J. E., Nease, R. F., Jr., Fowler, F. J., Jr., Ding, J., & Hynes, L. M. (1996). The importance of patient preference in the decision to screen for prostate cancer. *Journal of General Internal Medicine, 11*(6), 342–349.

Florin, D. (1994). Decisions about cardiopulmonary resuscitation: Time to talk. *British Medical Journal, 308*(6945), 1653–1654.

Flynn, L. M. (1997 May 8). *Issues concerning informed consent and protections of human subjects in research.* Hearing held before House Committee on Government Reform and Oversight, Subcommittee on Human Resources. Washington, DC: U.S. Government Printing Office.

Folkemer, D., Jensen, A., Lipson, L., Stauffer, M., & Gox-Grage. (1996). *Adult foster care for the elderly: A review of state regulatory and funding strategies,* Vol. I, #9604A and Vol. II., #9604B. Washington, DC: American Association of Retired Persons, Public Policy Institute.

Fortinsky, R. H., & Raff, L. (1995–96). The changing role of physicians in nursing homes. *Generations, 19*(4), 30–35.

Fowler, F. J., Jr. (1995). Prostate conditions, treatment decisions, and patient preferences. *Journal of the American Geriatrics Society, 43,* 1058–1060.

Fox v. Cohen, 406 NE2d 178 (Ill.App., 1980).

Frank, J. A. (1993). Guardianship procedures: A clinical program to assist in the decision-making process. *Thomas M. Cooley Law Review, 10*(1), 91–114.

Frasca, T. A. (1996). Issues of confidentiality in the information age. *Pharos, 59*(1), 17–19.

Freedman, B. (1993). Offering truth: One ethical approach to the uninformed cancer patient. *Archives of Internal Medicine, 153,* 572–576.

Freeman, I. C. (1995). One more faulty solution is novelty without progress. *Journal of Ethics, Law, and Aging, 1*(2), 93–96.

Freeman, M. D. A. (1989). The abuse of the elderly: Legal responses in England. In J. Eekelaar & D. Pearl (Eds.), *An aging world: Dilemmas and challenges for law and social policy.* Oxford: Clarendon Press.

Fried, T. R., Miller, M. A., Stein, M. D., & Wachtel, T. J. (1996). The association between age of hospitalized patients and the delivery of advanced cardiac life support. *Journal of General Internal Medicine, 11*(5), 257–261.

Fried, T. R., Stein, M. D., O'Sullivan, P. S., Brock, D. W., & Novack, D. H. (1993). Limits of patient autonomy: Physician attitudes and practices regarding life-sustaining treatments and euthanasia. *Archives of Internal Medicine, 153,* 722–728.

Fries, B. E., Hawes, C., Morris, J. N., Phillips, C. D., Mor, V., & Park, P. S. (1997). Effect of the national resident assessment instrument on selected health conditions and problems. *Journal of the American Geriatrics Society, 45,* 994–1001.

Frolik, L. A. (1990). Elder abuse and guardians of elderly incompetents. *Journal of Elder Abuse and Neglect, 2*(3/4), 31–56.

Furner, S. E., Brody, J. A., & Jankowski, L. M. (1997). Epidemiology and aging. In C. K. Cassel, H. J. Cohen, E. B. Larson, D. E. Meier, N. M. Resnick, L. Z. Rubenstein, & L. Sorensen, (Eds.), *Geriatric medicine* (3rd ed.). New York: Springer-Verlag.

Galanos, A. N., Gardner, W. A., & Riddick, L. (1989). Forensic autopsy in the elderly. *Southern Medical Journal, 82,* 462–466.

Gamble, E., McDonald, P. J., & Lichstein, P. R. (1991). Knowledge, attitudes, and behavior of elderly persons regarding living wills. *Archives of Internal Medicine, 151,* 277–280.

Ganzini, L., Lee, M., Heintz, R. T., Bloom, J. D., & Fenn, D. S. (1994). The effect of depression treatment on elderly patients' preferences for life-sustaining medical therapy. *American Journal of Psychiatry, 151,* 1631–1636.

Garrard, J., Chen, V., & Dowd, B. (1995). The impact of the 1987 federal regulations on the use of psychotropic drugs in Minnesota nursing homes. *American Journal of Public Health, 85,* 771–776.

Gasner, M. R. (1992). Financial penalties for failing to honor patient wishes to refuse treatment. *Saint Louis University Public Law Review, 11*(2), 499–520.

Gatz, M. (Ed.). (1995). *Emerging issues in mental health and aging.* Washington, DC: American Psychological Association.

Gazelle, G. (1998). The slow code: Should anyone rush to its defense? *New England Journal of Medicine, 338,* 467–469.

Geller, G., Botkin, J. R., Green, M. J., Press, N., Biesecker, B. B., Wilfond, B., Grana, G., Daly, M. B., Schneider, K., & Kahn, M. J. (1997). Genetic testing for susceptibility to adult-onset cancer: The process and content of informed consent. *Journal of the American Medical Association, 277,* 1467–1474.

Gerety, M. B., Chiodo, L. K., Kanten, D. N., Tuley, M. R., & Cornell, J. E. (1993). Medical treatment preferences of nursing home residents: Relationship to function and concordance with surrogate decision-makers. *Journal of the American Geriatrics Society, 41,* 953–960.

Ghusn, H. F., Teasdale, T. A., & Jordan, D. (1997). Continuity of do-not resuscitate orders between hospital and nursing home settings. *Journal of the American Geriatrics Society, 45,* 465–469.

Ghusn, H. F., Teasdale, T. A., & Skelly, J. R. (1995). Limiting treatment in nursing homes: Knowledge and attitudes of nursing home medical directors. *Journal of the American Geriatrics Society, 43,* 1131–1134.

Gillick, M. R. (1995b). Medical decision-making for the unbefriended nursing home resident. *Journal of Ethics, Law, and Aging, 1*(2), 87–92.

Gillick, M. R. (1995a). A broader role for advance medical planning. *Annals of Internal Medicine, 123,* 621–624.

Gillick, M. (1994). The high costs of dying: A way out. *Archives of Internal Medicine, 154,* 2134–2137.

Glaser, J. W., & Hamel, R. P. (Eds.). (1997). *Three realms of managed care: Societal, institutional, individual.* Kansas City, MO: Sheed & Ward.

Glass, K. C., & Somerville, M. A. (1991). Informed consent to medical research on persons with Alzheimer's disease: Ethical and legal parameters. In J. Berg, H. Karlinsky, & F. Lowy (Eds.), *Alzheimer's disease research: Ethical and legal issues.* Toronto: Thomson Publishing Company.

Glass, K. C., & Speyer-Ofenberg, M. (1996). Incompetent persons as research subjects and the ethics of minimal risk. *Cambridge Quarterly of Healthcare Ethics, 5*(3), 362–372.

Glick, S. M. (1997). Unlimited human autonomy: A cultural bias? *New England Journal of Medicine, 336,* 954–956.

Goldschmidt, P., & Bertram, D. (1994). *The influence of certainty of outcome on choice between treatments* (No. 9406). Washington, DC: AARP Public Policy Institute.

Goldstein, M. Z. (1995). Maltreatment of elderly persons. *Psychiatric Services, 46,* 1219–1221, 1225.

Gonzalez, R. (1993). Social security disability insurance benefits: A practitioner's guide through the administrative process. *Florida Bar Journal, 67*(4), 14–20.

Goodenough, G. K. (1988). The lack of objectivity of physician evaluations in geriatric guardianship cases. *Journal of Contemporary Law, 14*(1), 53–59.

Goodnight, D. R., & Davis, D. R. (1992). Spoliation of evidence: The unnecessary tort. *Journal of Health and Hospital Law, 25*(8), 232–241.

Goodwin, P. (1997). Oregon's physician-assisted suicide law: An alternative positive viewpoint. *Archives of Internal Medicine, 157,* 1642–1643.

Gordon, E. (1996). Multiculturalism in medical decisionmaking: The notion of informed waiver. *Fordham Urban Law Journal, 23,* 1321–1362.

Gordon, P. A. (1997). When a handshake just won't do. *Provider, 23*(4), 39–41.

Gostin, L. O. (1997). Deciding life and death in the courtroom: From *Quinlan* to *Cruzan, Glucksberg,* and *Vacco*—a brief history and analysis of constitutional protection of the "right to die." *Journal of the American Medical Association, 278,* 1523–1528.

Gottlich, V. (1994a). Beyond granny bashing: Elder abuse in the 1990s. *Clearinghouse Review, 28*[Special issue], 371–381.

Gottlich, V. (1994b). Protection for nursing facility residents under the ADA. *Generations, 28*(4), 43–47.

Gottlieb, G. L., & Reisberg, B. (1988). Legal issues in Alzheimer's disease. *American Journal of Alzheimer's Care, 3*(2), 24–36.

Gramelspacher, G. P. (1991). Institutional ethics committees and case consultation: Is there a role? *Issues in Law and Medicine, 7*(1), 73–82.

Grant v. Johnson, 757 F.Supp. 1127 (D.Or., 1991).

Grodin, M. A. (1993). Religious advance directives: The convergence of law, religion, medicine, and public health. *American Journal of Public Health, 83,* 899–903.

Gross, M. D. (1998). What do patients express as their preferences in advance directives? *Archives of Internal Medicine, 158,* 363–365.

Gunn, M. (1994). The meaning of incapacity. *Medical Law Review, 2*(1), 8–29.

Gutheil, T. G., & Appelbaum, P. S. (1991). *Clinical handbook of psychiatry and the law* (2nd ed.) New York: McGraw-Hill.

Hadler, N. (1982). Medical ramifications of the federal regulation of the Social Security disability program. *Annals of Internal Medicine, 96,* 665.

Hafemeister, T. L. (1990). Charting the course between life and death: The Supreme Court takes its first cautious steps in *Cruzan. Probate Law Journal, 10*(2), 113–140.

Hakim, R. B., Teno, J. M., Harrell, F. E., Jr., Knaus, W. A., Wenger, N., Phillips, R. S., Layde, P., Califf, R., Connors, A. F., Jr., & Lynn, J. (1996). Factors associated with do-not-resuscitate orders: Patients' preferences, prognoses, and physicians' judgments. *Annals of Internal Medicine, 125,* 284–293.

Halevy, A., & Brody, B. (1993). Brain death: Reconciling definitions, criteria, and tests. *Annals of Internal Medicine, 119,* 519–525.

Halevy, A., & Brody, B. A. (1996). A multi-institution collaborative policy on medical futility. *Journal of the American Medical Association, 276,* 571–574.

Halevy, A., Neal, R. C., & Brody, B. A. (1996). The low frequency of futility in an adult intensive care unit setting. *Archives of Internal Medicine, 156,* 100–104.

Haley, K., & Lee, M. (Eds.) (1998). *The Oregon Death with Dignity Act: A guidebook for health care providers.* Portland: Oregon Health Sciences University, Center for Ethics in Health Care.

Hall, M. A. (1997). *Making medical spending decisions: The law, ethics, and economics of rationing decisions.* New York: Oxford University Press.

Hammes, B. J., & Rooney, B. L. (1998). Death and end-of-life planning in one midwestern community. *Archives of Internal Medicine, 158,* 383–390.

Hansen, K. D. (1998). American legal and judicial system. In S. S. Sanbar, A. Gibofsky, M. H. Firestone, & T. R. LeBlang (Eds.), *Legal medicine* (4th ed.). St. Louis: C. V. Mosby.

Hanson, L. C., Danis, M., & Garrett, J. (1997). What is wrong with end-of-life care? Opinions of bereaved family members. *Journal of the American Geriatrics Society, 45,* 1339–1344.

Hanson, L. C., Danis, M., Mutran, E., & Keenan, N. L. (1994). Impact of patient incompetence on decisions to use or withhold life-sustaining treatment. *American Journal of Medicine, 97,* 235–241.

Hanson, L. C., & Rodgman, E. (1996). The use of living wills at the end of life: A national study. *Archives of Internal Medicine, 156,* 1018–1022.

Hanzlick, R. (1996). Protocol for writing cause-of-death statements for deaths due to natural causes. *Archives of Internal Medicine, 156,* 25–26.

Hanzlick, R., & Combs, D. (1998). Medical examiner and coroner systems: History and trends. *Journal of the American Medical Association, 279,* 870–874.

Hare, J., & Nelson, C. (1991). Will outpatients complete living wills? A comparison of two interventions. *Journal of General Internal Medicine, 6*(1), 41–46.

Harris, L. J. (1997). Semantics and policy in physician-assisted death: Piercing the verbal veil. *Elder Law Journal, 5*(2), 251–291.

Harris, M. G., & Thal, L. S. (1991). Retention of patient records. *Journal of the American Optometric Association, 62,* 430–435.

Harris-Wehling, J., Feasley, J. C., & Estes, C. L. (Eds.). (1995). *Real people, real problems: An evaluation of the long-term care ombudsman programs of the Older Americans Act.* Washington, DC: Institute of Medicine, National Academy of Sciences.

Harrold, J. K., & Lynn, J. (Eds.). (1998). *A good dying: Shaping health care for the last months of life.* New York: Haworth Press.

Harvard Law Review Staff. (1990). Developments in the law: Medical technology and the law. *Harvard Law Review, 103,* 1519–1676.

Hawes, C., Mor, V., Phillips, C. D., Fries, B. E., Morris, J. N., Steele-Friedlob, E., Greene, A. M., & Nennstiel, M. (1997). The OBRA-87 nursing home regulations and implementation of the resident assessment instrument: Effects on process quality. *Journal of the American Geriatrics Society, 45,* 977–985.

Hawes, C., Wildfire, J. B., & Lux, L. J. (1993). *The regulation of board and care homes: Results of a survey in the 50 states and the District of Columbia.* Washington, DC: American Association of Retired Persons, Public Policy Institute.

Hayley, D. C., Cassel, C. K., Snyder, L., & Rudberg, M. A. (1996). Ethical and legal issues in nursing home care. *Archives of Internal Medicine, 156,* 249–256.

Hazzard, W. R. (1995). Elder abuse: Definitions and implications for medical education. *Academic Medicine, 70,* 979–981.

Health Care Financing Administration. (1996). Do not resuscitate policy for LTC facilities (DHSQ Regional Program Letter No. 96-05). Washington, DC: Author.

Heckler v. Campbell, 461 U.S. 458 (1983).

Heffner, J. E., Barbieri, C., & Casey, K. (1996). Procedure-specific do-not-resuscitate orders: Effect on communication of treatment limitations. *Archives of Internal Medicine, 156,* 793–797.

Heilig, S., Brody, R., Marcus, F. S., Shavelson, L., & Sussman, P. C. (1997). Physician-hastened death: Advisory guidelines for the San Francisco Bay Area from the Bay Area Network of Ethics Committees. *Western Journal of Medicine, 166,* 370–378.

Hemp, S. J. (1994). The right to a remedy: When should an abused nursing home resident sue? *Elder Law Journal, 2*(2), 195–224.

Hermann, D. H. J. (1997). *Mental health and disability law in a nutshell.* St. Paul, MN: West Publishing Company.

Herr, S. S., & Hopkins, B. L. (1994). Health care decision making for persons with disabilities: An alternative to guardianship. *Journal of the American Medical Association, 271,* 1017–1022.

Hesse, K. A. (1995). Terminal care of the very old: Changes in the way we die. *Archives of Internal Medicine, 155,* 1513–1518.

High, D. M., Whitehouse, P. J., Post, S. G., & Berg, L. (1994). Guidelines for addressing ethical and legal issues in Alzheimer disease research. *Alzheimer Disease and Associated Disorders, 8*(Suppl. 4), 66–74.

Higuchi, N. (1992). The patient's right to know of a cancer diagnosis: A comparison of Japanese paternalism and American self-determination. *Washburn Law Journal, 31,* 455–473.

Hirschfeld, R. M. A., Winslade, W., & Krause, T. L. (1997). Protecting subjects and fostering research: Striking the proper balance. *Archives of General Psychiatry, 54*(2), 121–123.

Hirsh, H. L. (1998a). Cost containment and reimbursement. In S. S. Sanbar, A. Gibofsky, M. H. Firestone, & T. R. LeBlang (Eds.), *Legal medicine* (4th ed.). St. Louis: C. V. Mosby.

Hirsh, H. L. (1998b). Medical records. In S. S. Sanbar, A. Gibofsky, M. H. Firestone, & T. R. LeBlang (Eds.), *Legal medicine* (4th ed.). St. Louis: C. V. Mosby.

Hoffmann, D. E., Boyle, P., & Levenson, S. A. (1995). *Handbook for nursing home ethics committees*. Washington, DC: American Association of Homes and Services for the Aging.

Hoffmann, D. E., Zimmerman, S. I., & Tompkins, C. J. (1996). The dangers of directives or the false security of forms. *Journal of Law, Medicine and Ethics, 24*(1), 5–17.

Hoge, S. K. (1994). On being "too crazy" to sign into a mental hospital: The issue of consent to psychiatric hospitalization. *Bulletin of the American Academy of Psychiatry and Law, 22*, 431–450.

Holmes, O. W. (1911). The young practitioner. In O. W. Holmes, *Medical essays*. Boston: Houghton Mifflin.

Holroyd, S., Snustad, D. G., & Chalifoux, Z. L. (1996). Attitudes of older adults' on being told the diagnosis of Alzheimer's disease. *Journal of the American Geriatrics Society, 44*, 400–403.

Holstein, M. (1997). Reflections on death and dying. *Academic Medicine, 72*, 848–855.

Hommel, P. A. (1996). Guardianship reform in the 1980s: A decade of substantive and procedural change. In M. Smyer, K. W. Schaie, & M. B. Kapp (Eds.), *Older adults' decision-making and the law*. New York: Springer Publishing Company.

Hopper, K. D., Houts, P. S., McCauslin, M. A., Matthews, Y. L., & Sefczek, R. J. (1992). Patients' attitudes toward informed consent for intravenous contrast media. *Investigative Radiology, 27*, 362–366.

Horstman, P. (1975). Protective services for the elderly: The limits of parens patriae. *Missouri Law Review, 40*(2), 215–278.

Hsiao, W. C., Braun, P., Dunn, D., & Becker, E. R. (1988). Resource-based relative values: An overview. *Journal of the American Medical Association, 260*, 2347–2353.

Huffman, G. B. (1997). Death certificates: Why it matters how your patient died. *American Family Physician, 56*, 1287–1290.

Hughes, R., & McGuire, G. (1997). Neurologic disease and the determination of brain death: The importance of a diagnosis. *Critical Care Medicine, 25*, 1923–1924.

Hull, L., Holmes, G. E., & Karst, R. H. (1990). Managing guardianships of the elderly: Protection and advocacy as public policy. *Journal of Elder Abuse and Neglect, 2*(3/4), 145–162.

Hurme, S. B. (1991). *Steps to enhance guardianship monitoring*. Washington, DC: American Bar Association, Commissions on the Mentally Disabled and on Legal Problems of the Elderly.

Hurme, S. B. (1994). Limited guardianship: Its implementation is long overdue. *Clearinghouse Review, 28,* 660–670.

Hyde, L. (1988). *Essential dictionary of health care.* New York: McGraw-Hill.

Hyman, E. A. (1989). The Nursing Home and Community Residence Facility Residents' Protection Act of 1985: Boon or bane? *Howard Law Journal, 32*(1), 39–47.

Hyman v. Jewish Chronic Disease Hospital, 15 N.Y.2d 317, 206 N.E.2d 338, 258 N.Y.S.2d 397 (1965).

Hynes, D. M. (1994). The quality of breast cancer care in local communities: Implications for health care reform. *Medical Care, 32,* 328–340.

Iglehart, J. K. (1992). The American health care system: Medicare. *New England Journal of Medicine, 327,* 1467–1472.

Iglehart, J. K. (1993). The American health care system: Medicaid. *New England Journal of Medicine, 328,* 896–900.

In the matter of Gerkin, 434 NYS2d 607 (Sup.Ct., 1980).

In the matter of the Involuntary Discharge or Transfer of J.S. by Hall, 512 N.W.2d 695 (Minn.App., 1994).

In re Austwick, 275 Ill.App.3d 665, 656 NE2d 773 (1995).

In re Baby K, 16 F.3d 590 (4th Cir., 1994).

In re Conservatorship of Wanglie, Minnesota Dist. Ct. Prob. Div., (1991); reprinted, *Issues in Law and Medicine, 7*(3), 369–377.

In re Quinlan, 70 N.J. 10, 355 A.2d 647 (1976).

Institute of Medicine. (1986). *Improving the quality of care in nursing homes.* Washington, DC: National Academy Press.

Institute of Medicine. (1997a). *Approaching death: Improving care at the end of life.* Washington, DC: National Academy Press.

Institute of Medicine. (1997b). *Non-heart-beating organ transplantation: Medical and ethical issues in procurement.* Washington, DC: National Academy Press.

Iris, M. A. (1988). Guardianship and the elderly: A multiperspective view of the decisionmaking process. *Gerontologist, 28*(Suppl.), 39–45.

Iris, M. A. (1990). Uses of guardianship as a protective intervention for frail, older adults. *Journal of Elder Abuse and Neglect, 2*(3&4), 57–71.

Jablonski, D. F., Mosley, G. M., & Byrd, J. C. (1991). Informed consent for patient transfers to a Veterans Affairs Medical Center. *Journal of General Internal Medicine, 6*(3), 229–232.

Jackson, D., & Youngner, S. (1979). Patient autonomy and death with dignity. *New England Journal of Medicine, 301,* 404–408.

Jacobson, J. A., Kasworm, E., Battin, M. P., Francis, L. P., Green, D., Botkin, J., & Johnson, S. (1996). Advance directives in Utah: Information from death certificates and informants. *Archives of Internal Medicine, 156,* 1862–1868.

Jacobson, J. A., White, B. E., Battin, M. P., Francis, L. P., Green, D. J., & Kasworm, E. S. (1994). Patients' understanding and use of advance directives. *Western Journal of Medicine, 160*(3), 232–236.

Janofsky, J. S., McCarthy, R. F., & Folstein, M. F. (1992). The Hopkins competency assessment test: A brief method for evaluating patients' capacity to give informed consent. *Hospital and Community Psychiatry, 43*(2), 132–136.

Jardin, D. G. (1990). Liability issues arising out of hospitals' and organ procurement organizations' rejection of valid anatomical gifts: The truth and consequences. *Wisconsin Law Review, 1990,* 1655–1694.

Jayes, R. L., Zimmerman, J. E., Wagner, D. P., Draper, E. A., & Knaus, W. A. (1993). Do-not-resuscitate orders in intensive care units: Current practices and recent changes. *Journal of the American Medical Association, 270,* 2213–2217.

Jayes, R. L., Zimmerman, J. E., Wagner, D. P., & Knaus, W. A. (1996). Variations in the use of do-not-resuscitate orders in ICUs: Findings from a national study. *Chest, 110,* 1332–1339.

Jecker, N. S., & Pearlman, R. A. (1992). Medical futility: Who decides? *Archives of Internal Medicine, 152,* 1140–1144.

Jecker, N. S., & Schneiderman, L. J. (1992). Futility and rationing. *American Journal of Medicine, 92*(2), 189–196.

Jeremiah, J., O'Sullivan, P., & Stein, M. D. (1995). Who leaves against medical advice? *Journal of General Internal Medicine, 10,* 403–405.

Johns, A. F. (1997). Guardianship folly: The misgovernment of parens patriae and the forecast of its crumbling linkage to unprotected older Americans in the twenty-first century: A march of folly? Or just a mask of virtual reality? *Stetson Law Review, 27*(1), 1–90.

Johns, A. F., Gottlich, V., & Carson, M. (1992). Guardianship jurisdiction revisited: A proposal for a uniform act. *Clearinghouse Review, 26,* 647–651.

Johnson, A. B. (1990). *Out of bedlam: The truth about deinstitutionalization.* New York: Basic Books.

Johnson, R. F., Jr., Baranowski-Birkmeier, T., & O'Donnell, J. B. (1995). Advance directives in the medical intensive care unit of a community teaching hospital. *Chest, 107,* 752–756.

Johnson, S. H. (1990). The fear of liability and the use of restraints in nursing homes. *Law, Medicine and Health Care, 18*(3), 263–273.

Johnson, S. H., Gibbons, V. P., Goldner, J. A., Wiener, R. L., & Eton, D. (1997). Legal and institutional policy responses to medical futility. *Journal of Health and Hospital Law, 30*(1), 21–36.

Johnson, T. F. (1990). Guardianship in the South: Strategies for preserving the rights of older persons. *Journal of Aging and Social Policy, 2*(1), 33–50.

Johnson, T. F. (1995). *Elder mistreatment: Ethical issues, dilemmas, and decisions.* Binghamton, NY: Haworth Press.

Johnston, S. C., Pfeifer, M. P., & End-of-Life Study Group. (1998). Patient and physician roles in end-of-life decision making. *Journal of General Internal Medicine, 13*(1), 43–45.

Johnston, S. C., Pfeifer, M. P., & McNutt, R. (1995). The discussion about advance directives: Patient and physician opinions regarding when and how it should be conducted. *Archives of Internal Medicine, 155,* 1025–1030.

Joint Commission on Accreditation of Healthcare Organizations. (1995). *Home care survey and accreditation process guide.* Chicago: Author.

Joint Commission on Accreditation of Healthcare Organizations. (1999). *Accreditation manual for home care.* Chicago: Author.

Jones, J. S. (1994). Elder abuse and neglect: Responding to a national problem. *Annals of Emergency Medicine, 23,* 845–848.

Jones, J. S., Veenstra, T. R., Seamon, J. P., & Krohmer, J. (1997). Elder mistreatment: National survey of emergency physicians. *Annals of Emergency Medicine, 30,* 473–479.

Jones, M. A., & Keywood, K. (1996). Assessing the patient's competence to consent to medical treatment. *Medical Law International, 2*(1), 107–147.

Jonsen, A. R., Siegler, M., & Winslade, W. J. (1998). *Clinical ethics* (4th ed.). New York: McGraw-Hill.

Joos, S. K., Reuler, J. B., Powell, J. L., & Hickam, D. H. (1993). Outpatients' attitudes and understanding regarding living wills. *Journal of General Internal Medicine, 8*(5), 259–263.

Josefson, D. (1998). U.S. sees first legal case of physician assisted suicide. *British Medical Journal, 316,* 1037.

Kahana, J. S. (1994). Reevaluating the nursing home ombudsman's role with a view toward expanding the concept of dispute resolution. *Journal of Dispute Resolution, 1994*(2), 217–233.

Kane, R. A., Caplan, A. L., Urv-Wong, E. K., Freeman, I. C., Aroskar, M. A., & Finch, M. (1997). Everyday matters in the lives of nursing home residents: Wish for and perception of choice and control. *Journal of the American Geriatrics Society, 45,* 1086–1093.

Kane, R. A., & Wilson, K. B. (1993). *Assisted living in the United States: A new paradigm for residential care for frail older persons?* Washington, DC: American Association of Retired Persons.

Kane, R. S. (1996). The defeat of aging versus the importance of death. *Journal of the American Geriatrics Society, 44,* 321–325.

Kane, R. S., & Burns, E. A. (1997). Cardiopulmonary resuscitation policies in long-term care facilities. *Journal of the American Geriatrics Society, 45,* 154–157.

Kapp, M. B. (1982). Promoting the legal rights of older adults: Role of the primary care physician. *Journal of Legal Medicine, 3*(3), 367–412.

Kapp, M. B. (1983). Adult protective services: Convincing the patient to consent. *Law, Medicine and Health Care, 11*(4), 163–167, 188.

Kapp, M. B. (1989). Medical empowerment of the elderly. *Hastings Center Report, 19*(4), 5–7.

Kapp, M. B. (1991a). Health care decision making by the elderly: I get by with a little help from my family. *Gerontologist, 31,* 619–623.

Kapp, M. B. (1991b). Legal and ethical issues in family caregiving and the role of public policy. *Home Health Services Quarterly, 12*(4), 5–28.

Kapp, M. B. (1992a). Nursing home restraints and legal liability: Merging the standard of care and industry practice. *Journal of Legal Medicine, 13*(1), 1–32.

Kapp, M. B. (1992b). State statutes limiting advance directives: Death warrants or life sentences? *Journal of the American Geriatrics Society, 40,* 722–726.

Kapp, M. B. (1994a). Ethical aspects of guardianship. *Clinics in Geriatric Medicine, 10,* 501–512.

Kapp, M. B. (1994b). Implications of the Patient Self-Determination Act for psychiatric practice. *Hospital and Community Psychiatry, 45,* 355–358.

Kapp, M. B. (1994c). Proxy decision making in Alzheimer disease research: Durable powers of attorney, guardianship, and other alternatives. *Alzheimer Disease and Associated Disorders, 8*(Suppl. 4), 28–37.

Kapp, M. B. (1995a). Beyond Belmont: Critically assessing the adequacy of informed consent. *International Journal of Risk and Safety in Medicine, 7*(1), 43–54.

Kapp, M. B. (1995b). Elder mistreatment: Legal interventions and policy uncertainties. *Behavioral Sciences and the Law, 13*(3), 365–380.

Kapp, M. B. (1995c). Family caregiving for older persons in the home: Medical-legal implications. *Journal of Legal Medicine, 16*(1), 1–31.

Kapp, M. B. (1995d). *Key words in ethics, law, and aging.* New York: Springer Publishing Company.

Kapp, M. B. (1995e). Legal and ethical issues in family caregiving and the role of public policy. In R. A. Kane & J. D. Penrod (Eds.), *Family caregiving in an aging society: Policy perspectives.* Thousand Oaks, CA: Sage Publications.

Kapp, M. B. (1995f). Legal and ethical issues in home-based care. In L. W. Kaye (Ed.), *New developments in home care services for the elderly: Innovations in policy, program, and practice.* Binghamton, NY: Haworth Press.

Kapp, M. B. (1995g). Problems and protocols for dying at home in a high-tech environment. In J. D. Arras (Ed.), *Bringing the hospital home: Ethical and social implications of high-tech home care.* Baltimore: Johns Hopkins University Press.

Kapp, M. B. (1995h). Restraining impaired elders in the home environment: Legal, practical, and policy implications. *Journal of Case Management, 4*(2), 54–59.

Kapp, M. B. (1995i). Surrogate decision-making for the unbefriended: Social and ethical problem, legal solution? *Journal of Ethics, Law, and Aging, 1*(2), 83–85.

Kapp, M. B. (1996a). Alternatives to guardianship: Enhanced autonomy for diminished capacity. In M. Smyer, K. W. Schaie, & M. B. Kapp (Eds.), *Older adults' decision-making and the law.* New York: Springer Publishing Company.

Kapp, M. B. (1996b). Assessment of competence to make medical decisions. In L. L. Carstensen, B. A. Edelstein, & L. Dornbrand (Eds.), *The practical handbook of clinical gerontology.* Thousand Oaks, CA: Sage Publications.

Kapp, M. B. (1996c). Clinical practice parameters and nursing home medicine: Legal and ethical implications. *Nursing Home Medicine: Annals of Long-Term Care, 4*(7), 187–192.

Kapp, M. B. (1996d). Enhancing autonomy and choice in selecting and directing long-term care services. *Elder Law Journal, 4*(1), 55–97.

Kapp, M. B. (1996e). Medicolegal, employment, and insurance issues in APOE genotyping and Alzheimer's disease. *Annals of the New York Academy of Sciences, 802,* 139–148.

Kapp, M. B. (1996/97). Making medical decisions: Keeping medical decisions near the end of life in the family. *Preventive Law Reporter, 15*(4), 23–25.

Kapp, M. B. (1997a). Old folks on the slippery slope: Elderly patients and physician-assisted suicide. *Duquesne Law Review, 35*(1), 443–453.

Kapp, M. B. (1997b). Treating medical charts near the end of life: How legal anxieties inhibit good patient deaths. *University of Toledo Law Review, 28,* 521–546.

Kapp, M. B. (1997c). Who is responsible for this? Assigning rights and consequences in elder care. *Journal of Aging and Social Policy, 9*(2), 51–65.

Kapp, M. B. (1998a). *De facto* health care rationing by age: The law has no remedy. *Journal of Legal Medicine, 19*(3), 323–349.

Kapp, M. B. (1998b). Decisional capacity, older human research subjects, and IRBs: Beyond forms and guidelines. *Stanford Law and Policy Review, 9,* 359–371.

Kapp, M. B. (1998c). *Our hands are tied: Legal tensions and medical ethics.* Westport, CT: Auburn House.

Kapp, M. B. (1998d). The "voluntary" status of nursing facility admissions: Legal, practice, and public policy implications. *New England Journal of Criminal and Civil Confinement, 24*(1), 1–35.

Kapp, M. B., & Mossman, D. (1996). Measuring decisional capacity: Cautions on the construction of a "capacimeter." *Psychology, Public Policy, and Law, 2*(1), 73–95.

Kapp, M. B., & Wilson, K. B. (1995). Assisted living and negotiated risk: Reconciling protection and autonomy. *Journal of Ethics, Law, and Aging, 1*(1), 5–13.

Karetzky, M., Zubair, M., & Parikh, J. (1995). Cardiopulmonary resuscitation in intensive care unit and nonintensive care unit patients: Immediate and long-term survival. *Archives of Internal Medicine, 155,* 1277–1280.

Karlawish, J. H. T. (1997). Permissible risk and acceptable benefit: The ethics of research involving the cognitively impaired. *FORUM Trends in Experimental and Clinical Medicine, 7*(3), 277–285.

Karlawish, J. H. T., & Lantos, J. (1997). Community equipoise and the architecture of clinical research. *Cambridge Quarterly of Healthcare Ethics, 6*(4), 385–396.

Karlawish, J. H. T., & Sachs, G. A. (1997). Research on the cognitively impaired: Lessons and warnings from the emergency research debate. *Journal of the American Geriatrics Society, 45,* 474–481.

Kassirer, J. P. (1994). Incorporating patients' preferences into medical decisions. *New England Journal of Medicine, 330,* 1895–1896.

Katz, J. (1994). Informed consent: Must it remain a fairy tale? *Journal of Contemporary Health Law and Policy, 10*(1), 69–91.

Katz, P. R., Karuza, J., Kolassa, J., & Hutson, A. (1997). Medical practice with nursing home residents: Results from the national physician professional activities census. *Journal of the American Geriatrics Society, 45,* 911–917.

Kaufman, S. R. (1995). Decision making, responsibility, and advocacy in geriatric medicine: Physician dilemmas with elderly in the community. *Gerontologist, 35,* 481–488.

Kaye, J. M., Lawton, P., & Kaye, D. (1990). Attitudes of elderly people about research on aging. *Gerontologist, 30,* 100–106.

Keay, T. J., & Schonwetter, R. S. (1998). Hospice care in the nursing home. *American Family Physician, 57,* 491–494.

Keay, T. J., & Taler, G. A. (1992). Review of medical care in cited nursing homes: Key areas of deficiency. *Quality Review Bulletin, 18*(7), 222–228.

Keith, P. M., & Wacker, R. R. (1992). Guardianship reform: Does revised legislation make a difference in outcomes for proposed wards? *Journal of Aging and Social Policy, 4*(3/4), 139–155.

Kelly v. Methodist Hospital, 444 Pa.Super. 427, 664 A.2d 148 (1995).

Kemper, P., & Murtaugh, C. M. (1991). Lifetime use of nursing home care. *New England Journal of Medicine, 324,* 595–600.

Kennedy, W., & Jacobs, E. (1981). Literature review of legal aspects of medical records. *Topics in Health Record Management, 1,* 19.

Keville, T. D. (1993). Studies of transfer trauma in nursing home patients: How the legal system has failed to see the whole picture. *Health Matrix, 3,* 421–458.

Keyserlingk, E. W., Glass, K., Kogan, S., & Gauthier, S. (1995). Proposed guidelines for the participation of persons with dementia as research subjects. *Perspectives in Biology and Medicine, 38,* 319–361.

King, J. H., Jr. (1986). *The law of medical malpractice* (2nd ed.). St. Paul, MN: West Publishing Company.

King, N. M. P. (1996). *Making sense of advance directives* (rev. ed.). Washington, DC: Georgetown University Press.

Klassen, A. C., & Klassen, D. K. (1996). Who are the donors in organ donation? The family's perspective in mandated choice. *Annals of Internal Medicine, 125,* 70–73.

Klatt, E. C., & Noguchi, T. T. (1989). Death certification: Purposes, procedures, and pitfalls. *Western Journal of Medicine, 151,* 345–347.

Kleinschmidt, K. C. (1997). Elder abuse: A review. *Annals of Emergency Medicine, 30,* 463–472.

Klingenstein, R. J. (1992). Informed consent in medicine: One physician's perspective. *International Journal of Risk and Safety in Medicine, 3,* 263–270.

Knepper, K. (1996). Involuntary transfers and discharges of nursing home residents under federal and state law. *Journal of Legal Medicine, 17*(2), 215–275.

Koh v. Perales, 570 NYS2d 98 (NY App.Div., 1991), appeal denied 575 NYS2d 455 (NY Ct. App., 1991).

Korbin, J. E., Anetzberger, G., & Austin, C. (1995). The intergenerational cycle of violence in child and elder abuse. *Journal of Elder Abuse and Neglect, 7*(1), 1–15.

Kozak, E. A., Dittus, R. S., Smith, W. R., Fitzgerald, J. F., & Langfeld, C. D. (1994). Deciphering the physician note. *Journal of General Internal Medicine, 9*(1), 52–54.

Kramer, A. M. (1995). Health care for elderly persons: Myths and realities. *New England Journal of Medicine, 332,* 1027–1029.

Kramer, T. L. (1995). Section 784.08 of the Florida Statutes: A necessary tool to combat elder abuse and victimization. *Nova Law Review, 19,* 735–759.

Krasik, E. B. (1987). The role of the family in medical decisionmaking for incompetent adult patients: A historical perspective and case analysis. *University of Pittsburgh Law Review, 48,* 539–618.

Krasik, M. K. (1989). The lights of science and experience: Historical perspectives on legal attitudes toward the role of medical expertise in guardianship of the elderly. *American Journal of Legal History, 33*(3), 201–240.

Krumholz, H. M., Friesinger, G. C., Cook, E. F., Lee, T. H., Rouan, G. W., & Goldman, L. (1994). Relationship of age with eligibility for thrombolytic therapy and mortality among patients with suspected acute myocardial infarction. *Journal of the American Geriatrics Society, 42,* 127–131.

Krynski, M. D., Tymchuk, A. J., & Ouslander, J. G. (1994). How informed can consent be? New light on comprehension among elderly people making decisions about enteral tube feeding. *Gerontologist, 34,* 36–43.

Lachs, M. S., Berkman, L., Fulmer, T., & Horwitz, R. I. (1994). A prospective community-based pilot study of risk factors for the investigation of elder mistreatment. *Journal of the American Geriatrics Society, 42,* 169–173.

Lachs, M. S., & Pillemer, K. (1995). Abuse and neglect of elderly persons. *New England Journal of Medicine, 332,* 437–443.

Lachs, M. S., & Ruchlin, H. S. (1997). Is managed care good or bad for geriatric medicine? *Journal of the American Geriatrics Society, 45,* 1123–1127.

Lachs, M. S., Williams, C. S., O'Brien, S., Hurst, L., Kossack, A., & Siegal, A. (1997). ED use by older victims of family violence. *Annals of Emergency Medicine, 30,* 448–454.

Lamb, G. C., Green, S. S., & Heron, J. (1994). Can physicians warn patients of potential side effects without fear of causing those side effects? *Archives of Internal Medicine, 154,* 2753–2756.

Lamb, H. R., & Weinberger, L. E. (1992). Conservatorship for gravely disabled psychiatric patients: A four-year follow-up study. *American Journal of Psychiatry, 149,* 909–913.

Lamb, H. R., & Weinberger, L. E. (1993). Therapeutic use of conservatorship in the treatment of gravely disabled psychiatric patients. *Hospital and Community Psychiatry, 44*(2), 147–150.

Lantos, J. D. (1994). Futility assessments and the doctor-patient relationship. *Journal of the American Geriatrics Society, 42,* 868–870.

Lantz, M. S., Giambanco, V., & Buchalter, E. N. (1996). A ten-year review of the effect of OBRA-87 on psychotropic prescribing practices in an academic nursing home. *Psychiatric Services, 47,* 951–955.

Larson, E. J., & Eaton, T. A. (1997). The limits of advance directives: A history and assessment of the Patient Self-Determination Act. *Wake Forest Law Review, 32,* 249–293.

Lattanzi-Licht, M., Mahoney, J. J., & Miller, G. W. (1998). *The hospice choice: In pursuit of a peaceful death.* New York: Fireside Books.

Layson, R. T., & McConnell, T. (1996). Must consent always be obtained for a do-not-resuscitate order? *Archives of Internal Medicine, 156,* 2617–2620.

LeBlang, T. R., & Kirchner, J. L. (1996). Informed consent and Alzheimer disease research: Institutional review board policies and practices. In R. Becker & E. Giacobini (Eds.), *Alzheimer disease: From molecular biology to therapy.* Boston: Birkhauser.

Lee, J. M. (1993). Screening and informed consent. *New England Journal of Medicine, 328,* 438–440.

Lee, M., & Ganzini, L. (1992). Depression in the elderly: Effect on patient attitudes toward life-sustaining therapy. *Journal of the American Geriatrics Society, 40,* 983–988.

Lee, M., & Ganzini, L. (1994). The effect of recovery from depression on preferences for life-sustaining therapy in older patients. *Journal of Gerontology: Medical Sciences, 49*(1), M15–M21.

Lester v. Chater, 69 F.3d 1453 (9th Cir., 1995).

Levine, M. L. (1980). Themes and issues in gerontology and law. *Law Library Journal, 73,* 259.

Levine, R. J. (1983). Informed consent in research and practice: Similarities and differences. *Archives of Internal Medicine, 143,* 1229–1231.

Levine, R. J. (1986). *Ethics and regulation of clinical research* (2nd ed.). Baltimore: Urban & Schwarzenberg.

Levine, R. J. (1996). Proposed regulations for research involving those institution-alized as mentally infirm: A consideration of their relevance in 1996. *IRB: Review of Human Subjects Research, 18*(5), 1–5.

Levinsky, N. G. (1996). The purpose of advance medical planning: Autonomy for patients or limitation of care? *New England Journal of Medicine, 335,* 741–743.

Levinson, W., Roter, D. L., Mullooly, J. P., Dull, V. T., & Frankel, R. M. (1997). Physician-patient communication: The relationship with malpractice claims among primary care physicians and surgeons. *Journal of the American Medical Association, 277,* 553–559.

Levit, K. R., Lazenby, H. C., Sivarajan, L., Stewart, M. W., Braden, B. R., Cowan, C. A., Donham, C. S., Long, A. M., McDonnell, P. A., Sensenig, A. L., Stiller, J. M., & Won, D. K. (1996). National health expenditures, 1994. *Health Care Financing Review, 17*(3), 205–242.

Levitt, S. J., & O'Neill, R. J. (1997). A call for a functional multidisciplinary approach to intervention in cases of elder abuse, neglect, and exploitation. *Elder Law Journal, 5*(1), 195–212.

Lidz, C. W., Appelbaum, P. S., & Meisel, A. (1988). Two models of implementing informed consent. *Archives of Internal Medicine, 148,* 1385–1389.

Lidz, C. W., Mulvey, E. P., & Gardner, W. (1993). The accuracy of predictions of violence to others. *Journal of the American Medical Association, 269,* 1007–1011.

Lifton, R. J. (1986). *Nazi doctors: Medical killing and the psychology of genocide.* New York: Basic Books.

Lloyd, B. D. (1996). Toward a pragmatic model of judicial decisionmaking: Why tort law provides a better framework than constitutional law for deciding the issue of medical futility. *Seattle University Law Review, 19,* 603–632.

Lo, B. (1991). Unanswered questions about DNR orders. *Journal of the American Medical Association, 265,* 1874–1875.

Lo, B., Rouse, F., & Dornbrand, L. (1990). Family decision making on trial: Who decides for incompetent patients? *New England Journal of Medicine, 322,* 1228–1231.

Loewy, E. H. (1998). Ethical considerations in executing and implementing advance directives. *Archives of Internal Medicine, 158,* 321–324.

Loewy, E. H., & Carlson, R. W. (1994). Talking, advance directives, and medical practice. *Archives of Internal Medicine, 154,* 2265–2267.

Loftus, I. P. (1990). Note, I have a conscience, too: The plight of medical personnel confronting the right to die. *Notre Dame Law Review, 65,* 699–730.

Lombardo, N. B. E., Fogel, B. S., Robinson, G. K., & Weiss, H. P. (1996). *Achieving mental health of nursing home residents: Overcoming barriers to mental health care.* Boston: Hebrew Rehabilitation Center for the Aged.

Long, J., & Marin, A. (1982). Profile of patients signing against medical advice. *Journal of Family Practice, 15,* 551, 556.

Luce, J. M. (1990). Ethical principles in critical care. *Journal of the American Medical Association, 263,* 696–700.

Luce, J. M. (1994). The changing physician-patient relationship in critical care medicine under health care reform. *American Journal of Respiratory and Critical Care Medicine, 150*(1), 266–270.

Luchins, D. J., Hanrahan, P., & Murphy, K. (1997). Criteria for enrolling dementia patients in hospice. *Journal of the American Geriatrics Society, 45,* 1054–1059.

Lynn, J. (1997). An 88-year-old woman facing the end of life. *Journal of the American Medical Association, 277,* 1633–1640.

Lynn, J., Teno, J. M., & Harrell, F. E., Jr. (1995). Accurate prognostications of death: Opportunities and challenges for clinicians. *Western Journal of Medicine, 163,* 250–257.

Macolini, R. M. (1995). Elder abuse policy: Considerations in research and legislation. *Behavioral Sciences and the Law, 13,* 349–363.

Magrane, B. P., Gilliland, M. G. F., & King, D. E. (1997). Certification of death by family physicians. *American Family Physician, 56,* 1433–1438.

Maguire, C. P., Kirby, M., Coen, R., Coakley, D., Lawlor, B. A., & O'Neill, D. (1996). Family members' attitudes toward telling the patient with Alzheimer's disease their diagnosis. *British Medical Journal, 313,* 529–530.

Mahler, J. C., Perry, S., & Miller, F. (1990). Psychiatric evaluation of competency in physically ill patients who refuse treatment. *Hospital and Community Psychiatry, 41,* 1140–1141.

Makarushka, J., & McDonald, R. (1979). Informed consent, research, and geriatric patients: The responsibility of institutional review committees. *Gerontologist, 19,* 61.

Malloy, T. R., Wigton, R. S., Meeske, J., & Tape, T. G. (1992). The influence of treatment descriptions on advance medical directive decisions. *Journal of the American Geriatrics Society, 40,* 1255–1260.

Marek, K. D., Rantz, M. J., Fagin, C. M., & Krejci, J. W. (1996). OBRA '87: Has it resulted in better quality of care? *Journal of Gerontological Nursing, 22,* 28–36.

Margolis, W. M. (1992). The doctor knows best? Patient capacity for health care decisionmaking. *Oregon Law Review, 71,* 909–937.

Marks, D. T. (1996). Neglect in nursing homes. *Trial, 32*(2), 60–62.

Marks, E. S. (1989). Poor medical records [Letter to the editor]. *Annals of Internal Medicine, 110,* 1037.

Markson, L. J., Fanale, J., Steel, K., Kern, D., & Annas, G. (1994). Implementing advance directives in the primary care setting. *Archives of Internal Medicine, 154,* 2321–2327.

Markson, L. J., Kern, D. C., Annas, G. J., & Glantz, L. H. (1994). Physician assessment of patient competence. *Journal of the American Geriatrics Society, 42,* 1074–1080.

Marsden, A. K., Ng, G. A., Dalziel, K., & Cobbe, S. M. (1995). When is it futile for ambulance personnel to initiate cardiopulmonary resuscitation? *British Medical Journal, 311,* 49–51.

Marsh, F. H., & Staver, A. (1991). Physician authority for unilateral DNR orders. *Journal of Legal Medicine, 12*(2), 115–165.

Marson, D. C., Hawkins, L., McInturff, B., & Harrell, L. E. (1997). Cognitive models that predict physician judgments of capacity to consent in mild Alzheimer's disease. *Journal of the American Geriatrics Society, 45,* 458–464.

Marson, D. C., McInturff, B., Hawkins, L., Bartolucci, A., & Harrell, L. E. (1997). Consistency of physician judgments of capacity to consent in mild Alzheimer's disease. *Journal of the American Geriatrics Society, 45,* 453–457.

Martinez, R. (1995). Older drivers and physicians. *Journal of the American Medical Association, 274,* 1060.

Mason, J. K., & Mulligan, D. (1996). Euthanasia by stages. *Lancet, 347,* 810–811.

Mazur, D. J., & Hickam, D. H. (1993). Patient preferences: Survival vs. quality-of-life considerations. *Journal of General Internal Medicine, 8*(7), 374–377.

Mazur, D. J., & Hickam, D. H. (1994). Patients' willingness to accept risk of medical treatments. *International Journal of Risk and Safety in Medicine, 6,* 129–137.

Mazur, D. J., & Hickam, D. H. (1997). Patients' preferences for risk disclosure and role in decision making for invasive medical procedures. *Journal of General Internal Medicine, 12*(2), 114–117.

Mazur, D. J., & Merz, J. F. (1993). How the manner of presentation of data influences older patients in determining their treatment preferences. *Journal of the American Geriatrics Society, 41,* 223–228.

Mazur, D. J., & Merz, J. F. (1994). How age, outcome severity, and scale influence general medicine clinic patients' interpretations of verbal probability terms. *Journal of General Internal Medicine, 9*(5), 268–271.

Mazur, D. J., & Merz, J. F. (1996). How older patients' treatment preferences are influenced by disclosures about therapeutic uncertainty: Surgery versus expectant management for localized prostate cancer. *Journal of the American Geriatrics Society, 44,* 934–937.

McAdams, R. W., Jr. (1997). *Home health agencies: Legal, regulatory and contractual issues,* Legal Analysis Plus monograph series. Washington, DC: National Health Lawyers Association/American Academy of Hospital Attorneys.

McClung, J. A., & Kamer, R. S. (1990). Legislating ethics: Implications of New York's do-not-resuscitate law. *New England Journal of Medicine, 323,* 270–272.

McCrary, S. V., Swanson, J. W., Youngner, S. J., Perkins, H. S., & Winslade, W. J. (1994). Physicians' quantitative assessments of medical futility. *Journal of Clinical Ethics, 5*(2), 100–105.

McCue, J. D. (1995). The naturalness of dying. *Journal of the American Medical Association, 273,* 1039–1043.

McGuire, P., & Fulmer, T. (1997). Elder abuse. In C. K. Cassel, H. J. Cohen, E. B. Larson, D. E. Meier, N. M. Resnick, L. Z. Rubenstein, & L. B. Sorensen (Eds.), *Geriatric medicine* (3rd ed.). New York: Springer-Verlag.

McIntyre, K. M. (1993a). Failure of "predictors" of cardiopulmonary resuscitation outcomes to predict cardiopulmonary resuscitation outcomes: Implications for do-not-resuscitate policy and advance directives. *Archives of Internal Medicine, 153,* 1293–1296.

McIntyre, K. M. (1993b). Loosening criteria for withholding prehospital cardiopulmonary resuscitation. *Archives of Internal Medicine, 153,* 2189–2192.

McIntyre, K. M. (1995). On advancing advance directives: Why should we believe the promise? *Archives of Internal Medicine, 155,* 2271–2273.

McLaren, P. (1991). The right to know. *British Medical Journal, 303,* 937–938.

Medical Consultants on the Diagnosis of Death to the President's Commission for the Study of Ethical Problems in Medicine and Biomedical and Behavioral Research. (1981). Guidelines for the determination of death. *Journal of the American Medical Association, 246,* 2184–2186.

Medical Research Council Working Party on Research on the Mentally Incapacitated. (1991). *The ethical conduct of research on the mentally incapacitated.* London: Author.

Meehan, F. (1991). DNR orders: judicial authorization or statutory mandate? *Journal of Health and Hospital Law, 24*(5), 144–145.

Meier, D. E., Fuss, B. R., O'Rourke, D., Baskin, S. A., Lewis, M., & Morrison, S. (1996). Marked improvement in recognition and completion of health care proxies: A randomized controlled trial of counseling by hospital patient representatives. *Archives of Internal Medicine, 156,* 1227–1232.

Meier, D. E., Gold, G., Mertz, K., Taylor, B., Cammer-Paris, Seckler, A., & Mulvihill, M. (1996). Enhancement of proxy appointment for older persons: Physician counselling in the ambulatory setting. *Journal of the American Geriatrics Society, 44,* 37–43.

Meisel, A. (1988). A dignitary tort as a bridge between the idea of informed consent and the law of informed consent. *Law, Medicine and Health Care, 16*(3–4), 210–218.

Meisel, A. (1995). *The right to die* (2nd ed., Vols. 1 & 2). New York: Wiley Law Publications.

Meisel, A. (1996). The "right to die." A case study in American lawmaking. *European Journal of Health Law, 3*(1), 49–74.

Meisel, A. (1997). Physician-assisted suicide: A common law roadmap for state courts. *Fordham Urban Law Journal, 24,* 817–858.

Meisel, A., & Kuczewski, M. (1996). Legal and ethical myths about informed consent. *Archives of Internal Medicine, 156,* 2521–2526.

Melden, M. (1995). The home and community-based waiver program under Medicaid: An update. *Clearinghouse Review, 29,* 142–151.

Melnick, V. L., & Dubler, N. N. (Eds.). (1985). *Contemporary issues in biomedicine, ethics, and society.* Clifton, NJ: Humana Press.

Melnick, V. L., Dubler, N. N., Weisbard, A., & Butler, R. N. (1984). Clinical research in senile dementia of the Alzheimer type: Suggested guidelines addressing the ethical and legal issues. *Journal of the American Geriatrics Society, 32,* 531–536.

Melton, G. B., Petrila, J., Poythress, N. G., & Slobogin, C. (1997). *Psychological evaluations for the courts* (2nd ed.). New York: Guilford Press.

Melton, L. J. (1997). The threat to medical records research. *New England Journal of Medicine, 337,* 1466–1470.

Menikoff, J. A., Sachs, G. A., & Siegler, M. (1992). Beyond advance directives: Health care surrogate laws. *New England Journal of Medicine, 327,* 1165–1169.

Meredith, P., Emberton, M., & Wood, C. (1995). New directions in information for patients. *British Medical Journal, 311,* 4–5.

Messite, J., & Stellman, S. D. (1996). Accuracy of death certificate completion: The need for formalized physician training. *Journal of the American Medical Association, 275,* 794–796.

Meyers, B. S. (1997). Telling patients they have Alzheimer's disease. *British Medical Journal, 314,* 321–322.

Meyers, R. M., & Grodin, M. A. (1991). Decisionmaking regarding the initiation of tube feedings in the severely demented elderly: A review. *Journal of the American Geriatrics Society, 39,* 526–531.

Mezey, M., Mitty, E., Rappaport, M., & Ramsey, G. (1997). Implementation of the Patient Self-Determination Act (PSDA) in nursing homes in New York city. *Journal of the American Geriatrics Society, 45*, 43–49.

Middleditch, L. B., Jr., & Trotter, J. H. (1997). The right to live. *Elder Law Journal, 5*, 395–406.

Miles, S. H. (1991). Informed demand for non-beneficial medical treatment. *New England Journal of Medicine, 325*, 512–515.

Miles, S. H., Koepp, R., & Weber, E. P. (1996). Advance end-of-life treatment planning: A research review. *Archives of Internal Medicine, 156*, 1062–1068.

Miles, S. H., Singer, P. A., & Siegler, M. (1989). Conflicts between patients' wishes to forgo treatment and the policies of health care facilities. *New England Journal of Medicine, 321*, 48–50.

Miller, D. K., Coe, R. M., & Hyers, T. M. (1992). Achieving consensus on withdrawing or withholding care for critically ill patients. *Journal of General Internal Medicine, 7*, 475–480.

Miller, D. L., Gorbien, M. J., Simbartl, L. A., & Jahnigen, D. W. (1993). Factors influencing physicians in recommending in-hospital cardiopulmonary resuscitation. *Archives of Internal Medicine, 153*, 1999–2003.

Miller, F. G., & Meier, D. E. (1998). Voluntary death: A comparison of terminal dehydration and physician-assisted suicide. *Annals of Internal Medicine, 128*, 559–562.

Miller, M. A. (1994). Your money for your life: A survey and analysis of Medicaid estate recovery programs. *Thomas M. Cooley Law Review, 11*, 585–611.

Miller, T. E. (1990). Public policy in the wake of *Cruzan*: A case study of New York's health care proxy law. *Law, Medicine and Health Care, 8*, 360–367.

Mion, L. C., Frengley, J. D., Jakovcic, C. A., & Marino, J. A. (1989). A further exploration of the use of physical restraints in hospitalized patients. *Journal of the American Geriatrics Society, 37*, 949–956.

Mirkin v. Medical Mutual Liability Insurance Society of Maryland, 572 A2d 1126 (Md.Ct.Special Apps., 1990).

Mitchell, J. (1995). A fundamental problem of consent. *British Medical Journal, 310*, 43–46.

Mitchell, S. L., Kiely, D. K., & Lipsitz, L. A. (1997). The risk factors and impact on survival of feeding tube placement in nursing home residents with severe cognitive impairment. *Archives of Internal Medicine, 157*, 327–332.

Mittelberger, J. A., Lo, B., Martin, D., & Uhlmann, R. F. (1993). Impact of a procedure-specific do not resuscitate order form on documentation of do not resuscitate orders. *Archives of Internal Medicine, 153*, 228–232.

Mixson, P. M. (1996). How adult protective services evolved, and obstacles to ethical casework. *Aging Magazine, 367*, 14–17.

Moak, G. S., & Fisher, W. H. (1990). Alzheimer's disease and related disorders in state mental hospitals. *Gerontologist, 30*, 798–802.

Moak, G. S., & Fisher, W. H. (1991). Geriatric patients and services in state hospitals: Data from a national survey. *Hospital and Community Psychiatry, 42*(3), 273–276.

Mollica, R. L., & Snow, K. I. (1996). *State assisted living policy*. Portland, ME: National Academy for State Health Policy.

Molloy, D. W., Clarnette, R. M., Braun, E. A., Eisemann, M. R., & Sneiderman, B. (1991). Decision making in the incompetent elderly: The daughter from California syndrome. *Journal of the American Geriatrics Society, 39,* 396–399.

Moon, A., & Williams, O. (1993). Perceptions of elder abuse and help-seeking patterns among African-American, Caucasian American, and Korean-American elderly women. *Gerontologist, 33,* 386–395.

Morreim, E. H. (1995). *Balancing act: The new medical ethics of medicine's new economics.* Washington, DC: Georgetown University Press.

Morris, L. A., Tabak, E. R., & Gondek, K. (1997). Counseling patients about prescribed medication. *Medical Care, 35,* 996–1007.

Morrison, R. S., Meier, D. E., & Cassel, C. K. (1996). When too much is too little. *New England Journal of Medicine, 335,* 1755–1759.

Morrison, R. S., Morrison, E. W., & Glickman, D. F. (1994). Physician reluctance to discuss advance directives: An empiric investigation of potential barriers. *Archives of Internal Medicine, 154,* 2311–2318.

Morrison, R. S., Olson, E., Mertz, K. R., & Meier, D. E. (1995). The inaccessibility of advance directives on transfer from ambulatory to acute care settings. *Journal of the American Medical Association, 274,* 478–482.

Moskovitz v. Mt. Sinai Medical Center, 69 Ohio St.3d 638 (Ohio Supreme Ct., 1994).

Mossman, D. (1994). Assessing predictions of violence: Being accurate about accuracy. *Journal of Consulting and Clinical Psychology, 62,* 783–792.

Mower, W. R., & Baraff, L. J. (1993). Advance directives: Effect of type of directive on physicians' therapeutic decisions. *Archives of Internal Medicine, 153,* 375–381.

Muncie, H. L., Jr., Magaziner, J., Hebel, J. R., & Warren, J. W. (1997). Proxies' decisions about clinical research participation for their charges. *Journal of the American Geriatrics Society, 45,* 929–933.

Munetz, M. R., Grande, T., Kleist, J., & Peterson, G. A. (1996). The effectiveness of outpatient civil commitment. *Psychiatric Services, 47,* 1251–1253.

Murphy, D. J. (1994). Can we set futile care policies? Institutional and systemic challenges. *Journal of the American Geriatrics Society, 42*(8), 890–893.

Murphy. D. J. (1990). Improving advance directives for healthy older people. *Journal of the American Geriatrics Society, 38,* 1251–1256.

Murphy, D. J., Burrows, D., Santilli, S., Kemp, A. W., Tenner, S., Kreling, B., & Teno, J. (1994). The influence of the probability of survival on patients' preferences regarding cardiopulmonary resuscitation. *New England Journal of Medicine, 330,* 545–549.

Murphy, D. J., & Finucane, T. E. (1993). New do-not-resuscitate policies: A first step in cost control. *Archives of Internal Medicine, 153,* 1641–1648.

Murphy v. Wheeler, 858 S.W.2d 263 (Mo.Ct.App., 1993).

Murtaugh, C. M. (1994). Discharge planning in nursing homes. *Health Services Research, 28,* 751–769.

Murtaugh, C. M., Kemper, P., & Spillman, B. C. (1995). Risky business: Long-term care insurance underwriting. *Inquiry, 32*(3), 271–284.

Myers, T. S. (1989). *How to keep control of your life after 60: A guide for your legal, medical, and financial well-being.* Lexington, MA: Lexington Books.

Naimark, D., Naglie, G., & Detsky, A. S. (1994). The meaning of life expectancy: What is a clinically significant gain? *Journal of General Internal Medicine, 9,* 702–707.

National Center on Elder Abuse. (1994). *Elder abuse: Questions and answers—an informational guide for professionals and concerned citizens* (4th ed.). Washington, DC: Author.

National Conference of Commissioners on Uniform State Laws. (1993). *Uniform Health-care Decisions Act.* Chicago: Author.

National Health Lawyers Association. (1991). *The long term care handbook: Legal, operational, and financial guideposts.* Washington, DC: Author.

National Hospice Organization. (1996). Medical guidelines for determining prognosis in selected non-cancer diagnosis. *Hospice Journal, 11*(2), 47–63.

National Institute on Aging/Alzheimer's Association Working Group. (1996). Apolipoprotein E genotyping in Alzheimer's disease. *Lancet, 347,* 1091–1095.

National Institutes of Health Clinical Center. (1986). *Research involving human subjects: Clinical Center policy for the consent process.* Bethesda, MD: Author.

Neale, A. V., Hwalek, M. A., Goodrich, C. S., & Quinn, K. M. (1996). The Illinois elder abuse system: Program description and administrative findings. *Gerontologist, 36,* 502–511.

Nease, R. F., Jr., & Brooks, W. B. (1995). Patient desire for information and decision making in health care decisions: The autonomy preference index and the health opinion survey. *Journal of General Internal Medicine, 10,* 593–600.

Nelson v. Gaunt, 125 Cal.App.3d 623, 178 Cal.Rptr. 167 (1981).

Neufeld, R. R., & Dunbar, J. M. (1997). Restraint reduction: Where are we now? *Nursing Home Economics, 4*(3), 11–15.

Neugebauer, R. (1989). Diagnosis, guardianship, and residential care of the mentally ill in medieval and early modern England. *American Journal of Psychiatry, 146,* 1580–1584.

New York State Bar Association v. Reno, No. 97-CV-1768, LEXIS 4796 (N.D.N.Y., 1997).

Nolan, B. S. (1984). Functional evaluation of the elderly in guardianship proceedings. *Law, Medicine and Health Care, 12*(5), 210–218.

Nolan, B. S. (1990). A judicial menu: Selecting remedies for the incapacitated elder. *Journal of Elder Abuse and Neglect, 2*(3/4), 73–88.

Nuland, S. B. (1994). *How we die: Reflections on life's final chapter.* New York: Alfred A. Knopf.

Nyberg, D. (1993). *The varnished truth: Truth telling and deceiving in ordinary life.* Chicago: University of Chicago Press.

O'Bannon v. Town Court, 447 U.S. 773 (1980).

O'Brien, L. A., Grisso, J. A., Maislin, G., LaPann, K., Krotki, K. P., Greco, P. J., Siegert, E. A., & Evans, L. K. (1995). Nursing home residents' preferences for life-sustaining treatments. *Journal of the American Medical Association, 274,* 1775–1779.

O'Brien, L. A., Siegert, E. A., Grisso, J. A., Maislin, G., LaPann, K., Evans, L. K., & Krotki, K. P. (1997). Tube feeding preferences among nursing home residents. *Journal of General Internal Medicine, 12,* 364–371.

Ohio State Medical Association. (1994). *Ohio physicians' elder abuse prevention project reference handbook.* Columbus, OH: Author.

Olshansky, S. J. (1997). The demography of aging. In C. K. Cassel, H. J. Cohen, E. B. Larson, D. E. Meier, N. M. Resnick, L. Z. Rubenstein, & L. B. Sorensen, (Eds.), *Geriatic medicine* (3rd ed.). New York: Springer-Verlag.

Onwuteaka-Philipsen, B. D., Muller, M. T., van der Wal, G., van Eijk, J. T. M., & Ribbe, M. W. (1997). Active voluntary euthanasia or physician-assisted suicide? *Journal of the American Geriatrics Society, 45,* 1208–1213.

Orentlicher, D. (1990). Advance medical directives. *Journal of the American Medical Association, 263,* 2365–2367.

Orr, R. D., Morton, K. R., deLeon, D. M., & Fals, J. C. (1996). Evaluation of an ethics consultation service: Patient and family perspective. *American Journal of Medicine, 101*(2), 135–141.

Ouslander, J. G. (1997). The physician and the care of the nursing home patient. In C. K. Cassel, H. J. Cohen, E. B. Larson, D. E. Meier, N. M. Resnick, L. Z. Rubenstein, & L. B. Sorensen (Eds.), *Geriatric medicine* (3rd ed.). New York: Springer-Verlag.

Ouslander, J. G., Osterweil, D., & Morley, J. (1996). *Medical care in the nursing home* (2nd ed.). New York: McGraw-Hill.

Ouslander, J. G., & Tangalos, E. G. (Guest Eds.). (1995). Medical direction in long-term care. *Clinics in Geriatric Medicine, 11,* 331–552.

Ouslander, J. G., Tymchuk, A. J., & Krynski, M. D. (1993). Decisions about enteral tube feeding among the elderly. *Journal of the American Geriatrics Society, 41,* 70–77.

Pace, B. P., & Sullivan-Fowler, M. (Eds.). (1997). The criteria of senility. *Journal of the American Medical Association, 278*(2), 93h. (Reprinted from *Journal of the American Medical Association, 29,* 88–89 [1897]).

Paris, B. E. C., Carrion, V. G., Meditch, J. S., Jr., Capello, C. F., & Mulvihill, M. N. (1993). Roadblocks to do-not-resuscitate orders: A study in policy implementation. *Archives of Internal Medicine, 153,* 1689–1695.

Paris, J. J., Schreiber, M. D., Statter, M., Arensman, R., & Siegler, M. (1993). Beyond autonomy: Physicians' refusal to use life-prolonging extracorporeal membrane oxygenation. *New England Journal of Medicine, 329,* 354–357.

Parker, K., & Miles, S. H. (1997). Deaths caused by bedrails. *Journal of the American Geriatrics Society, 45,* 797–802.

Parri, R. L. (1996). If I call 911, is my living will any good? The living will v. the DNRO. *Florida Bar Journal, 60*(1), 82–86.

Parry, J. W. (1990). The court's role in decisionmaking involving incompetent refusals of life-sustaining care and psychiatric medications. *Mental and Physical Disability Law Reporter, 14*(6), 468–476.

Parry, J. W., & Hurme, S. B. (1991). Guardianship monitoring and enforcement nationwide. *Mental and Physical Disability Law Reporter, 15*(3), 304–314.

Pauker, S. G., & Kassirer, J. P. (1997). Contentious screening decisions: Does the choice matter? *New England Journal of Medicine, 336,* 1243–1244.

Payne v. Marion General Hospital, 549 N.E.2d 1043 (Ind.Ct.App., 1990).

Payne, B. K., & Cikovic, R. (1995). An empirical examination of the characteristics, consequences, and causes of elder abuse in nursing homes. *Journal of Elder Abuse and Neglect, 7*(4), 61–74.

Pecora, A. K. (1990). The Constitutional right to court-appointed adversary counsel for defendants in guardianship proceedings. *Arkansas Law Review, 43*(2), 345–372.

Pellegrino, E. D. (1996). The autopsy: Some ethical reflections on the obligations of pathologists, hospitals, families, and society. *Archives of Pathology and Laboratory Medicine, 120,* 739–742.

Pellegrino, E. D. (1997). The Nazi doctors and Nuremberg: Some moral lessons revisited. *Annals of Internal Medicine, 127,* 307–308.

Pepper, B., & Rubenstein, D. P. (1994). What preadmission screening and annual resident review means for older people with mental illness. *Clearinghouse Review, 27,* 1447–1455.

Perl, M., & Shelp, E. (1982). Psychiatric consultation masking moral dilemmas in medicine. *New England Journal of Medicine, 307,* 618–621.

Perlin, M. L. (1994). *Law and mental disability.* Charlottesville, VA: Michie Company.

Peters, P. G., Jr. (1997). When physicians balk at futile care: Implications of the disability rights laws. *Northwestern University Law Review, 91,* 798–864.

Peters, R. M. (1994). Matching physician practice style to patient informational issues and decision-making preferences. *Archives of Family Medicine, 3,* 760–763.

Peters, T. G., Kittur, D. S., McGaw, L. J., First, M. R., & Nelson, E. W. (1996). Organ donors and nondonors: An American dilemma. *Archives of Internal Medicine, 156,* 2419–2424.

Petrila, J. P., & Sadoff, R. L. (1992). Confidentiality and the family as caregiver. *Hospital and Community Psychiatry, 34*(2), 136–139.

Petrisek, A. C., Laliberte, L. L., Allen, S. M., & Mor, V. (1997). The treatment decision-making process: Age differences in a sample of women recently diagnosed with nonrecurrent, early-stage breast cancer. *Gerontologist, 37,* 598–608.

Phillips, C. D., Morris, J. N., Hawes, C., Fries, B. E., Mor, V., Nennstiel, M., & Iannacchione, V. (1997). Association of the resident assessment instrument (RAI) with changes in function, cognition, and psychosocial status. *Journal of the American Geriatrics Society, 45,* 986–993.

Phillips, R. S., Wenger, N. S., Teno, J., Oye, R. K., Youngner, S., Califf, R., Layde, P., Desbiens, N., Connors, A. F., Jr., & Lynn, J. (1996). Choices of seriously ill patients about cardiopulmonary resuscitation: Correlates and outcomes. *American Journal of Medicine, 100*(2), 128–137.

Pierce v. Penman, 515 A2d 948 (Pa. Super., 1986).

Pilot Life Insurance Company v. Dedeaux. (1987). 107 S.Ct. 1549.

Pleak, R. R., & Appelbaum, P. S. (1985). The clinician's role in protecting patients' rights in guardianship proceedings. *Hospital and Community Psychiatry, 36*(1), 77–79.

Polisky, R. A. (1995). Criminalizing physical and emotional elder abuse. *Elder Law Journal, 3,* 377–411.

Pollack, S. (1996). Detours on the road to autonomy: A critique of the New York State do-not-resuscitate law. *Archives of Internal Medicine, 156,* 1369–1371.

Popovich, M., Goldberg, A. I., Haddad, A. M., Hutchinson, D., Marshall, P., Trubitt, M. J., & Kapp, M. B. (1996). Legal and ethical issues in home health care: A panel discussion. *Journal of Ethics, Law, and Aging, 2*(1), 15–32.

Popp, A. J., & Moore, D. L. (1994). Institutional review board evaluation of neuroscience protocols involving human subjects. *Surgical Neurology, 41*(2), 162–167.

Post, S. G., & Foley, J. M. (1992). Biological markers and truth-telling. *Alzheimer Disease and Associated Disorders, 6*(4), 201–204.

Post, S. G., & Whitehouse, P. J. (1995). Fairhill guidelines on ethics of the care of
people with Alzheimer's disease: A clinical summary. *Journal of the American
Geriatrics Society, 43,* 1423–1429.

Post, S. G., Whitehouse, P. J., Binstock, R. H., Bird, T. D., Eckert, S. K., Farrer, L. A.,
Fleck, L. M., Gaines, A. D., Juengst, E. T., Karlinsky, H., Miles, S., Murray,
T. H., Quaid, K. A., Relkin, N. R., Roses, A. D., St. George-Hyslop, P. H.,
Sachs, G. A., Steinbock, B., Truschke, E. F., & Zinn, A. B. (1997). The clinical
introduction of genetic testing for Alzheimer disease: An ethical perspective.
Journal of the American Medical Association, 277, 832–836.

Potamitis, T., Aggarwal, R. K., Tsaloumas, M., Rene, C., McLaughlin, J., & O'Neill, E.
(1994). Driving, glaucoma, and the law. *British Medical Journal, 309,* 1057–1058.

Pratt, C. C., Jones, L., Shin, H., & Walker, A. J. (1989). Decisionmaking among single older women and their caregiving daughters. *Gerontologist, 29,* 792–797.

Prendergast, T. J. (1995). Futility and the common cold: How requests for antibiotics can illuminate care at the end of life. *Chest, 107,* 836–844.

Prendergast, T. J., & Luce, J. M. (1997). Increasing incidence of withholding and
withdrawal of life support from the critically ill. *American Journal of Respiratory and Critical Care Medicine, 155*(1), 15–20.

Prendergast, T. J., & Raffin, T. A. (1996). Variations in DNR rates: The onus is on
physicians. *Chest, 110,* 1141–1142.

President's Commission for the Study of Ethical Problems in Medicine and Biomedical and Behavioral Research. (1981). *Defining death: Medical, legal and ethical issues in the determination of death.* Washington, DC: U.S. Government
Printing Office.

President's Commission for the Study of Ethical Problems in Medicine and Biomedical and Behavioral Research. (1982). *Making health care decisions: The
ethical and legal implications of informed consent in the patient-practitioner relationship.* Washington, DC: U.S. Government Printing Office.

President's Commission for the Study of Ethical Problems in Medicine and Biomedical and Behavioral Research. (1983). *Deciding to forego life-sustaining treatment.* Washington, DC: U.S. Government Printing Office.

Prosser, R. L. (1992). Alteration of medical records submitted for medicolegal
review. *Journal of the American Medical Association, 267,* 2630–2631.

Quill, T. E. (1989). Utilization of nasogastric feeding tubes in a group of chronically
ill, elderly patients in a community hospital. *Archives of Internal Medicine, 149,*
1937–1941.

Quill, T. E. (1992). New York's health care proxy law [Letter to the editor]. *New
England Journal of Medicine, 326,* 495.

Quill, T. E. (1996). *A midwife through the dying process.* Baltimore: Johns Hopkins
University Press.

Quill, T. E., & Brody, H. (1996). Physician recommendations and patient autonomy: Finding a balance between physician power and patient choice. *Annals
of Internal Medicine, 125,* 763–769.

Quill, T. E., Lo, B., & Brock, D. W. (1997). Palliative options of last resort: A comparison of voluntarily stopping eating and drinking, terminal sedation, physician-assisted suicide, and voluntary active euthanasia. *Journal of the American Medical Association, 278,* 2099–2104.

Quill, T. E., Meier, D. E., Block, S. D., & Billings, J. A. (1998). The debate over physician-assisted suicide: Empirical data and convergent views. *Annals of Internal Medicine, 128,* 552–558.

Quinn, M. J. (1985). Elder abuse and neglect raise new dilemmas. *Generations, 10*(2), 22–25.

Quinn, M. J., & Tomita, S. K. (1997). *Elder abuse and neglect: Causes, diagnosis, and intervention strategies* (2nd ed.). New York: Springer Publishing Company.

Rabeneck, L., McCullough, L. B., & Wray, N. P. (1997). Ethically justified, clinically comprehensive guidelines for percutaneous endoscopic gastrostomy tube placement. *Lancet, 349,* 496–498.

Rains v. Belshe, 32 Cal.App.4th 157, 38 Cal.Rptr.2d 185 (1995).

Ratzan, R. (1982). Cautiousness, risk, and informed consent in clinical geriatrics. *Clinical Research, 30,* 345–353.

Reed, K. (1994). Computerization of health care information: More automation, less privacy. *Journal of Health and Hospital Law, 27*(12), 353–368, 384.

Regan, J. (1981). Protecting the elderly: The new paternalism. *Hastings Law Journal, 32,* 1111–1132.

Reilly, B. M., Magnussen, C. R., Ross, J., Ash, J., Papa, L., & Wagner, M. (1994). Can we talk? Inpatient discussions about advance directives in a community hospital. *Archives of Internal Medicine, 154,* 2299–2308.

Reilly, B. M., Wagner, M., Magnussen, C. R., Ross, J., Papa, L., & Ash, J. (1995). Promoting inpatient directives about life-sustaining treatments in a community hospital: Results of a 3-year time-series intervention trial. *Archives of Internal Medicine, 155,* 2317–2323.

Reilly, R. B., Teasdale, T. A., & McCullough, L. B. (1994). Projecting patients' preferences from living wills: An invalid strategy for management of dementia with life-threatening illness. *Journal of the American Geriatrics Society, 42,* 997–1003.

Rein, J. E. (1992). Preserving dignity and self-determination of the elderly in the face of competing interests and grim alternatives: A proposal for statutory refocus and reform. *George Washington Law Review, 60,* 1818–1887.

Rein, J. E. (1998). Ethics and the questionably competent client: What the Model Rules say and don't say. *Stanford Law and Policy Review, 9*(2), 241–265.

Reinders, M., & Singer, P. A. (1994). Which advance directive do patients prefer? *Journal of General Internal Medicine, 9*(1), 49–51.

Reiser, S. J., & Knudson, P. (1993). Protecting research subjects after consent: The case for the "research intermediary." *IRB: Review of Human Subjects Research, 15*(2), 10–11.

Reuben, D. B. (1991). Dementia and driving. *Journal of the American Geriatrics Society, 39,* 1137–1138.

Reuben, D. B., & St. George, P. (1996). Driving and dementia: California's approach to a medical and policy dilemma. *Western Journal of Medicine, 164*(2), 111–121.

Reust, C. E., & Mattingly, S. (1996). Family involvement in medical decision making. *Family Medicine, 28*(1), 39–45.

Reynolds, S. L. (1995). Shedding light on old dilemmas: A critical approach to protective interventions. *Journal of Ethics, Law, and Aging, 1*(2), 107–119.

Richards, E. P., III, & Rathbun, K. C. (1993). *Law and the physician: A practical guide.* Boston: Little, Brown.

Richter, P. K., Langel, S., Fawcett, S. B., Paine-Andrews, A., Biehler, L., & Manning, R. (1995). Promoting the use of advance directives: An empirical study. *Archives of Family Medicine, 4,* 609–615.

Rind, D. M., Kohane, I. S., Szolovits, P., Safran, C., Chueh, H. C., & Barnett, G. O. (1997). Maintaining the confidentiality of medical records shared over the Internet and the World Wide Web. *Annals of Internal Medicine, 127,* 138–141.

Roach v. Kelly Health Care, Inc., 742 P2d 1190 (Or. App., 1987).

Robb, M. J. (1997). Living wills: The right to refuse life-sustaining medical treatment—a right without a remedy? *University of Dayton Law Review, 23*(1), 169–188.

Robbins, M. K. (1994). Nursing home reform: Objective regulation or subjective decisions? *Thomas M. Cooley Law Review, 11*(1), 185–211.

Robertson, J. A. (1991). Ethics committees in hospitals: Alternative strategies and responsibilities. *Issues in Law and Medicine, 7*(1), 83–91.

Rodwin, M. A. (1993). *Money, medicine and morals: Physicians' conflicts of interest.* New York: Oxford University Press.

Roe, J. M., Goldstein, M. K., Massey, K., & Pascoe, D. (1992). Durable power of attorney for health care: A survey of senior center participants. *Archives of Internal Medicine, 152,* 292–296.

Rosenblatt, D. E., Cho, K-H, & Durance, P. W. (1996). Reporting mistreatment of older adults: The role of physicians. *Journal of the American Geriatrics Society, 44,* 65–70.

Rosenfeld, K. E., Wenger, N. S., Phillips, R. S., Connors, A. F., Dawson, N. V., Layde, P., Califf, R. M., Liu, H., Lynn, J., & Oye, R. K. (1996). Factors associated with change in resuscitation preference of seriously ill patients. *Archives of Internal Medicine, 156,* 1558–1564.

Rost v. Board of Psychology, 659 A.2d 626 (Pa., 1995).

Roth, L. H., Meisel, A., & Lidz, C. (1977). Tests of competency to consent to treatment. *American Journal of Psychiatry, 134,* 279–284.

Rothman, D. J. (1991). *Strangers at the bedside.* New York: Basic Books.

Rouse, F. (1990). Where are we heading after *Cruzan? Law, Medicine and Health Care, 18,* 353–359.

Rozovsky, F. A. (1990). *Informed consent: A practical guide* (2nd ed.). Boston: Little, Brown.

Rozovsky, F. A., & Rozovsky, L. (1993). *Home health care law: Liability and risk management.* Boston: Little, Brown.

Rubin, R. M., & Koelln, K. (1993). Out-of-pocket health expenditure differentials between elderly and non-elderly households. *Gerontologist, 33,* 595–602.

Rubin, S. M., Strull, W. M., Fialkow, M. F., Weiss, S. J., Lo, B. (1994). Increasing the completion of the durable power of attorney for health care: A randomized, controlled trial. *Journal of the American Medical Association, 271,* 209–212.

Sabatino, C. P. (1996). Competency: Refining our legal fictions. In M. Smyer, K. W. Schaie, & M. B. Kapp (Eds.), *Older adults' decision-making and the law*. New York: Springer Publishing Company.

Sabatino, C. P., & Litvak, S. (1996). Liability issues affecting consumer-directed personal assistance services: Report and recommendations. *Elder Law Journal, 4*(2), 247–368.

Sachs, G. A. (1994a). Advance consent for dementia research. *Alzheimer Disease and Associated Disorders, 8*(Suppl. 4), 19–27.

Sachs, G. A. (1994b). Increasing the prevalence of advance care planning. *Hastings Center Report, 24*(6), S13–S16.

Sachs, G. A., & Cassel, C. K. (1990). Biomedical research involving older human subjects. *Law, Medicine and Health Care, 18*(3), 234–243.

Sachs, G. A., & Cohen, H. J. (1997). Ethical challenges to research. In C. K. Cassel, H. J. Cohen, E. B. Larson, et al. (Eds.), *Geriatric medicine* (3rd ed.). New York: Springer-Verlag.

Sachs, G. A., Rhymes, J., & Cassel, C. K. (1993). Biomedical and behavioral research in nursing homes: Guidelines for ethical investigations. *Journal of the American Geriatrics Society, 41*, 771–777.

Sachs, G. A., Stocking, C. B., & Miles, S. H. (1992). Empowerment of the older patient? A randomized, controlled trial to increase discussion and use of advance directives. *Journal of the American Geriatrics Society, 40*, 269–273.

Sachs, G. A., Stocking, C. B., Stern, R., Cox, D. M., Hougham, G., & Sachs, R. S. (1994). Ethical aspects of dementia research: Informed consent and proxy consent. *Clinical Research, 42*, 403–412.

Scallet, L. J., & Robinson, G. K. (1991). Deinstitutionalization and mental health. *Caring, 10*(3), 5–13.

Schloendorff v. Society of New York Hospitals, 211 N.Y. 125, 105 N.E.2d 92 (1914).

Schmidt, W. C. (1996). Assessing the guardianship reform of limited guardianship: Tailoring guardianship, or expanding inappropriate guardianships? *Journal of Ethics, Law, and Aging, 2*(1), 5–14.

Schmidt, W. C., Jr. (1995). *Guardianship: The court of last resort for the elderly and disabled*. Durham, NC: Carolina Academic Press.

Schmidt, W. C. (1986). Adult protective services and the therapeutic state. *Law and Psychology Review, 10*, 101–121.

Schneider, E. K. (1997). The ADA: A little used tool to remedy nursing home discrimination. *University of Toledo Law Review, 28*, 489–519.

Schneiderman, L. J., Jecker, N. S., & Jonsen, A. R. (1996). Medical futility: Response to critiques. *Annals of Internal Medicine, 125*, 669–674.

Schoenenberger, R. A., von Planta, M., & von Planta, I. (1994). Survival after failed out-of-hospital resuscitation: Are further efforts in the emergency department futile? *Archives of Internal Medicine, 154*, 2433–2437.

Schonwetter, R. S., Walker, R. M., Kramer, D. R., & Robinson, B. E. (1993). Resuscitation decision making in the elderly: The value of outcome data. *Journal of General Internal Medicine, 8*(6), 295–300.

Schonwetter, R. S., Walker, R. M., Solomon, M., Indurkhya, A., & Robinson, B. E. (1996). Life values, resuscitation preferences, and the applicability of living wills in an older population. *Journal of the American Geriatrics Society, 44,* 954–958.

Schouten, R. (1989). Informed consent: Resistance and reappraisal. *Critical Care Medicine, 17,* 1359–1361.

Schuck, P. H. (1994). Rethinking informed consent. *Yale Law Journal, 103,* 899–959.

Schwartz, R. (1981). Some ethical and legal considerations. *Psychopharmacology Bulletin, 17,* 64.

Scofield, G. (1991). Is consent useful when resuscitation isn't? *Hastings Center Report, 21*(6), 28–36.

Scogin, F., & Perry, J. (1986). Guardianship proceedings with older adults: The role of functional assessment and gerontologists. *Law and Psychology Review, 10,* 123–128.

Scott v. Bradford, 606 P.2d 554 (Okla., 1979).

Segal, S. P. (1989). Civil commitment standards and patient mix in England/Wales, Italy, and the United States. *American Journal of Psychiatry, 146*(2), 187–193.

Semla, T. P., Palla, K., Poddig, B., & Brauner, D. J. (1994). Effect of the Omnibus Budget Reconciliation Act 1987 on antipsychotic prescribing in nursing home residents. *Journal of the American Geriatrics Society, 42,* 648–652.

Sharpe, V. A., & Faden, A. I. (1996). Appropriateness in patient care: A new conceptual framework. *Milbank Quarterly, 74*(1), 115–138.

Sheiman, S. L. (1996). Tube feeding the demented nursing home resident. *Journal of the American Geriatrics Society, 44,* 1268–1270.

Shelton v. Tucker, 364 U.S. 479 (1960).

Shepardson, L. B., Youngner, S. J., Speroff, T., O'Brien, R. G., Smyth, K. A., & Rosenthal, G. E. (1997). Variation in the use of do-not-resuscitate orders in patients with stroke. *Archives of Internal Medicine, 157,* 1841–1847.

Shiferaw, B., Mittelmark, M. B., Wofford, J. L., Anderson, R. T., Walls, P., & Rohrer, B. (1994). The investigation and outcome of reported cases of elder abuse: The Forsyth County aging study. *Gerontologist, 34,* 123–125.

Shorr, R. I., Fought, R. L., & Ray, W. A. (1994). Changes in antipsychotic drug use in nursing homes during implementation of the OBRA-87 regulations. *Journal of the American Medical Association, 271,* 358–362.

Shuster, E. (1997). Fifty years later: The significance of the Nuremberg code. *New England Journal of Medicine, 337,* 1436–1440.

Siegler, E. L., Capezuti, E., Maislin, G., Baumgarten, M., Evans, L., & Strumpf, N. (1997). Effects of a restraint reduction intervention and OBRA '87 regulations on psychoactive drug use in nursing homes. *Journal of the American Geriatrics Society, 45,* 791–796.

Siemon, D., Hurme, S. B., & Sabatino, C. P. (1993). Public guardianship: Where is it and what does it need? *Clearinghouse Review, 27,* 588–599.

Silberfeld, M., Nash, C., & Singer, P. A. (1993). Capacity to complete an advance directive. *Journal of the American Geriatrics Society, 41,* 1141–1143.

Silverman, M., McDowell, B. J., Musa, D., Rodriguez, E., & Martin, D. (1997). To treat or not to treat: Issues in decisions not to treat older persons with cognitive impairment, depression, and incontinence. *Journal of the American Geriatrics Society, 45,* 1094–1101.

Simonoff, L. A., Arnold, R. M., Caplan, A. L., Virnig, B. A., & Seltzer, D. L. (1995). Public policy governing organ and tissue procurement in the United States: Results from the National Organ and Tissue Procurement Study. *Annals of Internal Medicine, 123,* 10–17.

Sirmon, M., & Kreisberg, R. (1996). The invisible patient. *New England Journal of Medicine, 334,* 908–911.

Skodol, A. E., Shaffer, D., & Gurland, B. (1997). Psychopathology across the life cycle. In A. Tasman, J. Kay, & J. A. Lieberman (Eds.), *Psychiatry.* Philadelphia: W. B. Saunders.

Slobogin, C. (1994). Involuntary community treatment of people who are violent and mentally ill: A legal analysis. *Hospital and Community Psychiatry, 45,* 685–689.

Smith, G. P., II. (1995). Utility and the principle of medical futility: Safeguarding autonomy and the prohibition against cruel and unusual punishment. *Journal of Contemporary Health Law and Policy, 12*(1), 1–39.

Smith v. Sup. Ct. for City of Los Angeles, 198 Cal.Rptr. 829 (Cal.App., 1984).

Social Security Administration. (1996). *Social Security: A guide for representative payees* (SSA Publication No. 05-10076). Washington, DC: Author.

Society of Critical Care Medicine, Ethics Committee. (1992). Attitudes of critical care medicine professionals concerning forgoing life-sustaining treatments. *Critical Care Medicine, 20,* 320–326.

Society of Critical Care Medicine, Ethics Committee. (1997). Consensus statement regarding futile and other possibly inadvisable treatments. *Critical Care Medicine, 25,* 887–891.

Sorum, P. C. (1995). Deciding about cardiopulmonary resuscitation: The contributions of decision analysis. *Archives of Internal Medicine, 155,* 513–521.

Sosna, D. P., Christopher, M., Pesto, M. M., Morando, D. V., & Stoddard, J. (1994). Implementation strategies for a do-not-resuscitate program in the prehospital setting. *Annals of Emergency Medicine, 23,* 1042–1046.

Spicker, S. F. (Ed.). (1998). *The healthcare ethics committee experience.* Malabar, FL: Krieger Publishing.

Spillman, B. C., & Kemper, P. (1995). Lifetime patterns of payment for nursing home care. *Medical Care, 33,* 280–296.

Spitzer-Resnick, J., & Krajcinovic, M. (1995). Protecting the rights of nursing home residents: How tort liability interacts with statutory protections. *Nova Law Review, 19,* 629–646.

Spring, J. (1987). Applying due process safeguards. *Generations, 11*(4), 32–39.

Sprung, C. L., & Winick, B. J. (1989). Informed consent in theory and practice: Legal and medical perspectives on the informed consent doctrine and a proposed reconceptualization. *Critical Care Medicine, 17,* 1346–1354.

State v. Warren, 462 N.W.2d 195 (S.D. Supreme Ct., 1990).

Stiegel, L. A. (1995). *Recommended guidelines for state courts handling cases involving elder abuse.* Washington, DC: American Bar Association and State Justice Institute.

Stollerman, G. H. (1989). Assessment of the person. *Hospital Practice, 24*(4A), 13–17.

Stolman, C. J., Gregory, J. J., Dunn, D., & Levine, J. L. (1990). Evaluation of patient, physician, nurse, and family attitudes toward do not resuscitate orders. *Archives of Internal Medicine, 150,* 653–658.

Stone, D. A. (1985). *The disabled state.* Philadelphia: Temple University Press.

Strachan v. JFK Memorial Hospital, 109 N.J. 523, 538 A.2d 346 (1988).

Strahan, G. W. (1997). An overview of nursing homes and their current residents: Data from the 1995 national nursing home survey. *Advance Data* (National Center for Health Statistics, Centers for Disease Control and Prevention, U.S. Department of Health and Human Services), *280,* 1–10.

Sullivan, M. D., & Youngner, S. J. (1994). Depression, competence, and the right to refuse lifesaving medical treatment. *American Journal of Psychiatry, 151,* 971–978.

Sullivan v. Zebley, 110 S.Ct. 885 (1990).

Sulmasy, D. P., Song, K. Y., Marx, E. S., & Mitchell, J. M. (1996). Strategies to promote the use of advance directives in a residency outpatient practice. *Journal of General Internal Medicine, 11,* 657–663.

SUPPORT Principal Investigators. (1995). A controlled trial to improve care for seriously ill hospitalized patients: The study to understand prognoses and preferences for outcomes and risks of treatments. *Journal of the American Medical Association, 274,* 1591–1598.

Sutton, T. D. (1996). The physician's role in determining disability. *Journal of General Internal Medicine, 11,* 565–566.

Swan, J. H., de la Torre, A., & Steinhart, R. (1990). Ripple effects of PPS on nursing homes: Swimming or drowning in the funding stream? *Gerontologist, 30,* 323–331.

Swartz, M. S., Burns, B. J., Hiday, V. A., George, L. K., Swanson, J., & Wagner, H. R. (1995). New directions in research on involuntary outpatient commitment. *Psychiatric Services, 46,* 381–385.

Sweeney, L. (1997). Weaving technology and policy together to maintain confidentiality. *Journal of Law, Medicine and Ethics, 25,* 98–110.

Swidler, R. N. (1988). The health care agent: Protecting the choices and interests of patients who lack capacity. *New York Law School Journal of Human Rights, 6*(1), 1–61.

Swig, L., Cooke, M., Osmond, D., Luce, J. A., Brody, R. V., Bird, C., & Luce, J. M. (1996). Physician responses to a hospital policy allowing them to not offer cardiopulmonary resuscitation. *Journal of the American Geriatrics Society, 44,* 1215–1219.

Szabo, E., Moody, H., Hamilton, T., Ang, C., Kovithavongs, C., & Kjellstrand, C. (1997). Choice of treatment improves quality of life: A study on patients undergoing dialysis. *Archives of Internal Medicine, 157,* 1352–1356.

Taeuber, C. M. (1992). Sixty-five plus in America. In U.S. Department of Commerce, Bureau of the Census, *Current population reports* (Special Studies, P23-178). Washington, DC: U.S. Government Printing Office.

Tarnow, W. J. (1996). Recognizing a fundamental liberty interest protecting the right to die: An analysis of statutes which criminalize or legalize physician-assisted suicide. *Elder Law Journal, 4,* 407–457.

Tatara, T. (1995). *An analysis of state laws addressing elder abuse, neglect, and exploitation.* Washington, DC: American Public Welfare Association, National Center on Elder Abuse.

Taylor, R. M. (1997). Re-examining the definition and criterion of death. *Seminars in Neurology, 17,* 265–270.

T.D. v. New York State Office of Mental Health, 650 N.Y.S.2d 173 (1996).

Teno, J. M., Branco, K. J., Mor, V., Phillips, C. D., Hawes, C., Morris, J., & Fries, B. E. (1997). Changes in advance care planning in nursing homes before and after the Patient Self-Determination Act: Report of a 10-state survey. *Journal of the American Geriatrics Society, 45,* 939–944.

Teno, J. M., Hakim, R. B., Knaus, W. A., Wenger, N. S., Phillips, R. S., Wu, A. W., Layde, P., Connors, A. F., Jr., Dawson, N. V., & Lynn, J. (1995). Preferences for cardiopulmonary resuscitation: Physician-patient agreement and hospital resource use. *Journal of General Internal Medicine, 10*(4), 179–186.

Teno, J. M., Licks, S., Lynn, J., Wenger, N., Connors, A. F., Jr., Phillips, R. S., O'Connor, M. A., Murphy, D. P., Fulkerson, W. J., Desbiens, N., & Knaus, W. A. (1997). Do advance directives provide instructions that direct care? *Journal of the American Geriatrics Society, 45,* 508–512.

Teno, J. M., Lynn, J., Wenger, N., Phillips, R. S., Murphy, D. P., Connors, A. F., Jr., Desbiens, N., Fulkerson, W., Bellamy, P., & Knaus, W. A. (1997). Advance directives for seriously ill hospitalized patients: Effectiveness with the Patient Self-Determination Act and the SUPPORT intervention. *Journal of the American Geriatrics Society, 45,* 500–507.

Teno, J. M., Murphy, D., Lynn, J., Tosteson, A., Desbiens N., Connors, A. F., Jr., Hamel, M. B., Wu, A., Phillips, R., Wenger, N., Harrell, F., Jr., & Knaus, W. A. (1994). Prognosis-based futility guidelines: Does anyone win? *Journal of the American Geriatrics Society, 42,* 1202–1207.

Terry, M., & Zweig, S. (1994). Prevalence of advance directives and do-not-resuscitate orders in community nursing homes. *Archives of Family Medicine, 3*(2), 141–145.

Thapa, P. B., Meador, K. G., Gideon, P., Fought, R. L., & Ray, W. A. (1994). Effects of antipsychotic withdrawal in elderly nursing home residents. *Journal of the American Geriatrics Society, 42,* 280–286.

Thomas, B. (1995). Medicare at a crossroads. *Journal of the American Medical Association, 274,* 276–278.

Thomas, B. L. (1994). Research considerations: Guardianship and the vulnerable elderly. *Journal of Gerontological Nursing, 20*(5), 10–16.

Tolle, S. W. (1998). Care of the dying: Clinical and financial lessons from the Oregon experience. *Annals of Internal Medicine, 128,* 567–568.

Tombaugh, T. N., & McIntyre, N. J. (1992). The mini-mental state examination: A comprehensive review. *Journal of the American Geriatrics Society, 40,* 922–935.

Tonelli, M. R. (1996). Pulling the plug on living wills: A critical analysis of advance directives. *Chest, 110,* 816–822.

Tong, R. (1995). Towards a just, courageous, and honest resolution of the futility debate. *Journal of Medicine and Philosophy, 20*(2), 165–189.

Topol, E. J., & Califf, R. M. (1992). Thrombolytic therapy for elderly patients. *New England Journal of Medicine, 327,* 45–47.

Tor, P. B., & Sales, B. D. (1994). A social science perspective on the law of guardianship: Directions for improving the process and practice. *Law and Psychology Review, 18*(1), 1–41.

Torrey, E. F., & Kaplan, R. J. (1995). A national survey of the use of outpatient commitment. *Psychiatric Services, 46,* 778–784.

Tresch, D. D., Sims, F. H., Duthie, E. H., Goldstein, M. D., & Lane, P. S. (1991). Clinical characteristics of patients in the persistent vegetative state. *Archives of Internal Medicine, 151,* 930–932.

Truog, R. D., Brett, A. S., & Frader, J. (1992). The problem with futility. *New England Journal of Medicine, 326,* 1560–1564.

Truog, R. D., & Fackler, J. C. (1992). Rethinking brain death. *Critical Care Medicine, 20,* 1705–1713.

Tucker, K. L. (1998). The death with dignity movement: Protecting rights and expanding options after *Glucksberg* and *Quill. Minnesota Law Review, 82,* 923–938.

Tulsky, J. A., Chesney, M. A., & Lo, B. (1995). How do medical residents discuss resuscitation with patients? *Journal of General Internal Medicine, 10*(8), 436–442.

Tulsky, J. A., Chesney, M. A., & Lo, B. (1996). See one, do one, teach one? House staff experience discussing do-not-resuscitate orders. *Archives of Internal Medicine, 156,* 1285–1289.

Turkington, R. C. (1997). Medical record confidentiality law, scientific research, and data collection in the information age. *Journal of Law, Medicine and Ethics, 25*(2 & 3), 113–129.

Ubel, P. A. (1996). Informed consent: From bodily invasion to the seemingly mundane. *Archives of Internal Medicine, 156,* 1262–1263.

Underwood, M. (1992). The older driver: Clinical assessment and injury prevention. *Archives of Internal Medicine, 152,* 735–740.

University of Texas Medical Branch at Galveston v. York, 808 SW2d 106 (Tex.Ct. App., 1991).

U.S. Congress, House Select Committee on Aging. (1980). *Future directions for aging policy: A human service model.* 96th Congress, 2nd sess. Washington, DC: U.S. Government Printing Office.

U.S. Congress, House Select Committee on Aging, Subcommittee on Housing and Consumer Interests. (1989). *Model standards to ensure quality guardianship and representative payeeship services* (Committee Pub. No. 101-729). Washington, DC: U.S. Government Printing Office.

U.S. Congress, Office of Technology Assessment. (1993). *Protecting privacy in computerized medical information* (OTA-TCT-576). Washington, DC: U.S. Government Printing Office.

U.S. Congress, Senate Committee on Aging. (1975). *Nursing home care in the United States: Failure in public policy;* [Supporting paper No. 3], *Doctors in nursing homes: The shunned responsibility.* 94th Congress, 1st sess. Washington, DC: U.S. Government Printing Office.

U.S. Department of Health, Education, and Welfare. (1971). *Institutional guide to DHEW policy on protection of human subjects* (DHEW Publication No. (NIH) 72-102). Washington, DC: U.S. Government Printing Office.

U.S. Department of Health and Human Services. (1995). *The threshold of discovery: Future directions for research in aging* (report of the Task Force on Aging Research). Washington, DC: U.S. Government Printing Office.

U.S. General Accounting Office. (1992). *Social Security: Beneficiary payment for representative payee services* (GAO/HRD-92-112). Washington, DC: Author.

U.S. General Accounting Office. (1993). *Organ transplants: Increased effort needed to boost supply and ensure equitable distribution of organs* (GAO/HEHS-93-56). Washington, DC: Author.

U.S. General Accounting Office. (1995). *Patient Self-Determination Act: Providers offer information on advance directives but effectiveness uncertain* (GAO/HEHS-95-135). Washington, DC: Author.

U.S. General Accounting Office. (1996a). *Long-term care: Some states apply criminal background checks to home care workers* (GAO/PEMD-96-5). Washington, DC: Author.

U.S. General Accounting Office. (1996b). *Scientific research: Continued vigilance critical to protecting human subjects* (GAO/HEHS-96-72). Washington, DC: Author.

U.S. General Accounting Office. (1996c). *SSA disability: Program redesign necessary to encourage return to work* (GAO/HEHS-96-62). Washington, DC: Author.

U.S. General Accounting Office. (1997a). *Long-term care: Consumer protection and quality-of-care issues in assisted living* (GAO/HEHS-97-93). Washington, DC: Author.

U.S. General Accounting Office. (1997b). *Social Security disability: SSA must hold itself accountable for continued improvement in decision-making* (GAO/HEHS-97-102). Washington, DC: Author.

Vacco v. Quill, 117 S.Ct. 2293 (1997).

Vaisrub, S. (1981). Violence begins at home. *Journal of the American Medical Association, 245*, 1852.

Vaughan, C., & Ingman, S. R. (1989). Reconceptualizing elder abuse. *Gerontology Review, 2*(1), 77–84.

Veatch, R. M. (1988). Justice and the economics of terminal illness. *Hastings Center Report, 18*(4), 34–40.

Veatch, R. M. (1993). The impending collapse of the whole-brain definition of death. *Hastings Center Report, 23*(4), 18–24.

Veatch, R. M. (1994). Why physicians cannot determine if care is futile. *Journal of the American Geriatrics Society, 42*, 871–874.

Velick, M. D. (1995). Mandatory reporting statutes: A necessary yet underutilized response to elder abuse. *Elder Law Journal, 3*(1), 165–190.

Virmani, J., Schneiderman, L. J., & Kaplan, R. M. (1994). Relationship of advance directives to physician-patient communication. *Archives of Internal Medicine, 154*, 909–913.

Vladeck, B. C. (1996a). New Medicare physician payment to reflect relative resources. *Journal of the American Medical Association, 275*, 978.

Vladeck, B. C. (1996b). The past, present, and future of nursing home quality. *Journal of the American Medical Association, 275*, 425.

Volicer, L. (1997). Hospice care for dementia patients. *Journal of the American Geriatrics Society, 45*, 1147–1149.

Volicer, L., & Hurley, A. (Eds.). (1998). *Hospice care for patients with advanced progressive dementia.* New York: Springer Publishing Company.

Wagner v. Fair Acres Geriatric Center, 49 F.3d 1002 (3d Cir., 1995).

Wagner, E. H., Barrett, P., Barry, M. J., Barlow, W., & Fowler, F. J., Jr. (1995). The effect of a shared decisionmaking program on rates of surgery for benign prostatic hyperplasia. *Medical Care, 33,* 765–770.

Waisel, D. B., & Truog, R. D. (1995). The cardiopulmonary resuscitation-not-indicated order: Futility revisited. *Annals of Internal Medicine, 122,* 304–308.

Walker, L., & Blechner, B. (1995–96). Continuing implementation of the Patient Self-Determination Act in nursing homes. *Generations, 19*(4), 73–77.

Walker, R. M., Schonwetter, R. S., Kramer, D. R., & Robinson, B. E. (1995). Living wills and resuscitation preferences in an elderly population. *Archives of Internal Medicine, 155,* 171–175.

Waller, A. A., & Fulton, D. K. (1993). The electronic chart: Keeping it confidential and secure. *Journal of Health and Hospital Law, 26*(4), 104–109.

Waltzer, W. (1983). Procurement of cadaveric kidneys for transplantation. *Annals of Internal Medicine, 98,* 536–539.

Wang, L., Burns, A. M., & Hommel, P. A. (1990). Trends in guardianship reform: Roles and responsibilities of legal advocates. *Clearinghouse Review, 24,* 561–569.

Ward, H. W., Ramsdell, J. W., Jackson, J. E., Renvall, M., Swart, J. A., & Rockwell, E. (1990). Cognitive function testing in comprehensive geriatric assessment: A comparison of cognitive test performance in residential and clinic settings. *Journal of the American Geriatrics Society, 38,* 1088–1092.

Washington v. Glucksberg, 117 S.Ct. 2302 (1997).

Webster, J. R., & Berdes, C. (1990). Ethics and economic realities: Goals and strategies for care toward the end of life. *Archives of Internal Medicine, 150,* 1795–1797.

Wecht, C. H. (1998). Forensic use of medical information. In S. S. Sanbar, A. Gibofsky, M. H. Firestone, & T. R. LeBlang (Eds.), *Legal medicine* (4th ed.). St. Louis: C. V. Mosby.

Wecker v. Amend, 22 Kan.App.2d 498, 918 P.2d 658 (1996).

Weiler, K. (1994). Legal aspects of nursing documentation for the Alzheimer's patient. *Journal of Gerontological Nursing, 20*(4), 31–40.

Weiler, K., Helms, L. B., & Buckwalter, K. C. (1993). A comparative study: Guardianship petitions for adults and elder adults. *Journal of Gerontological Nursing, 19*(9), 15–25.

Weiler, P. C., Hiatt, H. H., Newhouse, J. P., Johnson, W. G., Brennan, T. A., & Leape, L. L. (1993). *A measure of malpractice: Medical injury, malpractice litigation, and patient compensation.* Cambridge, MA: Harvard University Press.

Weinberg, A. D. (1998). *Risk management in long-term care: A quick reference guide.* New York: Springer Publishing Company.

Weintraub, M. (1984). Ethical concerns and guidelines in research in geriatric pharmacology and therapeutics: Individualization, not codification. *Journal of the American Geriatrics Society, 32,* 44–48.

Weintraub, M. I. (1996). Driving and Alzheimer disease [Letter to the editor]. *Journal of the American Medical Association, 275,* 182.

Weisman, E. (1990). Liability for medical record disclosure is real but rare. *Hospitals, 64*(16), 28–32.

Weiss, B. D., Reed, R., Kligman, E. W., & Abyad, A. (1995). Literacy and performance on the Mini-Mental State Examination. *Journal of the American Geriatrics Society, 43*, 807–810.

Welch, D. D. (1989). Walking in their shoes: Paying respect to incompetent patients. *Vanderbilt Law Review, 42*, 1617.

Welch, H. G., Wennberg, D. E., & Welch, W. P. (1996). The use of Medicare home health care services. *New England Journal of Medicine, 335*, 324–329.

Wendland v. Sparks, 574 NW2d 327 (Iowa Supreme Ct., 1998).

Wenger, N. S., Pearson, M. L., Desmond, K. A., Brook, R. H., & Kahn, K. L. (1995). Outcomes of patients with do-not-resuscitate orders: Toward an understanding of what do-not-resuscitate orders mean and how they affect patients. *Archives of Internal Medicine, 155*, 2063–2068.

Wenger, N. S., Pearson, M. L., Desmond, K. A., Harrison, E. R., Rubenstein, L. V., & Rogers, W. H. (1995). Epidemiology of do-not-resuscitate orders: Disparity by age, diagnosis, gender, race, and functional impairment. *Archives of Internal Medicine, 155*, 2056–2062.

Wettstein, R. M., & Roth, L. H. (1988). The psychiatrist as legal guardian. *American Journal of Psychiatry, 145*, 600–604.

White, B. D., Siegler, M., Singer, P. A., & Iserson, K. V. (1991). What does *Cruzan* mean to the practicing physician? *Archives of Internal Medicine, 151*, 925–928.

White, L. J. (1994). Clinical uncertainty, medical futility and practice guidelines. *Journal of the American Geriatrics Society, 42*, 899–901.

White, M. L., & Fletcher, J. C. (1991). The Patient Self-Determination Act: On balance, more help than hindrance. *Journal of the American Medical Association, 266*, 410–412.

Wichman, A., & Sandler, A. L. (1997). Research involving critically ill subjects in emergency circumstances: New regulations, new challenges. *Neurology, 48*, 1151–1177.

Wickline v. California, 192 Cal.App.3d 1630, 239 Cal.Rptr. 810 (1986).

Wiener, J. M. (1996). Can Medicaid long-term care expenditures for the elderly be reduced? *Gerontologist, 36*, 800–811.

Wiesner, I. S. (1995). OBRA '93 and Medicaid: Assets transfers, trust availability, and estate recovery statutory analysis in context. *Nova Law Review, 19*, 679–734.

Wilber, K. H. (1990). Material abuse of the elderly: When is guardianship a solution? *Journal of Elder Abuse and Neglect, 2*(3&4), 89–104.

Wilkes, M. S., & Schriger, D. L. (1996). Caution—the meter is running: Informing patients about health care costs. *Western Journal of Medicine, 165*(1&2), 74–79.

Williams, C. C., & Finch, C. E. (1997). Physical restraint: Not fit for woman, man, or beast. *Journal of the American Geriatrics Society, 45*, 773–775.

Williams, M. A., & Suarez, J. I. (1997). Brain death determination in adults: More than meets the eye. *Critical Care Medicine, 25*, 1787–1788.

Wilson, K. B. (1995). *Assisted living: Reconceptualizing regulations to meet consumers' needs and preferences.* Washington, DC: American Association of Retired Persons, Public Policy Institute.

Wilson, R. F. (1998). Hospital ethics committees as the forum of last resort: An idea whose time has not yet come. *North Carolina Law Review, 76*(2), 353–406.

Winick, B. J. (1995). The side effects of incompetency labeling and the implications for mental health law. *Psychology, Public Policy and Law, 1*(1), 6–42.

Wolf, A. M. D., & Becker, D. M. (1996). Cancer screening and informed patient discussions: Truth and consequences. *Archives of Internal Medicine, 156,* 1069–1072.

Wolf, A. M. D., Nasser, J. F., Wolf, A. M., & Schorling, J. B. (1996). The impact of informed consent on patient interest in prostate-specific antigen screening. *Archives of Internal Medicine, 156,* 1333–1336.

Wolf, R. S., & Pillemer, K. (1994). What's new in elder abuse programming? Four bright ideas. *Gerontologist, 34,* 126–129.

Wolf, S. M. (1998). Pragmatism in the face of death: The role of facts in the assisted suicide debate. *Minnesota Law Review, 82,* 1063–1101.

Wood, E., Stiegel, L. A., Sabatino, C. P., & Edelstein, S. (1993). Overview of 1992 state law changes in guardianship, durable powers of attorney, health-care decisions, and home equity mortgages. *Clearinghouse Review, 26,* 1277–1286.

Young, W. F., Jr. (1997). Informed consent. *Annals of Emergency Medicine, 30,* 350–351.

Youngner, S. J. (1995). Medical futility and the social contract. *Seton Hall Law Review, 25,* 1015–1026.

Youngner, S. J., & Arnold, R. M. (1993). Ethical, psychosocial, and public policy implications of procuring organs from non-heart-beating cadaver organ . *Journal of the American Medical Association, 269,* 2769–2774.

Zimmer, J. G., Watson, N. M., & Levenson, S. A. (1993). Nursing home medical directors: Ideals and realities. *Journal of the American Geriatrics Society, 41,* 127–130.

Zimny, G. H., Diamond, J. A., Mau, M. M., Law, A. C. K., & Chung, C. (1997). Six-year longitudinal study of finances of elderly wards under guardianship. *Journal of Ethics, Law, and Aging, 3*(2), 91–101.

Zinberg, J. M. (1989). Decisions for the dying: An empirical study of physicians' responses to advance directives. *Vermont Law Review, 13,* 445–491.

Zinermon v. Burch, 494 U.S. 113 (1990).

Zinn, W., & Furutani, N. (1996). Physician perspectives on the ethical aspects of disability determinations. *Journal of General Internal Medicine, 11*(9), 525–532.

Zusman, J. (1990). Utilization review: Theory, practice, and issues. *Hospital and Community Psychiatry, 41,* 531–536.

Zusman, J. (1997). *Restraint and seclusion: Improving practice and conquering the JCAHO standards.* Marblehead, MA: Opus Communications.

Zweig, S. (1996). The challenges of teaching and learning about cardiopulmonary resuscitation in the nursing home. *Archives of Family Medicine, 5*(4), 213–214.

Zweig, S. C. (1997). Cardiopulmonary resuscitation and do-not-resuscitate orders in the nursing home. *Archives of Family Medicine, 6*(5), 424–429.

Index

Errors, medication, 48
Estate planning, 41
Estate recovery, 69
Ethics committees, 183–184, 187, 197,
    209–210
Ethics consultants, 210
Ethnic influences on decisions, 202
Euthanasia, 212, 213
Ex post facto, 6
Exclusive Provider Organizations
    (EPOs), 166
Executive branch, *see* Administrative
    law
Expert witnesses, 25, 107, 124, 174
Exploitation, 93, 126, 128, 244
Extension doctrine, 33
Extraordinary versus ordinary
    treatment, 196

Facilities, informed consent duties,
    20–22
Falls, 159–161, 162
Family consent statutes, 7, 31, 118, 196
Federal health care facilities, 54
Federal Insurance Contributions Act
    (FICA), 64, 80
Federal Privacy Act, 54
Fee for Service plans, 65
Feeding tubes, *see* Nutrition and
    hydration
Fees, professional, 46, 247
Females, *see also* Demography, 102
Fetuses, research on, 228
Fidelity, 13, 48
Fiduciary, 16, 41, 45, 58, 125, 128, 130
Financing, health care, 63–78
Fire codes, 143
Food and Drug Administration, 8,
    154, 158–159
Forensic medicine, 5
Foster care, 93
Foundation for Hospice and Home
    Care, 171
Fraud, 17, 48, 68–69, 89, 170
Freedom of Information Act, 158, 171
Futile treatment, 40, 207, 209, 212,
    215–218

Genetic testing, 30, 61
"Golden rule," 8
Granny bashing, 93
Gravely disabled, 104, 114
Graying of America, 2–4
Great Britain, 6, 93, 114, 192
    see also England
Great Society, 64
Guardian *ad litem*, 116, 123
Guardian, health care professional as,
    124
Guardian, responsibilities of, 125–126,
    128
Guardianship, alternatives to, 117,
    118–120, 122–123, 130–132,
    191
Guardianship, emergency, 115
Guardianship, estate, 116
Guardianship, generally, 5, 6, 8,
    31–32, 94, 98, 101, 105–106, 108,
    109–126, 127, 129, 133, 155, 191,
    217, 240
Guardianship, limited, 116–117, 242
Guardianship, motives for, 117–119
Guardianship, partial, 116–117
Guardianship, plenary, 116–117
Guardianship, public, 115
Guardianship, termination of, 125–126

Harvard brain death criteria, 219–220
Harvard School of Public Health, 67
Health care agent, *see* Proxy
Health care declaration, 199
Health Care Financing
    Administration (HCFA), 65, 67,
    71–73, 140–142, 143, 158, 168
    see also Interpretive Guidelines,
Health Care Quality Improvement
    Act, 148
Health Insurance Portability and
    Accountability Act (HIPAA),
    61, 68, 70, 251
Health Maintenance Organizations
    (HMOs), 64, 70, 137, 166, 204
Health planning, 10, 170, 214
Hearsay, 47
Heroic treatment, 196